Governing Prisons

GOVERNING PRISONS

A Comparative Study of Correctional Management

John J. DiIulio, Jr.

THE FREE PRESS
A Division of Macmillan, Inc.
NEW YORK

Collier Macmillan Publishers
LONDON

The Free Press
A Division of Macmillan, Inc.
866 Third Avenue, New York, NY 10022

Collier Macmillan Canada, Inc.

Printed in the United States of America

printing number
1   2   3   4   5   6   7   8   9   10

Library of Congress Cataloging-in-Publication Data

DiIulio, John J.
    Governing prisons.

    Bibliography: p.
    1. Prison administration—United States.
2. Prisons—United States.   3. Prisoners—United States.
I. Title.
HV9469.D54   1987   365'.068   87–8478
ISBN 0–02–907881–4

OCLC 15549219

AI MIEI GENITORI,
Grace and John Sr.

Man, when perfected, is the best of animals; but if he be isolated from law and justice he is the worst of all . . . . We assume that the man who is to become good must first be trained and habituated properly, and then go on to spend his time, in the spirit thus engendered, on worthy occupations—doing nothing base or mean either willingly or unwillingly. We also assume that this object can be attained if men live their lives in obedience to some sort of wisdom and under some form of right order—provided this order has sufficient force.

—ARISTOTLE, *Politics*, Book I, and *Ethics*, Book X

Contents

Acknowledgments

My principal debt is to the men and women of the Texas, Michigan, and California departments of corrections. Without their cooperation this study would not have been possible. In the Texas Department of Corrections (TDC), I owe special thanks to Dr. George Beto, Mr. W. J. Estelle, Mr. Raymond Procunier, Mr. O. L. McCotter, Warden Jack B. Pursley, Warden David L. Myers, Warden Billy R. Ware, Warden Bobby D. Morgan, and Mr. Larry Farnsworth. In the Michigan Department of Corrections (MDC), I am indebted to Mr. Perry M. Johnson, Mr. William Kime, Mr. Robert Brown, Warden Robert Redman, Warden John Jabe, Warden Dale Foltz, Warden John Prelsnick, the late Dr. Robert Richardson, Ms. Adria Libolt, and Mr. Terry Murphy. In the California Department of Corrections (CDC), I am grateful to Mr. Daniel J. McCarthy, Warden Wayne Estelle, Superintendent Alan Stagner, Warden Joseph Campoy, Warden Daniel Vasquez, Mr. James W. Park, Mr. James Kane, Ms. Ruth Younger, and Mr. Robert Dickover.

A list of the scores of others in each department who deserve a hearty note of thanks would run on for several pages. I hope that they will accept my gratitude without specific mention. While this is probably not the study that any of them would have had me write, I trust that they will find in it something that rings true and brings honor both to their individual departments and to their noble profession.

Mr. Norman A. Carlson, Director of the Federal Bureau of Prisons, responded kindly to my requests for advice. Professor Norval Morris, Dean of the University of Chicago School of Law, provided an early note of encouragement as did Ms. Charlotte A. Nesbitt of the American Correctional Association (ACA). Professor Mark H. Moore of the Kennedy School of Government, Harvard University, gave me a chance to present my preliminary findings to an interested group and reviewed drafts of the opening chapters. Professor Jameson W. Doig of the Woodrow Wilson School of Public and International Affairs, Princeton University, made a number of helpful suggestions. My friend and colleague, Dr. Ethan Nadelmann, read several chapters and was a source of advice and encouragement. My thanks to each of them.

Professor Samuel P. Huntington, Eaton Professor of the Science of Government, Harvard University, guided my first few years of graduate study and teaching and was the second reader of my dissertation. I owe him much.

My greatest debt is to Professor James Q. Wilson, Collins Professor of Management at UCLA, formerly Henry Lee Shattuck Professor of Government at Harvard. My earlier study of a Massachusetts prison and my first research expeditions to Texas, Michigan, and California were supported by the Alfred P. Sloan Foundation through grants administered by Professor Wilson. He supported me in obtaining an H. B. Earhart Fellowship and again in obtaining a generous grant from the Smith Richardson Foundation. For his role in this project, and still more for enabling me to study under and teach with him, he has my deepest professional respect and personal affection.

My wife, Rosalee, helped in more ways than I can count. What is good in this book is due to her and the others mentioned above. The rest is due to me.

Introduction

*If men were angels, no government would
be necessary.*

—JAMES MADISON, *Federalist* No. 51

Before entering the maximum-security prison in Walpole, Massachusetts, I had read a fair amount of the scholarly literature on prisons, studied the reports of various blue-ribbon panels, and reviewed as many newspaper accounts, magazine articles, and even prison novels as I could digest. None of that prepared me, intellectually or otherwise, for what I observed at Walpole. What I observed was something akin to a literal version of what the political philosopher Thomas Hobbes called a "state of nature," "wherein men live without other security, than what their own strength, and their own invention shall furnish them withall. . . . And the life of man, solitary, poore, nasty, brutish, and short."[1]

Inmates roamed about virtually unimpeded, glaring, making threatening gestures, often shouting profanities at the officers. One cellblock was "trashed" by the inmates who lived there to underscore some grievance that nobody, including the inmates themselves, was willing or able to articulate. Officers wearing rub-

1

ber boots and carrying shovels waded ankle-deep into the mess and were showered with insults and debris and human excrement. The inmates were rarely more charitable to each other than they were to the staff, and most assaults were inmate on inmate. Inmates spent their days in idleness punctuated by meals, violence, and weightlifting.

Virtually every correctional officer I talked to was quick to confide that "the inmates run the joint" and "can take over whenever they want to." The officers, unarmed and vastly outnumbered, had but two ways of maintaining control on a routine basis. First and foremost, they had their individual personalities; some would use humor ("clowns"), others would act insane ("crazies"), while still others would command respect based on their reputation for being "firm but fair" and calm under pressure ("statesmen").

The officers' second way of keeping order was formal. They could write a disciplinary report (known as a "ticket" or "D-report") on any inmate who violated the official rules. But they were reluctant to do so for several reasons. First, there was formal pressure not to "write." The officers' handbook advised that "the officer who succeeds in maintaining [order] with the lowest number of punishments deserves the highest commendation." This formal injunction was reinforced by peer pressure. Most officers held that "any guy who has to write all the time can't handle it and has no sway [influence] with the inmates." Finally, given the sheer number of rule violations (major and minor), it would be impossible for any officer to cite all or even most infractions. A popular bit of wisdom around the prison was that officers must "let everything go but the convicts."

To the extent that my study of Walpole squared with any established notions of how prisons run, it appeared to fit neatly into the sociological understanding of prison life as developed by such scholars as Gresham M. Sykes. In his classical monograph *The Society of Captives* (1958), Sykes painted a vivid portrait of a "prison society" in which the "keepers" were forced, for lack of other means of control, to enter into a corrupt alliance with the inmates, "tolerating violations of 'minor' rules and regulations" so as to "secure compliance in the 'major' areas of the custodial regime."[2]

The general lesson to be learned from Sykes, from most of the rest of the prison literature, and presumably from my own little study was that higher-custody prisons could be run in no other way. There was, so it seemed, virtually nothing that prison managers could do to make their institutions better places to live and work. Indeed, if Sykes and most other experts were to be believed, any attempt by prison personnel to run a tighter, cleaner ship would only result in more problems.[3]

But for several reasons this lesson did not sit well with me. I found it difficult to swallow the notion that the "society of captives" was somehow beyond better government. I began to dig more carefully through the literature on prisons, scrutinizing its empirical findings and tugging at its first assumptions. At the same time I began to gather information on higher-custody prisons in several states. Contrary to much of what I had read, the data indicated that these prisons were not all alike but differed significantly in one or more dimensions of their quality of life: some were clean, others filthy; some were orderly, others riotous; some offered many treatment programs, others few. I wanted to know why. More precisely, I wanted to know under what, if any, conditions better prisons were possible and how, if at all, we could foster such conditions.

But it seemed that the more I searched, the less I found. Instead of knowledge about prisons I found only lore, bare statistics, untested theories, colorful anecdotes, and questionable sociological assumptions. Much of this material was expressed in a bitter, defeatist spirit: prisons have been, and will continue to be, filthy, violent, unproductive places. The solutions offered ranged from political revolution to doing nothing.

The present study was conceived in a different spirit and guided by a different set of assumptions. The central assumption, unusual among scholars if not among average citizens, was that prisons could and should be run by the duly constituted state authorities—directors, wardens, officers, counselors, and so on. Prisons need not resemble Hobbesian states of nature. They can and should be governed. But this was only an assumption. Was it possible for prisons to be governed at an acceptable human and financial cost?

In framing this study, four things seemed essential. First, the study should focus on the formal prison administration. It seemed to me that one reason for the dismal state of knowledge about prisons was the extent to which most researchers had concentrated on the inmates while ignoring the staff. For instance, correctional officers are arguably the key actors in any prison setting, yet prison researchers have tended to neglect or unduly malign them.

Second, the study should be comparative. While a detailed study of a single prison, or of a single prison system, would certainly be useful, its findings might not be generally relevant. Better, I supposed, to study two or more prison systems that are known (or alleged) to differ in significant ways. By searching for the administrative, budgetary, political, or other factors associated with these differences, one might discover what, if any, opportunities exist for improving prisons by changing the way they are managed.

Third, the study should be of higher-custody prisons in major state prison systems. There are some 660 state and 47 federal prisons. Most of the nation's over 525,000 inmates are confined in prisons designated medium-, close- or maximum-security. Higher-custody institutions are the most costly, violent, and troubled. They are also the best known; they include Jackson, San Quentin, and Attica. Some state prison systems have several hundred inmates while others have upwards of 35,000. These larger systems, having the greatest number of prisons and prisoners, appeared to have a disproportionate share of the problems. Also, I hoped that the bigger systems would afford me the opportunity to observe intra- as well as inter-state differences.

Fourth, the study should be exploratory in nature. Exploratory studies do not provide settled answers. They are a beginning where none has been made. Exploratory research is appropriate at the earliest stages of our knowledge, when we do not know what variables are important, how they relate one to the other, or how (if at all) they can be measured. The explorer has to get out into the field, talk to people, and observe things first-hand. Exploratory research can be characterized as qualitative research, participant observation, or (the most apt description I have encountered) "soaking and poking—or just hanging around."[4] It also involves gathering statistics and other harder data where little or none exists—soaking, poking, and computing. To conduct such research in two or more state prison systems would probably be difficult to arrange, time-consuming, expensive, and hard on the legs. It might even be dangerous. But there appeared to be no good alternative.

In essence, the study should be framed to help open up the study of prison management by exploring closely a few departments of corrections, selected not because they were representative of all departments but because they differed from one another in important ways.[5]

I chose the Texas, California, and Michigan prison systems. A 1980 study by the Rand Corporation suggested that these three prison systems differed in interesting and significant ways.[6] Scholars and correctional practitioners I consulted agreed that this was the case.[7] Texas prisons ran on a "control model" that emphasized inmate obedience, work, and education. Michigan prisons ran on a "responsibility model" that de-emphasized paramilitary operations and stressed inmate classification and elaborate grievance procedures. California prisons ran on a mix of both models, closer to Texas on some dimensions (paramilitary operations) while closer to Michigan on others (inmate grievance procedures). When I began the research, Texas, California, and Michigan were, respectively, the first, second, and fifth largest prison systems in the country. All three systems were overcrowded and operating under court orders. Each system had attracted national attention, and each was the object of heated controversies.

Following a year of waiting and negotiating for access to the prisons, I made three trips to Texas and two each to Michigan and California. I conducted scores of interviews with prison personnel at every level, from present and former directors to junior correctional officers. Many of the interviews were conducted at the various department headquarters (Sacramento, Lansing, Huntsville), but the bulk of them were conducted on the fly in the course of observations inside the several prisons I examined in each state.

People and institutions do not stand still to be studied. They do not exist to suit the researcher's desire for methodological rigor or theoretical elegance. This is especially true for correctional people and prisons. In the case at hand, the choice of research sites, the quantity and quality of available information, and the precision of the "recording instrument" (me) were conditioned by things having little or nothing to do with the purposes of the study—the willingness of a given administrator to cooperate, ready access to a copying machine, the state of the department's library (or one's ability to crawl in and out of dusty old cardboard boxes). The original research plan had to be modified in light of such realities, and the research itself was affected by them. For instance, two of the three directors changed in the course of the work, and more than one interview was punctuated by an "all available hands" alarm.[8]

The prison managers I studied cooperated fully with me, thus making it possible to search systematically for answers to most of the questions about prisons with which I began. Here I will summarize a few of the more important answers.

I argue that key differences among the systems are rooted in differences of correctional philosophy. As the quotes in the pages ahead will attest, there are few "bleeding hearts" in the field of corrections. To paraphrase Calvin, no one in corrections believes that convicts are fit to be trusted. But there are differences among prison practitioners regarding the extent to which inmates should be mistrusted, the causes of criminality, and the proper scope of prisoners' rights (or, in the language of correctional staff, "what an inmate has coming.") In corrections as in most other fields, different ideas give rise to different practices, and different practices produce different outcomes.

Those philosophical differences, however, are variations on a common and widely shared set of beliefs. Prison personnel in each system share what in corrections circles is known as the "keeper philosophy," a basically nonpunitive outlook on convicted criminals that is often contrasted with the more punishment-centered "catcher philosophy," attributed by correctional workers to other law enforcement officials, lawmakers, and the public at large. Contrary to popular perceptions, prison employees do not share a "get tough" or "lock 'em up and throw away the key" approach. Most people who work in prisons do not believe that their primary mission is, or ought to be, punishment. The varieties of correctional management I found represent three distinct versions of this keeper philosophy.

A second and more general set of findings worth noting here concerns my working hypothesis about the governability of prisons. From everything that I was able to learn in the course of this research, it seems that the quality of prison life depends far more on management practices than on any other single variable. Indeed, the evidence leads me to conclude that, given certain administrative conditions, prisons can be improved, even in the face of crowded cells, tight budgets, faulty architecture, and inmate populations polarized along racial and ethnic lines. Prison officials can form a government behind the walls that produces safe, civilized conditions. These officials are neither pawns of inmate society nor captives of broader sociopolitical developments. Prisons are no more likely to fail than are schools, armies, state hospitals, regulatory agencies, or other important public organizations. If most prisons have failed, it is because they have been ill-managed, under-managed, or not managed at all.

The closest analogues to this book can, perhaps, be found in the literature on schools. Some twenty years ago a study found that differences in the readily measurable features of schools—expenditures, amount of teacher training, and the like—had virtually no effect on academic achievement once one controlled for the family background of the pupils.[9] More recent studies have confirmed that student performance is more strongly affected by such hard-to-measure factors as how the teacher conducts his class, how the principal guides his teachers, and how the superintendent directs his principals.[10] Indeed, it appears that even inner-city public high schools—places where many students are unruly or ill prepared, resources are slight, and the physical plant is in disrepair—can be improved, given strong leadership, clear teaching objectives, a disciplined classroom environment, high expectations for all pupils, and routine monitoring of student work and behavior.[11]

By the same token, it may be that where prison managers effect a strong administrative regime that enforces adherence to the norms and values of a civilized, noncriminal, "straight" way of life—dressing neatly, washing regularly, being punctual, working hard, speaking respectfully to peers and authorities, delaying gratifications for the sake of future rewards—serious disorders are less frequent, meaningful treatment programs more plentiful, and recidivism rates less startling.

Major differences of opinion exist concerning the impact of court intervention into prison affairs. There remain, in addition, important but little-researched questions about how the path to better prisons is opened (or blocked) by correctional officer unions, legislators, professional associations, reform groups, and the media. I address these and related issues in light of a Madisonian conception of the prison as a constitutional government: we must enable prison managers to control the inmates yet oblige them to control themselves. It seems possible to steer an administrative middle course between the violent rule of inmate predators and the arbitrary rule of autocratic wardens.

Prison administration in a free society poses important questions of political theory and governmental practice. Prison managers govern men who are far from being angels. How ought they to govern? What are the ends of good government in the "society of captives," and how can they be achieved? The evidence and arguments presented in this book hint strongly that, far from being a cruel and unusual sanction, imprisonment, properly instituted, may be a just and merciful one which serves both the convicted criminal and the free community. But I do not pretend to any definitive answers; the reader who wishes untempered policy prescriptions would do well to look elsewhere. While this account ends with a call for more and better prison research, it is probably true that the art of governing prisons, like the art of government itself, admits of no precise knowledge.

ONE

UNDERSTANDING PRISONS

Good order is the foundation of all good things.
—EDMUND BURKE, *Reflections on the Revolution in France*

sion. By *service* I mean anything that is intended to improve the life prospects of the inmates: programs in remedial reading, vocational training, work opportunities. I define a good prison as one that provides as much order, amenity, and service as possible given its human and financial resources. Policy-oriented knowledge about prisons would tell us the conditions under which good prisons are possible and how, if at all, we could foster such conditions.

The lack of policy-oriented knowledge about prisons is no mere intellectual problem. Judges, administrators, and prison reformers are recommending policies based on the assumption that if the policy is adopted, then something good will happen—if budgets are increased, or double-celling eliminated, or correctional officers better trained, or prisoners' rights enlarged (or contracted), then the quality of prison life will improve.[1]

In recent years, serious consideration has been given to proposals to do away with prisons ("tear down the walls"), to privatize prisons ("sell the walls"), to deinstitutionalize prisoners (community corrections), to let the inmates run the prisons (participative prison management), to stop building prisons (moratoria on construction), to make prisons rehabilitate (treatment-oriented prisons), and to make prisons simply incapacitate ("warehousing"). In my judgment, none of these proposals have proved both feasible and desirable. In the absence of genuine knowledge, those most responsible for making prison policy have been grasping at straws.[2]

The lack of policy-oriented knowledge about prisons has contributed to the popularity of unduly negative, pessimistic opinions about them. The leftist opinion centers on the notion that prisons are "inherently unjust and inhumane," the ultimate expressions of "injustice and inhumanity in the society at large."[3] The rightist opinion is based on the belief that prisons can and should merely protect society by punishing criminals, and do so as cheaply as possible.[4] Both conceal the truth that, for all the enormous failures, our penal history is a "history of good intentions" in which substantial progress has been made, and can still be made, against great odds.[5]

As Norval Morris has written, imprisonment is "the largest power that the state exercises in practice, on a regular basis, over its citizens."[6] Yet remarkably little is known about how to make the institutions charged with this responsibility perform as desired. Anyone who has thought seriously about American prisons, especially those few who have ventured behind the walls in the quest for policy-oriented knowledge about them, will be inclined to agree with the authors of a textbook on correctional administration when they say there is a need for "exploratory, descriptive, comparative, and experimental research into the problems of correctional management. . . . This kind of research is difficult to conduct but extremely valuable."[7] James Q. Wilson echoes this point when he writes that "prison is an essential component of the criminal justice system, a vital resource we must learn to manage more rationally and efficiently if it is to serve any of the objectives—retribution, deterrence, or incapacitation—we may have for it."[8] As Gordon Hawkins has observed, of all the impediments to improving prisons, "none is more fundamentally disabling than our lack of knowledge."[9]

There exists, to be sure, a good deal of scholarly research on prisons, but the bulk of that research is about the prison as a social system. Sociologists have written important studies about the effects on the inmates of prisonization and the prison ethos, about the racial and ethnic cleavages that exist within prisons, about the consequences of rehabilitative programs, about inmate argot and roles, and about the informal distribution of authority that develops in prison settings.[10]

But while this literature contains some outstanding research monographs, it supplies few immediate policy recommendations. Indeed, most of it suggests that nothing can be done: if prisons develop a distinctive social system along racial and ethnic lines, reinforced by an informal but powerful distribution of authority, policy makers can do little more than take notice, while prison managers must compromise their formal authority.

Unlike sociologists, my colleagues in political science have paid virtually no attention to prisons. A 1983 publication heralding the birth of a "political science of criminal justice" is more promise than fulfillment.[11] Of the American criminal justice system's three key components—"courts, cops, and corrections"—political scientists have paid most attention to the first, some attention to the second, and negligible attention to the third. Work in this area by political scientists remains sparse, uneven in quality, and of dubious relation to the rest of the discipline.[12]

THE SOCIOLOGICAL VIEW OF PRISONS

In the absence of any major intellectual alternative, the view of prisons put forth by sociologists has reigned supreme. For the last several decades it has colored how Americans think about prisons and shaped the course of correctional policy. Recite the names of Gresham Sykes, Norman Polansky, or Oscar Grusky before most correctional policy makers or administrators, and you will almost certainly draw blank stares. But ask these same people what causes prison violence, how officers should handle inmates, or how inmates behave, and the ideas of Sykes and other leading figures of prison sociology will pour forth.

To paraphrase Lord Keynes, many of those now responsible for shaping prison policy are the slaves of some defunct sociologist. Over the last five decades, the correctional theories of sociologists have become the conventional wisdom of numerous legislators, judges, prison reformers, journalists, prison administrators, inmates, academics in other fields, and others. To trace the channels through which so many minds were captured by prison sociology would be a fascinating project for students of intellectual history.

For the purposes of this study, however, we require only a basic understanding of what prison sociology is, how it has developed, and how it helps or hinders the development of a policy-oriented body of knowledge about prisons. But before proceeding any further, a few words of caution are in order.

What follows in this chapter is not equivalent to what all sociologists, or any particular sociologist, believes about prisons. Rather, it is a summary and analysis of the key ideas that run through a large body of writings about prisons. Sociologists have contributed more, and more important, ideas to this literature than any other identifiable group. The worth of scholarly writings on prisons (or any other subject) does not depend simply on their usefulness in telling us how to overcome practical problems. The sociological perspective on prisons may or may not teach us how to solve correctional conundrums, but it does enrich our understanding of them.

THE SOCIOLOGICAL VIEW OF CRIME AND CORRECTIONS

Most citizens hardly need to be persuaded that if crime did not pay, then fewer crimes would be committed. We naturally suppose that if would-be criminals had fewer opportunities to break the law; expected to be caught; and feared certain, swift, and severe punishment, then there would be less crime. This common sense of crime control is evident in everything from the popularity of home security devices, to the willingness of most taxpayers to spend more for police and prisons, to the way that all but a few of us slow down and check the speedometer when a highway patrol car appears.[13]

In many respects, the sociological view of crime is a standing rejection of such commonsense notions. From the sociological perspective, crime springs from any number of less obvious factors—unstable family life, lower-class culture, disadvantaged economic conditions, deviant personality development, association with delinquent or criminalistic others. The conditions that spawn crime are complex and multitudinous. To prevent or reduce crime requires more than double bolts on doors or stiffer penalties for offenders or other such commonsense measures.[14]

This split between the sociological and the commonsense understanding of crime is repeated when we turn to corrections. From the sociological viewpoint, prisons are highly complex institutions. Prison phenomena—how people behave in prison and what results from their behavior—are both difficult to understand and virtually impossible to control.[15]

On hearing about a prison disturbance, for instance, one might suppose that the trouble resulted from some obvious and easily identifiable security failure—poorly searched inmates or cells; readily available weapons (or objects that can be fashioned as weapons); or a breakdown in the official routine of numbering, counting, checking, and locking.

In the sociology of prisons, however, such suppositions are considered naïve. Understood sociologically, prison disorders are the product of complex underlying factors—inequities in the judicial system, deep racial and ethnic divisions among inmates or between inmates and correctional personnel, underfunding, overcrowding, the inadequacy or unavailability of educational programs or work opportunities, or a breakdown in the inmate social system.[16]

SOCIOLOGY AND INMATE SOCIETY

In the sociological vision, the reality of prison life is invisible to the untrained eye. The father of modern prison sociology, Donald

Clemmer, identified the prison's "unseen environment"[17] as the inmate social system. As Gresham M. Sykes defined it, the inmate social system is "not simply the social order decreed by the custodians, but also the social order which grows up more informally as men interact in meeting the problems posed by their particular environment."[18] It is the "society within a society," the "prison community," the "society of captives" or "prisoner subculture" that, sociologists have argued, develops in prison settings unless inmates are kept totally separate from one another.

In the early nineteenth century prison administrators in Pennsylvania isolated each prisoner for the entire period of his confinement. Inmates ate, worked, and slept in individual cells, seeing and talking with only a handful of prison officers and selected visitors. By most accounts, the results of this system were disastrous.[19] By moral choice and by practical necessity, all succeeding American prison systems incorporated a great deal of inmate movement and interaction behind the walls. The sociological significance of this fact is enormous. In the words of Sykes, if prison inmates associate, they cannot remain "an aggregate rather than a social group, a mass of isolates rather than a society."[20] It is the "patterns of release and reconfinement" that characterize the modern prison that give birth to inmate society, what Sykes termed the society of captives.[21]

Inmate society is "analogous to other types of social organization," a "social microcosm" with its own language, leaders, laws, rites, and rituals.[22] The members of this society are incarcerated criminals who speak in "the pungent argot of the dispossessed" and have their own vocabulary for everything from sex roles ("wolves," "punks") to dispositions vis-à-vis the official administration ("rats," "center men").[23] It is the ethos of this society to resist the authority of the "keepers."[24]

In probing the complex world of incarcerated criminals, sociologists have left no stone unturned, writing studies on everything from how inmates dream to how they adjust to life behind bars.[25] In the literature on prisons inmates are the stars while directors, wardens, correctional officers, and counselors are cast in a supporting role. Clemmer's pioneering work of modern prison sociology, *The Prison Community* (1940), provides but "a quick survey of the prison as an administrative unit,"[26] and Lee H. Bowker, in his 1977 survey of major works of prison sociology, praises one monograph as "a corrective to those proadministration studies that are more relevant to managing prisoners than understanding them."[27]

Why have sociologists paid so much attention to inmates and so little to prison workers? Why have they been more interested in inmate society than in prison administration? More than most of us, sociologists believe that human groupings of all sorts are to a large degree self-governing. They are interested in tracing the less visible bonds that somehow unite men in organizations, families, schools, churches, and prisons. Rather than viewing order in human societies mainly in relation to written laws and the formal machinery that exists to enforce them, sociologists are more inclined to focus on the natural adjustments that people make to each other via customs, traditions, norms, language, and in countless other ways. Where prisons are concerned, the intellectual orientation of sociologists naturally leads them to spotlight the informal order of the inmates over the formal order of the warden and his staff.

For instance, in a highly influential sociological treatise, Erving Goffman characterized prisons, mental hospitals, and military organizations as "total institutions" by which he meant places of "residence and work where a large number of like-situated individuals, cut off from the wider society for an appreciable period of time, together lead an enclosed, formally administered round of life."[28] He understood the prison as that total institution, "organized to protect the community against what are felt to be intentional dangers to it, with the welfare of the persons thus sequestered not the immediate issue."[29] It would seem obvious that those who administer this total institution have enormous power over the lives of the inmates. They keep the inmates behind locked doors, high walls, and barbed wire. They regulate the inmates' work, sleep, recreation, food intake, and so on. They are authorized to shoot and kill any inmate who tries to escape.

But even in this situation, sociologists have argued, people will associate informally in ways that limit the power of the formal machinery that exists to govern them.[30] According to Sykes, through "apathy, corruption, and the hard bedrock of informal human ties" prison inmates will curtail the power of prison administrators.[31] Indeed, as numerous scholars of the prison have argued, under certain conditions, the leaders of inmate society will come to run the prison.

SOCIOLOGY AND PRISON MANAGEMENT

Most scholars have recognized two basic approaches to managing prisons. As Donald R. Cressey identified them, "one is to keep inmate society as unorganized as possible, to prevent individuals from joining forces;" the other is "to enlist, unofficially, the aid of the inmates themselves" in running the prison.[32] From the sociological perspective, however, these two approaches present prison managers with a Hobson's choice in which they must choose the latter.

Political scientist Richard H. McCleery argued that control in the modern prison rests not on "the instruments of force" but on "peer-group formulation and enforcement of norms;" prison personnel must delegate "a large share in management of internal disorder to inmate society," clothing "its leaders with authority by the simple expedient of looking the other way."[33] To inmates, prison officials are "hacks," "bulls," "cops," or "the Man." In the inmate ethos, resisting these authorities is a great virtue while complying with them is a great vice. Prison administrators are thus forced to rely on what McCleery called "procedures for creating consensus."[34] They must recognize inmate society, form bonds of cooperation with its leaders, and hope that inmate conformity with key custodial ends—no escapes or riots—will thereby be achieved. In reward for helping to keep things quiet, inmate leaders must receive special privileges. "Prison government," McCleery concluded, "rests essentially on a basis of compliance and consent."[35]

A persistent theme in the sociology of prison management is that efforts to govern inmate society strictly through formal administrative controls will only beget disorders.[36] In his analysis of the New Jersey State Prison insurrections of 1952, Sykes observed that the administration's relation to "the social system of the prison" did not fit "the free community's image of what a maximum-security institution should be like."[37] The administration relied on inmate leaders, rewarded them illicitly, and was willing to let inmates behave pretty much as they pleased so long as they did not attempt escapes or incite riots. Sykes stressed that it was the very attempt to do away with this arrangement through "a general tightening of security measures" that moved the prison "toward disaster."[38] Echoing Sykes, sociologist James G. Fox has argued that prison administrators should run institutions in which strict rule enforcement is de-emphasized, for the more officials strive to achieve "control goals" the more they will foster inmate "alienation and conflict" within the prison.[39]

According to accepted sociological wisdom, prison management is an attempt to manipulate inmate society. Inmates must be coaxed, not coerced. Paramilitary features of prison management should be kept to a minimum. The symbols and substance of formal controls—weapons and badges for officers, restrictions on inmate movement—should be reduced or abolished.

THE EVOLUTION OF PRISON SOCIOLOGY

Over the last several decades the sociological perspective on prisons has undergone at least two major shifts. First, early sociologists of the prison were less convinced than their successors have been that inmate society is both inevitable and desirable. They were more inclined to see the society of captives as one in which the weak are prey to the strong and all manner of incivil and criminal behavior are commonplace. Consequently, they were somewhat sympathetic to the need for formal management controls on inmate behavior. Second, as was also true of writing in other academic fields, beginning in the 1960s much of the sociological writing on prisons became informed by countercultural assumptions, chief among them that prisons are the oppressive instruments of an oppressive, racially discriminatory, and vengeful society. An intellectual orientation that focused on the more complex causes of prison phenomena was thus combined with an ideological perspective that pronounced prisons microcosms of an illegitimate sociopolitical order. The combination was a powerful one. Riots in the cellblocks, like riots in the streets, could now be explained as reflections of the deeply rooted and legitimate grievances of an oppressed American underclass, a disproportionate component of which was black.

Thus, in the 1940s the reader of prison sociology would be told that inmate society is an unwanted by-product of formal administrative controls (or the lack of same). In the 1950s he would learn that the society of captives was an inevitable feature of prison life, which, nevertheless, could be harnessed to official ends mainly via inmate leaders. In the 1960s and 1970s he would learn that all of the old informal harnesses had been worn thin by the politicization of the prisoner population; thus the administration would have to share power with the inmates. In the 1980s he would be asked to doubt that incarcerated criminals are a less angelic bunch than the rest of us, and to believe that if the society of captives is to be governed at all it must govern itself.

The extent of shifts in sociological perspective is well illustrated by comparing Donald Clemmer's *The Prison Community* (1940) to John Irwin's *Prisons In Turmoil* (1980).

In his seminal study, Clemmer was able to show that the extent of inmate associations in prison had previously been exaggerated. He found that about 40% of prison inmates were "ungrouped," a fact attributable in part to the formal system of administrative controls. It was only the more hard-core convicts who wanted to play a big role in inmate society. The others just wanted "to keep out of all trouble in prison . . . by avoiding intimate contacts."[40] Clemmer discovered that, "for the most part, it is among the men who do not become deeply integrated into the prison culture that reform takes place."[41] In his preface to the 1958 edition of the book, Clemmer stressed that what "remains to combat in most modern prisons is the unseen environment, which is a stronger force for evil than the programs are for good."[42]

There was little malice and even a note of praise in Clemmer's brief portrait of prison workers. Prison inmates, he wrote, "are not a gentle, easily-managed folk. . . . Our prisoners have not abided by the laws in a less restricted milieu than that of the prison."[43] The need for discipline in prison is "not a simple problem."[44] He quoted a famous warden as follows: "All prison administration savors of the nature of despotism."[45] Clemmer called for "reasonable, commonsense methods" of prison discipline.[46]

Forty years later, sociologist John Irwin introduced his important study of prisons with these words: "I hate prisons; that is, I hate what happens to convicts in prison (my people, I suppose)."[47] Most correctional officers, he asserted, are ill-educated racists.[48] Inmates, on the other hand, are "humans like us and . . . will act honorably, given a real choice."[49] Give inmates "the resources to achieve self-determination," and prisons will be better places.[50] Inmate society, he concluded, should be made more self-governing via formal prisoner organizations.[51]

SOCIOLOGY AND THE CONTEMPORARY PRISON

These changes in the sociological perspective on prisons were grounded in a particular reading of post–World War II prison history. In the 1940s and 1950s, sociologists have argued, most inmate leaders were white convicts who shared, or could be persuaded to share, the administration's basic aims. These "con bosses" would help to prevent major disturbances and keep other inmates from joining forces or associating in ways that might upset the administration. In the language of corrections, these convict leaders would see to it that other inmates "did their own time." As Kathleen Engel and Stanley Rothman have argued, "the inmate social system, when operating free from interference, produced exactly the purposes of the security force . . . little violence, and a stable, peaceful regime and population."[52]

Beginning in the 1960s the prison population became increasingly black and Hispanic. The old con bosses, sociologists have argued, were replaced by a younger, more aggressive, more politicized breed of convict chieftains.[53] These new inmate leaders were far less willing and able to get other inmates to go along with even the most basic wishes of the administration. Inmate society became factionalized along racial and ethnic lines. The pliable con boss was succeeded by the inflexible prison gang leader. To these gangs and their leaders, the administration became practically superfluous. Their real battles were intramural. In the southwest, for instance, bloody feuds among Hispanic prisoners gave rise to two opposing gangs, the Mexican Mafia and La Nuestra Familia. Meanwhile, white prisoners joined the neo-Nazi Aryan Brotherhood and fought pitched battles with the Black Guerrilla Family.[54]

With the sociological interpretation of prisons in hand, John Conrad and Simon Dinitz explained the violence of the contemporary prison as follows: "The kinds of accords to each other which custodial officers and convicts used to make, as described in the literature on prison organization, seem no longer to be maintained."[55] Kathleen Engel and Stanley Rothman offered a similar explanation, arguing that court-imposed reforms undermined the "complex relationships among inmates," which once "contributed to the maintenance of order and inmate solidarity."[56]

From the sociological perspective, if the contemporary prison is more troubled than its predecessors, if inmates are more unruly and killings are more frequent, this is to be explained by reference to a change in the inmate social system: today's inmates are less willing to be governed than were yesterday's. The prison administrators of the 1940s and 1950s are to be understood as reluctant rulers coaxed by the circumstance of limited power to compromise their official authority through bargains with inmates and their leaders.[57] Contemporary prison administrators are to be understood as deposed rulers forced into a shared-powers model of correctional management.[58]

EVALUATING PRISON SOCIOLOGY

Nobody can question the intellectual merits of prison sociology. As Morris Janowitz has stated, sociologists "have a rich tradition of exploring the social organization of the prison. . . . The literature on prisons contains some of the most outstanding research monographs in sociology."[59] It is, however, fair to ask whether the sociological perspective on prisons yields insights that are useful to those interested in improving the quality of prison life.

Quite naturally, most sociologists are inclined to answer that question in the affirmative. Sykes argued that inmates are enmeshed in "a complex social system with its own norms, values, and methods of control; and any effort to reform the prison . . . which ignores this social system is as futile as the labors of Sisyphus."[60] Bowker counseled that "mastering the art of sociological analysis formally or informally is the only way" for prison managers to control inmate society.[61] Before agreeing or disagreeing with these assertions, it makes sense to examine how sociological analysis has fared when applied to important correctional issues. There are at least four major correctional topics that lend themselves to such an examination: (1) prison violence, (2) participative prison management, (3) inmate treatment and custody, and (4) administrative change and its consequences.

Prison Violence: Are Lax or Tight Controls to Blame?

Sociologists have argued that prison violence results from a breakdown in the inmate social system caused by the attempts of prison administrators to gain (or regain) formal control of the institution by enforcing official rules and regulations.[62] Efforts to run the prison "by the book" undermine informal inmate–staff relations and spark disorders.[63] When the special privileges conferred upon inmate leaders are withdrawn, these leaders cease to exercise informal power over other inmates in the interests of institutional order.[64] Disturbances follow as an expression of inmate frustration with the new formal order, or as a by-product of a power struggle among newly competitive inmate factions, or as an attempt by deposed inmate leaders to stifle reform and restore the old, informal order.[65] "The eventual response . . . is a riot."[66]

The Prison Riots of 1951–1953

The classic statement of this theory was made by Sykes in the penultimate chapter of his *The Society of Captives* (1958). Under the heading "Crisis and Equilibrium," Sykes wrote that "it is the cohesively-oriented prisoner committed to the values of inmate loyalty, generosity, endurance, and the curbing of frictions who does much to maintain the prison's equilibrium. When the custodians strip him of his power—when the custodians destroy the system of illicit privileges, of preferential treatment and laxity which has functioned to increase the influence of the cohesively-oriented prisoner who stands for the value of keeping things quiet—the unstable elements in the inmate population have an opportunity to capitalize on the tensions of prison life and rise into dominance. The stage has been set for insurrection."[67]

Sykes attempted to show how this theory explained two prison riots that occurred in 1952 at the New Jersey State Prison at Trenton. As Sykes noted, these riots were "part of a general wave of unrest which swept over custodial institutions in the United States between 1951 and 1953."[68] Over a dozen states experienced prison riots. By the end of 1953 scores of prison and jail disturbances had occurred. Before we examine how well the sociology of prison violence explains more recent incidents, it is important to examine it in light of these earlier disorders, for it is through the analysis of these disorders that the sociology of prison violence as we know it was born.

To examine Sykes's seminal analysis we must retrace his steps beginning with his own factual account of the riots:[69] To summarize, the first riot at the Trenton prison involved an inmate who complained to the officer on duty of being ill. An orderly from the prison hospital arrived promptly, checked the inmate, and phoned the doctor, who prescribed medication to be taken to the prisoner's cell. When the medicine arrived, the inmate refused it. Instead, he groaned and threw himself from his bunk to the floor. Inmates in nearby cells began chanting, "Take that boy to the hospital, take that boy to the hospital. . . ." The chanting grew louder, and inmates threatened to "take the joint apart." One inmate screamed "If I start smashing things, will you go along with me?" Inmates trashed the cellblock, knocking out lights, destroying washbasins, and tossing the debris to the floor. Soon prisoners were seen at large in the wing. Two shells of tear gas were fired into the cellblock but the rioting continued. There were fifty-two inmates in the wing. By noon the next day, twenty had given themselves up. The rest surrendered that evening. All were taken to the hospital and examined. Only seven or so could be positively identified as rioters. These seven were given forty-five days in solitary confinement.

The second riot at Trenton occurred the next month in the print shop. There was evidence of careful planning. Sixty-nine inmates seized two officers and two shop instructors. They went on "a wildly destructive spree," smashing machinery, tools, and supplies. Prison officials responded by locking other inmates in the institution in their cells and summoning reinforcements. Fearing for the safety of the hostages, the warden opted to negotiate rather than use force. On the third day of negotiations a disturbance began at the New Jersey Prison Farm at Rahway. "Some 230 inmates seized 9 hostages, barricaded themselves in a dormitory, and surrendered five days later. The immediate effect of the Rahway riot on the rebellion at the Trenton Prison, however, was to rob the latter of much of its publicity."[70] Weakened by "thirst and hunger, the rioters in the Print Shop gave up the struggle . . . and marched out into the hands of waiting guards."[71] The Trenton prison rioters, however, had won some "concessions from their captors." An inmate council was established and the inmate who had led the print shop riot eventually became its chairman.

Sykes asked "Who was to blame for the riots?"[72] Citizens and journalists, he noted, blamed the governor and his appointees. Prison officials blamed the inmates. The committee appointed to investigate the riots was "more sophisticated."[73] It blamed the "impersonal forces at work in the prison—overcrowding, idleness, heavy turnover in the custodial force, archaic disciplinary practices, inadequacies of the physical plant, heterogeneity of the inmate population, indifferent rehabilitation program, careless work assignments," and so on.[74] Sykes liked the committee's explanation because it avoided "the pat explanation of an individual scapegoat" and recognized the complex nature of "disturbances in the social system that we call the prison."[75] But he dismissed the investigating committee's report as "unsatisfactory because it fails to give an explanation of how the prison reaches the point of explosion."[76]

Why then did these prison riots occur? Sykes argued that "our understanding of the riots must rest on an understanding of the larger evolutionary sequence of which they are a part," most especially "the shifting status of what has been called the 'semi-official self-government' exercised by the inmate population."[77] Specifically, the "effort of the custodians to 'tighten up' the prison undermines the cohesive forces at work in the inmate population and it is these forces which play a critical part in keeping the society of the prison on an even keel."[78] In other words, the "system breeds rebellions by attempting to enforce the system's rules. The custodians' efforts to secure a greater degree of control result in the destruction of that control, temporary though it may be, in those uprisings we label riots."[79]

Did the New Jersey State prison authorities attempt to "tighten up" their control and did that cause the 1952 riots? The careful reader of Sykes's fascinating account will learn only that somewhere in the mid-1940s, New Jersey prison officials moved "in the direction of ever greater inmate control. The problem was attacked on many fronts and ranged from a severe curtailment of hobby work . . . to a general tightening of security measures."[80] No more detailed statement of what these new control measures were, how they were implemented, or how their implementation caused a crisis in the prison's "social equilibrium" is forthcoming. Nor does Sykes specify how these measures caused the riots in question. Instead, he argues his case purely on theoretical grounds, claiming that "even if this interpretation stands in need of a good deal more evidence and development to serve as a theory for prison riots in general or the insurrections in Trenton Prison in 1952 in particular, it has the initial, presumptive advantage of analyzing the disturbances in the prison not as isolated, fortuitous events but as an integral part of the nature of confinement."[81]

But no empirical theory, however interesting, can be its own justification. Sykes mustered very little evidence to support his interpretation of prison violence. Indeed, from his own account of the 1952 New Jersey prison riots, the opposite explanation seems equally plausible: the riots occurred not because prison officials "tightened up" but because they failed to do so; the riots occurred not because they destroyed the system of lax controls but because their control measures were never rigorous enough. How was it possible for inmates in the first riot to empty out freely into the wing? How was it possible for the inmates who staged the second riot to plan for the seige by stashing away food? How was it possible that "other prisoners hurried to the scene"? That all of these things did occur seems to indicate a breakdown of security management, the daily routine of numbering, counting, checking, searching, locking, monitoring inmate movement, controlling contraband, and general rule-enforcement that is the heart of formal administration in higher-custody prisons.

Was there greater evidence for the sociological theory of prison violence in the other riots of this period? Vernon Fox analyzed these riots together with scores of others, from the 1855 riot at New York's Sing Sing prison to the 1955 riot at the Deer Island jail in Massachusetts.[82] He contrasted the explanations of prison violence favored by criminologists, journalists, prison officials, and the inmates themselves. Based on his own investigation, however, Fox could corroborate none of them. No factor or cluster of factors was present at all prison riots. Indeed, some prisons remained calm even though all of the factors said to cause riots were present. Thus the only hypotheses that Fox could venture were highly general: "riots cannot begin in the absence of a real problem."[83]

Fox paid special attention to the 1952 riot at the State Prison of Southern Michigan at Jackson. Other writers, such as John Bartlow Martin, also made a study of the Jackson riot.[84] The Michigan Department of Corrections produced its own detailed analysis of the "causal and contributory factors" behind the disturbance. No tightening of security measures had preceded the riot. What, if any, role other general factors—inmate idleness, inadequate physical plant, and so forth—played in bringing about the riot has remained a matter of conjecture. The only thing that seems clear is that the riot began with a simple security slip committed by an inexperienced correctional officer. Disregarding the rules, the officer opened a cell door for an inmate after the evening lockup. The inmate exited his cell wielding a knife and the disturbance was underway. Such security management failures were commonplace at Jackson prison at this time. In his 1961 work on the Michigan Department of Corrections, Robert Vinter wrote that the riot "revealed serious weaknesses in the organization and administration of the Department."[85]

The prison riots of 1951–1953 do not appear to furnish much support for the sociological interpretation of prison violence. Analyses of particular riots aside, the simple fact that so many riots occurred during this period is hard to reconcile with certain lessons of prison sociology. As was discussed earlier, sociologists have explained recent increases in prison violence by positing a change in the inmate social order: pliable con bosses were succeeded by aggressive, politicized prison gang leaders. The 1940s and early 1950s was supposedly the heyday of the old system of informal controls. That being the case, one must wonder what the legendary con bosses were doing between 1951 and 1953.[86] It is difficult to imagine that in the same three-year period correctional administrators in over a dozen jurisdictions decided to "tighten up" formal controls. It is still harder to suppose that in each case the result was a prison riot.

An examination of the prison riots of 1951–1953 inspires what, from the sociological perspective, is a heretical speculation; namely, that the prison gang leader of the contemporary prison is more the offspring than the antithesis of the con boss of the 1940s and 1950s; that both are brought to life by lax administrative controls, and if the former is more violent, it is because controls in the contemporary prison are more lax. But this is only a speculation, and a highly tentative one at that. Before we can draw any conclusions we must examine the sociology of prison violence more closely.

Prison Riots of the 1980s

In early 1980 the Penitentiary of New Mexico at Santa Fe experienced the worst prison riot since 1971, when 43 inmates and hostages lost their lives at New York's Attica Correctional Facility. Thirty-three inmates (average age, twenty-seven) were murdered, many after being mutilated with blowtorches. Twelve correctional officers were held hostage. Some of the hostages were beaten. Many inmates were raped repeatedly. Millions of dollars worth of state property was destroyed.

The New Mexico Attorney General's Report on the riot concluded that "a series of security lapses" allowed inmates to gain control of the prison in just twenty-two minutes.[87] After overpowering four correctional officers in the prison's medium-security wing, the inmate assailants had no difficulty in seizing the prison control room and freeing other inmates, including those in the maximum-security unit. But the report stressed that "these security failures do not explain why the riot occurred in the first place."[88] The report noted "the underlying problems" which the riot brought to light and asserted that the carnage occurred because "a new group of violent inmates" had assumed leadership positions.[89] The accompanying Report of the Citizen's Advisory Panel stated: "For all such events, of course, there are both obvious and hidden causes."[90]

What were the "hidden causes" of this tragic prison riot? Several analyses of the riot have been published.[91] There is little evidence in any of them that would enable us to identify these causes. At the time the riot began, conditions in the prison—the level of crowding, the extent of educational and work opportunities, the quality of recreational facilities, and so on—had not changed in months. Most of the correctional officers, like most of the inmates, were Hispanic. Hence, it is difficult to suppose that festering racial and ethnic animosities were behind the violence. The administration had made no significant attempts to tighten its grip on the inmates. If anything, the administration of the prison had grown more lax in the weeks leading up to the riot, as even major rule violations by inmates went unreported. The rioters made no coherent package of demands until after the destruction had begun.

If such factors as overcrowding, inadequate recreational facilities, and official callousness were responsible for the violence, we would expect the prison to become less violent when these causes were removed. Following the riot, New Mexico prison officials reduced the inmate population by 40 percent, increased recreational services, bolstered officer training, and increased the officers' take-home pay. Despite these changes, however, eleven people, nine inmates and two officers, were murdered in a period of less than a year following the riot.[92]

The 1980 riot at the Santa Fe prison appears to furnish little support for the sociological intepretation of prison violence. A simpler and perhaps more accurate explanation for the riot might point to basic security-management failures. On the afternoon before the riot an officer reported "an unusually large congregation of inmates in the corridor."[93] This indicates that mass gatherings of inmates in the prison halls, even large ones, were not unusual. As the New Mexico Attorney General's Report observed, unlocked doors and open corridor grills were commonplace at the prison. Such security lapses occurred with "predictable frequency."[94] The merciless nature of the inmates' violence raises profound questions about human nature, but there is nothing profound in the fact that lax security procedures made blowtorches and other instruments of destruction readily available to the rioters.

Is there greater support for the sociological view of prison violence in other recent riots? It is hard to find anything other than simple security-management failures behind the 1981 disturbance at Pennsylvania's Graterford prison. Compared to the 1980 riot at the Santa Fe penitentiary, the human and financial costs suffered at Graterford prison were mild: several injuries, some property damage, no fatalities. But most observers agree that the outcome at Graterford could have been much worse. The trouble started when prison authorities mistakenly placed an inmate known to be a security risk in a low-supervision work assignment. This inmate led the disturbance. Six prison employees were gone for nearly an hour before anyone recognized or reported that they were missing. Two junior correctional officers and a lieutenant were among the hostages.[95]

In 1983, New York's Ossining (Sing Sing) prison was the scene of a hostage crisis. A seige began which lasted for two days. Drawing parallels to the 1971 riot at Attica prison, some observers attributed the trouble to the administration's failure to address a variety of longstanding inmate grievances. In truth, however, affirmative responses to inmate demands for liberalization of censorship and the like had preceded the Attica riot, while the hostage-takers at Ossining had no list of grievances. The Ossining disorder began when a sergeant gave orders contrary to standard operating procedures. Inmates armed with broom handles and other weapons overpowered correctional officers during a recreational period. In fact, for the 1500 inmates confined at the prison when the incident occurred, daily life had been nothing but one extended "recreational period." Fewer than 1 percent were in educational programs; 80 percent were awaiting transfers; 90 percent were kept idle and were allowed to "hang out" in the cellblocks or on the yards. The official report on the disturbance related these simple management failures, but in the context of an analysis that read like a page from a prison sociology text. Almost as if it were a self-evident truth, the report claimed that the transient status of most of the prison population had an "inhibiting effect on inmate social structure" and "stunted the growth of constructive inmate leadership which could have been useful in preventing or helping to more quickly resolve the uprising."[96] The factual record of the disturbance, however, revealed nothing about "stunted" socialization and much about unsound security.

Analyses of other prison disturbances of this decade tell much the same story. In 1981 the State Prison of Southern Michigan at Jackson, scene of the 1952 riot discussed earlier, experienced a major disturbance. The Report of the Governor's Special Committee on Prison Disturbances made some sixty specific recommendations. Among other things, the Governor's report mandated an improvement in the quality of food preparation and "increased and intensive training in the area of black urban experience and culture."[97] There is, however, little evidence that the riot was caused by poor food or racially insensitive officers. There is still less evidence that the implementation of measures to deal with such problems has resulted in a decrease in the level of violence at Jackson or other Michigan prisons.

On the contrary, a major 1982 riot at Michigan's Huron Valley Men's Facility (HVMF) occurred when inmates in the segregation unit took advantage of a defective locking system, installed when the institution, designed originally as a reception center, was hastily modified for use as a maximum-security prison. Subsequent disturbances at this institution arose through a combination of physical-plant defects and lax security procedures. Beginning in 1985, the installation of internal fencing, a tightening of restrictions on inmate movement, and a host of related measures reduced disorders at HVMF.

The 1981 riot at Jackson prison, the 1982 disturbance at HVMF, and escapes, stabbings, and murders at numerous other prisons around the country have left clear traces of breakdowns in security but few traces of breakdowns in inmate society.[98] The prison disorders of the 1980s, like those of the 1950s, appear to be simple tales of failed prison management.

Sociology and Prison Violence

Are lax administrative controls the root of prison violence? As James B. Jacobs has noted, "the management of the opportunities and instrumentalities of violence . . . are rather prosaic topics for academic commentators."[99] A theory of prison disorders that stresses the basic stuff of security management is by no means as stimulating intellectually as one which points to a complex and paradoxical relationship involving the dynamics of inmate society. To suggest that tight administrative controls and prison violence vary inversely is to utter a commonplace; to posit that they vary directly is to offer an intriguing and counterintuitive hypothesis. By the same token, a theory of prison disorders that focuses on the obvious and proximate factors related to management controls is easier to document than one which probes the less obvious and more remote factors that may move an inmate, or a group of inmates, to commit violent acts in prison.

In his 1976 essay on collective violence in prisons, Richard W. Wilsnack wrote that "prison riots appear to develop from preconditions at three different levels: inmate deprivation and social disintegration, administrative conflict and instability, and pressure and publicity from outside the walls."[100] It is probably true that such factors as overcrowding, racial tensions among inmates, and the depth (or shallowness) of public concern about prisons bear some relationship to prison violence. To date however, scholars of the prison have been unable to specify or document those relationships.[101]

It is hard to believe that most or all of the violence in prison is gratuitous. Most sociologists search for the causes of prison violence in nonobvious and remote places. From Sykes on down, they have viewed prison violence as a crisis in the prison's social equilibrium. The sociological view of prison violence revolves around the notion that anything that disturbs the inmates must inevitably disturb the prison. If inmates make persistent demands (legitimate or not) for a reduction in double-celling, or an increase in the amount of "yard time," or an instant improvement in the way food is prepared or served, or better wages for prisoner labor, then prison managers had better respond in a prompt and sympathetic manner—or else.[102]

As we have seen, there does not appear to be much evidence with which to support the sociological interpretation of prison violence. But for the sake of argument, let us suppose that such evidence does exist. Suppose, for example, that the kinds of security lapses discussed earlier merely allow festering inmate grievances to get out of control. In other words, suppose that such management failures are but froth on the waves of more complex and deeply rooted troubles affecting inmate society.

In most cases, we have neither the knowledge nor the resources to alleviate these problems. They are by definition difficult to understand and hard to remedy. Even if we could somehow identify and eliminate all of the underlying factors that lead to violence in prisons, it would take some time to do so. Would inmates be better off in the interim if we did nothing to prevent, reduce, and control the assaults, rapes, and riots that result from these underlying causes? By analogy, should we hesitate to deprive a group of potential arsonists of blowtorches on the ground that we have yet to understand and remedy the social, biological, or other factors that cause pyromania?

In a review of the literature on riots and disturbances published by the American Correctional Association, we learn that prison disorders "are complex phenomena for which simple explanations do not exist."[103] But the evidence seems to suggest that much of the explanation for prison violence relates to such banal matters as whether inmates have easy access to objects which can be fashioned into knives (or "shanks" in prison argot), whether doors are locked according to schedule, and the regularity and thoroughness with which inmates are frisked, cells searched, crowds dispersed, and contraband controlled.[104]

That sociologists favor sociological explanations of prison violence is not surprising. What is surprising, however, is that many prison managers also favor sociological explanations of prison violence. Of the scores of prison officials I interviewed, only a few explained prison violence primarily by reference to the practical mechanics of correctional administration. Still fewer explained it specifically in terms of security management. Rarest of all were comments such as the following: "Prison violence represents a failure of prison management. It occurs when staff are unable or unwilling to follow the rules governing security. When violence occurs the question to ask is 'Who in charge failed to do what he was supposed to do? Who in charge failed to be where he was supposed to be?' "

Instead, most officials explained prison violence, including major riots and disturbances, by reference to such factors as negative attitudes among inmates, race hatred, judicial interference, a lack of funds for treatment programs, inmate frustrations related to crowded conditions, and so on. While only a handful of these officials made explicit reference to works of prison sociology, each of them were effective exponents of the sociological view of prison violence. A few of them had learned their sociology in academic settings, but most had come to it as the conventional wisdom of corrections enshrined in their respective departmental training programs.[105]

The popularity of sociological theories of prison violence among correctional practitioners, however, may be less surprising than it seems. Prison managers can hide behind the "hidden causes" to deflect blame for rapes, assaults, murders, or riots that might otherwise be credited to their own managerial shortcomings. Some of those I talked to admitted to doing just that. One prison manager said: "If they blame the budget, blame the programs, blame the overcrowding, and blame the inmates they won't blame me." Another stated: "Every time there's a riot, half of us cries and half is happy because we know it means more attention and probably more money for everything—salaries, programs, you name it."

By the same token, it is no doubt easier for governors, judges, attorneys general, state legislators, and corrections commissioners to accept abstract explanations than to shoulder responsibility for appointing incompetent prison personnel or for failing to oversee them properly. As one state official remarked: "Nobody wants to say in public that they screwed up the prisons. It's best to say that the prisons are just screwed up." For journalists, a story about the complex and deep-rooted forces that caused a prison to explode in violence makes better, more colorful copy than a story which relates how Sgt. Smith failed to lock the cell of violent inmate Jones.

Some sociologists have urged correctional researchers and practitioners to focus on the more obvious and proximate causes of prison violence.[106] To date, however, the relationship between management practices and how they increase (or diminish) the instrumentalities and opportunities for violence has gone little investigated. The existing evidence seems to suggest that formal controls vary inversely with violence. To the extent that sociologists have studied prison management, however, they have recommended fewer such controls and a greater degree of inmate self-government.

Participative Prison Management: Should Inmates Be Self-Governing?

In 1979 Thomas O. Murton, a former Arkansas prison warden, captured the essential idea behind participative prison management in these words: "If inmates are allowed to participate in decision-making, they will tend to act more responsibly toward themselves, others, and prison society."[107] The reader may be surprised to learn that the former warden was not describing the idea in order to refute it. Quite to the contrary, Murton argued that participative prison management was the only hope for the ills of America's prisons.[108]

In the foreword to John Irwin's *Prisons In Turmoil* (1980), Donald Cressey described the author as one of his "sociological children."[109] Irwin's book, wrote Cressey, "is more than a book about prisons. It is a discourse on democracy."[110] Irwin was the leader of a "prison reform movement that would resolve the tensions of the contemporary prison democratically."[111] Irwin stated his idea as follows: "We need a new system of control over prisoners that is not based on arbitrary decision making or on the old informal convict social system and its single prisoner code. There is only one possibility, a formal system of decision making in which all diverse parties (prisoners and guards included) have some input and in which the conditions of work and confinement, the rules of the institution, and the special problems and grievances of different parties (individuals and groups) are negotiated."[112]

Intellectual Origins of Prison Democracy

The idea of giving inmates a role in the administration of the prison was not invented by modern-day wardens or sociologists. There were experiments with prison democracy in the eighteenth and nineteenth centuries. The latest and boldest trials of participative prison management began in the 1960s. Numerous correctional scholars and practitioners saw inmate involvement in prison administration as a sensible response to the social disintegration and violence of the contemporary prison. The administration, it seemed, was unable to govern the inmates. Owing to the budding racial and political splits among prisoners, inmate leaders were no longer willing or able to help. Given the anarchic conditions of the contemporary prison, participative prison management seemed worth a try. In John Irwin's words, "formal prisoner organizations with input in decision making and access to independent grievance processes will be necessary to reestablish a safe prison and for the first time a prison free from excessive punishment and malicious practices."[113]

There was, it seemed, a solid intellectual foundation for democratizing the prison. For years, a number of influential organizational theorists had been arguing that democratic management practices were most effective. Managers of business firms, schools, and even armies were encouraged to be "open" to their subordinates, to issue orders informally, and to otherwise de-emphasize the symbols and substance of formal organizational authority. Management was to be understood and practiced as the art of human relations.[114]

To my knowledge, architects of the human-relations school of management made no reference to prisons in building their case. From the 1950s onward, however, prison scholars wrote studies that would have enabled them to do so. In 1952, Harry Elmer Barnes and Negley K. Teeters attacked prison managers who rigidly enforced rules and regulations, judging such "asinine injunctions" unnecessary to security and positively antithetical to treatment.[115] A few years later Sykes wondered aloud whether prison officials "overestimate the amount of disorder which would occur in the absence of rigid controls reaching far into what seem to be irrelevant areas of [inmate] life."[116] Sykes and Sheldon Messinger prodded future researchers to discover whether "the suspicion and distrust of the conforming world embedded in the inmate code" could be broken down by loosening formal controls and making the prison environment "less rigorous."[117]

From at least the mid-1950s, therefore, the sociological study of prisons was headed towards support for some species of inmate self-government. The germinal theories in support of participative prison management were based on evidence gathered largely from studies of lower-custody prisons. For example, in 1958, Oscar Grusky reported that, contrary to the "traditional penological view," inmate leaders are not necessarily "a source of constant instigation of the inmates, promoting riots, dissension, and antiadministration behavior."[118] "In return for the promotion of the organization's goals of treatment and custody," inmate leaders at Camp Davis (Grusky's fictitious name for Michigan's Camp Brighton) received special privileges (upper bunks, better jobs). "The inmate culture at Camp Davis was organized not around the most hostile, but rather around the most co-operative, offenders."[119] The result, according to Grusky, was fewer problems than occurred at a comparable but more custody-oriented minimum security vocational prison.

In both his published essay and in the paper he delivered to Michigan prison officials, Grusky stressed that his findings were to be received with caution. Quite rightly, he recognized that his theory was "very much in the exploratory stage"[120] and noted that "comparative data, collected under more highly controlled conditions from a number of prisons of both the traditional custodial and the treatment type" were needed.[121] Interesting studies of youth institutions, prison camps, and other facilities followed.[122] Like Grusky's analysis, these studies implied that "different patterns of formal organization and structure may produce differences in inmate organization and in attitudes toward the prison experience."[123]

But precisely what kinds of formal organization produce what kinds of differences in inmate life, and what, if any, differences exist between inmates (and their self-selected leaders) in lower- and higher-custody settings such that official efforts to "co-opt" serious convicts might be more fraught with risks and unintended consequences? The literature simply did not permit any answer to this question. Neither, however, did it foreclose the enchanting possibility that the best way to manage populations of incarcerated criminals, even large populations of violent offenders, was to offer inmates all sorts of programs, reward the inmate leaders for supporting both custodial and treatment goals, and trust that these leaders would somehow induce other inmates to behave in civil and law-abiding ways. After all, the studies hinted that the anti-administration ethos of prisoners tended to melt in more open institutions that developed "a fairly rich and complex set of treatment goals and programs."[124]

Never mind that the studies hinted much but proved no such thing. For here was the recipe for an ostensibly new and better form of prison government, one apparently informed by years of sociological research and obviously more enlightened than the reigning alternative—forsake the traditional emphasis on guard-centered custody, invest responsibility in inmate leaders, build a "rich and complex" daily routine around these leaders, and everything from inmate–staff relations to recidivism rates will improve. In essence, this was the recipe for participative prison management. To many of those whose only education about inmates and prisons came from years of working in the cellblocks, it seemed like a recipe for disaster. As one veteran of two experiments with participative prison management recalled:

Boil it down, and the thing was to be nice to the inmates, to let them have a real hand in running the show. Some so-called experts discovered that these men had never had enough responsibility for themselves and that was why they had killed people, beat up teachers, raped, and so forth. So that was the main thing now, to give them athletic equipment, shrinks, job training, and let them organize themselves. We used to say "do your own time." Now we said "do time in your own way"—you organize the place, you run it. Just don't try to escape or get too crazy on us. Common sense said the whole damn thing from A to Z was ridiculous, but sometimes folks have to get burnt before they stop playing with matches. And sometimes the more educated or high-and-mighty they are, the less they learn.

Lessons of Experience: Walla Walla Penitentiary

In the 1970s one of the most forthright experiments in inmate self-government was made at Walla Walla Penitentiary in Washington State. The experiment occurred in response to inmate strikes and threats to riot. The formal prison administration abdicated in favor of inmate leaders. Among those who came to rule the prison were the "Bikers," a prison gang which, when not terrorizing other inmates or the staff, extended its members the privilege of racing their motorcycles on the prison yard. The experiment ended when the internal situation became so thoroughly chaotic that public pressure mounted to regain control of the institution. As one vivid nonscholarly account of the Walla Walla venture in participative prison management concluded, the "explosive prison violence of the 1970s" discredited most ideas about inmate self-government and opened the door to "hard-line administrators" who argued that "the more freedom inmates have, the more unsafe prisons will be."[125] "At Walla Walla, the reformers may not have had a fair chance, but they did have their turn."[126]

Quite a different lesson, however, was drawn by the authors of the leading scholarly account of the episode. Charles Stastny and Gabrielle Trynauer described the Walla Walla experiment as "the heir to past attempts to bring democracy to the autocratic prison setting."[127] The failure of participative prison management at Walla Walla, they argued, ought not to discourage us from making other experiments in inmate self-government. Instead, they concluded that prison democracy can work where inmates, correctional administrators, and the surrounding community make more of a joint effort than was apparent at Walla Walla: "more open environments must be created, attuning the prison regime to democratic values."[128]

Sociology and Inmate Self-Government

The evidence needed to support the idea that inmate participation in prison management makes for safer, cleaner, more productive prisons has never been forthcoming. That democratic management works better than the alternative when applied to business firms, schools, and armies is debatable. That democratic management works better than the alternative when applied to prisons seems highly questionable at best.

In his survey of inmate involvement in prison administration from 1793 to 1973, J. E. Baker asked why some correctional administrators were unfavorable to the idea "while others turn to the concept for succor in periods of program malaise and in the aftermath of disaster?"[129] Correctional administrators' principal objection to inmate advisory councils and the like "was that they permitted one inmate to have authority over another."[130] Baker found this objection unconvincing. A properly drawn plan, he argued, "can easily and effectively rule out any possibility of this occurring."[131] On "the basis of professional wisdom," he concluded, correctional administrators should assure every prisoner "the right to participate in matters relating to his personal welfare by contributing his point of view."[132]

There is, however, little evidence with which to support the belief that prisons where inmates enjoy more self-government are better than prisons where they enjoy less. What evidence does exist suggests that where inmates come to participate in the formulation and administration of prison policy, prisons change little or become worse. There is not a single example of a system of inmate self-government—formal or informal—in a higher-custody prison that has resulted in a safer, cleaner, more productive facility. Where prison officials have been unable or unwilling to run the prison without the assistance of inmates, the quality of prison life has suffered, often resulting in the rule of inmate predators.

The legendary con-boss system was an informal but potent form of inmate self-government. To the extent that these con bosses helped the administration to keep the inmate population in line, they did so not by friendly persuasion or personal charisma but by brute force. In Mississippi, Louisiana, and other states, con bosses were issued pistols and other weapons with which to "coax" the other inmates. Reformers such as Clinton Duffy of San Quentin were credited with bringing the con-boss system to an end.[133]

The truth, however, is that the system continued unabated at San Quentin and most other higher-custody prisons. Beginning in the 1960s the con-boss system merely assumed a new shape. In many prisons, inmate advisory councils replaced the con-bosses. Inmate self-government was thereby formalized and, in the minds of some observers, improved. These councils have official standing and are supposed to negotiate with prison administrators on behalf of the rest of the prison population. The leaders of these councils, however, are often prison gang leaders or their representatives. Prisons that have inmate councils or equivalent systems of inmate self-government have been no less troubled, and in many cases are more troubled, than those that do not.

Each of the three state prison systems to be discussed in the subsequent chapters of this work have at one time or another relied on inmates to control other inmates. California and Michigan prisons have used con bosses and inmate advisory councils. In these states neither system of inmate self-government improved the quality of prison life. Texas prisons have used what was known as the "building-tender" system. Building tenders were inmates selected by the administration to aid in controlling other inmates. So long as the building tenders were selected with extreme care and monitored closely, they served their purpose and rarely abused their special status. But as soon as the tight administrative controls on the building tenders were relaxed—that is, as soon as the system became one of genuine inmate self-government—terrible abuses of inmates by other inmates followed; the building tender system became a con boss system, powerful gangs came into being, and the administration tried to cope with these gangs through inmate grievance bodies and related measures. As we shall see, the attempt was unsuccessful.

The experiences of most prison systems seem to count against participative prison management. On the grounds of sociological theory, the idea that inmates can and should enjoy a significant degree of self-government seems plausible. From the existing evidence, however, it appears that the quality of prison life has been best where those formally responsible for running the prison have done so with minimal reliance on the inmates or their leaders.

Inmate Treatment and Custody: Are They in Conflict?

In his introduction to a major 1960 work by leading prison sociologists, George H. Grosser noted that the book set forth "a pessimistic view."[134] If the researchers were correct, there was no way that the prison could achieve both "the aims of custody, or punishment, on the one hand, and treatment and reform, on the other."[135] That "the same institution" cannot reconcile these "conflicting mandates," he concluded, "is obvious from these studies."[136]

From the sociological perspective, prisons are torn between treatment-oriented and punitive-custodial goals. The key assumption in the sociology of prison organizations is that, given its multiple and contradictory goals (punishment, incapacitation, deterrence, rehabilitation) the Big House must be a house divided. Prison administrators, sociologists have argued, are caught between the rock of custody and the hard place of treatment: to prevent escapes and maintain control over a large body of inmates, they are driven to paramilitary procedures and tight discipline; to create the treatment milieu necessary for education, counseling, and other programs, they are driven to a looser, more decentralized organizational regime. The incarnation of the administration's necessarily split personality is the correctional officer whose task is inmate "care and custody" and whose role is that of "cop and counselor."[137]

There is, to be sure, some truth in this organizational portrait of the prison. As one prison official stated: "Think of the convicted criminal as a man who never learned to dance. Think of rehabilitation and treatment programs as his dance instruction. We can't teach a man to dance and tie his legs at the same time. But that's precisely what we're supposed to do."

It is true that the modern prison administrator has multiple tasks. But is it true that these tasks are in opposition, or can inmate treatment and custody be reconciled in a rational administrative routine? The belief that treatment and custody are opposed is based on the widely held assumption that custodial routines are somehow inimical to the ends of treatment or inmate self-development. To employ a few of the terms defined in the opening pages of this chapter, sociologists have assumed that there is a basic incompatibility among the goals of order, amenity, and service such that greater order (custody) can be purchased only at the cost of fewer amenities and services (treatment), and vice versa.

Custody as a Condition of Treatment

But there is evidence to suggest that the relationship is one of mutual dependence: no order without amenity and service, no amenity and service without order; custody may be a necessary condition of effective treatment. As Charles E. Silberman has observed, "prison officials' ability or inability to maintain order affects inmates' well being more directly, and far more profoundly, than does any other aspect of prison life."[138] The most comprehensive survey ever undertaken of prison homicides in the United States suggests that a "nucleus of internal order must be present before counseling, educational, and vocational programs can be developed."[139] Where such programs already exist, the inmate who constantly fears for his safety or who cannot be certain of how things will run from one day to the next is unlikely to derive the full benefit of them; he may even forgo these treatment opportunities entirely for the sake of greater protection.[140]

George Beto, a professor of criminal justice and former director of the Texas prison system, has characterized the relationship between inmate treatment and custody as follows: "To offer successfully a wide range of educational and other programs, it is first necessary to establish and maintain safety and security. Work and recreational opportunities can be pursued meaningfully only in an orderly environment. 'Orderly' does not mean repressive. Quite to the contrary, it means simply that degree of formal control which inmates have a right to expect and society has a duty to provide."[141]

Over the last decade or so the idea that custody is a necessary condition of effective treatment has been gaining some ground. In the 1974 edition of their famous criminology text, Edwin Sutherland and Donald Cressey argued that "contemporary conditions of imprisonment are such that the lack of rather uniform conformity to rules by inmates may have adverse effects on any prospects for rehabilitation. Compulsion, thus, might be more conducive to rehabilitation than poor discipline which gives inmates an opportunity to exploit other inmates" and does not keep them from obtaining "things in an illegal manner" just as they did "while on

the outside."[142] In his *Prison Victimization* (1977), Lee Bowker
concluded: "In the case of adult correctional institutions, the emphasis on rehabilitation has been misplaced in that it has tended to
obscure the necessity for devoting significant resources to the
mundane goal of protecting prisoners from each other."[143] In his
recent essay on prison violence, Steve Lerner concluded: "In effect, we made the mistake of trying to rehabilitate inmates before
providing them with a safe place to live. . . . If prisons have a high
density of violent people, they should also have a high density of
law enforcement supervision."[144] The same conclusion was reached
by Clemens Bartollas in his *Correctional Treatment* (1985): "The
lack of a safe and lawful environment presents a major problem in
conducting programs in Big House prisons. Inmates who may otherwise be disposed to treatment will have little interest in anything but survival when they feel unsafe or victimized."[145]

Custody as a Part of Treatment

There is little reason to suppose that a tightly administered prison
regime is in and of itself inimical to the purposes of rehabilitation.
Enforced adherence to rules requiring work, cleanliness, punctu-
ality, and a civil disposition toward others is a form of habituation
to the values, norms, and responsibilities of a non-criminal way of
life. Prisons thus may habituate inmates to civil, law-abiding behavior. Sociologists have tended to reject this idea on the grounds
that it reinforces "the traditional low priority" attached to "the
task of reform" and is no guarantee that the inmate will continue
to behave in a civil and noncriminal way when he is released.[146]
Most contemporary correctional experts have scoffed at the notion
that custody is a part of treatment, judging it to be the intellectual
province of old-fashioned wardens.

It is difficult, however, to dismiss the idea so casually, for the
belief that civil behavior is learned through habituation is present
in Aristotle, runs through the writings of modern philosophers
such as John Stuart Mill, and is consistent with much of contemporary behavioral psychology.[147] Of course, wardens and other
prison workers have normally come to this belief through the
nonacademic channels associated with their practical experiences.
Many of their charges come from backgrounds where life is unstable, and there is little actual (or perceived) relationship between
doing what is right and being rewarded and doing what is wrong

and being punished. In a strict custodial regime, inmates are made to behave in ways consistent with the standards of the "straight" community—dressing neatly, showering regularly, being punctual, working, speaking respectfully to peers and authorities, learning to delay immediate pleasures for the sake of greater future enjoyments, and so on. Breaking the laws of the prison results in punishment (e.g., loss of recreation, solitary confinement) while consistent obedience to the rules is rewarded (e.g., elevation to a trustyship, greater privileges, a reduction in sentence).

The Sociological View of Treatment Versus Custody

Sociologists have objected that forcing criminals to live life on the straight-and-narrow while in prison does not guarantee that they will "internalize" the values and norms of law-abiding society. When the custodial restraints are lifted or relaxed, or when the inmates are released from prison, they may return to a criminal way of life—showing little concern for personal hygiene; treating others in a coarse, incivil manner; stealing; raping; killing. This may be true, but the relationship between the prison's custodial character and rates of recidivism has gone little investigated. Numerous studies of the relationship between treatment programs and recidivism rates have indicated that these programs do little if anything to keep released prisoners from returning to a life of crime.[148] Even if studies of the relationship between custody and recidivism were to produce similar findings, it would not necessarily follow that custodial controls should be loosened or abandoned. Tight custody may be a condition of effective treatment, a form of treatment, and the only way yet devised to keep higher-custody prisoners from physically assaulting and exploiting each other and the staff.

Administrative Change and Its Consequences

The foregoing discussion of prison violence, participative prison management, and inmate treatment and custody has shed a few doubts on the sociological interpretation of prisons. An important test of any mode of analysis is how well it enables one to explain and predict. If the sociological view of prisons is correct, then the best explanation of change in the prison relates to the dynamics of inmate society. If we were to accept the sociological approach, we would predict that moving from tight to loose administrative controls, giving inmates a greater measure of self-government, and tending separately to the tasks of inmate treatment and custody would affect inmate society in ways that would make for less prison violence, more inmate freedom, and better treatment programs.

The Case of Stateville Penitentiary

Most scholars of the prison would probably agree that James B. Jacobs's *Stateville: The Penitentiary in Mass Society* (1977) is the finest single work of prison sociology to be published in the last decade. This high opinion is shared by most correctional practitioners. In Jacobs's words, the study was built upon "a distinguished tradition of sociological studies of the prison community."[149] It is itself a classic contribution to that rich literature.

Jacobs examined administrative change and its consequences at Stateville, a maximum-security prison in Illinois. Stateville was famous for two reasons. First, the prison was built according to the design of political philosopher Jeremy Bentham. It is a circular "panoptican" structure that enables one to stand in the center and see into every cell. As distinctive as Stateville's architecture was its longest-reigning warden, Joseph Ragen.

A man of little formal learning, Ragen ran Stateville for nearly thirty years. By all accounts, including his own[150], the prison was one of the nation's toughest and Ragen ruled it with an iron fist. Of inmates and staff alike, he required rigid adherence to formal rules and regulations covering virtually every aspect of prison life. Under Ragen's highly security-conscious management, Stateville was remarkably clean and free from violence. For prison staff who abused their authority and for inmates who abused other inmates the punishments were swift and certain. In the early 1950s when other prisons were experiencing riots, Stateville remained calm. Still, evaluations of Ragen's regime vary.[151]

In Jacobs's account, Ragen emerges as a transitional figure akin to those last village chieftains who vanish as their societies reach the threshold of political modernization. A new professional breed of prison administrators, many with advanced college degrees, came to run Stateville. For the most part, they dismantled the custodial system of rules and regulations institutionalized by Ragen.

In Jacobs's interpretation, the post-Ragen administrators transformed Stateville "from a patriarchal organization based upon traditional authority to a rational-legal bureaucracy" in which a "professionally oriented central administration" formulated policy, promulgated "comprehensive rules and regulations," and monitored the prison's day-to-day activities.[152] Part of the prison's bureaucratization involved the creation of the nation's first Unified Code of Corrections and an Adult Advisory Board "dominated by academic specialists."[153] The code mandated extensive staff training and development, a separate program of research and long-range planning, "a grievance mechanism whereby the prisoners could complain of their institutional treatment," and a requirement that the prison maintain extensive written records.[154]

According to Jacobs, these changes in the administration of the prison were the result of the rise of such politicized prisoner groups as the Black Muslims, the dawn of court intervention into prison affairs, and other developments that made the "prison's boundaries . . . permeable to the outside."[155] By 1970 "the forces of bureaucratization, politicization and the penetration of judicial norms had undermined the traditional system of authority to the extent that control itself had become problematic."[156] But while the reform administrations that succeeded Ragen encountered serious difficulties, Jacobs concluded that there was a good chance that Stateville would "reemerge in the next few years as a leading model of prison administration for the nation."[157]

Unfortunately, events did not conform to Jacobs's sociological analysis.[158] In the late 1970s, rapes and stabbings at Stateville became commonplace, cleaning ceased, drugs proliferated, and staff turnover rose dramatically. Inmate gangs took over parts of the prison, declaring certain areas off-limits to officers and threatening to kill anyone who trespassed. In the administration's frantic efforts to regain some semblance of control, inmates at Stateville came to enjoy less freedom of movement than they had under Ragen.

Limits of Prison Sociology

Jacobs's masterful case study suggests the limits of the sociological analysis of the prison. As we have seen, from the sociological perspective, prison phenomena are both difficult to understand and hard to control. From this viewpoint, modern prison administrators are to be understood as pawns of the inmate social system buffeted about by contradictory organizational goals and captive to broader social changes. But, as Donald Clemmer noted, "Perspective is everything."[159] While the sociological perspective yields a number of highly interesting ideas about prison life, it appears that few of these ideas are supported by the existing evidence.

For the sake of argument, however, let us suppose that the reality about prisons is essentially as sociologists have been painting it for the last several decades. Suppose, for instance, that the sociological view of prison violence is correct in that a wide range of complex maladies are at the root of inmate assaults, rapes, and riots. Prison managers are hardly in a position to remedy these ills. If the sociological view of prisons is correct, then the most that prison managers can do is to practice what the criminologist Austin McCormick called "paregoric penology,"[160] brokering their official authority through bargains or power-sharing arrangements with the inmates in the hope that these measures will keep the peace.

Whatever its other merits, the sociological view of prisons does not seem to yield insights that are useful to those interested in improving the quality of prison life. Sociological knowledge about prisons does not yet amount to a body of policy-oriented knowledge about them. A different approach to understanding prisons seems necessary.

CONCLUSION: A GOVERNMENTAL PERSPECTIVE ON PRISONS

Unlike contemporary students of the prison, Gustave de Beaumont and Alexis de Tocqueville believed that inmate societies were neither inevitable nor to be welcomed. In what then stood as the most comprehensive study of American prisons ever undertaken, they anticipated much of the sociological literature on prisonization by arguing that where inmates are permitted to associate freely, they are bound to think and act in ways that make them less manageable and "still more corrupted."[161] They did not believe in what we would term rehabilitation and were certain that prison could do little to effect "the radical change of a wicked person into an honest man—a change which produces virtues in the place of vices."[162] But they did believe that in an orderly, well-administered prison where the convict is governed not by other convicts but by disciplined, honorable, and caring officials, he may contract "honest habits" and become "at least more obedient to the laws; and that is all which society has a right to demand."[163] They added that "it is also important for society, that he, whom it punishes, in order to set an example, should correct, if possible, his morals in the prison."[164] They denied flatly that this could be achieved where inmates are in any respect self-governing; and with great prescience they cautioned against attempts "to see liberty restored to the criminal as soon as there is a presumption of his regeneration" or to make "the duration of his sentence depend upon the convict's behavior in prison."[165]

As guides to contemporary corrections, Beaumont and Tocqueville point away from prison sociology and toward what may be termed a governmental perspective on prisons. A governmental perspective on prisons does not provide practical solutions to particular correctional conundrums. Rather, it is a way of thinking about and studying prisons that may lead us to such knowledge. From this perspective, the key actors in any prison setting are the prison administrators, from the director to the warden to the most junior correctional officer in the cellblock. They are the government of the prison, and it is assumed that the quality of prison life will depend mainly, if not solely, on what they do or fail to do. It is the government of keepers, not the society of captives, that is of primary importance. A governmental perspective on prisons asks whether, given the lawless and uncivilized character of their citizens, inmate societies ought not to be subject to strong official controls and a tight, mandatory regime of work and programs. In essence, it admits the possibility, so long foreclosed by prison sociology and its minions, that given appropriate checks on the authority of the keepers, those prison managers may govern best who govern most.

The first question to be asked about government in the society of captives is the same as that to be asked about government in society at large—what are its proper ends and how can they best be achieved?[166] The ends of prison government must be conceived with prison administrators clearly in view. In the words of the late Richard A. McGee, former director of the California prison system, it is prison administrators—directors, wardens, officers, and so on—who have the "pragmatic task" of managing a "miscellaneous lot of people who have one universal characteristic: each has been found guilty of a prohibited act and given a legal sentence by a court of law."[167]

As defined earlier, order, amenity, and service are three ends of good prison government. What kinds of administrative systems are best able to produce order, amenity, and service in prisons? In the remainder of this book, we shall attempt to answer this question through a comparative study of correctional institutions in three states. The Texas, Michigan, and California prison systems furnish us with three strong but distinct approaches to prison management. We compare them not so that we may rank them from best to worst. Rather, we look across these systems in order to discover what their experiences tell us about the mechanics of good prison government. We want to discover the administrative, budgetary, political, or other conditions that make for good prisons in order to determine how, if at all, we can foster such conditions. In short, we are going to look for "what works" in the way of prison government by comparing the past and present practices of three major state prison systems. By examining these varieties of correctional administration, we may begin to learn something of intellectual and practical import about the governability of prisons.

2

The Quality of Prison Life

To many readers the title of this chapter may seem odd. It is widely assumed that prisons are simply horrible places. As Chief Justice Warren E. Burger has observed, "No one has ever suggested that there is any such thing as a good prison."[1] An inmate of the Texas Department of Corrections has stated, "To be confined, to be restricted . . . if that's your future life, then being locked up for thirty years in the Shamrock Hilton would be bad."[2] In the words of criminologist Marvin E. Wolfgang, "prison remains because we are imperfect specimens of our vision of proper humanity."[3]

Prisons are, indeed, quite depressing places. But some prisons are better and less depressing than others. Prisons differ in their levels of order, amenity, and service.

To convey some immediate idea of what this means, on the first day of my study at Walpole prison in Massachusetts, most inmates were confined to their cells because of a murder that had occurred there the night before. Classes, counseling, visits, and work activities were delayed or cancelled. The next morning, I made the rounds with a junior officer in the protective custody wing. I saw inmates lying in beds with sheets tucked tightly around them mummy-style. The reason for this, the officer said, was "to keep the cockroaches from bothering them too much." Later that morning inmates grumbled about the lack of hot coffee. Some days the coffee flowed freely; other days there was barely a cup for each man. Depending on which officer was on duty when the coffee wagon arrived, inmates either would or would not be permitted additional cups.

On any given day, the prison's schedule of treatment and work activities was as erratic as the availability of hot coffee. The prison's industrial plant was scarcely a beehive of productive activity. When counselors or volunteer teachers did meet with inmates, the atmosphere was usually not conducive to communicating problems or to learning. There was shouting, aggressive horseplay, and occasional violence. Even when no violence occurred the threat of violence seemed omnipresent, and both officers and inmates reported being tense. One mid-afternoon, for instance, an inmate (one who had grumbled loudly about the lack of coffee) grabbed a stick with a nail on its tip, used to pick up papers and debris in the yard, and feigned attack by swinging the stick within inches of the officer standing next to me. This man had assaulted both inmates and officers in the past. On another day, an inmate threatened to throw an officer from the third tier of a cellblock. One-third of the state's disciplinary infractions and most of its inmate-on-inmate assaults occurred at Walpole.

If killings, assaults, and threats were less common and administrative routines more predictable (order), if program and work opportunities were offered more regularly and utilized more effectively (service), and if cups of hot coffee (but not cockroaches) were in abundance (amenity), then the quality of prison life at Walpole would have been better than it was.

MEASURING THE QUALITY OF PRISON LIFE: ORDER, AMENITY, AND SERVICE

We can move beyond such anecdotal accounts to more precise ways of measuring and comparing levels of order, amenity, and service in prisons. Of these three aspects of the quality of prison life, order is the most easily measured. One important measure of order relates to prison violence: rapes, assaults, homicides, riots, and so on. There are, however, precious few systematic studies of prison violence. Even if many such studies did exist, the statistics contained in them could not be accepted uncritically. Different departments define infractions, including incidents of violence, differently. They keep varying amounts of information on given indicators of disorder. As I have seen first hand in three different states, there is no end to the number of reporting errors and omissions that can occur at each stage of the reporting process, from the officer in the cellblock who writes the initial disciplinary report to the research analyst at headquarters who codes, records, and files it.

Still, it is possible to make measurements and comparisons of prison order. The data are hard to come by, but they do exist and can be used as a crude but suggestive indicator of how orderly or disorderly a given prison system, or a given prison, has been. Wherever possible, however, it makes sense to supplement the statistics with other types of information about the level of prison order. Such information might include everything from reports about the level of tension in the prison to rates of turnover among prison personnel to the opinions offered by disinterested parties who have investigated conditions or ventured behind the walls.

Order in prison has both an objective and a subjective dimension. Objectively, a prison is orderly if there is little or no overt violence—assaults, rapes, riots, murders, and so on. Subjectively, a prison is orderly if life behind the walls is mostly calm, stable, and predictable. In theory it is possible that a prison that ranks high on objective order may rank low on subjective order, and vice versa. For instance, in some places, prison officials in decades past maintained discipline among inmates by heavy-handed measures which included arbitrary punishment. In these old prisons rates of inmate violence were low, but levels of tension and fear were high. By all accounts, daily life for inmates and staff at these prisons was terribly unpleasant and highly volatile. On the other hand, if the sociological interpretation of prisons is correct, then the contemporary prison may rank high on subjective order but low on objective order—assaults and other violent acts are frequent, but inmate gangs are organized accordingly, know what to expect, and move about calmly; officers adapt to the situation by retreating to the walls; peace reigns so long as nobody upsets the inmate balance of power or violates its informal code of behavior.

As we shall see, however, prisons and prison systems that rank high (or low) on objective order tend to rank high (or low) on subjective order as well. In addition, we shall see that the impressions of disinterested observers normally match the statistics on prison violence.

It is harder to measure amenity and service. Data are scarce, and objective indicators are lacking or controversial. For instance, if prison A has more prisoners enrolled in remedial reading classes than prison B, or if A offers its inmates more hours of instruction per week than B, this tells us little about the quality of the service. How intensive is the instruction? How unruly is the class? How able are the teachers? If A offers inmates work but few other opportunities while B offers them no work but a plethora of programs, which prison should rank higher on service? The problem is even more pronounced in the case of amenity. Food may be abundant, but are the meals nutritious, are the buns hot, is the meat tasty? What constitutes an acceptable level of cellblock cleanliness, and how do we measure it? Is television (or a pool table) a luxury or a necessity for confined persons?

Nevertheless, knowing how many inmates are enrolled in given types of treatment programs gives us a rough measure of prison services. As in the case of order, wherever possible, levels of service should be measured on both objective (number participating, hours spent) and subjective (classroom atmosphere, teacher competency) grounds. The same is true for levels of prison amenity, though in this case the measure is bound to be mostly subjective.

ORDER IN TEXAS, MICHIGAN, AND CALIFORNIA PRISONS

The Texas, Michigan, and California prison systems were compared over time in terms of their respective levels of order, amenity, and service. In terms of prison order, the comparison revealed at least three interesting sets of differences.

1. *Intersystem:* higher levels of order in Texas prisons.

2. *Historical:* a decline in the level of order in Texas prisons.

3. *Intrasystem:* a disparity in the level of order between comparable California prisons.

Texas: The Most Orderly Prisons

By every measure, the Texas prison system was for many years the most orderly of the three, and perhaps the most orderly prison system in the country. Tables 2.1 through 2.3 show that for most of the decade beginning in 1973, Texas has a lower rate of homicides, assaults, suicides, riots, and total critical incidents than either California or Michigan. From 1973 through 1980 Texas had a total of 19 homicides, while California had 139. The average annual homicide rate for these years in California was about eight times higher than in Texas. For most of the period 1977 to 1983 the rate of assaults in Texas was less than half that in Michigan. The same was true for the rate of total incidents in Texas versus both California and Michigan.

In 1980, the Rand Corporation published a study based on data gathered in these three states. Rand's findings are summarized in Tables 2.4 and 2.5. For most of the seven infraction types counted, the percentage of Texas inmates with at least one major infraction is less than that of either Michigan or California inmates. When Rand weighted the infraction score by the severity of each incident, the gap between Texas and the other states widened, suggesting that the infractions in Texas were not only less frequent but less severe than those in Michigan and California. Table 2.6, adapted from a study conducted in 1982, indicates that Texas has had a lower rate of assaults on staff and a lower escape rate than five other large prison systems. Table 2.7 indicates that Texas has had a lower violent death rate than Michigan, California, and several other major prison systems.

In most states, a person is more likely to be murdered inside of prison than on the streets. In Texas, however, the reverse has been true. Bruce Jackson has reported that in California the prison homicide rate has been seven times higher than the state homicide rate. In other large states, such as Minnesota, the prison homicide rate has been over fifty times as great as the state homicide rate. "Among the larger states," Jackson concluded, "only Texas prisoners were at less risk in prison than outside of it."[4]

By most measures, therefore, Texas prisons have been more orderly than California or Michigan prisons. The statistics tend to confirm the observations about Texas prisons made over the years by scores of reporters, academics, visiting practitioners, and others. The Rand study noted that in achieving security "the Texas

Table 2.1: Serious Incidents in the California Department of Corrections (CDC)

Year	Pop.	Hom.	Asslt.	Suic.	Escp.	Rts.	Total
1973	18,080	20	289	18	38	—	777
1974	24,233	23	341	14	39	—	1,022
1975	23,988	16	322	09	20	—	1,089
1976	20,345	20	335	07	25	—	1,385
1977	21,525	17	418	12	41	—	1,815
1978	20,629	16	517	04	36	—	2,060
1979	22,534	14	698	08	50	—	2,427
1980	23,511	13	775	11	46	—	2,848
1981	26,768	17	927	12	56	—	3,084
1982	32,127	14	1,105	24	—	6	3,625
1983	37,218	10	1,438	19	—	5	3,904
Rates per 1,000 Inmates (rounded)							
1973		1.10	16	0.99	2.00	—	43
1974		1.00	14	0.57	1.60	—	42
1975		0.66	13	0.37	0.83	—	45
1976		0.98	16	0.34	1.20	—	68
1977		0.79	19	0.55	1.90	—	84
1978		0.77	25	0.19	1.70	—	100
1979		0.62	31	0.35	2.20	—	108
1980		0.55	33	0.46	1.90	—	121
1981		0.63	35	0.44	2.00	—	115
1982		0.43	38	0.74	—	0.18	112
1983		0.26	38	0.51	—	0.13	104

Abbreviations: Pop. = population. Hom. = homicides. Asslt. = assaults. Suic. = suicides. Escp. = escapes. Rts. = riots. Total = total incidents.

Compiled from *Incidents in the Institutions*, California Department of Corrections (1973 through 1983) and *California Prisoner*, California Department of Corrections (1973 through 1983). In 1982 the former source included the number of riots but not the number of escapes. Under assaults are counted attacks with and without weapons. Prior to 1982 the latter category was labelled "fights." Riots are not defined. Total incidents also include possession of a weapon, attempted suicide, sex offenses, narcotics offenses, and "other." They do not include "less serious attacks" such as "throwing cold liquid, food or cards." The incident reports detail the institution and method of homicides; for example, of the 17 persons murdered in 1981, one was a supervisor in the wood shop at San Quentin who was clubbed to death; the rest were inmates: one strangled at San Quentin, three stabbed to death at San Quentin, one shot and four stabbed to death at Folsom, four stabbed to death at the California Medical Facility, and three stabbed to death at the Deuel Vocational Facility.

system is regarded as the most successful and efficient in the nation. . . . The facilities are extraordinarily clean and free from disturbances."[5] The author of a 1978 article in a Texas magazine wrote that "Texas is ranked number one among the nation's penal

Table 2.2 Serious Incidents in the Michigan Department of Corrections (MDC)

Year	Pop.	Hom.	Asslt.	Suic.	Escp.	Rts.	Total
1977	13,823	2	524	6	60	5	1,257
1978	14,944	4	432	2	66	8	1,079
1979	15,002	5	718	2	78	8	1,528
1980	15,124	0	781	9	22/48	6	1,457
1981	14,964	3	799	7	13/32	27	3,809
1982	14,737	3	658	6	8/46	14	3,640
1983	14,470	3	813	4	3/12	11	3,478
Rates per 1,000 Inmates (rounded)							
1977		0.14	38	0.43	4.30	0.36	91
1978		0.26	29	0.13	4.40	0.53	72
1979		0.33	48	0.13	5.20	0.53	101
1980		0.00	52	0.59	1.40	0.39	96
1981		0.20	54	0.46	0.87	1.80	255
1982		0.20	45	0.40	0.54	0.95	247
1983		0.20	56	0.27	0.20	0.76	241

Abbreviations: Pop. = population. Hom. = homicides. Asslt. = assaults. Suic. = suicides. Escp. = escapes. Rts. = riots. Total = total incidents.

Compiled from *Annual Statistical Reports*, Michigan Department of Corrections, 1977 through 1983. Riots are defined as "riot/mutiny/strike." Escape figures for 1977 through 1979 are for escape attempts. In 1980 and thereafter the reports list escapes (first figure) and escape attempts (second figure). Rates for 1977 through 1979 are based on attempts and rates for 1980 through 1983 are based on escapes. Among the other categories counted under total incidents are suicide attempts, weapons offenses, smuggling, drug offenses, insubordination, money offenses, and extortion.

systems. TDC annually hosts scores of prison administrators from other states, and even other countries, who visit the Texas system to study its operation and management."[6] A 1978 article in the *Christian Science Monitor* described the Texas prison system as a "highly disciplined industrial dynasty" that had progressed "about as far into the 20th century as any in the country."[7] A 1978 article in a leading magazine for corrections professionals stressed that the Texas prison system was widely acknowledged to accomplish security "better than any other prison system."[8]

In their 1978 essay on prison discipline, John P. Conrad and Simon Dinitz argued that "Texas has proved that it is possible to organize a prison for the primary purposes of control and economic productivity."[9] Texas, they wrote, has achieved "lawful and safe" prisons. Leading practitioners, such as Director of the Federal Bureau of Prisons Norman Carlson, are among those who have

Table 2.3: Serious Incidents in the Texas Department of Corrections (TDC)

Year	Pop.	Hom.	Asslt.	Suic.	Escp.	Rts.	Total
1973	16,224	2	130	—	24	1	468
1974	17,113	1	178	—	19	1	648
1975	18,377	1	248	—	22	1	985
1976	20,266	0	327	—	14	0	856
1977	21,382	5	271	—	3	0	970
1978	23,935	0	259	—	11	2	963
1979	25,260	3	234	[a]	9	0	1,100
1980	28,032	7	—	[a]	19	0	—
1981	30,855	12	—	[a]	11	8	—
1982	35,088	6	887[b]	[a]	6	0	2,504[b]
1983	36,945	10	3,411[c]	[a]	14	0	4,462[c]
Rates per 1,000 Inmates (rounded)							
1973		0.12	8	—	1.40	0.06	29
1974		0.05	10	—	1.10	0.05	38
1975		0.05	13	—	1.20	0.05	54
1976		0.00	16	—	0.69	0.00	42
1977		0.23	13	—	0.14	0.00	45
1978		0.00	11	—	0.46	0.08	40
1979		0.11	9	—	0.35	0.00	44
1980		0.25	—	—	0.67	0.00	—
1981		0.38	—	—	0.35	0.25	—
1982		0.17	57[b]	—	0.40	0.00	76
1983		0.27	95[c]	—	0.37	0.00	120

Abbreviations: Pop. = population. Hom. = homicides. Asslt. = assaults. Suic. = suicides. Escp. = escapes. Rts. = riots. Total = total incidents.

[a] From 1979 to 1983 there were 25 suicides. Source: Sheldon Eckland-Olson, "Judicial Decisions and the Social Order of Prison Violence: Evidence From the Post-Ruiz Years in Texas" (University of Texas, Department of Sociology, 1984)."

[b] Data are for period 8/7/81 to 8/18/82. Rates calculated on pop. of 33,000.

[c] Data are for period 4/1/83 to 3/3/84. Rates calculated on pop. of 36,000.

Compiled from *Bi-Monthly Disciplinary Reports*, Texas Department of Corrections (January 1973 through March 1984) and *Fiscal Year Statistical Report*, Texas Department of Corrections (1973 through 1983). Data on riots are derived from "Texas Department of Corrections Riots," Texas Department of Corrections, 1974. A riot is defined as an incident involving fifteen or more inmates. Because it did not meet this standard, a 1974 riot at the Huntsville Unit was not noted in the report but was counted here because of its severity. Assaults 1973–1979 include inmate attacks with and without weapons. Assaults 1981–1983 include these attacks plus fighting and striking an officer. Total incidents also include destroying property, fighting, sex malpractice, and escape attempts.

Table 2.4 Percentage of Inmate Population with at Least One Disciplinary Infraction During Their Present Term

Infractions Type

Administrative: Minor violations, disobedience, gambling, theft, horseplay, out-of-place, noncoercive homosexuality, work-related and other non-serious charges.

Contraband: Having concealed or in possession of items in violation of rules (e.g. drugs, weapons, literature).

Threat: Statement or gesture indicating intent to harm, coerce, intimidate, etc.

Violence Without Injury: Destruction of state property, fight or assault not resulting in an injury (but more serious than horseplay).

Minor Injury: Fight or assault resulting in cut, bruise, needing only slight medical treatment, i.e. antiseptic or bandaids.

Major Injury: Fight or assault resulting in injury requiring medical treatment or observation, i.e. broken bone, unconsciousness, cut requiring stitches.

Escape: Plots, attempts, conspiracies.

	California	Michigan	Texas
Administrative	45	60	48
Contraband	24	30	08
Threat	04	14	01
Violence without injury	15	28	18
Minor injury	02	05	01
Major injury	03	01	01
Escape	01	08	00

SOURCE: Joan Petersilia et al., *The Prison Experience of Career Criminals* (Santa Monica, CA: Rand Corporation, May 1980), pp. xiv, 67.

Table 2.5 Average Number of Infractions per Inmate

Infractions Type
Serious: Escape, Injury, Violence Without Injury
Nonserious: Threat, Possession of Contraband, Administrative Rule Violations

Infractions Type	California (n = 337)	Michigan (n = 363)	Texas (n = 583)
Serious	.30	.69	.29
Nonserious	1.69	3.70	1.38
Total	1.99	4.39	1.67

SOURCE: Joan Petersilia et al., *The Prison Experience of Career Criminals* (Santa Monica, CA: Rand Corporation, May 1980), p. 69.

Table 2.6 Assaults on Staff and Escapes (1981–1982) per 1,000 Inmates for Five Prison Systems with Average Daily Populations over 10,000

	Assaults	Escapes
Florida	40.2	29.9
Georgia	—	21.1
Maryland	22.0	19.6
North Carolina	20.1	42.3
Texas	05.9	00.4

Adapted from *Adult Correctional Systems: Report to the Southern Legislative Conference Council of State Governments* (October 1982), p. 19.

Table 2.7 Deaths (1980–1983) per 1,000 Inmates for Ten Prison Systems with Average Monthly Populations of over 10,000 Ranked by Total Violent Death Rate

	Total	Homicide	Suicide
California	1.01	.46	.55
Maryland	.97	.51	.46
Federal	.84	.48	.36
Michigan	.67	.17	.50
Georgia	.50	.35	.15
Florida	.47	.30	.17
Texas	.47	.30	.17
Ohio	.46	.10	.36
Pennsylvania	.37	.05	.32
North Carolina	.24	.13	.11

SOURCE: Sheldon Eckland-Olson, "Judicial Decisions and the Social Order of Prison Violence: Evidence from the Post-Ruiz Years in Texas" (University of Texas, Department of Sociology, 1984).

openly admired the Texas prison system for its achievements in prison safety. A 1980 Masters thesis covering the history of corrections in Texas was lavish in its praise for the system's orderliness.[10] A 1981 textbook on correctional administration concluded its chapter on institutional custody and security with the transcript of an interview with Dr. George Beto, Director of the Texas Department of Corrections from 1962 to 1972, and chief architect of what was commonly considered to be the country's safest prison system.[11]

The comparative lack of violence in Texas prisons may be partially responsible for the system's low rate of personnel turnover for most of the 1970s and early 1980s. A 1981 Ph.D. thesis on Texas correctional officers found that the system's correctional personnel did not believe that working in prison was very stressful. The author concluded that this "could be due to the safety and security of the Texas system."[12] Such an inference seems plausible in light of the fact that more violent prison systems generally have higher rates of staff turnover. For example, in California, rates of correctional staff turnover at some prisons have run over 50 percent. In Texas, turnover rates at most institutions ran below 10 percent.

In each of their annual agency reports from 1964 to 1981, Texas prison officials pointed proudly to their system's safety record. In Michigan, on the other hand, there was little such horn-blowing. Indeed, following the major 1981 riot at Michigan's State Prison of Southern Michigan (SPSM-Jackson), the department's annual report began by harking back to an earlier riot and noting "the injuries, the destruction, the opportunities lost to stop the spinning top, wobbling crazily out of control."[13] Michigan, however, has not often been the object of reports, studies, and commentaries about prison disorder. California, on the other hand, has been alternately praised for its emphasis on inmate treatment and criticized for the widespread violence and gang activities inside its prisons.

The Decline of Order in Texas Prisons

While the level of order in California and Michigan prisons has not changed significantly over the last few years, the level of order in Texas prisons plummeted dramatically between 1983 and 1986. In 1984 the system experienced twenty-five murders. In 1985 there were twenty-seven homicides in Texas prisons. Table 2.8 shows that the rate of total infractions in Texas prisons has climbed in this decade. Tables 2.9 and 2.10 isolate this systemwide trend as it pertains to homicides and inmate-on-officer violence, respectively. Tables 2.11 and 2.12 offer a closer view of this rise in violence as it has occurred at one Texas prison. Table 2.11 shows that between 1981 and 1984 the total rate of violence among inmates at this prison almost tripled. The most spectacular rise, however, was in the rate of inmate attacks on officers. Table 2.12 shows that between 1981 and 1984 the total rate of inmate-on-officer aggression at this prison increased over fivefold.

There was no shortage of essays, newspaper reports, and commentary to mark this decisive decline in the orderliness of Texas prisons.[14] What in 1975 was being touted as one of the most or-

Table 2.8 Rates per 1,000 Inmates of Escapes, Homicides, and
All Major and Minor Infractions for the Texas Prison System from
1964 to 1984

Year	Escapes	Homicides	All Infractions
1964	0.41	0.08	97.3
1965	0.47	0.07	79.6
1966	0.64	0.08	60.4
1967	0.39	0.00	44.9
1968	0.56	0.24	54.6
1969	0.08	0.00	70.0
1970	0.15	0.07	105.3
1971	0.46	0.26	90.7
1972	0.55	0.00	99.1
1973	1.40	0.12	165.8
1974	1.10	0.05	189.2
1975	1.20	0.05	224.3
1976	0.69	0.00	246.1
1977	0.14	0.23	234.3
1978	0.46	0.00	313.2
1979	0.35	0.11	254.0
1980	0.67	0.25	270.6
1981	0.35	0.38	374.7
1982	0.40	0.17	597.5
1983	0.37	0.27	657.5
1984	—	0.70[a]	——

[a]In 1984 the Texas prison system had 25 homicides and an average daily population of 35,256.

Compiled from *Disciplinary Reports*. Texas Department of Corrections, 1964 through 1983.

derly prison systems in the country had, by 1985, become one of the nation's most unsafe places to serve time.

Intrasystem Differences in Order: California Prisons

Prisons in the same system have differed markedly in their rates of disorder. While Texas and Michigan display some such intrasystem differences, they are not so pronounced as those that can be observed among otherwise comparable California prisons. One intrasystem difference is between California's Correctional Training Facility, better known as Soledad prison, and its California Men's Colony, called CMC. Both are (in the parlance of California corrections) "level-3" institutions, higher-custody prisons that are designated to hold all but the worst criminals and security

Table 2.9 Homicide Rates and Population Levels in the Texas Prison System from 1968 to 1983

Years	Homicides per 1,000 Inmates
1968–70	.24
1969–71	.30
1970–72	.41
1971–73	.32
1972–74	.30
1973–75	.36
1974–76	.28
1975–77	.26
1976–78	.19
1977–79	.35
1978–80	.36
1979–81	.77
1980–82	.97
1981–83	1.01

SOURCE: Sheldon Eckland-Olson, "Judicial Decisions and the Social Order of Prison Violence: Evidence from the Post-Ruiz Years in Texas" (University of Texas, Department of Sociology, 1985), p. 33.

Table 2.10 Rates of Striking an Officer or Other Employee in the Texas Prison System from 1973 to 1983

Year	Rate per 1,000 Inmates	Rate per 1,000 Staff
1973	2.29	—
1974	2.40	—
1975	3.05	—
1976	3.64	—
1977	2.53	—
1978	3.97	—
1979	3.66	39.95
1980	4.35	48.02
1981	6.24	65.02
1982	12.46	105.40
1983	13.71	106.20
1984	40.03[a]	273.40[a]

[a] Approximate, based on data through November 1984.

SOURCE: Sheldon Eckland-Olson, "Judicial Decisions and the Social Order of Prison Violence: Evidence from the Post-Ruiz Years in Texas" (University of Texas, Department of Sociology, 1985), p. 34.

Table 2.11 Rates per 1,000 Inmates of Inmate-on-Inmate Weapons Offenses by Type at the Eastham Unit of the Texas Department of Corrections

Infraction	1981	1982	1983	1984
Fighting with a weapon	8.5	9.6	14.6	11.8
Striking an inmate with a weapon	7.1	7.7	12.6	21.8
Possession of a weapon	13.6	7.7	18.7	51.4
Homicide	0.0	0.3	0.0	1.1
Total	29.2	25.3	45.9	86.1
Population	2,938.0	3,224.0	3,150.0	2,607.0

Adapted from James W. Marquart and Ben M. Crouch, "Judicial Reform and Prisoner Control: The Impact of Ruiz v. Estelle on a Texas Penitentiary," Revised version of a paper delivered at the annual meeting of the Southern Sociological Society (Charlotte, NC, April 1985).

Table 2.12 Rates per 1,000 Inmates of Inmate-on-Officer Infractions, by Type, at the Eastham Unit of the Texas Department of Corrections

Infraction	1981	1982	1983	1984
Striking an officer	1.3	6.5	12.0	49.4
Attempting to strike an officer	2.3	2.7	5.7	8.0
Threatening to strike an officer	1.3	1.5	12.0	41.0
Refusing or failing to obey an order	30.6	20.1	22.8	81.7
Use of indecent or vulgar language	3.7	4.3	28.2	36.0
Total	39.0	35.0	81.0	216.0
Population	2,938.0	3,224.0	3,150.0	2,607.0

Adapted from James W. Marquart and Ben M. Crouch, "Judicial Reform and Prisoner Control: The Impact of Ruiz v. Estelle on a Texas Penitentiary," Revised version of paper delivered at the annual meeting of the Southern Sociological Society (Charlotte, NC, April 1985).

risks. The most dangerous offenders are supposed to serve their sentences in either of the state's two "level-4" institutions, San Quentin and Folsom prison. Historically, rates of homicide, assault, and other disorders have been lower at CMC than at Soledad. Table 2.13 shows that from 1977 to 1983 CMC had lower total incident rates than Soledad. In some years (1977, 1979, and 1980) the differences were rather sharp. In no year has Soledad had lower total incident rates than CMC. CMC has been widely regarded as the safest higher-custody prison in California.

Table 2.13 Incident Rates per 100 Average Daily Institutional
Population for the California Men's Colony (CMC) and the California
Training Facility (CTF-Soledad) from 1977 to 1983

	1977	1978	1979	1980	1981	1982	1983
CMC	5.57	7.60	4.63	5.13	7.00	6.21	7.96
CTF	15.22	17.57	20.70	16.45	11.60	10.46	9.96

SOURCE: *Inmate Incidents in the Institutions, Summary*, California Department
of Corrections, April 6, 1984.

EXPLAINING DIFFERENCES IN PRISON ORDER

What accounts for such differences in levels of prison order? There
are several possibilities. The Rand study noted that a detailed
examination of each state's administrative policies and practices
might explain the intersystem differences.[15] Such an examination,
however, was beyond the scope of that study. Managerial differences might also explain the increase in Texas prison disorder and
the intrasystem difference between comparable California institutions. There are, in fact, many possible explanations. Eleven of
them are as follows:

1. Inaccurate or biased data
2. Characteristics of the inmate population
3. Level of expenditures
4. Level of crowding
5. Inmate-to-staff ratios
6. Level of formal training
7. Architecture
8. Inmate social system
9. Level of inmate treatment
10. Inmate–staff race relations
11. Repressive measures

These are not the only possibilities; they are, however, the ones
most often cited when differences in prison order and wider differences in the quality of prison life are debated. Nor are these

explanations mutually exclusive. For example, it may be that Texas was more orderly because it concentrated on custody to the virtual exclusion of treatment, had more docile inmates, experienced little crowding, spent much money, underreported violent infractions, had wall-to-wall officers, devoted lots of resources to officer training, did nothing to upset inmate society, had newer and more secure facilities, brutalized and repressed inmates, and had a more racially homogeneous inmate population. Finally, these factors are not fully independent of prison management. Levels of staff training and staffing, for instance, can be highly influenced by administrative policies and practices.

Inaccurate or Biased Data

In any empirical research, one has to confront the possibility that one's data are flawed, bogus, or incomplete. In the case at hand, it might be that the differences in levels of prison order are more apparent than real. For instance, one might speculate that the differences in infraction rates between Texas and Michigan arise because Michigan has been more scrupulous than Texas in reporting and recording inmate misdeeds. Also, the impressions of outside observers about the orderliness of Texas prisons may have been biased by official misinformation, unduly colored by the tug of conventional correctional wisdom about Texas prisons, or distorted by exaggerated accounts of disorder in, say, California prisons. By the same token, the upturn in Texas prison violence and the difference between CMC and Soledad may be artifacts of flaws in the data.

More will be said on this subject in the succeeding chapters and in the appendix on studying prisons. For now, however, it should be noted that various precautions were taken to guard against such data problems. The Rand study hinted that the differences in order between Michigan and the other two states arose because Michigan prison personnel were most scrupulous about taking official action against inmate rule infractions. "In our opinion," the study noted, "the Michigan infractions data probably reflect more accurately the actual level of inmate behavior problems. In California . . . minor transgressions are often ignored as a tradeoff for continued order in prison. . . . Texas prison officials spoke of informal procedures (short of writing a disciplinary report) for handling some minor infractions."[16]

But my own research—from archival digging, to interviews, to extended on-site observations—leads me to conclude that, if anything, the amount of disorder in Texas prisons has been overreported while that in California and, especially, Michigan prisons has been underreported. Texas correctional officers, for instance, were far more likely than those in the other two states to act on minor rule violations by inmates. Senior officers in Texas were also more likely to report and discipline junior officers for misconduct. On the other hand, officers in California and Michigan (like those I had observed in Massachusetts) were more prone to ignore many minor, and even some major, infractions by inmates and staff. In Texas, prison personnel acted on rule violations pretty much as they were instructed to in basic training. To quote from a typical passage of a Texas training manual, "Whatever the rules, enforce them. . . . [Any officer who fails to do so] is not only useless . . . but a positive menace . . . to the security of the institution. . . . Do not be satisfied with anything less than complete compliance with orders."

Document 2.1 lists the ninety-eight rule infractions that until recently could land a Texas inmate in solitary confinement. The offense recorded on the sample disciplinary report (number 45: laziness) has not been considered a major offense in the other two states and would, in most cases, go unreported where it occurred. The offenses listed under Document 2.1 range from escape (number 25) to "unauthorized piddling" (number 68). The point is not that the Texas Department of Corrections has been right (or wrong) to enforce the rules regarding these behaviors, but rather that in Texas prison officials have been at least as likely to report and act on violations of the official rules, and to do so through formal channels, as have officials in either California or Michigan. Given that Texas has been most rigorous (even fetishistic) about acting on disciplinary problems, the actual intersystem difference in level of order was probably wider than the numbers indicated, with Texas still more orderly and the other two systems less orderly than the numbers suggest.

This conclusion, however, is not beyond a reasonable challenge. With respect to the intersystem differences, for instance, some Michigan prison officials are convinced that their system has actually performed much better, and the Texas system much worse, than is indicated by the bare statistics. One high-ranking Michigan Department of Corrections (MDC) official argued:

DOCUMENT 2.1

CODE	DESCRIPTION
01	Act defined as felony by State of Texas
02	Act defined as misdemeanor by State of Texas
03	Use of narcotics
04	Possession of narcotics
05	Buying narcotics
06	Selling narcotics
07	Use of marijuana
08	Possession of marijuana
09	Buying marijuana
10	Selling marijuana
11	Use of alcohol
12	Buying alcohol
13	Selling alcohol
14	Possession of alcohol
15	Distilling alcohol
16	Brewing alcohol
17	Use of intoxicating inhalents
18	Possession of intoxicating inhalents
19	Selling intoxicating inhalents
20	Buying intoxicating inhalents
21	Use of unauthorized drugs
22	Possession of unauthorized drugs
23	Selling unauthorized drugs
24	Buying unauthorized drugs
25	Escape
26	Attempt to escape
27	Aiding escape
28	Aiding attempt to escape
29	Fighting without weapon
30	Fighting with weapon
31	Possession of weapon
32	Committing sex malpractice oral active
33	Committing sex malpractice oral passive
34	Committing sex malpractive anal active
35	Committing sex malpractive anal passive
36	Soliciting sex malpractice
37	Inciting sex malpractice by threat
38	Creating unnecessary noise
39	Indecent language, use of; and/or vulgar language
40	Inmate verbally threatening another inmate
41	Mutiny
42	Agitating mutiny
43	Inciting mutiny
44	Refuse medical treatment for communicable disease
45	Laziness: Refuse to work

DOCUMENT 2.1 *(cont.)*

Page Two

CODE	DESCRIPTION
46	Laziness: Failure to work
47	Laziness: Refuse to obey orders
48	Laziness: Failure to obey orders
49	Damaging or destroying State property
50	Damaging or destroy another person's property
51	Mutilation - self-inflicted
52	Mutilation - permit other to inflict
53	Mutilation - assist infliction of injury
54	Talking to non-authorized people
55	Writing to non-authorized people
56	Non-authorized publication
57	Giving unauthorized information
58	Possession of unauthorized clothing
59	Use of unauthorized clothing
60	Possession of money
61	In living quarters without permission
62	Leaving assignment without permission
63	Disrespectful attitude
64	Disrespectful action
65	False soliciting of money
66	False soliciting of gifts
67	Refusal to attend school
68	Unauthorized piddling
69	Abuse treatment of animal
70	Carnal relations with animal
71	Creating disturbance
72	Stealing State property
73	Stealing from inmate
74	Possession of contraband
75	Wasting food
76	General agitation
77	Inmate protection
78	Lying to officer
79	Running a store
80	Trafficking and trading
81	Solicit assistance from an officer to violate rule
82	Solicit assistance from an inmate to violate rule
83	Withholding information during an interview
84	Failure to cooperate during interview
85	Malingering
86	Sleeping on job
87	Attempting to strike an officer
88	Threatening an officer
89	Striking an officer
90	Gaming

DOCUMENT 2.1 *(cont.)*

```
Page Three


  CODE        DESCRIPTION

   91         Possession of gaming paraphernalia
   92         Tattooing
   93         Possession of tattooing paraphernalia
   94         Aggravated assault on inmate
   95         Aggravated assault on inmate with weapon
   96         Unauthorized cell
   97         Possession of contraband for planning escape
   98         Aiding and abetting in planning escape
```

We in Michigan have attempted to provide a sort of internal uniform crime report. . . . What officers report to their supervisors and what gets into official statistics may be two different things. . . . (I am convinced) that the Texas system condoned and allowed exploitation and brutality to an extent which could not occur here. . . . We believe it very likely that violence was systematically unreported to the central office in the Texas system, as it was in many prisons in the U.S. prior to the 60s and 70s.

Other Michigan officials, however, including many who have spent years in the system's cellblocks, ridiculed as naïve any belief in the efficacy of MDC's own reporting system. One veteran officer stated: "We've always let lots of things go without reporting them—fights, roughing a guy up, more serious stuff too. See for yourself. . . ." In none of the several probes of MDC conducted by the Department of Justice and investigative committees has the system been accused of such violations. When pressed with this fact, the officers' typical response was "They buy the fancy paperwork." Or as one veteran official said: "Like in baseball, you can't hit what you can't see, all the infractions that we let go on a daily basis are invisible . . . a way of life."

So far as one can discover, the upturn in Texas prison disorder was no mere artifact of reporting changes or greater scrupulousness in recording violations. If anything, between 1983 and 1986, officers and other Texas prison officials had become somewhat less likely than they were in previous years to act on rule infractions. Hence, the upturn in Texas prison disorder may be a bit understated. There are no clear differences between the official reporting of inmate or staff misdeeds at CMC and Soledad.

It is hard to imagine that prison officials in any state still can misrepresent the number of homicides. It is much less possible than it once was for them to grossly underreport other serious disorders. In the cases at hand, one doubts that even substantial inaccuracies in reporting would explain the very large differences in measures of order.

Characteristics of the Inmate Population

One clear possibility is that differences in the level of prison order result from differences in the character of the inmate population. A plausible guess is that more orderly prisons (or prison systems) have less violent (or violence-prone) inmates. Or to state this hypothesis more colloquially, maybe some prisons are less violent because the "cookies" in them are not so tough.

An immediate problem with this hypothesis, however, is that there is no clear consensus in the research literature regarding what, if any, relationship exists between negative prison behavior, such as assaultiveness, on the one hand, and objective inmate characteristics, such as race, offense of conviction, or prior prison terms, on the other. But there is some consistent evidence that inmate age and prison disciplinary problems vary inversely such that younger inmates are more prone to disorderly behavior than older inmates.[17] Inside prisons as on the streets, it appears that younger criminals are more violent than older ones.

To the extent that this relationship between age and inmate behavior holds, we would expect to find that Texas inmates are older than either California or Michigan inmates. We would also expect to find that the percentage of younger inmates in Texas grew as the system became more violent. Finally, we would guess that CMC has had an older inmate population than Soledad.

In fact, however, none of these suppositions appears to hold. Table 2.14 shows that in the Rand sample younger inmates were more common in Texas than in either California or Michigan. Table 2.15 summarizes the leading characteristics of the statewide Texas prison population over the last several years. Not only the age of the inmate population but every other objective characteristic investigated has remained virtually constant as Texas prisons have become more disorderly.

As noted earlier, CMC and Soledad are both so-called level-3

Table 2.14 Characteristics of Inmate Populations (in percent, rounded)

	California	Michigan	Texas
Race			
Anglo	41	38	38
Black	35	56	43
Hispanic	22	02	18
Age			
23 or younger	25	39	52
24–30	49	31	23
31 or older	26	30	25
Conviction Offense			
Homicide	18	08	14
Robbery	28	16	22
Burglary	15	24	26
Drugs	07	06	08
Prior Prison Term(s)	63	61	67

SOURCES: Figures on age, Michigan conviction offense, and prior prison term(s): Joan Petersilia et al., *The Prison Experience of Career Criminals* (Santa Monica, CA: RAND Corporation, 1980), p. 9. Figures on conviction offense for Texas: *Fiscal Year Statistical Report 1980* (Huntsville, Texas: Texas Department of Corrections). Figures on conviction offense for California: *California Prisoners* (Sacramento, CA: California Department of Corrections): Figures on race: Texas, Michigan, and California departments of corrections.

institutions. But because of levels of overcrowding in the system, both prisons have had to house a number of level-4 inmates. In California corrections circles, one frequently hears CMC's comparative advantage in orderliness attributed to its relative lack of level-4 felons. In fact, however, over the last few years about 25 percent of the inmate population at both CMC and Soledad has consisted of level-4 inmates. Most of the rest of the inmate population at each prison has consisted of level-3 felons. The level-3 inmates at CMC have been less disorderly than the level-3 inmates at Soledad.

The Rand research suggested that the typical Texas inmate had fewer and less serious self-reported crimes than the typical inmate in California or Michigan. Conceivably, this might account in part for the lower levels of disorder in Texas. We do not know, however, what, if any, relationship exists between an offender's preinstitutional criminality and his propensity to commit infractions inside the prison. In any case, no intersystem difference in the inmates' preinstitutional criminal profiles could account for ei-

Table 2.15 Characteristics of the Texas Inmate Population
(in percent, rounded)

	1980	1981	1982	1983	1984
Race					
Anglo	38	38	38	37	37
Black	43	44	44	44	43
Hispanic	18	18	18	19	19
Age					
25 or younger	40	39	39	38	37
31 or older	67	67	67	66	65
Conviction Offense					
Murder	14	14	14	14	14
Robbery	22	23	22	22	21
Burglary	26	25	25	26	26
Drugs	08	07	06	06	06
Sex	06	06	06	06	06
Prior Term					
Texas	41	40	39	39	42
Other	12	13	12	12	11
Recidivist age 22–25	10	10	10	10	10
Mean I.Q.	88	87	87	87	88

Compiled from *Fiscal Year Statistical Report* (1980 through 1984) (Huntsville, Texas: Texas Department of Corrections).

ther the upturn of disorder in Texas prisons or the intrasystem difference in California.

Nor do the characteristics of the inmate population help to explain an earlier historical change in the level of prison order in Texas. Between 1947 and 1961, the average annual rate of killings per 1,000 inmates was .45. Over the years 1962 to 1972 the rate dropped to .14. During the earlier period, the average annual total infraction rate per 1,000 inmates was 84. In the latter period, the rate dropped to 75. This decrease in prison disorder occurred even though the Texas inmate population had increased by about 50 percent, was more diverse racially, and had a higher proportion of violent offenders. As we shall learn in some detail later, a different administration governed Texas prisons in the latter period.

None of this should be taken as proof that characteristics of the inmate population do not matter in determining the level of prison order. The fact is that higher-custody prisons have more troublesome inmates than lower-custody prisons. (Corrections people have a chest full of terms for such inmates, among the more printable of which are "heavies" and "hard asses.") Common sense suggests that this has something to do with the almost uniformly higher levels of violence in higher-custody prisons.

Rather, the evidence suggests only that, in the three cases at hand, characteristics of the inmate population were not the whole story. Instead of concluding that inmate characteristics do not matter, it would be wiser to infer cautiously that in each case there may have been some intervening variable at work (the character of prison management) that conditioned (strengthened or restrained) the propensity to violence of a given inmate population.

Level of Expenditures

Successive blue-ribbon panels and numerous scholars have argued that America's prisons are so wretched because so little money is spent on them. Perhaps Texas prisons achieved greater order than Michigan or California prisons by spending more money per inmate. One might also posit that the decline in order in Texas was associated with a cutback in prison expenditures, while the greater order of CMC over Soledad has been purchased with more tax dollars per inmate.

Table 2.16 Annual Expenditures per Inmate in Dollars, Ranked by State from Lowest to Highest (1977)

Rank	State	Expenditure
1	Texas	2,241
17	Michigan	4,990
36	California	8,173
50	New Hampshire	15,946

Adapted from Joan Mullen and Bradford Smith, *American Prisons and Jails, Volume III; Conditions and Costs of Confinement* (Washington, D.C.: National Institute of Justice, October 1980).

Table 2.17 Annual Expenditures per Inmate in Dollars for the Texas, Michigan, and California Prison Systems

	Texas	Michigan	California
1980	2,300	10,000	12,000
1981	5,121	14,545	17,594
1982	4,545	15,332	17,625
1983	6,951	18,337	19,339

SOURCE: Texas, Michigan, and California departments of corrections.

Tables 2.16 and 2.17 cast doubt on this hypothesis. They show that Texas has spent far less per prisoner than California, Michigan, and most other states. Indeed, for most of the last two decades, Texas has spent less per prisoner than any prison system in the country. Table 2.18 shows that the per-diem expenditure per inmate in Texas has been less than one-third the national average.

Texas prison expenditures were increasing as the system became less orderly. Table 2.19 indicates that both the absolute level and the rate of increase in Texas prison expenditures were increasing as the system was becoming more violent.

CMC has normally spent less per inmate than the California average, while Soledad has normally spent at or above this average. For instance, in 1983–1984, CMC had the lowest per capita cost in the California prison system (15 percent below the system average).

In each case, therefore, greater order was being achieved where less money was being spent.

Table 2.18 Texas Prison System Expenditures per Inmate per Day in Dollars Versus National Average

	Texas	National Average
1979	7.34	27.00
1981	9.80	31.00
1983	14.57	43.37

SOURCE: *Strengthening TDC's Management Effectiveness: Final Report* (Dallas, Texas: McKinsey and Company, May 14, 1982), p. 8.

Table 2.19 Texas Prison System Expenditures per Inmate per Day in Dollars and Spending Increases

	Expenditure	Increase (percent)
1977	7.32	not applicable
1978	7.15	−2.3
1979	7.34	2.6
1980	8.61	17.3
1981	9.80	13.8
1982	12.11	23.5
1983	14.57	20.3
1984	17.70	21.4

Compiled from *Fiscal Year Statistical Report, 1984* (Huntsville, Texas: Texas Department of Corrections).

Level of Crowding

It is widely believed that crowding increases violence in prisons. There are a number of studies that suggest that it has this effect.[18] Perhaps Texas prisons were less crowded than California and Michigan prisons during those years when Texas prisons were most orderly. By the same token, recent disorder in Texas prisons might be explained by increased crowding in that system. The differences between CMC and Soledad might be ascribed to less crowding in the former and greater crowding in the latter.

The evidence, however, does not support these contentions. Table 2.20 shows that, in 1978, Texas had the most crowded prisons in the nation and was far more crowded than either California or Michigan. The same is true for most of the period 1973 to 1983. Table 2.21 shows that population density in Texas prisons was actually decreasing as violence in that system was rising. In 1984 and 1985 Texas prisons were less crowded but more violent than at any time in the system's recent history. Until the 1980s, levels of

Table 2.20

Inmates held in cells occupied by two or more with less than 60 square feet of floor space per inmate ranked by state from most to least crowded (1978)

Rank	State	Percent
1	Texas	90
39	Michigan	11
44	California	06
50	North Dakota	03

Inmates held in crowded cellblocks or dormitories occupied by more than 50 inmates ranked by state from most to least crowded

Rank	State	Percent
1	Mississippi	73
12	Texas	14
19	Michigan	03
50	California[a]	00

[a] Twenty-eight other states also have no crowded cellblocks.

Adapted from Joan Mullen and Bradford Smith, *American Prisons and Jails, Volume III: Conditions and Costs of Confinement* (Washington, D.C.: National Institute of Justice, October 1980).

Table 2.21 Population Density and Rates of Violence in the Texas Prison System

	1979	1980	1981	1982	1983	1984
Average Population[a]	24,846	27,352	30,292	32,424	36,838	35,619
Rated Capacity[b]	24,750	27,083	29,900	36,892	38,868	NA
Population Density[c]	1.10	1.14	1.15	0.94	0.96	NA
Living Area[d] (sq. feet per inmate)	27.49	26.70	28.16	29.61	32.41	35.20
Violence Rate[e]	9.29	4.65	8.95	11.87	12.92	18.87

[a] Taken from Fiscal Year Statistical Reports, Management Services, Texas Department of Corrections.

[b] Rated capacity depends on the standards employed. Here cell capacity was defined in terms of two inmates per cell. Dorm capacity was defined in terms of forty square feet per inmate. Tents were used between 1981 and 1984. Tent capacity was calculated on the basis of twelve men per tent.

[c] Population density is the ratio of average population to rated capacity.

[d] Based on report from Management Services, Texas Department of Corrections. Does not include temporary housing (mostly tents) added in 1981 and 1982.

[e] Violence rates include homicide and suicide incidents plus the number of major incident reports filed on inmate-on-inmate and inmate-on-staff assaults.

SOURCE: Sheldon Eckland-Olson, "Judicial Decisions and the Social Order of Prison Violence: Evidence from the Post-Ruiz Years in Texas" (University of Texas, Department of Sociology, 1985), p. 31.

crowding in CMC and Soledad did not diverge sharply. In recent years, however, Soledad has been far more crowded than CMC. In 1983–1984, for instance, Soledad was operating at 99 percent over rated capacity while CMC was operating at only 18 percent over rated capacity. But since 1984, CMC's population has expanded dramatically. By April 1986, CMC had about 6,300 inmates, making it the most heavily populated and overcrowded prison in California. In the face of this increased crowding, levels of disorder at CMC actually went down, widening the gap between CMC and Soledad.

Hence, with regard to the intersystem and historical differences in prison order, crowding does not appear to have played the role that most observers would expect. With respect to the intrasystem difference, the data are more ambiguous but seem to weigh against the belief that crowding causes disorder.

Inmate-to-Staff Ratios

Judges, prison reformers, and scholars have suggested that a key to order in prisons is staff size. Judges, for instance, have ordered state corrections agencies to decrease their inmate-to-staff ratios on the assumption that such decreases will result in greater protection and better services.[19] From this assumption, we would hypothesize that Texas prisons were most orderly because their inmate-to-staff ratios were lowest. Similarly, we would expect to find rising ratios accompanying the rise of prison violence in Texas. By the same token, we would expect that CMC has had a lower inmate-to-staff ratio than Soledad.

Contrary to these assumptions, it turns out in each case that prisons with the highest inmate-to-staff ratios have been the most orderly: fewer rather than more staff were associated with a higher level of prison order. With regard to the intersystem difference, the authors of a comprehensive 1978 statistical portrait of American prisons and jails concluded that "Texas has been in a class by itself with staffing ratios for both custodial and service staff three times the national median."[20] Similarly, a 1978 study by the Texas Department of Corrections found that, in the two previous years, Texas had the highest inmate-to-staff ratio of all but one of thirty-two states surveyed.[21] Table 2.22 shows that from 1980 to 1983 Texas had higher inmate-to-staff ratios than either Michigan or California. In 1984 and 1985, the most violent years in the system's recent history, Texas had its lowest inmate-to-staff ratios ever.[22] CMC's inmate-to-staff ratios have been higher than Soledad's; indeed, they have been the highest in the California system.

Level of Training

Perhaps prisons are most orderly where staff are best trained. Formal training includes preservice educational requirements, the length and intensity of basic training, and the amount and quality of in-service training. We might suppose that prison personnel in

Table 2.22 Inmate-to-Staff Ratios

	1980	1981	1982	1983
California	7.0	7.7	7.1	7.3
Michigan	6.0	7.4	5.6	6.4
Texas	13.0	10.1	9.0	8.8

SOURCE: Texas, Michigan, and California departments of corrections.

Texas have spent more hours and undergone more elaborate training than their counterparts in the other two states, that as the Texas system grew more violent, its level of training declined, and that CMC has somehow attracted better-trained workers than Soledad.

In point of fact, however, the level of formal training in Texas has been far lower than in either California or Michigan. In 1983, Texas provided only 80 hours of preservice and in-service training for correctional staff, while California provided 400 hours, and Michigan provided a national high of 640 hours. (The national average in 1983 was around 180 hours of training.) Prior to 1983 Texas prison workers received even less formal training compared to those in Michigan and California.

It is commonly acknowledged that correctional officers are the backbone of any prison operation. In Texas most of the training for correctional officers has been simple, security-oriented, and on-the-job. In fact, most Texas officers reported learning their craft as cellblock apprentices under the tutelage of seasoned officers. By contrast, in Michigan, officer training has been more complex, less purely security-minded, and more in-class. For instance, while Michigan officers have received extensive training on how to frisk inmates and search cells, much of their training has focused on such topics as race relations, human relations, working with people, due process, and theories of criminal justice. Document 2.2 is one of the "human/race relations" tests which Michigan officers take while in training. Stacked up, their written training materials weigh over eighteen pounds and stand over a foot high. California's officer training materials are almost as bulky, while those of Texas have consisted of a few copybook-style manuals.

Michigan training officials believe that the study of such topics as personality development and human motivation is an integral part of security training; hence, the amount of training time spent on such subjects has rivalled that devoted to custodial basics such as key control or how to make an accurate count of inmates. In Texas, most of the formal training has consisted of just such custodial basics and a detailed examination of the department's history. As Document 2.3 suggests, the training emphasis in California has been more balanced.

Until recently, the lack of a high school diploma was no bar to employment in the Texas Department of Corrections and would scarcely hinder one from rising to the top as a warden or as an

DOCUMENT 2.2

MICHIGAN DEPARTMENT OF CORRECTIONS

HUMAN/RACE RELATIONS EXAMINATION

TRUE/FALSE QUESTIONS:

1. _____ GENDER ROLES ARE BEHAVIORS, EXPECTATIONS, AND ROLE SETS DEFINED BY SOCIETY AS MASCULINE OR FEMININE WHICH MAKE UP THE BEHAVIOR OF A INDIVIDUAL MAN OR WOMAN AND ARE CULTURALLY REGARDED AS APPROPRIATE TO MALES OR FEMALES.

2. _____ RACE IS A MEANS OF DIVIDING MANKIND.

3. _____ RACE RELATIONS ARE SUBSTANTIALLY DIFFERENT FROM HUMAN RELATIONS.

4. _____ INSTITUTIONS ARE BUILDINGS.

5. _____ SEXISM IS DEFINED AS ANY ATTITUDE, ACTION, OR INSTITUTIONAL STRUCTURE WHICH ONLY CONSCIOUSLY DEVALUES, RESTRICTS, OR DISCRIMINATES AGAINST A PERSON OR GROUP BECAUSE OF BIOLOGICAL SEX.

6. _____ RACISM CAN ONLY BE PRACTICED BY WHITE MALES.

7. _____ GENERAL ROLE CONFLICT AND SEXISM CAN PRODUCE CONSIDERABLE STRESS FOR MEN AND WOMEN.

8. _____ PERCEPTIONS ARE THE GLASSES THROUGH WHICH PEOPLE SEE REALITY.

9. _____ AN INSTITUTION HAS PROCEDURES BUT NO VALUES.

10. _____ AN INDIVIDUAL MUST CHANGE ATTITUDES IN ORDER TO CHANGE BEHAVIOR.

MULTIPLE CHOICE

11. HOMOPHOBIA IS:

    (A) FEAR OF HOMOSEXUALS
    (B) FEAR OF BEING HOMOSEXUAL
    (C) BELIEFS, MYTHS AND STEROTYPES ABOUT GAY PEOPLE
    (D) ALL OF THE ABOVE
    (E) NONE OF THE ABOVE

12. CONTROL IS:

    (A) A NEGATIVE NECESSARY MOVEMENT OF PEOPLE
    (B) TO REGULATE, RESTRAIN, OR TO HAVE OTHERS OR SITUATIONS UNDER ONE'S COMMAND
    (C) A KNOB TO REGULATE PRISONER BEHAVIOR
    (D) ALL OF THE ABOVE
    (E) NONE OF THE ABOVE

DOCUMENT 2.2 *(cont.)*

HUMAN/RACE RELATIONS EXAMINATION

MULTIPLE CHOICE CON'T.

13. POWER IS:

      (A) TO OBTAIN AUTHORITY OVER OTHERS
      (B) TO OBTAIN INFLUENCE OVER OTHERS
      (C) TO OBTAIN ACSENDANCY OVER OTHERS
      (D) ALL OF THE ABOVE
      (E) NONE OF THE ABOVE

14. THE AFFIRMATIVE ACTION POLICY:

      (A) PROTECTS ONLY WOMEN
      (B) PROTECTS ONLY RACIAL MINORITIES
      (C) PROTECTS ONLY HANDICAPPED PERSONS
      (D) PROTECTS ALL UNDER REPRESENTED EMPLOYEES
      (E) NONE OF THE ABOVE

15. EVERY INSTITUTION HAS TWO TYPES OF FUNCTIONS TO PERFORM (INTENDED AND BELIEVED):

      (A) PURSUIT OF ITS OBJECTIVES IN A WORLD WHICH IS OFTEN INDIFFERENT OR HOSTILE TO THESE OBJECTIVES
      (B) PURSUIT OF CHANGE IN A CHANGING SOCIETY
      (C) PRESERVATION OF ITS OWN INTERNAL COHESION SO THAT IT MAY SURVIVE
      (D) A AND B
      (E) B AND C
      (F) A AND C

FILL IN THE BLANKS

16. LIST FIVE (5) OF THE SITUATIONAL CRITERIA TO ASSESS GENDER ROLE CONFLICT:

      (A)_____

      (B)_____

      (C)_____

      (D)_____

      (E)_____

DOCUMENT 2.2 *(cont.)*

HUMAN/RACE RELATIONS EXAMINATION

FILL-IN THE BLANKS CON'T.

17. THE _____ OF WOMEN BY MEN, AND TO A LESSER
    DEGREE THE _____ OF MEN BY WOMEN, IS A
    CENTRAL CONCEPT IN UNDERSTANDING HOW PERSONAL AND INSTITUTIONAL
    SEXISM OPERATE IN SOCIETY.

18. _____PERCEPTIONS OFTEN SERVE AS A BASIS
    FOR ASSUMING DIFFERENCES.

19. _____PERCEPTIONS REQUIRE TIME AND DISCUSSION
    TO EVALUATE.

20. DEFINE SEXUAL HARASSMENT: _____
    _____
    _____

21. DEFINE RACISM:_____
    _____
    _____

22. TELL HOW INSTITUTIONAL RACISM DIFFERS FROM PERSONAL RACISM:_____
    _____
    _____
    _____

23. FROM WHAT SOURCE DOES A PERSON GET STEROTYPES? NAME FOUR SOURCES:
    1._____   3._____
    2._____   4._____

24. STATE THE MAJOR OBJECTIVE OF AFFIRMATIVE ACTION:_____
    _____

DOCUMENT 2.2 *(cont.)*

```
                           ANSWER SHEET

PRE AND POST TEST

HUMAN/RACE RELATIONS


1.  TRUE                    17.  Devaluation

2.  TRUE                    18.  Surface

3.  FALSE                   19.  In-depth

4.  FALSE                   20.  Unwanted physical and/or verbal contact

5.  FALSE                        which is repetitive

6.  FALSE                   21.  Policies, practices, procedures, etc.

7.  TRUE                         that restrict the opportunities of

8.  TRUE                         minority groups which may or may not be

9.  FALSE                        intentional but which produce harmful

10. FALSE                        results (irrational base)

11. D                       22.  Accept answers which refer to systems

12. B                            which perpetuate unequal treatment such

13. D                            as irrationally restrictive requirements

14. D                            which are not bona fide occupational

15. F                            requirements.  Personal racism can not

16. A. Negative Consequences     have the continuity of generations as is

    B. Restriction               generally based solely on practices.

    C. Mental or Physical Tension   23.  Family, friends, newspaper, television,

    D. Incongruence or discrepancy       radios, schools, books, etc.

    E.  Violation or restriction of our rights

    F.  Violation or restriction of other people's rights

    G.  Self devaluation         24.  Accept Dept. of Corrections affirmative

    H.  Devaluation by others         action objective.

    I.  Loss or threat
```

DOCUMENT 2.3

CORE CURRICULUM IN-SERVICE TRAINING CLASSES TO BE OFFERED ANNUALLY

1. Application and Use of Restraint Gear - 2 Hrs. - APRIL
2. Canteen Procedures - 1 Hr. - SEPTEMBER
3. Career Development Workshop - 8 Hrs. - QUARTERLY (AUG.-NOV.-FEB.-MAY)
4. Classification Procedures - 1 Hr. - JANUARY
5. Clothed and Unclothed Body Searches - 1 Hr. - MARCH
6. Collection and Preservation of Evidence - 1 Hr. - JUNE
7. Communication - 1 Hr. - JUNE
8. Count Procedures - 1 Hr. - FEBRUARY
9. C.P.R. - 8 Hrs. - SIX TIMES PER YEAR - (JULY-SEPT.-NOV.-JAN.-MAR.-MAY)
10. Crime Scene Preservation - 1 Hr. - MAY
11. Departmental Manuals, Procedures & Post Orders - 1 Hr. - MAY
12. Dining Room Procedures - 1 Hr. - SEPTEMBER
13. Disciplinary Procedures - 1 Hr. - SEPTEMBER
14. Disturbance Control - 1 Hr. - FEBRUARY
15. Drug Identification - 1 Hr. - MARCH
16. Employee Discipline - 1½ Hrs. - DECEMBER
17. First Aid - 8 Hrs. - SIX TIMES PER YEAR - (APRIL-JUNE-AUG.-OCT.-DEC.-FEB.)
18. Housing Unit Operation - 1 Hr. - AUGUST
19. Human Relations - 1 Hr. - AUGUST
20. Inmate/Staff Relations - 1 Hr. - JANUARY
21. Investigative Officer - 1 Hr. - JUNE
22. Key Control - 1 Hr. - AUGUST
23. Mail Room Procedures - 1 Hr. - MAY
24. Overview of California Department of Corrections - 1 Hr. - NOVEMBER
25. Overview of Criminal Justice System - 1 Hr. - DECEMBER
26. Prison Gangs - 1 Hr. - JULY
27. Report Writing - 1 Hr. - QUARTERLY (AUGUST-NOVEMBER-FEBRUARY-MAY)
28. Sallyport and Gate Procedures - 1 Hr. - DECEMBER
29. Search of Cells - 1 Hr. - APRIL
30. Sexual Harassment - 1 Hr. - OCTOBER
31. Straight Stick Baton - 2 Hrs. - QUARTERLY - (JULY-OCTOBER-JANUARY-APRIL)
32. Stress Reduction - 2 Hrs. - NOVEMBER
33. Supervision of Inmates - 1 Hr. - MARCH
34. Transportation of Inmates/Hospital Coverage - 2 Hrs. - QUARTERLY -
                                    (JULY-OCTOBER-JANUARY-APRIL)
35. Use of Central Files/Microfische - 1Hr. - MARCH
36. Visiting Room Procedures - 1 Hr. - NOVEMBER
37. Work Incentive Law - 1 Hr. - JULY

upper-level administrator in the central office. Preservice educational requirements in Michigan and California, on the other hand, have always been much stiffer. Indeed, in Michigan, it is not uncommon for higher-level administrators, including wardens, to possess advanced college degrees. In recent years, the same has been true for California.

The training programs of both California and Michigan have

been more elaborate than those of Texas. The former departments have been heavily influenced by the American Correctional Association (ACA). Founded in 1870, the ACA is the nation's oldest and most respected independent association of corrections professionals. Over the last few decades it has been at the forefront of what might be termed the professionalization of corrections. The ACA is to corrections professionals and prisons what the American Medical Association (AMA) is to most doctors and hospitals. As described by one California prison official, the ACA is "a lobby, professional standards-setter, peer review group, public relations mill, seller of prison-related junk, and a place where people in this business can get credibility, lift their prestige, make connections, pop-off and retire." Despite the less-than-flattering tone of this description, it is the case that most upper-level prison administrators in California have embraced the ACA's ideas about how to run prisons. This is even more true for top officials in the Michigan Department of Corrections. In Texas, on the other hand, the ACA's role as a provider of professional expertise and guidance (including the accreditation of prisons) has, until recently, been virtually nil. Traditionally, Texas prison officials have not cared a great deal about what the ACA has had to say about prisons in general or about Texas prisons in particular. Hence, whereas officers in California and Michigan have been trained according to ACA-influenced programs, and whereas upper-administrators in these states have pursued and studied ACA publications, the level and scope of training in Texas have been unleavened by the ACA and its battery of corrections guidebooks.

It would thus be difficult to explain the higher level of order in Texas prisons by pointing to a higher (or more sophisticated) level of training for Texas correctional officers. Such an explanation becomes even less tenable when we consider that the level of formal training in Texas has increased as the system has become more violent. Beginning in 1983, Texas increased the time devoted to training by about 20 percent and introduced more material on subjects such as human relations and race relations. Whereas previous generations of Texas correctional officer trainees were assured in class that they would learn most of what they needed to know once they "hit the blocks," trainees were now instructed to avoid learning their craft from "old school" officers. Whereas the underlying theme of Texas training had been that good correctional workers are born not made, the new theme was that the job required no natural talents and could be learned through study. Career advancement became more and more contingent upon the possession of college degrees.

More will be said about training and related matters in succeeding chapters. For the present, however, the point is that the level of formal training in Texas was lower than that in either Michigan or California. The level of such training in Texas was increasing and becoming more elaborate as the system was becoming more violent. Finally, there are no observable differences between formal training for staff at CMC and Soledad. Based on my talks with officers at each institution, however, it appears that officers at CMC have been more prone to learn on the job and from senior officers. When asked how they had learned their job, most of those at CMC mentioned a particular senior coworker, while a greater proportion of those at Soledad mentioned the training academy.

Architecture

There is reason to suppose that the physical plant of a prison is a highly important determinant of prison violence.[23] Perhaps Texas facilities have been better designed than those in Michigan, California, and most other states. It is also possible that CMC's physical layout has been more conducive to the control of violence than Soledad's.

The reader who has never ventured inside a prison may be a bit puzzled by this hypothesis. After all, the physical plant does not rape or kill anybody, the inmates do. While this is true in a literal sense, the fact is that architecture may matter enormously in controlling (increasing or decreasing) the opportunities and instrumentalities of prison violence. Most of the nation's inmates are housed in prisons built before 1950. Looked at from the outside, these fortresslike structures appear quite secure. On the inside, however, one can easily spot numerous out-of-the-way, hard-to-monitor, and hard-to-reach places that furnish ideal physical traps for stabbings, beatings, and other types of violence. In some places, locks are worn and faulty. Iron pipes running beneath sinks are easily made into weapons. A list of such security-threatening architectural features could run on for dozens of pages. The point, however, is that the physical structure of the prison may be a great ally or a great adversary in any attempt to establish and maintain orderly institutions.

Based on my own observations inside numerous prisons, the observations of scores of correctional professionals, and facts about the age and structure of the facilities in each state, it would be very difficult to conclude that Texas has been more orderly because its architecture has been more favorable to security. The system's Huntsville ("Walls") unit, for instance, is the oldest prison in the system, one simply teeming with unsafe physical features (not least of which were numerous cell doors that did not lock). Yet that prison has been, and continues to be, one of the system's most orderly higher-custody institutions. In 1980 over half of the Texas prison stock was fifty to one hundred years old; in Michigan and California about half of each state's facilities were only one to twenty-five years old.

Even with the benefit of unworn, modern facilities, however, some prisons have lots of security trouble. For instance, in 1981, Michigan opened its Huron Valley Men's Facility (HVMF). HVMF has a college-campus design with brightly painted housing units circling a broad open space flanked by recreational centers. Inmate-to-staff ratios at the prison have been among the lowest in the Michigan system. HVMF has rarely been crowded and has held as few as 400 inmates. In 1985, the prison won accreditation from the American Correctional Association.

Since it opened, however, HVMF has been plagued by major disturbances, including a 1982 riot in the prison's segregation unit, which required nearly 200 outside law enforcement officers to quell, and a spate of escapes and stabbings. The physical design of the prison deserves part (though by no means all) of the blame. For instance, one inmate, known as the "sewer monster," was repeatedly able to clog the prison's drainage system and flood the cellblock. Apart from being malodorous and messy, this created tensions and security problems, as inmates had to be moved out of their cells at irregular hours so the cells could be cleaned and repaired. The prison has no bars and inmates have shattered or simply removed its "unbreakable" glass. The angle of gun coverage from the towers is less than ideal, making it easy for guards to shoot at the fence but not inside the compound. The control centers in each housing unit (except segregation) are totally open. Officers sit at desks around which inmates roam freely. Electronically controlled locks on doors have proven less efficient and more of a security hazard than predicted.

The evidence can hardly lead one to a position of architectural determinism. In Texas, the administration of the Huntsville unit has achieved a high degree of order, despite a decrepit physical plant, inhospitable to security. In Michigan, prisons with an architecture similar to that of the Huntsville unit have done much less well. At Michigan's HVMF, with the blessing (or curse) of a spanking new facility, one wholly unlike the old fortress prisons, the security record has been poor. At CMC, it does appear that the prison's orderliness is due in part to its favorable design. CMC's West Facility opened in 1954 and its East Facility opened in 1961. The prison was designed by a group of security-conscious wardens. Its physical layout makes it easier than at most prisons to control and monitor inmate movement.

At the same time, however, it is difficult to ascribe CMC's comparative success in maintaining prison order wholly to its physical plant, just as it would be difficult to ascribe Soledad's lesser success to its physical design. While not as conducive to security as CMC's physical plant, Soledad's is nonetheless far from poor. It was built in the late 1940s and early 1950s at a cost of nearly 11 million dollars. Designed in contrast to the old fortress prisons, Soledad was intended to be the showplace of the California prison system, a "model prison" physically and in every other respect. In the prison's higher-custody units, cellblocks are situated off of a long, heavily gated hall. Some correctional experts consider this design highly favorable for security purposes.

In summary, architecture does not appear to be a good explanation for either the intersystem or the historical differences in question here. In deference to the unique design of CMC, however, architecture should be counted as a factor in explaining the intrasystem difference.

Inmate Social System

In chapter one, we discussed the sociological theory regarding the relationship between prison violence and the state of inmate society. Sociologists, it was noted, have explained prison disorder as the consequence of a breakdown in the prison's social system. Such breakdowns, sociologists have argued, are often the result of administration attempts to tighten up discipline, run things "by the book," or make it more difficult for inmates to behave as they wish or to associate freely.

In succeeding chapters, a great deal more will be said about the administrative regime of prisons in each state. For now, however, it is important to note that, contrary to sociological theory but in keeping with common sense, prison order and official attempts to enforce it seem to vary directly rather than inversely. As was mentioned in the discussion of data problems, Texas has tended to run its prisons strictly according to official rules and regulations, while prisons in the other states have been administered more loosely. Both California and Michigan have long had elaborate inmate grievance mechanisms and have experimented with various forms of participative prison management and inmate self-government. While the Texas approach to inmate society has been more complex than this overview suggests, in general, it is correct to say that Texas has been far less accommodating of inmate society and its leaders than the other two states. As John P. Conrad and Simon Dinitz have observed, in Texas the emphasis has been on "the atomization of the prison culture. Prisoner groups are not allowed to form."[24] Conrad and Dinitz aptly labelled Texas inmate society a "prison non-community."[25] Michigan and California, on the other hand, have done less to stifle inmate society and more to recognize and share power with its leaders. Prison managers in these two states have often responded to inmate demands through negotiations with groups of prisoner representatives, generally referred to as inmate advisory councils. By contrast, in Texas, prison authorities have simply vetoed or ignored inmate demands. For instance, despite a history of so-called work bucks by inmates working on the system's farms and in its industries, inmate wages in Texas have been zero.

Regarding the intrasystem difference in California, the administration of CMC has by most accounts been far less solicitous of inmates and their leaders than that of Soledad. For example, at Soledad inmates have been permitted to wear (or drape from their cell doors) colored bandanas showing their gang affiliation, to sit where they want (rather than in the next available seat) in the dining hall, and to fraternize freely in large groups in the yard or in the cellblocks. At CMC, on the other hand, the administration has been more resistant to "flying your colors" and other such inmate activities. At Soledad, personnel have been prone to entertain inmate complaints about everything from crowding to the lack of fresh socks; at CMC, such complaints have been less likely to elicit a favorable or sympathetic response from prison workers.

If the sociological view of inmate society were correct, then Texas should have been more disorderly than the other two states and become more orderly as it took greater pains to loosen formal controls, bargain with inmate leaders, and accommodate inmate demands and grievances. By the same token, CMC should have been more violent than Soledad. In fact the reverse has been true: greater order has been associated with more strenuous efforts at formal governance and less accommodation of inmate society.

There is, of course, another hypothesis—that California and Michigan are in a "transitional" stage of disorder while moving toward a more self-governing regime, and that Texas is now experiencing an acute initial bout of such transitional violence. The evidence for this intriguing hypothesis, however, is nonexistent. Beginning in the last quarter of 1985, for example, the rising rate of disorder in Texas prisons was slowed after prison officials imposed greater restrictions on inmate movement, curtailed the free flow of inmate mail, and tightened a few of the formal controls on inmates that had been relaxed. We shall have more to report along these lines in the chapters that follow.

Level of Inmate Treatment

If we took our cue from the sociological literature on prisons, we would suppose that prison order has been greatest where the emphasis on inmate treatment has been weakest. As was discussed in chapter one, sociologists have argued that order (custody) and amenity and service (treatment) are antithetical and that greater order can be purchased only at the cost of less amenity and service, and vice versa. Treatment and custody are said to impose conflicting organizational mandates on prison managers: to prevent escapes and minimize inmate violence they are driven to paramilitary procedures and tight discipline; to create the treatment milieu necessary for education, counseling, and other programs, they are driven to de-emphasize the symbols and substance of formal administrative controls over inmates.

If this were true, then with regard to the intersystem difference, we would expect that Texas, having the most orderly prisons, would have achieved less amenity and service than California and Michigan, while these latter states achieved less order but greater amenity and service than Texas. By the same token, we might expect to see some increase in the level of amenity and service in Texas prisons as the system became less orderly. Finally, we would predict that CMC, which achieved more in the way of order, would have less in the way of amenity and service than Soledad.

In the Rand study, it was found that 66 percent of Texas inmates were enrolled in some major treatment program versus 80 percent of Michigan inmates and 64 percent of California inmates (Table 2.23). Using various other measures of treatment orientation, the Rand report concluded that Michigan prisons could be regarded as slightly more treatment-oriented than either Texas or California prisons.

The Rand study, however, contained little information on the quality of programs in each state's prisons and did not document the conditions under which these programs were offered. For instance, the Rand report noted but did not elaborate on the Texas system's Windham School District. Funded by the State Minimum Education Program through the Texas Education Agency, Windham was the nation's first fully accredited prison school system. Table 2.24 records the number of inmates who have received degrees or certificates in Texas prisons. The point is not that inmates in California, Michigan, and other prison systems have been unable to attend school or to earn degrees and certificates. Rather, the point is twofold. First, the fact that so many Texas inmates have completed educational programs (while serveral times more have participated in them) counts against the hypothesis that Texas

Table 2.23 Inmates Involved in Treatment Programs (percent)

	California (n = 340)	Michigan (n = 363)	Texas (n = 583)
Major Program[a]	64	80	66
Misc. Program[b]	14	5	11
Work Only	13	5	11
Idle[c]	9	10	12

[a] Major programs include education, vocational training, substance abuse rehabilitation, and individual and group counseling.

[b] Miscellaneous programs include community activities, religious programs, self-help groups, prerelease programs, and work furloughs.

[c] Idle means in neither work nor treatment activity.

SOURCE: Joan Petersilia et al., *The Prison Experience of Career Criminals* (Santa Monica, CA: Rand Corporation, May 1980), pp. 26–27.

Table 2.24 Educational and Vocational Services of the Texas
Department of Corrections

Number of Inmates Receiving Degrees/Certificates	
High school and high school equivalency 1970–1984	27,570
Vocational 1970–1984	10,047
Associate 1967–1984	2,519
Baccalaureate 1974–1984	215

SOURCE: *1984 Annual Report* (Huntsville, Texas: Texas Department of Corrections), pp. 13–14.

purchased order at the expense of service or has been preoccupied with custody to the exclusion of treatment.

Second, Texas prison schoolrooms have been places of learning staffed by competent educational instructors who have been able to spend most of their time teaching rather than combating unruly inmate pupils. At the system's Huntsville unit, for instance, classrooms were remarkably clean, calm, and quiet (except when the teacher was speaking).

Teachers in Michigan prisons, on the other hand, report on years of frustration in trying to achieve anything in their behind bars version of the blackboard jungle. One Michigan teacher said, "Look here, is this a real educational environment? You've got the numbers, but what's behind them? . . . They don't make it possible for us to shape their minds or their characters." A teacher who had spent nearly two decades in the system said, "Do you want me to speak truthfully? . . . I do not run this room, they [the inmates] do." My own observations and experiences confirmed these statements. Shouting, aggressive horseplay, and even taunts and threats directed at the teacher (and myself) were the norm. Only in the prison's vocational center, staffed by a man who bragged about his no-nonsense approach to instructing inmates, did anything approaching constructive learning appear to be underway.

In addition, while none of the prison instructors observed in Texas appeared to be less than competent, the same could not be said for those in Michigan. One veteran Michigan instructor, for instance, spoke to the inmates in their (mostly ungrammatical) idiom on the grounds that it was both necessary and appropriate to "talk their trash." This same teacher discounted the disadvantages of illiteracy, stressed the virtues of "street sense," and was unable to show the one inmate pupil who seemed interested how to perform simple arithmetic.

While each of the three systems boasts an impressive array of prison industries that employ inmates, here too there are differences in the quality of the service. In general, the percentage of the Texas inmate population engaged in prison industries has been higher than that of either California or Michigan. As Table 2.25 suggests, Texas also has outdistanced other large prison systems as a provider of this service. Again, however, qualitative points are at least as telling as numerical ones. The Texas system's dental lab, textile mill, bus repair facility, printing operation, and other plants have been remarkably clean beehives of productive activity and vocational learning. My observations are shared by others. For instance, after taking a tour of the industrial operations at the system's Ellis I unit, Richard Neely, then chief justice of the state supreme court of West Virginia, could barely contain his enthusiasm and spoke of "building one just like it in my state." With a few notable exceptions, the industrial workplaces in California and Michigan were somewhat less impressive; some were little more than alternate centers of inmate idleness and disorder.

For our purposes, however, the point is less that Texas has performed as well (or better than) California, Michigan, and other states in providing this type of service than it is that it has done so without making any apparent trade-off in terms of prison order.

Table 2.25 Inmates Employed in Prison Industries for Five State Prison Systems with Average Daily Populations of 10,000 or More (1982)

State	Percent
Maryland	3.3
Georgia	4.1
Florida	6.9
N. Carolina	8.1
Texas	12.6

SOURCE: *Adult Correctional Systems: Report to the Southern Legislative Conference Council of State Governments* (October 1982), pp. 25–26.

This point is reinforced when we consider that, in 1982, Texas began a substance abuse program comparable to the drug rehabilitation programs which have existed in Michigan, California, and other states. It has also provided psychological counseling, medical and related services, computer programming, and other postindustrial vocational programs for inmates. In addition, unlike the other states, Texas long maintained a system of full employment and a forty-hour work week for inmates.

It would, therefore, be difficult to contend that a depressed level of inmate treatment underwrote the comparative success of Texas in achieving orderly prisons. This contention becomes even less plausible as we broaden the comparison to include levels of amenity. Like their counterparts in California and Michigan, Texas inmates have long enjoyed regular and easy access to weightlifting equipment, color televisions, ping pong tables, and other things which help to relieve monotony and boredom. For those experiencing what Gresham Sykes termed the "pains of imprisonment,"[26] good meals can make a pleasant difference. On a given day in January 1982, for instance, Texas inmates could have hot oatmeal, creamed ham, and fried eggs for breakfast; cheeseburgers, french fries, and assorted relishes for lunch; and salisbury steak, mashed potatoes, and assorted condiments for dinner. Since most of the food was grown on the system's farms it was normally fresh. (Having taken meals in all three systems, I would hesitate to take them again anywhere but Texas.) Diversions from the daily routine and a chance to see a little of the countryside are coveted by the imprisoned. In Texas, every inmate who has no disciplinary infractions against him come October is free to attend the system's annual prison rodeo where he can watch his fellow inmates ride bulls and milk wild cows for fun, profit, and bragging rights. The rodeo is held each Sunday in October at the system's Huntsville unit stadium.

It would thus be hard to maintain that the order that existed in Texas prisons was achieved at the expense of treatment. Nor does it appear that the lesser degree of custodial control in the other states was compensated for by greater amenity and service.

In 1984 and 1985, the level of amenity and service in Texas prisons decreased substantially. Work schedules were frequently interrupted by violence. Classrooms became battlegrounds. At one point in 1984 all programming at several institutions was curtailed as administrators locked down the prisons and tried to regain some semblance of control. The Texas inmate newspaper and other sources reported that college classes and other treatment programs had been cancelled, curtailed, or made more erratic in the wake of rising prison violence. Greater restrictions on inmate movement and reduced access to day rooms, gyms, and the like also followed the upturn in disorder. In short, the level of inmate treatment in Texas prisons appears to have varied directly rather than inversely with the level of custodial control: as order decreased the levels of amenity and service decreased.

CMC, the most orderly higher-custody prison in the California system, is also widely acknowledged to be the most treatment-oriented. CMC's programs have included basic schooling, vocational training, and work assignments for every prisoner. Inmate crews at CMC have been trained and organized to assist the National Guard, the Forestry Service, and the city of San Luis Obispo. CMC's industrial operations have been highly productive both financially and as centers of vocational learning. Likewise, the level of amenity at CMC has been outstanding. The Center of the prison is a neatly manicured and well tended garden. There is no lack of athletic equipment. Where cleanliness is concerned, CMC has compared favorably to any prison in Texas.

Inmate–Staff Race Relations

Numerous scholars and others have argued that improving race relations is the key to improving prisons.[27] Inmates must learn to respect the racial or ethnic backgrounds of their peers. Officers must be trained to be sensitive to the life experiences of inmates from backgrounds other than their own. It would be expected, therefore, that race relations in Texas prisons have been demonstrably better than those in other states. A related guess would be that the officer corps in the more orderly prisons reflected the racial and ethnic mix of their respective inmate populations more closely than did those of the less orderly prisons.

As was noted in the discussion of training, correctional personnel in California and Michigan have received far more training in the area of race relations than correctional personnel in Texas. In relation to the inmate population, correctional staff in each of the three states are disproportionately white. But through affirmative action and departmental recruiting initiatives, staff in California and Michigan have mirrored their respective inmate clienteles more closely than Texas staff has mirrored its. CMC and Soledad have differed little from one another in this respect.

As we saw earlier, in Texas and California, there are a significant percentages of black, white, and Hispanic inmates. In Michigan most inmates are black or white. In each state, racial violence has occurred, but most of the disorder has not been clearly linked to interracial animosities. A good deal of violence in California prisons has been intraracial, involving battles among Hispanic prisoners.

There is, in any case, little dependable evidence that race relations are a major factor in promoting or suppressing prison violence. While, in particular cases, inmate violence may certainly have a racial component, generally speaking the state of race relations appears to be neither a clear threat nor a clear boon to prison order.

Repressive Measures

Critics (and supporters) of the Texas prison system have claimed that the system was so orderly for so long because it used repressive administrative tactics. Texas used inmates to control other inmates. These inmates, known in Texas as building tenders, are widely credited (or blamed) for the low rates of violence that until recently characterized Texas prisons. The upturn in Texas prison disorder has been explained by the supposed "power vacuum" created when federal court intervention brought the building-tender system to an end.

There is a germ of truth, but a far greater measure of oversimplification and misunderstanding, in this explanation. We shall explore this issue in detail in chapter five. Here, it is enough to note that both the critics and the advocates of the Texas building-tender system have had a poor understanding of this system. A truer understanding about Texas prisons was contained in the conclusion reached in 1982 by a blue-ribbon commission impaneled to study the Texas criminal justice system. In their preliminary report to the governor, they noted that the Texas prison system has been described both as "the best example of slavery remaining in the country" and "probably the best prison system in the world." As the report stated, the reality "lay somewhere in between."[28]

Simply as a matter of logic, if it were true that order in Texas prisons was achieved mainly or solely through brutal tactics, then one would suppose that similar measures employed elsewhere would have similar effects. We know, however, that, in other places, prison managers have used what was described in chapter one as the highly repressive con-boss system. In its various forms, that system was associated with some of the most disorderly prisons in the history of corrections. As we shall see, in Texas and elsewhere, prison order has been achieved only where managers have employed a mix of legal and duly authorized carrots and sticks. Merely repressive correctional measures simply do not work.

THE QUALITY OF PRISON MANAGEMENT

The foregoing analysis proves nothing of a definitive nature about the determinates of prison order. The evidence applies only to the cases under consideration. Even in these cases further probing may lead one to conclude that (for example) crowding or the level of expenditures were more important factors than they first appeared. At the same time, however, there is now reason enough to doubt popular conjectures about these factors. For instance, those who wish to maintain that more money, more staff, or more repressive measures are necessary to safer prisons will have to qualify their assertions in light of the contrary evidence provided above.

There is a case to be made that not only the level of prison order, but the overall quality of prison life depends mainly on how prisons are organized and managed. In the introduction to the revised edition of his *Thinking About Crime* (1983), James Q. Wilson noted correctly that no one has ever "explained why some prisons are humane and others are unspeakable."[29] The answer to be offered in the rest of this book is that the quality of prison life varies according to the quality of prison management. The evidence will lead us to the conclusion that prison management is the strategic variable, one that may be subject to change with predictable and desirable consequences. The first bit of evidence is presented in the next chapter, beginning with an introduction to correctional management in Texas, Michigan, and California.

TWO

GOVERNING PRISONS

Good orders make evil men good and
bad orders make good men evil.

—JAMES HARRINGTON, *A System of Politics*

3

Governing Prisons in Three States

Whether a prison (or a prison system) is safe, humane, and treatment-oriented, on the one hand, or violent, harsh, and unproductive, on the other, may depend mainly on the character of its prison governance. Managerially, the Texas, Michigan, and California prison systems have differed dramatically. In this decade, the Texas prison system has undergone an administrative revolution. There have been, and continue to be, intrasystem differences in prison management, especially in California. These three sets of managerial differences—intersystem, historical, and intrasystem—parallel and, it will be argued, account for the differences in the quality of prison life discussed in the previous chapter.

Unfortunately, this explanation for differences in the quality of prison life is far more messy and complex than most of its rivals—expenditure levels, overcrowding, staffing ratios, and so on. It may, however, have the virtue of being true. Let us begin to explore this thesis by way of a brief tour of the Texas, Michigan, and California prison systems.

A TOUR THROUGH TDC, CDC, AND MDC: THREE MODELS OF CORRECTIONAL MANAGEMENT

If you were blindfolded and taken into the building which is head-quarters for the Texas Department of Corrections, within seconds of uncovering your eyes, you would probably know that you were someplace having to do with prisons. To your left you would see a showcase of weapons (crudely fashioned knives, handmade guns); makeshift escape ladders; and the "bat," a wooden-handled, raw-hide belt, 3¼ feet long and 2½ inches wide, once used to admin-ister whippings of twenty lashes to those guilty of rule infractions. If you read the index cards beneath each object in the case and studied the photos on the walls, including pictures of present and past governors, prison board members, directors, and inmates, you would learn more than a little about the history of this prison bureaucracy. Even as a casual observer you would not miss the clean-shaven men in the crisp white uniforms, names written in black over their shirt pockets, busily washing windows, polishing floors, and nodding a greeting to each person who walked by them. Nor would you miss the other men (and women) in the crisp grey uniforms, some of them with silver bars on their shoulders or sergeant's stripes on their sleeves. But if, after these and similar observations, you were still in doubt about where you were, all doubts would end the moment you walked through the building and stepped out on the other side. There you would see a massive red brick structure with high walls, gun towers at each corner, and grey-and-white uniforms in every direction.

If, on the other hand, you were blindfolded and taken into the building which is headquarters for the Michigan Department of Corrections, you would probably guess that you were someplace that housed government or business offices. Reading the office directory, you would know that you were in a government build-ing. Exit the elevator a few floors up and, if you bothered to read the fine print on some of the notices hanging on the bulletin boards, you would believe that you were in the central offices of the Mich-igan prison system. You would, however, be only half right. To find the personnel or training offices of the department you would have to leave the building and drive (unblindfolded) several miles to another nondescript building. Once you stepped outside and looked across the street, you would see high brick walls, but they would belong to the Michigan Civic Center.

If, alas, you were blindfolded and taken to the building that is headquarters for the California Department of Corrections, you would not have the foggiest idea of where you were, unless and until you were past the enclosed reception area on the inside. If the blindfold were removed before you entered the building, and if (as I did) you missed the state flag flying in front and the unobtrusive nameplate, you would be sure that you were standing before a store in a shopping mall. All around, you would see stores and shoppers. (In fact, the building that now houses CDC was once a J.C. Penney store.) Once inside, however, you would see a few pictures of buildings that look like prisons and various announcements asking for votes in some upcoming ballot to decide which union will represent the line correctional staff.

Let us now move from headquarters into the field. If you enter a Texas or California prison, you are unlikely to have any problem sorting out who is who or who is in charge. Inside the Texas prison you will see inmates in white, officers in grey, and senior officers wearing various signs of rank. When the men in white speak to the men and women in grey, they usually do so in a calm voice, addressing the officers as "sir" or "boss." Inside the California prison, you may have a bit more trouble sorting things out, but only slightly. The officers are the ones in the paramilitary green-and-tan uniforms. Some inmates are wearing state-issued blue pants and shirts, but most are in an assortment of "street duds"—jeans, T-shirts (often with lewd sayings on them), and (on cooler days) an occasional leather vest or jacket. When the inmates speak to the officers, it is not uncommon for them to do so in a very forward manner, often beginning with "Hey man!"

If you enter a Michigan prison, it is a fair bet that, unless you have been there before, you will have some initial difficulty telling who are the officers and who are the inmates. Even after you have spent much time inside the prison, you will be unable to tell senior officers from junior officers (unless, of course, you come to know and associate names, ranks, and faces). The officers wear no visible signs of rank—no stripes, no bars, no insignias. Instead, they sport black pants and green or white "airline pilot" shirts. Some wear green blazers and black baseball caps. The inmates are in every imaginable garb. Few wear their state-issued "blues and shoes." Many are in "cool threads"—silky shirts, expensive (but untied) sneakers, one to three hats (usually baseball caps) on their heads, and gold chains. Stick around for a few minutes, and you will almost surely hear inmates address officers with some vulgar epithet. Walk about alone or with a member of the nonuniformed staff (even the warden), and you are likely to hear much more of the same. If the staff person is female, much of the vulgarity will be sexual and threatening.

If you wished to avoid contacts with the inmates, you would be best able to do so in Texas and least able to do so in Michigan. In Texas inmates move about in a more or less orderly fashion with a correctional officer somewhere close at hand. There is little roaming about the cellblocks. It is rare for an inmate to initiate a conversation with a visitor and rarer still for a visitor to be shouted at, insulted, or threatened by inmates. In Michigan, it is virtually impossible to avoid interaction, friendly or unfriendly, with inmates. It is not uncommon for an inmate to demand an explanation of who you are and what you are doing. Indeed, it is common for inmates to bombard you (sometimes in groups of ten or fifteen) with their opinions about the institution, the administration, and other matters. The following is a sample of what you are likely to hear:

> You got these f—ing idiots here (pointing to officers). You got an asshole for a warden.
>
> Hey b——h, hey sweet b——h I want you. I'll beat/rip your ass motherf——er (shouted from various cells).
>
> Tell them. You know who. Tell them of the injustice you witnessed here today.

In Michigan, such behavior by inmates is considered typical, unexceptional, and requiring little or no response. In Texas, such behavior (the few times it occurs) will bring an immediate reprimand and in some cases disciplinary action. In California, how much of this type of inmate behavior you witness will depend largely on what prison you are visiting. San Quentin, for instance, is about as noisy and threatening as any prison could be. As you move from that prison to Folsom, Soledad, and CMC such behavior by inmates will become less likely. At CMC you will witness virtually none of this type of inmate behavior.

In California and Michigan prisons, inmates are more likely to register complaints with officers or other staff members in an aggressive way. Workers in both systems are as likely as not to respond to such complaints in a sympathetic manner and to do so in the inmates' argot. For instance, in Michigan an inmate screams in the face of a higher-level official: "I'm fed the f—— up with this s——t. I'll do my time! What can you do, put my ass in the hole? Big s——t! F—— the warden too." The official responds with repeated attempts to reason with the inmate, calling him by his nickname, making clear that he appreciates the problem, and repeating over and over the need to grasp the "real options." The inmate responds by shouting "I'm a man, I'm sick and tired," turning his back on the official, and returning to his cell. Similarly, a California inmate accosts a staff person as follows: "Hey lady, who are you? [*to me*] Who are you? Why the hell am I here? I'm supposed to be at another unit. Why don't I have any socks? Do you have any power?" The official responds: "I can't help you man, you'll just have to hang on. . . . Send me a kite." (A "kite" is a written request or statement from an inmate to a prison official.) In another California prison, an inmate, subjected to a frisk on his way out of the dining hall, curses and criticizes the officer who is frisking him as a "low status man trying to act bad." The officer completes the frisk and then says, "Well, what's your claim to fame?"

In Texas, inmates rarely accost officials in this manner. When they do, a disciplinary report normally follows. Rather than automatically sympathizing with the complaint, Texas prison workers are more likely to weigh its legitimacy and remind the inmate of the limits both of the institution's resources and of the inmate's rights. For instance, it is recreation period and from the window of the office of the major—the highest-ranking uniformed worker in the prison—you see inmates playing basketball in the yard. One of them leaves the game and approaches the major's door. Without bothering to knock—there is a sign hanging on the door which says (in English and in Spanish) "Knock and wait for permission to enter"—the inmate enters the office and complains loudly: "Yeah, I'm here because I'm tired of being jacked around. I'm tired of the bulls——t that's going on here. I been real sick since I come here, but I can't get to a lower bunk. Some other man got one . . . a transit." (A "transit" is an inmate housed at the prison en route to another unit.) The major asks, "Why do you need a lower bunk?" The inmate replies, "I just told you! . . . Look, I'm a man too. Why does one guy get it and not another? I'm needing a lower bunk." At that point the major orders the inmate out of his office. The inmate complies but slams the door on the way out. As instructed, he waits on the major's doorstep until, some thirty minutes later, he is told to reenter. The major then addresses him as follows:

> You slammed the door. Don't ever do that again. This is the penitentiary. There are rules to be followed. The man who is disrespectful isn't going to do well in here. . . . I checked on your request. You've been complaining about a hurt hand. You can't climb into an upper bunk, but you *can* play a mean game of basketball. The other man really did need that lower bunk. He has a bona fide medical problem. That is all. (Inmate says "Thank you, sir" and retires from the major's office, gently closing the door.)

If you looked into the cells of prisoners in each state, you would find those of the Texas inmates to be most spartan and those of the Michigan inmates to be bursting with all manner of personal property—television sets, radios, games, books, clothes, sewing machines, and so on. In Michigan, you would see huge green canvas baskets being wheeled about by correctional officers. The baskets are used to transport inmate property in the event that the inmate is transferred to a new cell or out of the unit.

In Texas and California, prison officials may tease you, the naïve visitor, about the facilities available to the inmates: "Want to see the swimming pool?" Having fallen for the joke in those two states, you will be prepared for it when your tour ends in Michigan. But do not be too quick to laugh. In at least one Michigan higher-custody prison, there was a heated, enclosed inmate swimming pool.

These and scores of like differences would impress you as your tour of prisons in each state came to an end. If you were then motivated to make some general sense out of what you observed, you would discover that the differences were indicative of three different models of correctional management: the Texas control model, the Michigan responsibility model, and what, for lack of an existing appellation, will be termed the California consensual model.

Elements of the Texas Control Model

Until recently, the Texas prison system ran according to what in corrections circles came to be known as the control model of correctional management. The chief architect of the control model was Dr. George Beto, director of the Texas Department of Corrections from 1962 to 1972. The control model was based on a correctional philosophy emphasizing inmate obedience, work, and education, roughly in that order.

One of the most telling facts about the control model is that, during its reign in Texas, a period stretching roughly from 1963 to 1983, every prison in the system was designated as a maximum-security institution and, for the most part, run accordingly. There were, to be sure, some differences in administrative practices from prison to prison, but in general the administrative routine inside Texas prisons was the same everywhere. In each prison, correctional officers were organized along strict paramilitary lines running from the warden and his assistants, to the major, all the way down to the most junior correctional officer. Official rules and regulations were followed closely and enforced rigorously. In the prison corridors, inmates were required to walk between lines painted on the floors rather than moving at random down the center. Talking too loud was a punishable offense. In short, daily life inside the prisons was a busy, but carefully orchestrated, routine of numbering, counting, checking, locking, and monitoring inmate movement to and from work activities and treatment programs.

As late as 1984, this system was still in existence at some Texas prisons. For instance, at the Huntsville "Walls" unit, the system's oldest and probably best-known institution, traces of the control model remained highly visible. Document 3.1 is a schedule of the prison's daily activities. Things happened precisely when (and how) they were supposed to at this prison. Inmate movement was regulated tightly. The chain of command was followed rigorously. Officers had a sense of mission, an ésprit de corps, and an amazing knowledge of the system's history. Treatment and work opportunities were offered on a regular basis and were well administered. Tension between treatment and custody personnel was virtually nonexistent. In short, life inside the Walls was in general safe, humane, productive, calm, stable, and predictable. Such was life at most Texas prisons in the years when the control model was in effect.

In essence, the control model involved a mixture of correctional carrots and sticks. For inmates who violated the rules, punishment in the form of solitary confinement or extra work assignments was swift and certain. For inmates who "did their own time" and kept

Document 3.1

SO-4 Rev. 10-75

TEXAS DEPARTMENT OF CORRECTIONS
Inter-Office Communications

From _Gøth ._

To _MR. Drøvjia_

Date _____

Subject _HUNTSVILLE UNIT TIME SCHEDULE_

05:45 AM SHIFT CHANGE - FINISH FEEDING BREAKFAST

06:00 AM PROCESS PAROLES & DISCHARGES (SHOWERS)

06:15 AM START PILL LINE

07:00 AM WORK TURN OUT (IE LOWER YARD,MECH.DEPT,TEXTILE)
START SICK CALL CHAIN BEGINS COMING IN.

08:00 AM TRANSIT SICK CALL-TRANSIT WRIT ROOM

08:45 AM SHUT DOWN PREPARE TO COUNT

09:00 AM COUNT TIME

10:00 AM OR AS SOON AS COUNT CLEARS START FEEDING LUNCH SHAKING
DOWN IN COMING CHAIN

11:00 AM FEED ADMIN. SEG.-LOWER YARD TURNS IN FOR LUNCH

11:30 AM YARD OPENS

11:45 AM START 2nd PILL LINE

12:00 PM LOWER YARD TURNS BACK OUT

12:30 PM CLOSE DOWN CHOW HALL

13:30 PM CLOSE YARD-TRANSIT COMMISSARY

13:45 PM SHIFT CHANGE-2nd SHIFT BEGINS

14:45 PM BEGIN FEEDING SUPPER

16:00 PM LOWER YARD TURNS IN FROM WORK-GO's TO CHOW

17:00 PM END OF CHOW-ALL CHAIN SHOULD BE IN

17:30 PM BEGIN 3rd PILL LINE

18:00 PM SHUT DOWNPREPARE TO COUNT

18:30 PM START COUNT

19:00 PM OR WHEN COUNT CLEARS BEGIN DAYROOM RECREATION

20:00 PM LAST PILL LINE

DOCUMENT 3.1 *(cont.)*

```
SO-4 Rev. 10-75          TEXAS DEPARTMENT OF CORRECTIONS
                            Inter-Office Communications

From  _____   Date  JUNE 18,1984 _____

To  _____   Subject HUNTSVILLE UNIT TIME SCHEDULE


      21:30 PM ADMIN SEG GO TO WRIT ROOM

      21:45 PM SHIFT CHANGE-3rd SHIFT BEGINS

      22:30 PM RACK UP

      23:30 PM 3rd SHIFT TEXTILE TURN OUT

      00:00 AM COUNT TIME

      02:00 AM COUNT TIME

      02:30 AM CHAIN TIME-BEGIN SHAKING DOWN & FEEDING OUT GOING CHAIN

      04:00 AM OUT GOING CHAIN TAKEN TO EAST GATE

      04:45 AM BEGIN FEEDING BREAKFAST,1st CHAIN BUSES ARRIVE

      05:45 AM SHIFT CHANGE 1st SHIFT BEGINS
```

out of trouble, the rewards were equally swift and certain. Indeed, given that Texas used solitary confinement and related punishments less frequently than other systems, the rewards were vitally important in securing inmate compliance with official rules and regulations. Texas offered inmates some of the most liberal "good time" provisions in American corrections. Under its 1982 good time policies, for instance, a Texas prison inmate could earn as much as two days off of his term for every productive, problem-free day he served (see Table 3.1). Inmates who scored below a fifth-grade competency level on prison-administered tests were required to attend school at least one day each week. Each inmate spent his first six months in the prison working on the prison

Table 3.1 Good Time in Texas Prison System (1982)

Time Earning Class	Sentence Serving Beginning 1-1-82	Time Served	Good Time Credited	Total Time Credited	Discharge Date
I	60 Mos	36 Mos	24 Mos	60 Mos	1-1-85
II	60 Mos	45 Mos	15 Mos	60 Mos	10-1-85
III	60 Mos	60 Mos	0 Mos	60 Mos	1-1-87
Trusty	60 Mos	30 Mos	30 Mos	60 Mos	7-1-84

farms. Better jobs—in the industrial plants, kitchens, or elsewhere—awaited those who performed well. There was a "point-
incentive system" whereby inmates could earn points for working,
going to school, and other such positive endeavors. In general, the
more points an inmate earned, the closer he moved to a trustyship.
But any good time or associated privileges earned by an inmate
could be taken from him for disciplinary reasons.[1]

By most accounts, this simple combination of—as one veteran
Texas officer described it—"prods and prizes" enabled the Texas
prison authorities to control the Texas prison inmates. One comparative measure of just how well the control model worked is the
degree to which antisocial or violent inmate associations appeared
in Texas versus other systems. Until 1983–1984, a time during
which the control model was rapidly disappearing from Texas prisons, the system experienced no significant gang problems, certainly nothing on the order of those that plagued California and
many other states. Indeed, in the 1970s researchers and practitioners who sought an answer to the problem of gang-based prison
violence looked to the large, racially diverse, but relatively gang-
free Texas system. To my knowledge, however, none of them took
away the most obvious lesson: Texas had little gang activity because prison gangs in Texas were few in number and weak; they
were so weak because the administration saw to it that inmates
were not allowed to associate freely in ways that might lead to the
formation of stable, powerful prisoner groupings.

In general, under the control model, inmate movement was
monitored too closely, rules were enforced too tightly, inmates
were kept too busy, the punishments for misbehavior were too
swift and certain, and the rewards to be earned in sentence reduction and other privileges were too great for inmates to commit
many infractions.

Under the control model, a cardinal rule, well-understood and
generally followed by all concerned, was that each inmate was to
serve his sentence on his own. Criminalistic associations among
inmates—to plot an escape, plan some violence, deal in contraband, or engage in some other form of misconduct—were checked.
The principle that every inmate must "do his own time" was advanced and realized in a variety of ways. At the system's Diagnostic Center, the induction point for incoming inmates, the
necessity of following the rules and avoiding troublesome contacts

with other inmates was spelled out in handbooks and lectures. When an inmate reached the unit to which he was assigned, he would receive more documents and lectures to reinforce this message. In the units, the lectures were often conducted by the major on duty when the new inmates arrived. In a typical scene, a group of six to ten newly arrived inmates would be marched single file into the major's office, usually located at some central point inside the prison. In one of the instances I recorded, the major began by handing each inmate a copy of the prison's rulebook and then spoke to the group as follows:

> You are in the custody of the Texas Department of Corrections. Stand where I can see you! [pause] That book I just gave you is the most important thing you'll ever receive here. It lists all the rules and regulations. You're responsible for knowing them. If you can't read, we'll have someone read it to you as many times as you need. . . . Now, if you need education—and we all do—we've got it right here. You can learn a skill in here, you can earn good time. . . . The best way to do time is to do your own time. Do your own time! Nobody else can do it for you. If you listen to some inmates inside, you'll have trouble for sure. You get in trouble, and you'll be right here with me for a longer time; I guarantee it. Now, you have family and friends waiting on you—don't let them down. Don't let yourself down. Do your own time, and you'll be fine. The rules are for your own protection and health. . . . There is a reason for each and every rule. They are to help you, to keep you whole.

The control model did more than rely on such exhortation as a means of preventing individual or group misconduct, especially the sort that might threaten the safety of others or make escapes more likely. All rules, even the most minor ones, were enforced. Casual groupings of inmates in the cellblocks, on the yards, out in the fields, or at work in the plants were simply not permitted. Almost reflexively, officers would shout "Break it up!" or "Move out!" at the incipient stages of such gatherings. In sum, the control model involved administrative measures tight enough to check individual misdeeds as well as the maldevelopment of inmate society, but not so tight as to preclude the degree of inmate movement and interaction necessary for work and treatment opportunities.

Evolution of the Control Model

Dr. Beto's predecessor as director of the Texas prison system was O. B. Ellis. Ellis had served as director from 1947 till his death in 1961 at a Board of Corrections meeting. Ellis had come to Texas from correctional work in Tennessee. Beto, on the other hand, came to the helm of Texas corrections from a more unconventional background. An ordained Lutheran minister with a Doctorate in Education, he came to Texas from Illinois, where he had served on the Illinois Board of Parole and been active in other areas of criminal justice. In addition, he had been president of Concordia College in Texas and Concordia Theological Seminary in Illinois. While at the former, he had served on the Texas Board of Corrections. In corrections circles Beto earned the nickname "Walking George" because of his practice of making frequent and usually unannounced visits to the prisons. In the next chapter we shall learn more about Beto's correctional legacy.

For now, however, it is important to note that one of the chief influences on Beto's thinking about prisons was Joseph Ragen, the famous warden of Illinois's Stateville penitentiary. As was noted in chapter one, Ragen's approach to correctional management was remarkably security-oriented. So far as the internal management of the prisons was concerned, Beto borrowed more than a few pages from Ragen's book, seeing to it that his subordinates at every level practiced an incredibly security-conscious yet treatment-oriented approach to running the prisons. In this effort, Beto was advantaged by having the kind of charismatic personality that led his subordinates to feel that he knew or could trace their every move; in fact, he normally could.

With Richard A. McGee, who directed the California prison system from 1944 into the 1960s, Beto was ahead of his time in being sensitive to the place of correctional agencies in the overall criminal justice system. Even more than McGee, however, Beto reached beyond the walls to master other parts of the criminal justice system and, more importantly, to bend the system's political environment to its best interests. Beto cultivated governors, legislators, prison board members, journalists, and other important constituencies beyond the walls. Largely because of his efforts, state laws were passed that, among other things, made it possible for the system to produce and sell a significant quantity of prison-made goods. This enabled the system to develop a thriving industrial complex which could employ vast numbers of the prison population. Together with the system's enormous agri-business complex, also developed largely under Beto's tutelage, it was possible for the system to keep per capita costs relatively low, far below the per capita costs of other major state systems. In Texas, a state where tax dollars for most public goods and services have traditionally been allocated in stingy and irregular amounts, this proved vital, for it helped to keep the system popular politically and enabled it to do more than merely warehouse inmates.

Beto's successor was W. J. Estelle. Estelle came to Texas after having been a ranking correctional worker in California and a warden in Montana. Estelle, whose family history in correctional administration stretches back to the late nineteenth century and includes the first warden of California's San Quentin prison, served as director of the Texas prison system from 1972 to 1983. He shared virtually all of Beto's correctional philosophy and saw it as his mission to further institutionalize the control model of management that, just about everybody agreed, had made Texas prisons safe, clean, treatment-oriented, and financially self-supporting.

As the Texas inmate newspaper noted in a 1984 article reviewing Estelle's administration. "his 11½ years as director of TDC were highly successful in leading the Texas prison system through what were perhaps the most precarious years of its 140-year existence."[2] Estelle expanded the system's industrial and agricultural complexes, personnel training, and treatment programs. The circumstances surrounding Estelle's resignation and the overriding role of federal court intervention in bringing about fundamental changes in the way that Texas runs its prisons are covered in chapter five.

Defects of the Control Model

There were at least two latent defects, one internal, the other external, in the model of prison administration bequeathed by Beto to Estelle. Internally, the control model involved what was known as the building-tender (BT) system.

BTs were inmates selected by the administration to assist correctional officers in running the cellblocks. The building-tender system grew out of Beto's theory, not untouched by readings of prison sociology, that inmates are bound to have leaders. Rather than allow the most aggressive and violent inmates to rule, Beto believed that prison officials could select exemplary inmates, give them special official status beyond a mere trustyship, and use them to preempt the influence of more hardcore, criminalistic, and violent inmates. "Either you pick their leaders," he explained, "or they do." Beto elaborated the idea as follows:

> In any contemporary prison, there is bound to be some level of inmate organization, some manner of inmate society. . . . The question is this: who selects the leaders? Are the inmates to select them? Or is the administration to choose them or at least influence the choice? If the former, the extent of control over organized and semi-organized inmate life is lessened; if the latter, the measure of control is strengthened.

The building-tender system was intended as a way of reducing the influence of aggressive, exploitative inmate leaders. It was, in effect, an attempt to make formal and legitimate what Gresham Sykes had characterized as the corrupt alliance between the inmates and the administration. It was designed as a way of avoiding a situation in which prison inmates rather than prison authorities determine the character of life behind bars. Under Beto, BTs were rewarded officially rather than informally with better job assignments and the like. But they were positively forbidden to use their positions for illicit gains and were, at least until the mid-1970s, largely prevented from doing so. Any BT who tried to exploit his position in this way would be in trouble with the authorities. Being a BT did not give an inmate the right to ignore the rules. In short, under Beto, the BT system worked as an alternative to the widely practiced con-boss system wherein favored inmates were given illicit privileges and allowed to abuse other inmates (and even the staff) in return for helping the administration to keep order.

But to keep the BT system from sliding into a con-boss system required enormous administrative energy spent selecting and monitoring the BTs. By all accounts, Beto saw to it that building tenders were chosen carefully and kept on a very short leash. As Beto himself recalled:

> We would not select someone likely to abuse his position. All building-tender appointments had to be cleared by me or by the director of classification. No inmate could be appointed simply on a warden's say so. One day, for instance, during one of my tours I observed an inmate acting as a building tender.

I knew this man's history. He was a very bad character, the type that would rape a snake through a brick wall. I said, "What in the world are you doing in this position?" He said that the warden or some other authority at the institution had given him the job. I saw to it that he was removed as a building tender—on the spot.

Estelle, like Beto, was a talented and energetic executive. During his tenure, however, the system more than doubled both in population and in number of units. Estelle was not given to the kind of superclose, hands-on supervision that marked Beto's directorship. Even if he were, however, it would have been virtually impossible for him to cover over two dozen institutions the way that Beto had covered twelve. Also, Estelle did not have the advantage of Beto's charismatic personality or reputation for omniscience concerning what was happening in the field. These factors combined to weaken the centralized control that was at the heart of the control model. Towards the end of Estelle's era, therefore, the BT system broke down and became a classical con-boss system. Under Estelle's successors, it evolved into a situation in which the leaders of various prison gangs, organized largely along racial and ethnic lines, ran major parts of the Texas prison system.

A second latent defect in the control model was essentially external and political. The Texas control model depended for its existence on an extraordinary degree of political support from powerful state leaders. For decades the Texas Board of Corrections, the body with immediate authority over the prison system, cast only unanimous votes in support of the administration's policies and was an effective public voice for the department's budgetary and other needs. Until the 1980s the board was composed almost entirely of the state's leading businessmen. Chief among them was H. H. "Pete" Coffield. Coffield, a member of the board since 1948, was its chairman from 1955 to 1974. He was a multimillionaire who had made money in a variety of endeavors. In his day, Coffield was considered to be, next to LBJ, the most powerful man in Texas.

Known affectionately as "Mr. Chairman," Coffield could be ruthless in pressing his will on state politicians and had much influence with the state's press. The Texas Department of Corrections was, in effect, the chief benefactor of his enormous power within the state. Beto used Coffield's influence sparingly but, nevertheless, had this political resource at his disposal to win key legislative or other battles. Coffield's dedication to the system was incredible. For example, on the department's behalf, he would sponsor (and pay for) lavish cocktail parties for the state's most influential citizens—legislators, corporate executives, and so on. He would come to the prisons and speak at inmate high school graduation ceremonies, a service valuable both for what he had to say and for the positive image it left with the public. In short, for twenty-eight years this important figure stood behind the Texas prison system in its efforts to become one of the nation's best. The system acknowledged his contributions when, in 1974, it dedicated a department-prepared history of the agency to him.[3]

Coffield, however, was not the only political pillar of the Texas control model. Equally important were key state legislators such as Bill Heatly, long-reigning chairman of the House Appropriations Committee. Known in Texas as the "Duke of Paducah" (Paducah being the Texas county from which he came), Heatly was for some twenty-eight years all-powerful in his control over the state's purse. Districts whose representatives opposed Heatly on even insignificant measures would get less funds for their roads, schools, and other state services. A "yellow dog" Texas Democrat (meaning a party loyalist who would "vote for a yellow dog over a Republican"), in 1972, Heatly was able to deliver his district for the wildly unpopular George McGovern. Heatly was a recovered alcoholic who was helped by Alcoholics Anonymous (AA). In gratitude, Heatly ran a loosely grouped AA chapter for people in state government. With one eye on the political significance of the act, Beto saw to it that the AA chapters in the prisons became an integral part of the formal treatment program. In later years Heatly repaid this gesture by giving Beto's agency what it needed (but not a penny more) budgetarily.[4]

Beto's ties to Heatly and other important state legislators were direct and intimate. Beto used various strategies to win and keep their support, but in general, he was simply relentless in his attempts to educate state political leaders about the system's needs. He encouraged them to visit and study the prisons. His powers of persuasion proved more than equal to the task of cultivating such support. Successive governors became highly interested in and supportive of his attempt to run the nation's best correctional agency.

In 1974, just two years into Estelle's tenure, the aging Pete

Coffield retired from his chairmanship on the Board of Corrections. In 1978, William P. Clements, Jr. became the state's governor. Clements was the first Republican governor elected in Texas in 105 years. He made a number of appointments, including some to the Board of Corrections, that were intended to shake things up. Key supporters of the system began to retire or saw their influence wane. At the same time, the system was undergoing major litigation in federal court in the form of a class-action suit challenging the constitutionality of conditions inside the state's prisons. The presiding judge was William Wayne Justice. Judge Justice was known in Texas for his generally liberal views on such matters as busing. In 1980 "Willie Wayne," as he was called, handed down a decision ordering changes in virtually every part of the Texas prison system.

Judge Justice's opinion came at a time when the system's political support was already declining, albeit slowly. Estelle was known as a stubborn administrator, one dedicated to certain correctional principles (those of the control model.) He was fiercely loyal to his subordinates and thoroughly opposed, on philosophical grounds, to the judiciary's attempt to order changes in prison operations and oversee their implementation. He thus made a vigorous defense of the system and its accomplishments against the court and its appointed monitors. By this time, the Board of Corrections was no longer solid in its support for the system. Unprecedented split votes were cast, and the Board, now composed of less powerful men and women of differing backgrounds, made its battles public. There soon followed an outpouring of news stories and editorials questioning, criticizing, or condemning the agency.[5] Clement's successor in the governor's office, Democrat Mark White, was no unbending supporter of the agency. In short, by 1984, the Texas prison system had gone from the sunniest political weather to a storm of thunderous dissent and protest.

Also during the latter part of Estelle's tenure, the state's oil revenues began to decline. The troubled prison system became a favorite target of those who wanted to spend less on the public sector. Estelle was unable to get the legislature to approve his package of budget requests. Recognizing that he had become a political liability to the agency, Estelle resigned in late 1983.

In a letter to me, former Texas Governor John Connally (1963–1969) summed up the transformation in the system's political environment leading up to Estelle's resignation:

. . . the success of the Texas Department of Corrections was
made possible by [a] supporting political environment which
consisted of its Board of Corrections . . . [the] State Legislature, and . . . a favorable press. . . . We had the cooperation
of men like Pete Coffield and Bill Heatly . . . and many many
other people including the strong support of the Speaker of
the House, Ben Barnes, who later became Lieutenant Governor.[6]

Connally implied that the loss of this support was responsible for
the system's difficulties. Former Texas governor Preston Smith
(1969–1973) made the same argument, though more directly. In a
letter to me, Governor Smith wrote:

. . . it is rather ironical, but true, that politics has played a
definite role in the overall operations of the Texas prison
system. It's too bad, but true, that our system has not had
the proper attention and support it had some years back.[7]

Smith went on to say that "we simply do not have the caliber of
people on the board nor the executive, legislative, public support
that was once available."

It is important to highlight the administrative consequences of
this change in the organization's political environment.[8] The most
important consequence was to undermine the system's organizational stability at all levels. From Beto's predecessor through
Estelle, the Texas prison system had three directors in thirty-six
years, a remarkable fact, given that the average tenure of state
prison directors is roughly three years. Estelle was followed by
D. V. "Red" McKaskle, who served several months as acting director. In mid-1984 Raymond P. Procunier, who had directed the
California prison system from 1967 to 1975, was appointed director. Procunier's tenure lasted under two years; he was succeeded
by his second-in-command O. L. McCotter, formerly an Army colonel in charge of the disciplinary barracks at Fort Leavenworth,
Kansas. Since 1983, therefore, the system has gone through three
directors, as many in the last few years as it had in the previous
thirty.

Rates of turnover at lower levels increased as well. Veteran
correctional officers, disgruntled by the administrative changes
brought on by the Justice Justice's order and the new directorships, began to leave the system or seek early retirement. New

recruits quit at rates as high as 90 percent per year. Meanwhile, policy and procedure manuals changed, multiplied, and thickened but the administrative routine grew less comprehensible and less predictable. Prison personnel became less certain about what rules were in effect, how to enforce them, and the extent of their authority in governing inmates. The sense of mission and esprit de corps of the lower ranks suffered. Officers who only months earlier had proudly boasted of their role in "the nation's best prison system" came to view their work as—in the words of one veteran officer—"just a job" in which the goal was to "get paid but not get injured, sued, or killed."

Though brief, Procunier's tenure as director of the Texas prison system was important and may be viewed as the final chapter in the demise of the Texas control model and the first in a sort of natural experiment in prison management. As noted, before coming to Texas, Procunier had been head of the California prison system. He had also served as director of the Virginia and Utah systems and was a consultant to the New Mexico prison system shortly before its major 1980 riot. Procunier was praised as a tough, energetic, and colorful administrator, a man of salty language who related to inmates and staff like an old-fashioned machine politician nailing down votes.

Procunier presided over California prisons during the years when four competing prison gangs became a major disruptive force in the system, a situation changed over the last decade only by the rise of new, still more violent gangs in that system. When he came to Texas, Procunier imported some of his old California subordinates with the idea that together they would implement changes in the way that Texas prisons were managed. Procunier took measures to dismantle the remaining elements of the control model and to erect something closer to the California consensual model of prison administration.

After an initial honeymoon period with state political leaders, prison reform groups, and the press, Procunier came under serious fire for unprecedented and rising levels of violence in the system. Then, as had occurred under his administration in California, Texas began to develop its first unabated prison gang problem. As the violence and the gang problem grew worse, Procunier's political support crumbled. As one local journalist stated, Procunier had been appointed to "come in, kick ass and clean house."[9] In the early months of his tenure, Procunier won a surprising measure of goodwill inside the organization from "old guard" wardens, the uniformed force, and other personnel. Soon, however, this internal support dwindled. For the first time ever Texas correctional officers began to unionize themselves. The sum of these and related developments proved too much, and Procunier, while having committed himself to two years at the helm of Texas prisons, retired from corrections in 1985.

As we shall see in chapter five, the rising violence and the overall decline in the quality of prison life that characterized Texas prisons between 1983 and 1986 is attributable to these and associated changes in prison management. Now, however, let us turn to a model of correctional administration as different from the Texas control model as can be imagined: the Michigan responsibility model.

Elements of the Michigan Responsibility Model

The best way to introduce the Michigan responsibility model is to compare it to the Texas control model. Whereas the control model placed a premium on administrative measures that maximized control over inmates, the responsibility model placed a premium on measures that maximized inmates' responsibility for their own actions. Whereas the control model mandated that every prison be designated and run as a maximum-security facility, the responsibility model established a number of security levels and, through an inmate classification system leagues more sophisticated and elaborate than anything that has yet been developed in Texas and most other systems, attempted to fit inmates into the most appropriate but least-restrictive prison setting. Whereas the control model involved policies and procedures intended to maximize the paramilitary content of prison life, the responsibility model involved measures that minimized the symbols and substance of formal administrative authority over inmates.

The chief architect of the responsibility model was Perry M. Johnson, director of the Michigan Department of Corrections from August 1972 through June 1984. In 1955, Johnson began his career in corrections as a counselor at the State Prison of Southern Michigan. In 1959, he became supervisor of a minimum-security facility. Four years later he returned to Jackson prison as an administrative assistant to the warden. Between 1964 and 1969, he served as assistant deputy in charge of custody, first at Marquette

Branch prison and later at Jackson. After about a year as deputy director of the department's Bureau of Correctional Facilities, he became warden of Jackson, a post he held until his appointment as director. After resigning as director, Johnson became deputy director of the department's Bureau of Field Services (BFS). As of this writing, Johnson is still deputy director of BFS.

Under the responsibility model, prisons are to be run in ways that impose minimum constraints on inmates. The 1979 *Employee Handbook* advised:

> An important principle of Corrections is that no more custody and security should be imposed than are really necessary. People should be classified properly as to their security needs. This is true not only for reasons of humanity but also for economy. Secure institutions are expensive to build and operate, and are counterproductive except where really needed.[10]

Tight security is "counterproductive" because inmates ought to be given a chance to behave in acceptable ways. Rather than having their every move monitored inmates ought to be given the greatest measure of freedom consistent with basic security requirements and then be held strictly accountable for their actions.

Unlike Texas, but like California, the administration of prisons in Michigan is headed by a director who is also responsible for probation, parole, and other postsentencing ("field services") operations. According to the premises of the responsibility model, convicted offenders should, if at all possible, be given sentences that do not necessitate imprisonment. Only dangerous offenders should be sent to prison and only the most dangerous of those imprisoned should live under maximum-security conditions. Even those offenders who do end up in maximum-security prisons should not have to lead thoroughly regimented lives. They, too, should be given a significant degree of freedom—what in corrections is sometimes called "air"—and then be held to account for their actions. One upper-level administrator, familiar with the Texas system, explained:

> We go by the idea that prison should be as unrestrictive as possible. Don't misunderstand. Order comes first. You have to keep control. Security is number one through one thousand. But we don't have to smother people to keep things under control. We try to show the inmates respect and expect it in

return. We are more willing than Texas to give them air and
then hold them accountable. . . . We attempt to operate safely
in the least restrictive environment possible. . . . If Texas
opts for the most restrictive, we opt for the least restrictive.

Predictably, the administrative routine of Michigan prisons has
been quite different from that of Texas prisons. In Texas, for
instance, there was an all-encompassing emphasis on the rules and
their official enforcement. In Michigan, on the other hand, the
rulebook reminded officers (in bold letters) that "there is no requirement that every rule violation" be treated formally, noting
that in "many cases verbal counseling or summary action should be
the first response to the apparent misconduct."[11] Rather than the
tight routine of numbering, counting, checking, and locking that
characterized Texas prisons, daily life inside Michigan prisons was
a more loosely supervised, somewhat anarchic round of inmate
movement punctuated by frequent counts of the population.

The responsibility model is highly consistent with attempts to
give inmates a greater voice in prison affairs as well as opportunities for individual growth. For instance, a policy directive issued
in 1981 stated that "prisoner organizations are to be encouraged as
a means of prisoner self-expression and self-development."[12] Under the terms of this policy, it was not required that a member of
the correctional staff be present to supervise inmate gatherings.
Instead, the directive authorized "community volunteers" to supervise the meetings, requiring only that a staff member be available "for drop-in supervision."

As mentioned earlier, under the responsibility model, a premium is placed on assigning inmates to the lowest security setting
consistent with basic custodial goals. This has necessitated the
development of a complex classification system.[13] Regardless of
security classification, Michigan inmates have been entitled to extensive visiting and other privileges such as frequent telephone
calls. Until recently, Texas inmates were extended few such privileges.

Under the responsibility model, minimal emphasis is placed on
exhorting or forcing inmates to "do their own time." Neither at the
Reception and Guidance Center nor upon arrival at their assigned
institutions are inmates encouraged to isolate themselves, physically or psychologically, from other inmates. Such isolation would
not be consistent with the attempt to "normalize" (a word com-

monly used by Michigan personnel in explaining their approach), so far as possible, life behind bars. If the Texas control model is an attempt to atomize the prisoner community, the Michigan responsibility model is an attempt to foster one. Many Michigan officials criticized the Texas approach as an attempt to "crush individuality" among the inmates.

Another element of the responsibility model is to invest in so-called Resident Unit Managers (RUMs) immediate authority for what goes on in the prison's living areas. RUMs are not correctional officers. They are, however, in charge of the officers in their units, adjudicate most minor disputes among prisoners, counsel inmates, and attempt to keep their areas clean. Michigan is by no means alone in its use of a unit management system. For instance, for most of the last decade virtually all federal prisons have used unit management. Michigan is unique, however, in that relatively few of its RUMs have risen through the custodial ranks or spent the bulk of their careers in uniform. In the federal system, and in several of the other states that have employed unit management, it is more common for unit supervisors to be ex-correctional officers.

As noted in the previous chapter, Michigan prison authorities have worked closely with the American Correctional Association (ACA) and sought accreditation wherever possible. In some units staff members have spent virtually all of their time preparing for accreditation inspections. Michigan has also been in the forefront of attempts to hire and promote women and minorities, having perhaps the most aggressive affirmative action policy of any correctional department in the country. As we shall see in more detail later, at some institutions these efforts have triggered conflicts between inmates and staff and between officers and their administrative superiors.

Evolution of the Responsibility Model

Almost as much a father of the responsibility model as Johnson was William Kime, deputy director of the department's Bureau of Programs. Some long-time members of the department credit the responsibility model and its emphasis on creating a minimally restrictive institutional environment chiefly to Kime. Prior to Johnson and Kime, Michigan prisons were headed for nearly two decades by Gus Harrison, a generally progressive but in many respects traditional prison executive. It was, for instance, under Harrison

that Michigan pioneered the concept of multiple security classifi-
cations, opening the country's first genuine medium-security prison
in 1958. Under Harrison, prisoners were permitted personal clothing, radios, and many other articles of personal property. The
movement away from paramilitary uniforms, featuring cloth "Ike"
jackets, began during his tenure. But by most accounts, Harrison
was a strong believer in the necessity of strict inmate and correctional officer grooming standards. He accepted, but did not cham-
pion, the demilitarization of the custodial ranks and was unfriendly
to the idea of even indirect inmate participation in running the
prisons.

It was not, therefore, until Johnson and Kime were in the ascendant that the Michigan responsibility model was implemented,
and then only gradually. According to Kime, "the de-militarization
was intentional. We chose to do it in order to lessen the tensions
and the distance between inmates and officers." But not all of the
innovations associated with the responsibility model's demilitarization were a part of the original concept. For instance, most MDC
personnel identified the system's elaborate inmate grievance procedures as a hallmark of the model. In fact, however, Johnson,
Kime, and other higher-ranking prison officials opposed the move
to a more intricate grievance and hearing process. As Kime observed:

> [The grievance procedure] was designed to cope with the law
> imposed on the Department of Corrections which created the
> Office of Legislative Corrections Ombudsman. We preferred
> the grievance system prior to that, which was simple and
> direct. . . . I know that a lot of people in the institutions don't
> understand that the current processes were forced on us. . . .
> In some instances these measures were written into law and
> court orders; some we adopted in advance to head off worse.

Still, most correctional officers resisted the demilitarization of the
system and blamed headquarters for everything that appeared to
come in its wake. Michigan, a state with a strong labor union
tradition, has long had some of the nation's most active, powerful,
and militant correctional officer unions. Basically, the officer unions
have pushed for measures contrary to both the letter and the spirit
of the responsibility model.[14] There is a belief, shared by virtually
all of the officers with whom I spoke, that in the effort to give the
inmates greater responsibility and to demilitarize the prison envi-

ronment, the system has forfeited most of its routine administrative controls.

In recent years the Michigan responsibility model of correctional management has been buffeted by adverse court opinions, rising violence, fluctuating political support, and overcrowding. Accused by the United States Department of Justice of running prisons characterized by "perverse racial tensions, high levels of violence, inhumane treatment of mentally ill prisoners and inadequate due process," the department negotiated and entered into a consent decree mandating major changes and improvements.[15]

To insulate itself from the pressures of overcrowding, the department had championed an "Emergency Powers Act" (EPA). Signed into law in 1981, the EPA was triggered whenever the state prison population exceeded the department's certified prison capacity for thirty straight days. The Corrections Commission would request that the governor declare a state of emergency; after fifteen days and with the governor's approval the minimum sentences of all prisoners were reduced by ninety days. The act was triggered several times and so shaved months, even years, from the terms of thousands of inmates. For example, an inmate with a 2-year sentence who entered the prison system in July of 1982 would serve only six months as a result of automatic good time credits and successive instances of the EPA; indeed, by a quirk of law, at the end of only six months behind bars he would be three months late for parole. After 1984, the state's political leaders responded to a public outcry against this policy, and the act died. Johnson's successor as director, former Bureau of Correctional Facilities deputy director Robert Brown, has come under fire for the system's increasing costs and rising violence.[16]

Defects of the Responsibility Model

The chief defect of the responsibility model seems to be internal and involves not just one aspect of the model but several major facets of it. Later we shall have more to say about correctional administration in Michigan. Here we shall highlight just a few of the system's apparent administrative shortcomings.

Whatever its presumed benefits in creating a better prison milieu, the responsibility model has done little to promote organizational morale and much to stimulate among correctional officers a feeling of animosity towards the "brass" at headquarters in Lansing. Officers in Michigan have little clear sense of mission and are often cynical, even bitter, about the organization and its policies. They are frustrated, for instance, by the generous personal property and visiting policies, which, they contend, make it easier for inmates to obtain and conceal weapons and other types of contraband. The following comments were typical:

> Lansing plays the spoiling grandparent. They come up with all sorts of goodies to spoil. They give the inmates their own way too much and then ask us to keep order and raise them properly. Bulls——t! They reap what they sow. We are made into scapegoats for their asshole schemes.
>
> We look like some bartenders' union. We got rid of the symbols of authority. But we lost more than the symbols.
>
> Property control is a nightmare.

If one measured bureaucracy simply by the scope and detail of an organization's policy manuals and the like, then the Michigan prison system would rank among the most bureaucratic in the nation. But if one measured by the ability of workers to translate these policies into a clear, simple routine of administrative action, then the department would, possibly, rank among the least bureaucratic. In the words of one veteran administrator:

> One of the major changes under the responsibility idea was the codification of rules and procedures. We used to have a thin book, a little thing you could hold between your fingers. Know what we have today? (He turns around in his desk.) This! (He holds up three fat volumes.) This happened in 1973. We've got more things written down but I don't think we follow even the basic guidelines the way we used to.

A 1982 policy directive (PD-BCF-53.01) contains over six pages of closely typed regulations intended to "establish uniform guidelines regarding property which inmates are permitted to have in their possession" and related matters. To know how much and what type of clothing an inmate is allowed, an officer would have to master this directive plus a few others. To enforce several key provisions, he would need to be able, among other things, to tell whether an inmate's gold earring was worth more than fifty dollars retail, have the time to count the number of cassette tapes in an inmate's cell (maximum 30), and make sure that the inmate's sewing machine is of the portable variety.

One alleged consequence of such policies has been the creation of innumerable security problems as inmates are more easily capable of creating and storing forbidden items on their persons or in their cells. One high-level administrator stated:

> The line has been, if it's not a verifiable and immediate problem, then let him have it—clothes, TV, you name it. . . . This stuff has to be processed; it necessitates more shakedowns [searches of cells]; it gives rise therefore to more conflicts over privacy and procedures. . . . Furthermore, much of this stuff is raw material for weapons. . . . The benefits of the attempt to normalize are intangible, the costs are more concrete. . . . property is hard to control, more conflicts, more violence. . . .

A second consequence has been the creation of a sort of caste system in which some inmates dress and live far more lavishly than others. As one official commented, "The freedom they have is good in principle but creates some practical problems—stolen coats, stolen shirts. . . . It makes them feel less institutionalized. But then you have some who are well dressed and others in less expensive, up-to-date clothes. That may be a source of friction." Another administrator stated, "we've created a caste system of haves and have-nots."

A third consequence has been that top administrators, both at departmental headquarters and in the field, find themselves buried behind mountains of paperwork, unable to get out into the institutions with any regularity. The perception among the institutional staff, including upper-level administrators and most officers, is that the system's top management simply does not know what is "really going on" in the prisons. This perception was largely confirmed when, in interviews with some of the officials at headquarters, it became clear that they were unaware of certain basic operational realities. For instance, some did not know that the officers had no visible signs of rank. Others were unaware of the actual levels of violence or crowding at given prisons. One high-ranking institutional official noted some of the absurdities produced by this isolation from actual happenings inside the prisons. "They [headquarters] insist," he said, "that we have fewer inmates than we do. They quote me the numbers over the phone. Meanwhile, I'm staring at bodies with no place to put them." The same official went on about how he was a captive of paperwork, unable to tour his own institution with any frequency.

There are other basic flaws in the responsibility model, not least of which is the limited efficacy of the elaborate classification procedure. There is no hard evidence that the Michigan classification system has worked as intended. In any case, overcrowding has necessitated assigning "high-risk" inmates to "low-risk" institutions. Nor is there any solid evidence to support the idea that greater inmate access to grievance mechanisms and participation on various advisory councils has worked to make the prisons more secure or to improve the overall quality of prison life. Indeed, many of the system's employees, at all levels, believe that such policies have had just the opposite effect, moving the system away from its goal (stated in PD-DWA-64.02) that inmates "be treated humanely and with dignity in matters of health care, personal safety and general living conditions."

It would be incorrect, however, to lay the entire blame for these problems at the door of the responsibility model and equally incorrect to assume that they make MDC compare unfavorably to most other prison systems. As one upper-level Michigan official stated:

> The responsibility model holds that people should be held accountable for the consequences of their choices. It calls not merely for rewarding people for doing the right thing, but also for sanctions for doing wrong. Examples to the contrary—and a number undeniably occur—are violations of the concept, not a part of it. . . . Also, the property and other policies did not evolve from the model but from the belief that the courts would allow restrictions only if compelling State interest could be shown. Our Sixth District Federal Court has been among the most sympathetic to prisoners' rights in the nation. . . . Most of the due process and liberal privileges would have been imposed on our system under any administrative model.

While a review of the prison litigation in Michigan during the 1970s reveals that there is much truth in this statement, it appears that, under the responsibility system, the momentum of court rulings and legislative initiatives was carried to an extreme. Johnson, Kime, and other top MDC officials opposed certain innovations as inimical both to the responsibility model and to the need for basic controls. But the perception which festered among the vast majority of the prison employees was that, without exception, these changes were less court-induced and more agency-sponsored, a by-product of the insensitivity and bad judgement of their administrative superiors. The ire of the custodial ranks, which in other systems has been directed mainly at judges, legislators, and others beyond the walls, was in Michigan directed largely at those sitting in headquarters or the warden's office. At a minimum, it is fair to say that the responsibility model served as a convenient conduit for certain measures of which even its founders disapproved.

A thirty-year veteran of the system summarized what to him were the defects of the responsibility model as a correctional management system:

> I'd love to have a prison that could run the way the model says. But we've got a little problem: impulsive convicts and human nature. . . . This system deprives inmates of the right to safety in the name of giving them other rights, then fails to deliver on these other rights. . . . A cellblock should be like a residential street. Would you want to live on a street where your neighbors were always shouting? Where most of what they shouted was vulgar and violent? Would you permit your neighbors to assault you and each other? That's what we do here on "Rock Street."

Despite these defects, the quality of life inside Michigan prisons has been superior to the quality of life in many other state prisons. In the next chapter we shall explore the philosophical assumptions underlying the responsibility model. Now, however, we turn to examine a model of correctional administration resting somewhere on the continuum between the responsibility model and the control model: the California consensual model.

Elements of the California Consensual Model

Strictly speaking, there is no founder or chief architect of the California model of correctional administration, no Dr. George Beto as in Texas, or Perry Johnson and Bill Kime as in Michigan. Correctional students and practitioners familiar with the history of California prisons may rush to point out that Richard A. McGee was the father of the post-World War II California Department of

Corrections. This is certainly true. But the California system that developed under his successors was not the one that McGee had worked to set in motion. Its policies and procedures departed in significant ways from those championed by McGee. More to the point, however, one cannot state just what the California model of correctional management is or how it has differed from other models of prison administration. Indeed, if the California model has any defining feature, it is its hodgepodge, crazy-quilt pattern of correctional principles and practices.

On the one hand, California prisons have appeared to run according to a weak version of the Michigan responsibility model. Like Michigan, California has developed elaborate classification procedures and inmate grievance mechanisms.[17] As in Michigan, California inmates have participated in a variety of inmate councils and been offered what are commonly considered to be a wide range of rehabilitation programs. Though not to the extent of Michigan, California has generally favored less rather than more restrictive correctional environments and has come down on the side of liberality in its policies governing inmate grooming, movement, property rights, and other matters. For instance, one of the system's "Institutional Orders" notes that inmates "may wear their hair at any length and in any style they desire . . ." Inmates may freely display tattoos, even ones that are clearly evocative of some prison-gang affiliation (e.g., swastikas for members of various white supremacy gangs).

On the other hand, California's officer force has been organized along paramilitary lines. While grooming standards for officers have been more relaxed than in Texas, California has had a similar emphasis on a "spit and polish" appearance. While California officers have been less formal in relations with their superiors and more informal in dealing with the inmates than officers in Texas, there has been a far greater emphasis on the chain-of-command and the organizational hierarchy than in Michigan. California's powerful officer unions have been militant about preserving and enhancing the paramilitary features of CDC's prison operations. In 1985, for instance, the officers fought for and won the right to carry firearms when off-duty. Their successful, widely publicized slogan is that correctional officers have "the toughest beat in the state."

At the same time, however, California officers handle inmates in a mostly informal, "go with the flow" manner. Many California officials, for instance, pride themselves on their ability to speak to inmates in the inmates' own argot. One administrator stated:

> People identify with different things, different music, food. . . . I can say to a Mexican inmate, *"Como estas?"* or to a black inmate "What's happening man?" or to a white inmate "How are you today?" This matters.

Even among themselves, officials adopt the inmates' argot, speaking of "righteous weapons" (dangerous ones), "bad ass dudes" (aggressive inmates or inmate predators), and so on. At Soledad prison, the officers' "post orders" read in part: "Rules shall be enforced firmly but fairly and impartially. Avoid nagging, threats, arguing. . . ." Disciplinary situations are often handled informally, sometimes with a serious but half-humorous verbal order to an inmate to stop his inappropriate behavior: "Mr. (inmate's name), you are asked to cut the crap."

If there is a single unifying principle of California's approach to correctional administration, it is the notion that prison government rests ultimately on the consent of the governed—that is, the inmates. Prison workers in each state expressed the view that the inmates were capable of seizing control of the prisons if they so desired. This opinion was expressed most frequently in California and least frequently in Texas. In a typical remark, one upper-level California administrator explained:

> Prisons were once an island, but now they're a part of society. The inmates were once total outcasts, but now they're looked upon as incarcerated citizens. The reality is that we who manage must manage by gaining their consent. To do this we must treat them fairly, honestly, and caringly. Guns don't manage.

To some degree this idea of management by consent grows out of the chief operational fact of life inside California prisons: prison gangs. In California, prison administrators have had to govern largely through brokering compromises among the system's most powerful four to six prison gangs. California prison officials are understandably touchy about this subject. The gang problem, they argue, has been severe only at San Quentin and Folsom, only two of the twelve major California prisons. As one Soledad official explained:

> In California we have identified five major gangs and consider members of these gangs to be dangerous and not suitable for general population programs. Further, several of these gangs are at war and pledged to kill each other. . . . They attempt to control most narcotic contraband "business" within the prison. . . . Now, in a setting such as the Correctional Training Facility [Soledad], your general population is—hopefully—not controlled by these gangs. The prison is greatly influenced rather by inmates who gain a certain degree of power by various means, i.e., money, narcotics/contraband trafficking, ingratiating themselves to staff. My perception is the more security-oriented, stable and professional your staff the less control these individuals exert.

The same analysis was made by scores of other California prison workers and is, so far as one can tell, essentially correct. There are, however, a few crucial qualifications to be made.

While it is true that the gang problem plagues some California prisons more than others, it is a major source of worry, trouble, and concern at all of the state's higher-custody facilities. At Soledad, for instance, the first question asked by administrators who learn about some violent incident is "Was it gang related?" Morning staff meetings are often consumed by such topics as what gangs are "making moves" inside the prison and rumor control concerning gang activities at other prisons.

In short, in California, the question of how to manage prisons has resolved itself into the question of how to manage prison gangs. The California model rests mainly on the assumption that the best way to manage gangs (or inmate associations generally) is via a mixture of—as one veteran officer put it—"a show of heavy artillery" plus a recognition of the need to win the inmates' cooperation. In the minds of most California prison administrators, any approach predicated on either a responsibility or a control model of correctional management is doomed to failure; somehow prison workers must realize both models. As one California administrator explained:

> There is always present a fine balancing between staff and inmates in this area because of mutual survival needs. I guess my point is that this . . . is not a gang phenomenon but rather is a necessary survival function. I can also say from hard experience that if either party (staff or inmates) gains too

much power, violence increases, i.e., inmates begin to traffic more heavily in contraband, which results in more violence, or tension between staff and inmates increases because of a paramilitary approach by staff. . . . We do not negotiate or "power share" with prison gangs. But we establish in general population settings "Advisory Councils" that work with staff and inmates. These groups are very effective if your management is security-oriented and if members are not allowed to become too powerful.

To a surprising degree, California prison workers have managed to steer an administrative middle course between the putative excesses and defects of the responsibility model, on the one hand, and the control model, on the other. Generally speaking, however, the system's prisons have fallen more on one or the other side of this administrative divide. As we shall see, CMC has been more of a control model institution while Soledad has been more of a responsibility model institution.

Evolution of the Consensual Model

During his years in California corrections, Raymond Procunier, director of the system from 1967 to 1975, enjoyed amicable relations with the state's governors, particularly Ronald Reagan. Indeed, in 1984 when he was considered for the director's position in Texas it was reported that the first two lines on his resume listed President Reagan and Edwin Meese as references. Known to friends, associates, and inmates as "the Pro," Procunier's earthy manner and philosophy of corrections inspired or offended just about everyone: "The simple way I put it is that if you find them [inmates] climbing over the fence you shoot them, and if you find them crying in the main yard you put your arm around them."

To the extent that the California consensual model can be said to have a father it is Procunier. On the one hand, he stressed the need for control. "If you don't have control," he stated, "you don't have programs, you don't have decent treatment. Everyplace I go, the convicts want me to run the prison. They don't want other convicts to run the prison." On the other hand, he stressed that most inmates will behave well if only "they get the sense that you're fair and square." According to Procunier, the highest compliment an inmate can pay a prison official is to say "That S.O.B.: he's tough; but he's decent." In general, his approach to corrections was to "kick ass when somebody screws up and to get my ass kicked when I screw up."

As noted earlier, it was under Procunier that California's prison gang problem first developed. As even the slim portrait of him given thus far should enable one to predict, Procunier's response to the problem was mainly shoot from the hip. At one point he would lock down the prisons; at another he would encourage the wardens and their staffs to communicate with the inmates, negotiate settlements among the gangs, or make non-security-threatening compromises with gang leaders. When in place, the restrictions on inmate movement worked to reduce the level of gang activity and violence, but in the view of most California officials (including Procunier) such measures were not to be institutionalized and so did not constitute a long-term solution to the problem.

Prison gangs were not entirely new in California. In the 1940s under McGee there were a variety of prison gangs. For several reasons, however, the gangs that began to develop in the 1960s were believed to pose a new type of correctional problem. First, these gangs were larger, younger, more politicized and tended to be organized along racial and ethnic lines. Blacks, in particular, joined prison gangs with the claim that they were "political prisoners." Second, officials perceived that the climate of public opinion combined with court rulings made any outright attempt to destroy the gangs impossible. For instance, due process requirements prevented officials from isolating inmates whose gang membership was known but could not be established beyond a reasonable doubt. Other laws hampered officials in their desire to separate inmates on the basis of race even where desegregating the prisons was alleged to pose greater dangers of inmate-on-inmate violence. Most important, however, was the officials' belief that certain gangs were so powerful and so well rooted that nothing could work to dissolve them. Retired CDC official James Park recalled:

Nobody predicted the development of gangs. Nobody could have. The traditional cure was to move them around, split them up. Then came the Mexican gangs. The old cure was up against a new culture. *La raza, la vida loco* ("the race, the crazy life"). They are not at all bothered or intimidated by sanctions. It's a question of honor and pride to be a gang member. You can split them up but they re-form overnight—new *commandantes*, new *generales*, new *soldados*. Machismo rules—they don't always stop stabbing when they hear shots.

By the time that Procunier resigned, high rates of prison violence, much of it caused by the gangs, were an established fact of prison life in California. Under Procunier, wardens had begun to act as power brokers for the gangs. One top official recounted how he had acted in this capacity following a series of attacks and counterattacks between the Mexican Mafia and the Black Guerrilla Family. "I would," he recalled, force "them to deal, to compromise, to have conferences."

Two of Procunier's successors as director were J. J. Enomoto and Ruth Rushen. Most California officials characterize their tenures as times when rifts between the officer unions and prison management deepened, the gang problem worsened, and the centripetal administrative force of Procunier's personality was replaced by the weakest brand of executive leadership. "The Pro" did not always follow through on new initiatives, made erratic personnel decisions, and blew hot and cold in his relations with the press. Still, his no-nonsense rhetoric and his histrionics—walking alone into a yard full of protesting inmates, offering himself as a hostage—had won him a measure of support at all levels of the department; even the CDC research chief, Robert Dickover, whose careful but unflattering assessment of the department's treatment programs Procunier had publicly labelled "a bunch of bulls——t," respected the colorful director.[18] Indeed, Dickover has stated:

> In assessing Procunier, one has to look beyond his flamboyance. He did lots of good here. For instance, he started family visiting, got the furlough program moving in the teeth of internal and external resistance, stimulated affirmative action in the agency, and in his own unique way was highly responsive to inmate and staff concerns.

Compared to Procunier, Enomoto and Rushen were correctional neophytes who lacked their predecessor's charisma and failed to develop any compensating levers of executive leadership.[19] The consensus among California officials is that during their directorships the system was more than ever the sum of what individual wardens happened to be doing at their prisons; in essence, following Procunier, there was an extended period of organizational drift.

Confronted with the gang problem, for instance, Enomoto turned to a CDC veteran for guidance.

> One day he asked me, "What the hell can we do?" He didn't have the foggiest idea. I said, "Let's pray."

Eventually, Enomoto decided to consult with the gang members themselves. As the same Enomoto confidante recalled:

> So we got some advice from—guess where?—the bastards themselves. Damn if they didn't give some good advice. The Mexican gangs especially. . . . They'd write it all out for us. Often, their proposals, their solutions, were quite good. Some of their ideas were better than ours.

The gangs fixed their position in the prison system. Where they promised to refrain from unprovoked violence, their right to associate in large numbers with fellow members in the dining halls or in recreation yards was not overly restricted by the administration. This de facto consent agreement was played out, with varying degrees of failure, as the staff at each prison adapted to the situation pretty much on its own.

For years CDC's official mission was to rehabilitate offenders. In 1978, however, the law was changed, and the department's chief duties became public protection and punishment. This change in the law added to the administrative confusion created by the lack of solid executive direction. As one veteran CDC administrator remarked, "The legislature wrote into the penal code that prison is for punishment, period. Go and read it. But what does it mean? How is that to be implemented?"

In 1983, Daniel J. McCarthy became CDC director. He was the first director since Procunier who had significant institutional experience, serving for many years as the warden of CMC. The most important influence on McCarthy's correctional thinking was Richard A. McGee. Referring to a copy of McGee's 1981 book *Prisons and Politics*, McCarthy said "that's my way too." McCarthy is a self-effacing, soft-spoken man, almost the exact opposite of the flamboyant Procunier. According to most CDC officials, McCarthy was appointed as director in the hope that he could rescue the system from its years of drift and initiate more effective measures to deal with the gang problem.

McCarthy did take measures to lessen the gang problem, including the formation of a task force composed of various top institutional officials. Thus far these measures have had limited but noticeable success. At a minimum, his efforts have given CDC personnel the chance to ponder the possibility of prisons where gangs are less prominent and have inspired them to work toward this goal. Also, McCarthy has lent his enormous prestige with the rank and file and his credibility with public officials to the start of a thoroughgoing reorganization of the system. This reorganization is being engineered by his immediate subordinates.

In considering this administrative restructuring of the California prison bureaucracy, the analogy that springs to mind is a distant one. When various rulers of Japan sought to promote what were essentially nontraditional concepts of government among a highly tradition-minded Japanese people, they drew upon the legitimacy of the most highly revered of all living symbols, the emperor. The modernizing reforms were taken in the emperor's name, often with his public blessing. Some of these reforms, however, would weaken the role of future emperors.

In essence, McCarthy has been presiding over administrative reforms designed to minimize the future influence in the department of correctional regulars like himself. His young immediate subordinates, brought into CDC from other state agencies, announce themselves as "professional managers, not corrections people." Their mission, in effect, is to make it impossible for the likes of a Dan McCarthy to rise through the ranks to a top institutional or central office position. As one official expressed it, the 1980s will be the decade in which CDC replaces its "ridiculous, crazy-quilt, asinine" operations with a "professional management system," grounded in techniques such as management by objectives (MBO): "There has been no attempt to bring contemporary management principles to this department—until now!" Another official noted: "We have no computerized information processing system—a billion dollar agency without basic information processing."

Those behind the changes have acted in the belief that there is nothing distinctive about correctional management. In the central office and the institutions, managers with absolutely no correctional experience, but a decent record in other state agencies, have been hired. There is no fear of an eventual loss of correctional expertise:

> . . . there are plenty of corrections guys around here—too many, that's the problem. . . . The good-ol'-boy system has ruled here forever. Guards rise to the top from the cellblocks.

Having already faced some stiff resistance from "the old guard," they have been quick to bring in "middle managers who are not corrections types and who see things our way."

> In a few years, hundreds of our top institutional personnel will be lured into retirement by our . . . benefits package, and the old boys network will be flushed out. We may get axed, but these civil servants will live on.

Although Procunier had been gone from the department for nearly a decade when this attempt to restructure CDC began, his influence has lingered so strongly that he has become the bête noire of those pushing the changes and a rallying point for those opposing them. One official remarked:

> Procunier was not even close to a professional manager. He ran this agency like hell—"I'll kick your ass; I like your style"—what crap! He tried his "follow me or f—— you" approach in the welfare department.[20] It failed. That doesn't work outside corrections, or maybe some primitive police departments.

Between the tenures of Procunier and McCarthy, it is claimed, the system gravitated more and more toward a situation in which "every institution is run in its own way by the lights of its warden":

> Why do you use X procedure here but not there, why do you use Y procedure here and here but nowhere else? Nobody knows. "That's what we've done for twenty years," they'll say. It's not a managed system. It's a system run by ritual, custom, and habit, each institution on its own.

According to some CDC officials, the costs of this lack of administrative uniformity have less to do with internal concerns (gangs, officer training, etc.) and more to do with the agency's external, mainly political, relations. One administrator observed:

> We're building ten new prisons in this state—an unprecedented venture. We've got a billion dollar budget. But these old-timers will send the legislature a one-page memo requesting 2.5 million dollars to hire new guards or for other new positions. Of course the legislature sends it back with a big question mark. . . . Likewise, the courts are becoming ever more involved in corrections. . . . [The courts] lead to greater

standardization. . . . You must have operating rules that apply everywhere. Otherwise the court reads your actions as arbitrary.

Another official remarked:

We go before the legislature and get the s——t kicked out of us. They ask very basic questions. "What's the procedure for X?" "Why build it that way?" This department couldn't, and still can't, give adequate answers. Staff see that you're getting the hell kicked out of you this way. Soon it dawns on them, "Hey, the public is demanding clearer operations, more accountability for how we do what we do, it's a public agency."

Defects of the Consensual Model

Unlike the Michigan responsibility model or the Texas control model, what we have been calling the California consensual model of correctional management presents us with no coherent pattern of correctional principles and practices. It would, therefore, be somewhat presumptuous to comment on the defects (or virtues) of the consensual model in the way that we have commented on the responsibility model and the control model. In any case, the shortcomings of CDC—violence, gangs, and so on—require little commentary. It is more appropriate to highlight the intrasystem differences in prison administration that California's approach has allowed. We shall do so in the next section of this chapter by comparing the character of prison governance at CMC and Soledad. The California prison experience, including the ongoing effort to replace the "old guard" with managers from outside of corrections, raises a number of important prison management issues. We shall address those issues in the concluding chapter. Now, however, let us return to each state's prisons in order to learn more about the differences in how they have been governed. We begin with the Walls unit in Texas, move to California's CMC and Soledad prisons, and finish in Michigan's Huron Valley Men's Facility (HVMF).

VARIETIES OF CORRECTIONAL ADMINISTRATION

That the character of an organization is an important determinant of its success or failure is taken as a rather unexceptional proposition when applied to business firms, hospitals, and (at least of late) schools. When applied to modern military organizations, the proposition appears to weaken in the face of the presumed role of high-technology weapons as the decisive factors in any battle. But even here there is a convincing case to be made that such things as regimentation, leadership, and ésprit de corps count in getting armies to fight—and win.[21]

By the same token, there have been striking and consequential differences in how prisons are managed. While most such differences are refracted through the behavior of corrections directors, wardens, officers, and other prison workers, it is well to remember that in many cases it is the inmates who are best able to discern and are most affected by varieties of correctional management. For instance, at a classification meeting in the prison's Ranier Hall, a Soledad inmate asked if he could receive a transfer back to Folsom prison. To me at least this came as a surprising request. After all, Folsom was a level-4 institution while Soledad was a level-3 institution. This meant, in effect, that the inmate was asking to be confined to a prison where his freedom of movement would be more restrained than it currently was, while his privileges would be fewer. The CDC officials conducting the meeting, however, did not bat an eyelash at this request. Then the inmate, who described himself as a "three-time loser" (a criminal imprisoned for the third time) spoke as follows:

> You've got a tighter operation there (Folsom). Here you have people running all over the place. At Folsom if somebody is running, you hit the ground. You don't run or they'll start shooting.

This inmate had been involved in homosexual activity during at least one of his prior confinements. He believed that for him Folsom was safer than Soledad. A similar observation was made by an inmate who worked in the watch commander's office inside the prison. After giving an unsolicited discourse on the impossibility of controlling prison violence and the inevitability of inmate social organization, he added: "Man, you can't stop the violence in here. . . . I prefer Folsom cause it's tighter."[22]

According to one CDC official, there were a number of inmates in the system who had served time in Texas prisons. While their experiences inside TDC were obviously ineffectual in keeping them out of trouble, these inmates told "horror stories" about how mean those Texas correctional officers could be, refusing to "cut any slack" in enforcing the pervasive rules governing inmate life.

In Michigan an inmate who had served time at Marquette Branch prison, Jackson prison, and was now at Huron Valley men's prison observed: "This is the place I feel unsafe. . . . It's a heaven when I want to move, but I have to watch my back all the time. You have no guns on the inside. That's why things can get out of hand. . . . I would take more safety if I had to choose. But I can defend myself good." Another inmate in the same prison asked: "What do you think of the control in here, man? Do you think you're safe: Do you think they (pointing to officers) are in control? It's up to us isn't it? We can make it or break it, right?" Looking up from his desk the officer interjected, "He's right!"

Only in recent years, however, could anything along these lines be said about conditions in Texas prisons. Prior to the 1980s, most Texas prisons were places where prison authorities were in firm control and inmates were, for the most part, safe and sound.

The Walls Unit: Huntsville, Texas

The rules are critical. The rules are the
institution. The rules must be enforced
evenhandedly.

A CAPTAIN OF THE WALLS

If you are an inmate of the Texas Department of Corrections (TDC), you are bound to spend at least a little time at the Huntsville "Walls" unit. The Walls is the prison which holds inmates as they move to and from other assignments. Each morning before the cock crows "the chain"—buses of inmates being transported within the system—is loaded up and moved out. Also located at the Walls is the department's central infirmary. Much of the aged physical plant consists of cellblocks, mechanical and print shops, a textile mill, a prison store, and an educational center.

The man indisputably in charge of the prison is Warden Jack B. Pursley. Pursley has spent over two decades as a TDC employee. Before becoming warden of the prison, Pursley spent about a decade running its mechanical shop. He also served roughly four years at the system's Ferguson unit. His predecessor as warden of the Walls was H. H. "Hal" Husbands, a man who had spent the better part of three decades at a variety of TDC units before his retirement in 1978.

Pursley presided over the Walls in the years when its population climbed over 2,000. His office is filled with prison artifacts, including a number of correctional awards he has won over the years. It is a comfortable office where the radio softly plays country music and the paperwork—organized for Pursley by a nineteen-year TDC veteran and former department secretary-of-the-year known as "Miss Molly"—never seems to stop. Nevertheless, Pursley leaves his office every day—sometimes several times a day—to make his rounds inside the prison. Sometimes the officers know he is coming, but often they do not. Pursley is clear about the reasons for these frequent tours:

> One is to keep everybody on their toes—officers and inmates both. . . . Second, there's just no other way to know what's going on. I can trust or rely on my staff, but I'd be a damn fool to sit over yonder all day and never get back here. . . . Most of all, though, you've got to make them know you're on top of things. . . . Look here, if it's true that the top boss doesn't know what's going on or hasn't thought his policies through or saw to it that they are being implemented properly, what'll happen? If it's true, there will be confusion on the line, in the cellblocks, in the yard. Officers will contradict one another. Inmates will say that the man don't know what's up. . . . That'll encourage them to behave badly. . . . Everybody in here has to know his job to perfection. . . . It's so that my job is knowing all jobs.

Pursley works incredibly hard at "knowing all jobs" and attributes any failures inside the prison to not "being on top of things half enough." The warden, he maintains, is "responsible for the whole place, for everyone on it." In Pursley's view, nothing happens inside the prison "that can't at some level be controlled. . . . In this prison it's my job to control things so that all are safe and sound."

In this and most other respects, Pursley thinks and acts according to the correctional credo of the man whose prison career and personal achievements he respects most, Dr. George Beto. Pursley does not think about his mentor's control model as an abstract body of correctional principles. To Pursley the control model is synonymous with how caring and commonsensical prison managers run things:

You have to have rigid discipline—that's the heart of the
Texas idea. . . . It begins with the most basic things . . . the
dress code and grooming standards. . . . Sloppy dress encourages sloppy behavior. No grooming standards gets you no
grooming, or damned little.

Pursley has practiced what he has preached. No issue concerning prison operations is too large or too small for his attention. For
example, the day after a new procedure regulating on-duty meals
for employees went into effect, Pursley summoned the responsible
officer. Their conversation went as follows:

WARDEN: Mr. [officer's name], do you got it straight? Are you logging people in? Do you summarize the daily meal attendance?
How are you reporting?

OFFICER: We send them there sheets? [referring to new form]

WARDEN: Aren't you summarizing it? You're to summarize and account on these forms. You need to get a good, clear understanding of that!

OFFICER: Warden, sir, I was missing bosses [TDC term for officers]
the other day.

WARDEN: Look, if someone is 13 [personnel rank] or above make
him sign in the third column. Everyone has got to sign! I watched
yesterday. A nurse lady come in with a box lunch, and she
grabbed her two pieces of bread.

Pursley was equally on top of things when it came to another
seemingly banal administrative issue, towel control. Informed by a
central office memo that the prison had used its quota of towels for
the month, Pursley contacted the laundry officer: "Mr. [officer's
name], I got a letter here says we use 7 towels per inmate, already
used 14,000, and we ain't getting any more. What's our balance?"
The officer responded by saying that he was having difficulty keeping inmates from taking extra towels. Pursley told him to make
each towel "cell-issue" by putting cell numbers on them: "What is
happening is they are tearing towels up—for headbands, to shine
shoes, to mop up, to use as hankies, and what else." The officer
sheepishly said that marking the towels as requested might "take
too much time." Pursley's retort was loud and decisive: "I don't
give a damn how much time it takes to mark them—it won't take
much at all. Do it so that each towel is cell-issue." Pursley then

summoned the major to ask his opinion. The major agreed that inmates should have a towel and endorsed the idea of having the towels issued to individual cells.

When the major or any other prison worker was in the presence of the warden they were practically at attention in the military sense, or perhaps it is more accurate to say that they left no doubts about the warden's authority. When the major brought the warden the count slip, the official latest count of the inmate population, before signing it, the warden would look straight into the major's eyes and ask, "Is this a good count, major?" The major would respond, "Yes sir, warden." Pursley saw to it that the prison's chain of command was followed and respected. An officer who had violated the chain of command by bypassing his immediate superiors was called into the warden's office and, with the major present, reprimanded severely:

> Mr., if you have a problem or idea, you take it on up the line. . . . Did you bother to tell your sergeant? . . . Do you see the major with his gold bars standing here? . . . You must not have much respect for us . . . but I didn't take this job to win no popularity contest.

When the warden made a decision, it was implemented quickly. It did not matter whether the decision involved major changes in operations (e.g., changes in procedures for inmate movement and supervision) or minor ones (e.g., the availability of benches in the cellblocks for TV watching), the word got out quickly and was followed to the letter. As Pursley himself stated:

> I can take a new policy and implement as quickly as I need to and as selectively as I need to, in one building tomorrow or all at once today. Say there's a new rule. . . . I call the major, he calls the captain, and on the line that night the ranking officer on the shift [often a lieutenant] will [follow it]. That's it. No talk. No BS.

Pursley uses various measures to make sure that rules are being followed. As noted, he gets out into the prison on a daily basis—through the kitchens, into the laundry area, up through the cellblocks, behind the textile mill, and so on. He even searches around in the prison's huge trash bin "to make sure that nothing is being wasted . . . that nothing is being hidden—contraband, knives, drugs, et cetera—and to see that nothing unusual is present, nothing out of the ordinary. You've heard that you can know a family by their trash? Well, you can know a prison by its trash too."

As he moves about the prison Pursley greets the officers and nonuniformed staff—counselors, teachers, doctors, and so on. His usual salutations are "Hey, bub" or "Alright buddy." Often his greetings will be questions about how things are going: "You having any trouble or flack from anybody, buddy? Any flack you let me know right away, OK boss?" Normally the answers are "Fine, sir" or "Thank you, warden." Sometimes, however, his tours inform him of trouble before the news "officially" reaches his office.

On one of his tours, for instance, Pursley learned that there was some trouble with the latest count. For obvious reasons, that is one of the most serious types of trouble that any prison administrator can face; for if the count is wrong, it means that some inmates are not where they are supposed to be: It may mean that some have escaped. Pursley stayed on top of the trouble until it was resolved. Had he not been on the scene or available at his office, the officers in charge would have attempted to "clear the count" by "reracking," that is, by stopping all activity in the prison, returning all inmates to their cells, and counting noses. Pursley, however, ordered that the inmates should be reracked only as a last resort, for the rerack would require the disruption of the schedule and the disruption of the inmates' work and treatment activities:

> You want things to go like clockwork, you try to make things go along machinewise, but it sometimes stalls.

Pursley gave those responsible ten minutes to account for the trouble and present an accurate count, after which time they were to begin reracking immediately. The drama moved back to his office and within a few minutes it was resolved. An officer on the previous shift had made some numerical mistakes in logging the count. The problem was resolved, but not for the officer who had made the mistake. Pursley did not reprimand the young officer; it had been an honest if critical mistake. Instead, he summoned the officer to his office. "I'm not getting all swolled [angry] at you, but you have to get it right. We can't be close, we must be exact, exactly on target. . . . If I messed up on your bank account by one digit I'd be close, but you might be out of some big money. You're putting undo stress on the next man, who can't trust your figures."

The officer was not removed from his post, but Pursley did review his list of officers, checking their intelligence test scores and coming up with a list of possible replacements should this officer continue to make errors. "That boy's not bad," remarked Pursley, "just slow."

In Pursley's view, one of the keys to prison discipline is whether rule infractions are punished appropriately: "You've got to keep the punishment proportionate. A major offense requires major punishment." He therefore personally reviews each and every disciplinary report filed by his officers. This enables him to see if there are any trends, to know where there are reported problems, and to judge whether his staff is being too hard or too soft on the inmates. Pursley throws out or changes (from major to minor or vice versa) about 5 percent of all disciplinary reports. This is a mammoth undertaking, and it would be much easier simply to sign off on the reports without reviewing them carefully. But if he did not review them, there would be more rather than fewer inconsistencies. For instance, an inmate who refused to move out of the dining hall when instructed to do so by an officer and then threatened and resisted the officers who came to remove him shouting "It'll take all five of you to move me!," received a minor disciplinary ticket calling for twenty-one days of cell restrictions and extra work assignments. Another inmate who refused to shave shouting "I ain't going to take no f——ing shave," but who then cooperated, received a major disciplinary ticket. Pursley saw to it that these kinds of inconsistencies were checked or ironed out.

One telling fact is that Pursley and his senior officers were able to make on-the-mark guesses about exactly how many disciplinary reports were being filed, the percentages that were major versus minor, and the type of punishments being given. They were, to be sure, educated guesses, but none of them had studied the aggregate statistics. As they had surmised, just under half of all infractions resulted in major disciplinary action, about 55 percent of those resulting in some loss of good time. A typical major report would read: "Cancel SAT 4 [State Approved Trusty status], reduce to line 2, lose 180 days."

Pursley repeatedly showed a masterful grasp of the prison's operations, down to the smallest details. Dictating a letter about fire safety to his secretary, he rattled off the following: "We have smoke detectors at eighty-one strategic points in the hospital. Inmates remove batteries for use in radios and other battery-driven

objects. We have thirty-nine fire extinguishers and six on order."
He did this while perusing a cryptic letter received in the morning
mail. The letter contained a vague threat against the warden's life.
After notifying a member of the department's intelligence staff,
the warden went about his business without any signs of preoccupation.

Pursley was constantly worrying, however, about the well-being
of the inmates. He insisted that all inmates be treated impartially
and live on an equal basis:

> Whatever their previous financial condition, whoever's son
> they are, whatever connections they might have, in here they
> are inmates, all equal and all alike in their rights. Prisons,
> well run, are levellers—rich, poor, smart, dumb—all are
> equal. All are treated the same.

Pursley would stay in contact with businessmen and community
officials to see if they had jobs for inmates who were about to be
released. He organized special July Fourth activities at the prison,
including a barbecue, saying "I'm concerned for the poor bastard
who doesn't have any help. Holidays around here can be tough for
inmates." Commenting on the need to encourage inmates' self-
betterment, Pursley stated:

> We use psychology more than most suppose. We work on
> building up a man's pride. These inmates are starved for a pat
> on the head. Most have never been recognized except for the
> bad things they've done. So you tell a man, "Terrific, way to
> fix that machine! Whew, you're learning one hell of a skill."
> You cannot force a man to learn a trade or even to do the
> work necessary to fix a car engine. You must persuade by
> force of reason, circumstance, and character.

The staff at the Walls unit had virtually nothing bad to say about
their warden. Of course, what is said to an outsider in this setting
is always subject to question. But extended observations revealed
that their expressions of respect were generally sincere. One officer (who insisted about ten times on not being identified) said "I
have deep respect and affection for the warden." To give their
commands added force or legitimacy, officers would preface their
orders to inmates and to each other with "Warden says" or "Warden wants." In any case, Pursley did his job in accordance with the
rules and saw to it that they did theirs. On Pursley's office wall

there hung a poster, which read in part, "as long as you are part of the institution, do not condemn it." As we shall now see, the staff's loyalty to Pursley was part and parcel of their loyalty to the department.

Next to the warden and the assistant wardens, the most powerful figure in a Texas prison was the major. At the Walls the major was a sort of uniformed warden, responsible for virtually all phases of the operation. Even more than the warden, however, the major would swirl about the institution to make sure that the rules were being followed. Major Scott of the Walls was typical of other top-ranking officers. His ideas about prison governance were simple and direct:

> I do believe—we all do—from the director, to the warden, to the boss in the cellblock—that prisons can be run well. Prisons don't have to be unsafe, unclean, uneducational. Good programs and good safety go together with good management.

"Good management" to the Major meant paramilitary operations and unflagging discipline. Trying to keep up with Scott, a hulking man who moves with incredible speed, was difficult.

Like most high-ranking prison workers, Scott faced a daily mountain of paperwork and office chores. But his "real work," as he called it, was "out there" in the prison. Barreling through the industrial plant Scott would notice inmates going through the motions of work. He would point at them and shout "You don't want these good jobs, huh? Y'all better find some right quick!," meaning that they had better start working in earnest. He then would go straight to the officer on duty in the area to reprimand him: "I saw people sitting on their asses bossman." After noting that one building had dirty windows he approached the officers in that area and told them to get them cleaned immediately. Most officers and inmates would rush to comply with Scott's orders. To any who hesitated or acted without complete courtesy he said, "You've got the wrong attitude, mister." When he surprised one day-dreaming officer in the cellblock, Scott began, "This ain't no good bossman," and ordered the officer to report himself to the lieutenant; eventually this man was reprimanded and placed on probation by the warden.

Scott's views on rehabilitation were typical of those held by most officers, not only in Texas but in California, Michigan, and, for that matter, Massachusetts as well. He argued that an inmate has to want to change his criminal ways. All that the prison agency could do, he said, was to provide the opportunity, to facilitate the self-motivated reform. Most inmates, he observed, were not "evil" or "wicked" people, just individuals who through poor life circumstances and unlucky breaks had gone wrong. But Scott added something to this set of ideas that was most often heard from prison workers in Texas. Based on his nearly two decades of correctional experience, Scott asserted:

> You see, you've got to want to help people to grow up. I guess that's how I see rehabilitation. If it means anything, it means making folks who were never responsible be responsible. People that were never respectful have to be respectful here. Maybe they learn that way, it can become a habit, I mean responsible ways of behaving.

Given his frequent use of the term *responsible*, the reader may wonder whether Scott's observation is not more evocative of the Michigan responsibility model than it is of the Texas control model. What makes it more evocative of the latter is his stress on "making" the inmates behave in a responsible way. They are not to be given freedom (or "air") and then held accountable, they are to be made to behave in rule-abiding ways and then be rewarded for a long period of problem-free behavior. In practice this meant checking even seemingly trivial instances of inmate misbehavior. For instance, as inmates lined up at the commissary, some would rush to the front of the line while others would jump over the turnstiles. The Major would yell, "Hey, you know there are no shortcuts. Go through the right way and stop the messing." In the cellblocks of every prison I have visited, inmates make a habit of "hanging out" on the tiers. Only in Texas was such behavior prevented routinely. Major Scott noted: "You didn't see anyone on the runs. That's because I wrote a couple up for it. Most times, if you crack down 90 percent will be dutiful."

Scott was typical of Texas officers in that he placed great stress on loyalty to the department and expressed pride in his work. To him, it did not matter what was going on with the courts or in the system's political relations so long as the prison's rules were fair, clear, and enforceable: "You lay down the law. You enforce it fairly. And you don't take any crap." "New policies," he observed, "will be implemented whether I or anyone else agrees. That's the way it ought to be. If not, you best quit."

No less vital to the prison's control style of prison management were the personnel below the warden, assistant wardens, and major. The next links in the prison's tight chain of command were the captains such as the Walls' Captain Schumacher. Schumacher thought and acted in accordance with the rulebook. In the dining halls, for instance, Schumacher stifled any inmate shouting, kept a close watch on knives, forks, and other utensils that might be used as quick and easy weapons, and saw to it that officers were positioned so as to control inmate movement in and out of the area. "In here," said Schumacher, "they [inmates] talk quietly. That's fine. The rules permit it. What I can't tolerate is screaming cross the hall or acting out [horseplay, etc]. The rules don't allow for it, and it just shouldn't be done. I'll tell an inmate to leave if necessary, but that's rare because everybody knows the rules and most go by them." At the same time, Schumacher tried to convey a relaxed manner. If one appears to be overly security-conscious, he said, then inmates will "think you're afraid of them, which we're not. It doesn't make sense to count every fork every five minutes." Still, during the recreation periods when large numbers of inmates roamed about freely in the main yard, Schumacher was all eyes and saw to it that his subordinates were too; that was the time each day when controls were most relaxed and violence was most likely.

Like other staff members, Schumacher would sometimes joke with inmates or address them in a familiar sort of way. For instance, one elderly inmate who worked in the prison's administrative offices kidded Schumacher: "Captain, I have to listen to you complain all day and to watch how incompetent you can be—that's cruel and unusual punishment." Laughter arose when at a disciplinary hearing presided over by the Captain an inmate admitted doing each and every thing he was accused of but then pled "not guilty." "Please tell us how can you admit it all and then plead not guilty?," asked Schumacher. The inmate replied, "Oh, I had to plead something!" There were, however, strict bounds placed on such lighter moments. In general, these types of episodes would be initiated by the senior officer and brought quickly to an end by him as soon as they started to get out of hand.

As noted earlier, the warden and other TDC officials laid great stress on treating inmates in an impartial way. Schumacher was adamant in this regard and strove to avoid any impression of favoritism. There was, for instance, an inmate who for medical reasons needed to take six or seven meals a day at times when the rest of the population was working, in school, or recreating. A more junior officer had allowed this man to take his meals as required in the prison's dining hall. Other inmates would see this man carrying bits of food to and from the dining hall at periods when they were not allowed to venture near the kitchen. Schumacher ordered an immediate change: "This ain't going to make it. No. No way! It looks unfair, and I've already heard complaints. If it has to be done, then he has got to eat in his house (cell). He can't be prancing in the yard with it. It makes it look like we're playing favorites. We can't let 'em feel that way. They're all equal and that's how they should be treated."

After the captains, the prison's next most important figures were the lieutenants. On the night shift, it is not uncommon for a lieutenant to be the highest-ranking prison official on the prison grounds. Most of the lieutenants at the Walls were veteran officers who thought and acted in ways resonant of their superiors and consistent with the control model. One lieutenant stated:

We try to be consistent. We try to enforce the rules. I've worked at other units. It's pretty much the same way there. It's pretty much the same all over. The rules are the thing that matters.

Another lieutenant agreed to be interviewed in the captain's office. As he described the procedures for handling a disturbance, he peered out the window, excused himself, and dashed out of the room. Two inmates were fighting and a large group of inmates had gathered to watch and cheer. The lieutenant yelled a command for them to disperse, assisted the officers who had wedged themselves between the combatants, and then followed to the letter the procedures he had just described, including filing a report on the bruises and scratches he had suffered.

In the evening, a lieutenant addressed the officers in their preshift meeting: "There are no special issues tonight. Do chase inmates off the runs as ordered. This has been more of a problem lately. When they're hanging out there, they're up to no good. Also, you're aware that we're short, so keep on your toes." The night shift was not always a quiet one. For instance, one evening an inmate slit his own throat. The lieutenant went to the scene and, together with other officers, brought the bleeding man to the prison hospital. There was no panic, no sense of drama. They simply moved quickly and without confusion. During the night shift, some inmates who were being disciplined would perform extra duties, such as polishing the brass bars in the prison's entranceway. Except for the relative lack of movement, the night shift was like the others. As one lieutenant observed: "This is a paramilitary operation. Even this shift, which is a quiet one usually, keeps in paramilitary form. There is a chain of command and it does not stop operating at night. This place runs just as if the warden were in his office." Sometimes Pursley was in his office and would pay this shift a visit.

The most revered officers in the prison were the sergeants. As one lieutenant said, "What he'll [a sergeant] go through in an eight-hour period is unbelievable. The big problems get filtered up through him. He'll see from six to eight officers on one or more matters and handle the specific needs of an odd dozen inmates—all in addition to his other regular duties."

The sergeants kept a tight reign on operations, making sure that everyone—inmates and officers—was in his place doing what he was supposed to do. One veteran sergeant stressed: "We have rules to live by. And you can't be inconsistent—you know, treat people differently, let somebody have or take advantage, play favorites. If you do, you won't be respected." On the one hand, the sergeants were the most dogged adherents of the control model. On the other hand, they were the ones who kept things in perspective and forced a recognition of the limitations on the officers' ability to control the inmates.

Nobody, least of all the inmates, doubted any sergeant's commitment to control. But the sergeants seemed to use their undisputed reputations for toughness as a brake on any unrealistic, hard-to-implement plans and goals of the administration. For instance, it was the sergeants who were strongest in the contention that officials must never—as one sergeant stated—"blow a problem out of proportion. Let them [inmates] work, take breaks. . . ." Another sergeant, commenting on the system's emphasis on inmate work, observed: "Look, getting work out of people that ain't getting paid for it is hell. That's the bottom line. . . . A lifer will tell you straight, 'Hey boss, I got life, I'll do my two hours a day.' " Another sergeant commented that the most important aspect of good prison management was "communication at all levels . . . as to what is expected and what in reality is necessary." Another cited "flexibility, to be able to deal with the same inmates day in and day out." At the Walls at least, the sergeants served to keep the control model on an even keel by, among other things, keeping junior officers from "riding" the inmates while at the same time insisting on firm enforcement of the rules.

The junior officers were engaged in a daily routine that afforded them little discretion about what to do or how to do it. Most, however, seemed to like their work and spoke of making sergeant, lieutenant, or captain some day. (Only a few of them were so hopeful as to mention major and warden; only one was sure that he would become the system's director.) Their manner in preshift meetings was formal but relaxed. There was a clear comradeship among them, evidenced by their knowledge of each other's names and assignments, expressions of mutual concern, offers to help each other in professional and personal matters, willingness to exchange (often biting) personal jokes and remarks, and after-hours get-togethers. Even more telling, however, was their individual knowledge of the department's history and their obvious pride in being a part of the "best prison system" in the nation. As one officer said, "We're the Dallas Cowboys of prisons." Most officers, even those with under a year in the department, knew about Dr. George Beto, who the wardens of various prisons were or had been, and what contributions they were credited with making to the system. It would be difficult for them not to know these sorts of things. Two of the system's prisons are named after Beto; another is named for H. H. "Pete" Coffield, the political pillar of TDC discussed earlier. The Walls was known to them as the oldest prison in the system. Many could give a mini-lecture on how the prison had come into being and how it had developed since the Civil War.

The department did much to foster this sense of history, sense of mission, and ésprit de corps. Through officer training, the folklore of the system, its "shameful past," and its "decades of progress" were stressed. There were numerous awards such as "rifleman-of-the-month." A few officers learned more about the system by studying at Sam Houston State University's Center for Criminal Justice. The campus and the prison are the two major institutions in Huntsville, Texas. Most of the system's other prisons are also in east Texas. TDC officers have even done original research on the system, one writing a detailed history of its development through the late 1970s.[23]

At the Walls, the relationship between the custodial staff and the noncustodial staff was totally lacking in the kind of tensions that the literature on prisons would prepare one to expect. This was not, as one might suppose, because noncustodial activities were somehow made wholly secondary or subordinate to custodial ends. There was, to be sure, a belief that security came first. But neither the officers nor the doctors, teachers, counselors, and other treatment personnel saw any inconsistency between treatment and custody: the latter, they thought, made the former possible. Hence, relations between, say, the majors and the school instructors were cordial, even warm. As one hospital employee said:

> We have six physicians, an RN for each floor, a psychiatrist, a psychologist, and other treatment personnel at work here. There are seven or so officers on duty. They work with us. There is a clear division of labor here. The line between security and health care is hard to fine tune. But we've all got the right, sensible attitude, and we all do our jobs accordingly.[24]

The prison's educational center was a model of cooperation between the uniformed security forces and the treatment staff. The result, according to the center's director, was that "We don't have many severe disciplinary problems. If we do we can deal with each as it arises."

Similarly, the relationship between the prison's officers and the treatment personnel on the one hand, and the central office staff on the other, was not adversarial. There was no negative talk about the "brass" or any sense that the system's top administrators did not know what was really happening inside the prison. There were various signs of this positive relationship, not the least of which was the way that the prison staff, from the warden on down, related to the system's director of research, Dr. Larry Farnsworth. Unlike in other systems I visited, the field personnel in Texas knew and generally liked the chief of research. In most public organizations, especially law enforcement agencies, the workers in the field look upon the research people as a bunch of do-nothings or cranks whose main purpose in life is to produce meaningless studies on unimportant topics. Usually, the ill feeling is mutual as the researchers have serious doubts about the intelligence and the commitment of those who work in the institutions.

In Texas, however, the research chief shared virtually all of the assumptions about prison management held by personnel in the field. Given that Farnsworth had begun as a correctional officer, this was not wholly surprising. What was surprising, however, was the degree to which he and other central office personnel identified with and supported those working in the institutions. Indeed, everyone from the personnel director to the office secretaries was an ardent advocate of the control-model approach to running prisons. Farnsworth's remarks were typical:

> Texas has a school system for its inmates. . . . And the prisons are clean here . . . cleaner than I've seen in some other states. . . . Most of all, nobody is afraid. I've worked these prisons and studied them, and I know this to be so. . . . There are rapes and disturbances, but the system works to minimize these troubles. . . .

Like other central office personnel, the researchers were required to respond to serious emergencies inside the prisons. The Michigan research director recalled with amazement how he had learned about this aspect of the Texas system: "The idea that people here would respond to calls is strange. . . . I once tried to phone the TDC training director and was told that he was out chasing an escapee!"

California Prisons: Soledad and CMC

Any California correctional officer who began his career in 1975 at Soledad and worked there for a decade would have served under five different wardens. The current warden, Al Stagner, is in most respects the antithesis of the Walls' Jack Pursley. For one thing, Stagner is not really a warden. His title is superintendent. To him, the difference is not merely semantic. As Stagner explained, the superintendent has a range of responsibilities and duties that far exceed those of the so-called warden. The superintendent must wear "many, many hats—inside dealing with the staff and the inmates, outside dealing with the community, the legislature, the central office. . . . You can't be captured by a vocal minority of inmates, or officers, or people in Sacramento, or community activists."

Stagner presides over what are really three separate institutions. There are Soledad-Central and Soledad-North, both of which house some of the state's highest security risks. Then there is Soledad-South, a lower-custody facility located a short drive from the main gates. As one top Soledad administrator noted, "Soledad is truly a microcosm of the system." In recent years the combined population of these three facilities has soared to around 6,000 inmates. Stagner relies on his deputies and associate superintendents to take care of the prison's day-to-day concerns and rarely gets out into the prison. He places a great deal of faith in his staff, saying that he "would rather have a good staff, a solid team of officers and administrators, than have a brand new prison with all the advantages that come with it; because in the last analysis it's the staff, the management, that counts most in determining how well, or how poorly, things go in here."

Stagner noted that, despite his correctional background, he does not look like somebody who runs a prison. Neatly dressed in a suit, the generally soft-spoken Stagner said: "I don't have heavy hands and I'm not heavy-handed; I'm not the ex-professional wrestler type. I don't curse and scowl. I don't have to." His "one absolutely firm principle is that you don't take something away from the inmates unless you have very strong reasons which can be articulated to them. You may have a list of things you would like to take back but you must proceed with great caution. . . ."

Stagner was true to this principle in implementing a new policy governing inmate lunches. To cut down on the number of large-scale inmate movements, it was decided that henceforth inmates would not be moved to the dining halls for lunch but instead would receive a box lunch brought to them in the cellblocks, work areas, and so on. This meant that inmates would no longer have a hot lunch. As Stagner observed, "going to a box lunch and doing away with the hot noon meal—this could cause a riot if done in an insensitive way. So we explained every detail to the inmates. We explained why. We even showed them how it would cost us more to provide the box lunch. . . . My focus is on the things that may lead to violence by frustrating the inmates—the frustrations, the anxieties, and so on. You can't simply look at your means of control and physical restraints." Stagner appeared on the prison's closed-circuit television station and addressed the inmates. Members of the inmates' advisory council were consulted. Officers were instructed to explain the policy to inmates.

After a few hectic days, the box lunch program was implemented. But despite the superintendent's efforts to smooth the path, there continued to be disgruntlement about the policy among both inmates and officers. The inmates simply refused to buy what "the Man" had to say. The officers were convinced that the box lunches created more rather than fewer security and other problems. The boxes, they maintained, could be used to conceal weapons or transport contraband, particularly drugs.

Stagner had worn the officers' uniform for years and had worked at seven CDC prisons, including San Quentin, before coming to the top post at Soledad. On more than one occasion he was attacked by inmates. Until he became a captain—the highest-ranking uniformed grade in the system—Stagner was a member of the officers' union. In short, he has the kind of career credentials that might translate into popularity with the officer force. In fact, however, the superintendent was not well liked by many of his uniformed subordinates. He was aware of his unpopularity: "I'm not the most popular guy out there. I'm known as rather quick with the pen" (meaning quick to take disciplinary action against officers). Among the officers, the consensus was that Stagner was "all for the inmates" and neither knew nor appreciated the difficulty of their task.

The prison's top administrators were far from insensitive to the need to develop a spirit of teamwork between management and the officers. As one official noted: "We take pains to recognize outstanding employee efforts—letters of recommendation, employee-of-the-month, and so forth." Each year the managers sponsor a barbecue at which they cook for the entire staff. "It's symbolic," said one Soledad manager, "our way of showing our heartfelt appreciation for what they do. . . ."

These measures, however, have not been fully successful in winning the support of the correctional ranks. To most officers, life inside the prison is just too "loose" and they blame management for making the "toughest beat in the state" so dangerous. Their negative feelings extend beyond the institution to the "kooks" in Sacramento.[25]

While the administrators of the respective units—North, South, and Central—stressed the necessity of teamwork, they were anxious to point out that the units were indeed separate administrative entities. "Don't judge Soledad just by Central," commented one administrator. A lieutenant at Central, frustrated by the limited cooperation given by the other two units in resolving an overnight crowding crisis, bitterly denounced them.

The officer unions have made a series of demands on Soledad's prison management that would effectively destroy the limited control exercised by the superintendent and his administrative staff.

For instance, they have demanded a pure bid system—a job assignment system based on seniority. As Stagner commented, to accede to such a request would "take control over who works and where" out of management's hands. Some of the union requests, such as that the superintendent censor the prison's inmate newspaper, have simply been beyond the administration's authority. "They don't see," said Stagner, "that I'm not the Supreme Court."

The gang problem occupies much of administrative life at Soledad. As discussed previously, the gangs are organized along racial and ethnic lines, and the prison authorities are careful not to mix inmates in ways that may lead to violence. A want-ad hanging on one of the bulletin boards in the colorfully painted quarter-mile corridor of the Central unit read: "White workers needed for first watch clean up crew. . . . No escape history, no "R" [sex offense], not a discipline problem. If interested, send request to Assignment Lieutenant. . . ."

Soledad administrators have relied on the inmates themselves to keep the peace and minimize intergang rivalries. One top administrator explained by way of an example how this problem has been handled at Soledad: "Always provide inmates a way out. . . . In this situation I removed the leaders and then brought the two groups face to face. Give us your word, I told them, give us your word that there will be no more conflict. They did, and it worked."

The officers at Soledad were not overly concerned about their lack of control over the inmates. They were confident in their ability to arrest major disturbances before they got out of hand. When shots were fired inside the institution or a fight would break out, officers responded, though usually with some confusion (gates opened or closed incorrectly, persons leaving their posts prematurely). In the prison's hallways inmates would strut back and forth more or less freely. In random fashion the officers would stop and frisk inmates. When the gangs were "flying their colors," the officers went on a sort of red alert, tightening up on inmate movement and passing the word up and down the line about what was afoot.

Inmates who challenged an officer's authority were given numerous chances to comply before any action was taken. In a typical instance, an inmate worker refused to leave the kitchen area when so instructed by his supervising officer. Only after several minutes of cursing back and forth did a lieutenant intervene, ordering the inmate to move out and promising swift disciplinary measures if he hesitated any further. The inmate complied, and no disciplinary action was taken against him. Similarly, an inmate who refused to return to his cell for the evening lock-up did so only when a lieutenant, carrying an electronic stun gun, appeared on the scene. As the lieutenant explained, "This thing [the stun gun] won't injure you, but it'll knock you on your ass."

About 130 miles from Soledad is the California Men's Colony (CMC). The Warden of CMC was Wayne Estelle. If the reader finds that last name familiar, he should. Wayne Estelle and former director of the Texas prison system W. J. Estelle are brothers. There is, however, more than this to link CMC to Texas prisons. The best way to describe the management system of CMC is by likening it to what we observed in Texas. California's Estelle has run a sort of mini-control-model system at CMC (minus, however, the building tenders). In effect, CMC presents us with another natural experiment in prison management, though just the reverse of the one that occurred when former California director Procunier came to the helm in Texas.

Unlike Soledad's Stagner, Estelle of CMC prefers the title warden to that of superintendent. The only difference Estelle acknowledged between the two titles is "$100 a month." Though he did not get out into the prison as often as he wished, Estelle pushed aside his paperwork and made it out into the 3,000-plus man institution at least once a day.* His correctional philosophy sounds much like that of most Texas officials, stressing inmate obedience, work, and education. Despite all of the changes in public attitudes about prisons and in the state laws governing their operations, Estelle maintained that the heart of good prison administration has never changed: "It all begins and ends with the guard in the block, or the overpromoted guard in the warden's chair, like me." In Estelle's view, "there's nothing complicated about running these places. It's tough but it's not complicated. . . ."

Inmate movement at CMC is closely controlled. As suggested in chapter two, such control is facilitated by CMC's unique physical plant. The prison is divided into an east wing and a west wing. It has four identical quadrangles. Each quadrangle is sealed off from the others. From many points inside the institution one can catch a glance of the beautiful town of San Luis Obispo.

---

*In 1986, CMC's inmate population climbed to over 6,000 (see chapter 2, page 75). Estelle's routine did not change.

Soledad's history has been troubled and, as one of the prison's chroniclers phrased it, melancholy.[26] CMC, on the other hand, has been an almost unparalleled, if far less well-known, prison success story. In John P. Conrad's words, CMC began "under a compulsive superintendent," who was determined to capitalize on the prison's security-conscious design.[27] CMC has always been led by men, including CDC director McCarthy and Estelle, who were "compulsive" when it came to running safe, clean, productive prisons. In California correctional circles, CMC's assorted excellences—lowest violence, least costly, cleanest, best programs, finest officers—are almost legendary. Even the wardens and administrators of other institutions, such as Warden Vasquez of San Quentin, were quick to say that "CMC is the best prison in California."

There was an ésprit de corps among the officers at CMC and an attention to the chain of command that simply did not obtain at most other CDC prisons. Officers were invariably neat and mannerly. Inmates were not allowed to roam about freely either on the quadrangles or inside the buildings. Nor were they permitted to "fly their colors." Estelle and his staff spared nothing in their attention to detail. There was a preoccupation with control reminiscent of the Walls. The noise level inside CMC cellblocks was shockingly normal. Still more shocking than the lack of noise was the relative lack of vulgar language. There was, to be sure, no chorus of choir boys at CMC, and both the inmates and the prison authorities used more than the average amount of foul language. But there was far less of it than at other prisons, certainly less than at Soledad. The reason for the low level of noise and cursing among inmates was that officers were simply unwilling to let the inmates get away with it, moving in to order quiet. Among officials, it was considered less than fully appropriate and something of a bad example for officers to speak to the inmates "on their own level."

As was clear through various disciplinary hearings, inmates at CMC recognized that they were living in a special prison. The officials who ran the meetings were quick to point out that the other places the inmate might be sent—usually Folsom or San Quentin—would afford him few of the amenities and services available at CMC. The administrators had an absolutely no-nonsense approach in dealing with inmates who misbehaved. At one disciplinary hearing, for instance, an inmate who had struck an officer began by cursing about how rotten the administration was. Before he could say much more, an administrator responded: "You listen to me! You hit an officer without provocation. Do you think you can get away with that? Do you think we'll listen to you blame it on everybody and everything but yourself? Behave yourself or your hearing is over." Relations between the prison's inmate advisory council and the administration were generally good, even though the administration rarely made any concessions. One top CMC administrator received a plaque from CMC's inmate advisory council thanking him for "saying no with a smile."

While the officer unions were as strong at CMC as they were at Soledad, there was virtually no tension between labor and management at the former prison. Some CMC employees who had worked at Soledad noted this difference in the working climate. Furthermore, Warden Estelle was highly respected among the officers; a few even spoke of him as a hero or model warden with an extraordinary knowledge both of corrections in general and of CMC in particular.

Michigan: Huron Valley Men's Facility (*HVMF*)

Don't promise what you can't deliver.

—WARDEN, HVMF

In 1981 HVMF was opened as the prototype of the smaller, more easily managed prison which corrections experts had been recommending for decades. It promised to be a showplace both of the latest correctional thinking and, more particularly, the Michigan responsibility model. Its campuslike design was described in chapter two. Inside the units, paintings graced the brightly colored walls. There were no steel bars, just laminated glass slightly under an inch thick. The prison was well staffed and well funded. An impressive array of treatment programs were developed, and even the prison's life-term inmates were encouraged to participate fully in them. Together with the Resident Unit Managers (RUMs), the green-blazered officers were instructed to create a "normal" environment for the inmates. HVMF inmates were free to roam about pretty much at will while minimal restrictions were placed on their dress, speech, work, and recreation. The prison received the enthusiastic accreditation of the American Correctional Association and was praised by prisoners' rights groups. It was, however, also racked by inmate disorders which continued through 1985. As of this writing, the latest major episode involved the taking of three hostages by two armed inmates who were attempting to escape through the prison's steam tunnels.

The prison's longest-reigning warden, Bob Redman, was a veteran of the Michigan prison system. He was a great admirer of Director Perry Johnson. Redman was a direct, no-nonsense administrator. Staff members who were unwilling to follow his orders were fired. Inmate leaders and "politicians"—inmates who through various means gain the ear of the authorities and can garner special privileges for themselves and their friends—were demoted in status or transferred out if they became disobedient or cocky. Officers who balked at central-office policies were told to go along or quit. Redman did not permit himself to become a captive of paperwork, making sure that he got out into the prison several times each day. He was, in short, a hands-on type of prison manager who did his best to keep both inmates and officers on a very short leash.

At HVMF, Redman was in charge of a maximum-security prison that was really more of a minimum-security operation; that was how the central authorities wanted HVMF to run. Watching the warden as he tried to run HVMF in a strict, high-security fashion was like watching a man pushing desperately on a string.

Rather than giving inmates commands, HVMF officers spent most of their time responding to the commands of inmates—to open an electronically-controlled cell door, to check on an appointment with a counselor, to answer some complaint. Most of the inmates were not the least bit respectful in lodging these requests. When a busy officer did not open a cell door seconds after an inmate had shouted for him to do so, the inmate yelled "Break [open] number [cell number] you jerk off!" Informed by a female officer that he had received a certain counseling assignment, an inmate jumped in front of her and screamed, "I told you I don't want no f——ing European!" ("Europeans" is the term that some of Michigan's black inmates use for whites.) Inmates would surround the officers' desk area, located at the entrance point of the unit, and "hang out" there. In the beehive of inmate movement—around the desks, up the steps, in and out of doors, and so on—it was virtually impossible for even the most experienced officers to know where inmates were or what they were doing. Out in the prison's various yards and recreation areas, no serious effort was made to regulate inmate behavior and nothing was done to keep inmates from associating together in large groups for extended periods of time.

Since there is, throughout the prison system, an emphasis on reducing the paramilitary aspects of prison life, officers showed little concern or even understanding of the chain of command. By the same token, sergeants were not the highly revered figures they were in Texas and to a lesser degree in California. Indeed, one officer at another Michigan prison had quit his post as sergeant to become a regular correctional officer again. "Being a sergeant," he said bitterly, "doesn't mean s——t around here." That sentiment was shared by many others who conveyed that, given the loose controls necessitated by the responsibility system, it was more or less every individual officer for himself. As another sergeant said: "We try to keep up a good front. . . . But honestly, morale is low. We want uniforms, the stripes. I shouldn't say so but it's true." A junior officer said: "This [prison] is ridiculous. You can't get how ridiculous it is till you've worked here."

The lack of ésprit de corps or sense of mission among the officers was the product of at least four factors. First, there was the officers' limited understanding and sympathy for what were regarded as unsupportive departmental policies which made it highly difficult for them to control the inmates or to protect themselves against the inmates. One veteran officer remarked: "I don't know why things are the way they are, I only know we don't think very highly of how we have to do this job." Second, the department has pursued affirmative action policies which have polarized the officers along racial and gender lines. Many veteran white male officers were resentful of younger minority and female officers who received promotions without "paying any dues." Some higher-level institutional officials resented having to wait to fill critical posts while the department searched for qualified minority applicants. (Two of every three positions in the department were held for persons in a minority job category.) Third, the officers were to some degree split between rival unions which competed for their allegiance by emphasizing and often exaggerating the extent to which "Lansing's policies" have caused a loss of control and resulted in officer injuries and deaths. The unions have battled each other by asserting that their competitors are "in bed" with the system's top management.[28] Fourth, apart from the affirmative action policies, the department has moved to make personnel changes at prisons where generations of rural white officers, often the sons and grandsons of retired workers, have been dominant. These changes have included the lateral transfer from other prisons of minority senior officers. Some of these minority officers spoke of being "undercut" by prejudiced junior officers while the latter group complained of being stereotyped, being treated unfairly, and being unable to obtain promotions on their merits.

Virtually no one at HVMF seemed unaware of the security risks posed by the loose management system. Some, however, argued that the lax controls improved security by reducing inmate frustrations. One RUM said:

> It reduces tensions. . . . No bubbles or security areas as such. It has its dangerous potential. . . . But we don't breathe down their necks. . . . It reduces barriers this way. . . . I visited a [name's state] prison. They had a paramilitary operation. The officers and the inmates didn't have any personal relationship beyond opening and closing doors. That's bad. We try to overcome it.

It was difficult, however, to observe how the loose controls fostered better officer-inmate interactions or made the inmates more cooperative as opposed to hostile. Inmates complained about everything and expressed little satisfaction with either their living areas or the facilities and programs available to them. One described the prison as a "psychiatric ward" designed to "make you mellow out."

In one instance, a group of inmates loudly berated an officer for their poor accommodations and then turned to me for some pronouncement. I told them that I was not in a position to make any such pronouncement to them but would say that there were prisons in other places, some of which I had visited, where inmates had to share a cell with two other inmates and did not have available to them pool tables, television sets, and the host of other amenities and services provided to inmates at HVMF. The crowd hushed until one inmate said, "S——t, maybe it ain't so bad." Usually, however, inmates railed about a lack of basic comforts and good programs. Some of the programs, such as the "confrontation group" meetings where they would "rap" about a variety of issues and problems, were criticized by inmates as a "big joke."

To some extent, the fact that inmates took the prison's services for granted and issued frequent complaints was taken by officials as a sign of success. As one Reception and Guidance Center official noted, "We emphasize rights. We tell them how they have recourse if they are treated unfairly. . . ." Others, however, considered this policy one of many basic flaws in how inmates are handled. Many officers argued that the inmates were under the impression that they had every right except the right to leave, so that any attempt by officers to regulate their behavior was taken personally rather than as a function of the officers' job. This seemed to be true. One inmate, for instance, complained about a particular officer: ". . . he's trouble. He goes by the book and makes it hard to get by. . . . He says go to your house [cell] when it's time. He don't cut no slack."

Given the earlier mentioned Emergency Powers Act, an inmate's term could be reduced by months or years independent of his behavior. Also, the system gave inmates their good time—often as much as 25 to 30 percent more than the specified legal maximum—the day they entered the prison. Most inmates kept their good time whether or not they had disciplinary problems. Hence, as the officers were quick to point out, the prison authorities had few correctional carrots and, in light of the least-restrictive management ethos, fewer correctional sticks. One senior HVMF administrator complained, "Everything should have to be earned." Another official described the policies as "stupid, unrealistic." Following an incident that resulted in one correctional officer being bloodied by an inmate, an officer said "Somebody has to get killed at the crossroads before they put up a stop sign. That's all I have to say about this so-called prison."

Unfortunately, the officer's heated remark proved rather prophetic. Officers and inmates at the prison have been subject to numerous attacks and several serious stabbing incidents. Johnson's successor as director of the system asked publicly whether HVMF staff had "gotten lax in those kinds of basic correctional measures that let those weapons accumulate?"[29] Measures were taken to tighten the operation. There were more frequent—and more surprise—shakedowns of cells and personal searches; certain parts of the prison yards were fenced off; internal fencing was erected; inmate movement in and out of the units was regulated, and the number who could gather in the cellblocks, dining halls, or exercise yards was limited; the use of metal detectors was initiated. Other basic facets of the operation, however, did not change: inmate dress and grooming standards, lack of paramilitary organization among the officers, unrestrictive inmate property policies, and so on.

SUMMARY AND CONCLUSION

Oddly, critics of the HVMF operation seemed to blame the prison's troubles on Warden Redman. The officers generally disliked the warden, other top administrators questioned his security-consciousness, and the press laid blame for escapes and violence at his office door. Redman, however, was simply carrying out so far as possible the rules and regulations that governed prison administration in Michigan. Throughout his tenure, Redman was fully aware of the security problems engendered by the model of correctional management that he was responsible for implementing. In general, he supported the notion of maximizing inmate responsibility while minimizing inmate restrictions, but he was never under any illusions about the costs of attempting to realize that ideal. Redman's favorite maxim on how to handle inmates was "Don't promise what you can't deliver"; and he had done as much as anyone could to deliver on the promises of the responsibility model at the prison. HVMF was new, uncrowded, well endowed financially, staffed by highly trained officers, responsive to inmate demands, respectful of the inmate social order, bursting with programs, and as well managed as it could be under the existing responsibility system.

In the concluding chapter of this book, we shall draw a host of lessons from these observed varieties of correctional administration. Based in part on this comparison of correctional institutions in three states, we shall attempt to answer the question with which we began: under what, if any, conditions are good prisons possible and how, if at all, can we foster such conditions?

But before we arrive at any general lessons or prescriptions, there is more to be learned about prison administration in Michigan, California, and Texas. Having gone on a brief tour of each system, been introduced to the models of correctional management on which each system has been based, and glanced at how each model has worked, we now turn to examine the philosophical roots of these differences, the role of correctional leadership, and the causes and consequences of correctional change.

Correctional Philosophy and Leadership

Those who know the most about what prisons can do have rarely taken part in the debates over what prisons are for. Prison directors, wardens, officers, counselors, and others who have actually spent their lives working with prisoners have ideas about the purposes of imprisonment, but their ideas on the subject have been less well attended than those of outside researchers who have concentrated on the beliefs and behavior of inmates. Our public discourse about prisons has been shaped more by the bitter accounts of ex-convicts than by the studied reflections of ex-prison workers.

This is unfortunate for several reasons. First, it has obscured the fact that prison officials at all levels do have beliefs, often well-reasoned and passionately held beliefs, about the purposes of imprisonment. Second, it has given rise to the incorrect notion that most prison workers have a purely punitive mind-set or favor a "lock 'em up and throw away the key" approach. Third, it has caused most observers to miss entirely the connection between what correctional officials think and how prisons run. Finally, it has concealed the degree to which seemingly slight philosophical differences among correctional workers give rise to marked differences in correctional policies, practices, and procedures.

Correctional workers themselves have been guilty of concealing truths and fostering misperceptions. Some prison workers, for instance, simply deny that correctional philosophies exist or have any bearing on what they do. As one California official asserted: "There is no philosophy as such. . . . Hell, we don't talk philosophy. Look at what we do and how we do it. Don't ask me about any silly philosophy. . . . So any administrator who says that this system has a philosophy is silly—he's probably just snowing you or insulting your intelligence." Five minutes later, however, this same official launched into a heated and unprompted discourse about the causes of criminality, the purposes of imprisonment, the rights of inmates, and the moral necessity of postrelease supervision by caring parole agents. His beliefs on these matters were shared by most (though by no means all) California correctional workers but not by most Texas and Michigan correctional workers; members of the latter departments had their own respective bodies of beliefs on such matters—their own distinct correctional philosophies.

Most correctional administrators, however, were highly conscious that a particular correctional philosophy was at work in the way they governed their state's prisons. As Michigan's Warden Redman explained: "Every warden or superintendent has the same basic functions. But your ideas will influence the way you meet these problems and carry out your functions. Here, most of the institution heads have the same creed, or if you want, philosophy." Furthermore, most correctional officials attributed the operational differences among prisons to differences in correctional philosophy. Warden Vasquez of California's San Quentin, for instance, observed that it might be "easier" to run his prison "the Texas way" but then added: "I don't agree with taking extreme measures for the sake of control. . . . There are good guys and bad guys on all sides—in blue [inmates] and in tan [officers]." Similarly, a California central office administrator observed that the lack of any weapons showcase or prison paraphernalia at CDC headquarters was indicative of a difference in the way that Texas and California prison officials see their work: "Those kinds of symbols are just bulls——t. It paints an oversimple picture of what corrections is really supposed to be about." Indeed, when California's ex-director Procunier came to Texas, the weapons showcase and some of the pictures disappeared from TDC headquarters.

But before learning how the correctional philosophies of the Texas, Michigan, and California prison systems are different, we must first understand how they are fundamentally alike, for the philosophy of each system is derived from a common body of beliefs which in corrections circles is sometimes called the "keeper philosophy."

THE KEEPER PHILOSOPHY

I feel that it's our responsibility when we get them to keep them and keep them safely.

—CDC DIRECTOR DANIEL J. MCCARTHY

There are two basic principles which together constitute the keeper philosophy. The first is that, whatever the reasons for sending a person to prison, the prisoner is not to suffer pains beyond the deprivation of liberty. Whatever the law says, and whatever the prevailing wisdom among commentators and outside experts, prisoners should not suffer any punishments inside prison except those which may be incidental to their confinement: confinement itself is the punishment. A corollary to this principle, and the second basic tenet of the keeper philosophy, is that regardless of his crime, a prisoner should be treated humanely and in accordance with how he behaves inside the institution. Even the most heinous offender is to be treated with respect and given privileges if he behaves well once behind the walls.

Underlying these two principles are a constellation of assumptions about the nature of confinement. The overwhelming majority of prison workers, especially the more seasoned ones, believe that imprisonment is a heavy burden to place on any individual. They are amused by charges that the state "coddles" convicted criminals when it affords prisoners amenities (pool tables, exercise equipment, etc.) and services (educational programs, vocational training, etc.). As prison workers in each state were quick to argue, such charges are the product of gross ignorance about what it means to be confined for extended periods. Former Texas director W. J. Estelle observed:

No matter what you call them, what color you paint them, or the scent of the disinfectant, a prison is still a place of confine-

ment and limited freedoms and exceptional discipline. . . .
Even under the best of conditions prisons are lousy places.

Michigan's Ron Gach, a deputy at the state's Michigan Reformatory, echoed Estelle:

> We are here to have them serve their terms, not to punish
> them inside here. You can't leave when you want to—that's
> the punishment. Then there are the incidental deprivations of
> life in a prison . . . what you eat, the basics. Anybody who
> thinks that is not a severe punishment ought to spend a little
> time confined. You don't have to be confined in a place this
> depressing. Confine yourself to your house for two weeks. . . .
> The inmates have to swallow it whole for as long as the court
> says.

Similarly, California's Warden Wayne Estelle said of crowded
prisons: "If you want to find out what double-celling is like, lock
yourself in your bathroom over a weekend with your spouse and
don't come out."

Rather than worrying about affording the inmates too many
undeserved comforts, most prison officials worry about making the
inmates' confinement easier without compromising security. In a
remark typical of correctional workers, Warden Joseph Campoy of
Folsom prison argued: "Inmates should be respected. For instance,
if you need to see a man at dinner time, wait till he's through
eating, don't disturb him without need. Or if a man is sleeping,
don't make loud noises. . . . You can make your counts without
waking a guy—just so long as you're sure it's a man and not a
bunch of pillows." CDC's chief training official, Conrad Holmes,
observed that while certain security functions were unavoidably
bothersome to inmates, it was important to execute them as pleasantly as possible. Referring to routine frisks and inmate trans-
ports, Holmes said: "You must pat them down gently, not giving
any rough chops to the groin. You must speak in a normal tone. . . .
There's no nice way to put handcuffs on somebody, but we try."

In Texas, Warden Wallace M. Pack of the Ellis unit would belie
his reputation as the system's toughest warden by reaching into
his own pocket to purchase special baked goods for long-confined
inmates. Warden Pursley of the system's Walls unit argued for the
necessity of inmate work programs not as rehabilitative or cost-
saving measures but in terms of their immediate benefits to the

prisoner: "The product is the inmate himself. . . . It makes him healthy mentally and physically. . . . Otherwise, you've got them tearing at their own insides. . . ."

To most of us outside of the corrections profession, it may seem odd, even perverse, that prison workers are so concerned about easing the inmates' burden of confinement. For one thing, it is prison workers who are often the targets of inmate abuse and violence. For instance, in 1981 the aforementioned Warden Pack of Texas and farm manager Billy M. Moore were slain on the prison grounds. Why then do prison workers care to make the inmates' lives—the lives of convicted rapists, murderers, thiefs, and other criminals—less hard and unpleasant?

It is tempting to explain their concern for the inmates as a mere reflection of occupational self-interest. Since, as we have already seen, many prison workers believe that inmates can "take over" whenever they so desire, perhaps such measures are attempts to buy the inmates' goodwill so that, in the event of an uprising or a hostage-taking incident, they may go unharmed. There is, no doubt, a germ of truth in this explanation. But correctional workers do discipline inmates. Those prison workers who have reason to be least concerned about the inmates' ability to harm them are often the ones most concerned abut reducing the inmates' pains of imprisonment; Texas workers shared the keeper philosophy no less than Michigan and California workers; the keeper mentality of central office personnel in each state was shared by the correctional officers in the cellblocks.

Instead, the keeper philosophy seems to be the product of the nature of the task confronted by prison workers. Wardens, officers, and other prison authorities must deal on a daily basis with people whom most of us would be both frightened and disgusted to be near. Through a mixture of legal, operational, and professional imperatives, they respond to their occupational chores as keepers. Referring to one of his correctional mentors, Michigan's Ron Gach explained:

He taught me the toughest, most important lesson in this business: If you are in corrections, you are not the public, you are not the judge, you are not the victim's family. Your job is to forget the crime and to work with him. Some people can't work with a baby raper. I'm not trying to be sensationalistic with you, but there are those types in here. . . . Some can't

work with a guy who beat up some old lady. It's a lousy sort
of professionalism, but being a professional in corrections
means being able to work with these sorts of people. . . . The
outsiders generally don't care about the inmates. We have to
care about them. We have to protect them from themselves
and from each other. . . . We keep them till [release] or till
they die, whichever comes first.

Similarly, former TDC director Estelle explained:

We deal with people that others have discarded, people that
nobody else wants to take charge of or care for . . . not the
sort of people that most of us care or dare to be around. . . .
We in corrections take the lowest of the low and sometimes
succeed in raising them.

Or as CDC director McCarthy explained, "There are a lot of people
in institutions who made a mistake and want to do something about
it. . . . I think we should provide them a safe environment to live
in."[1]

Occupationally, people who work in prisons are like doctors or
nurses who work in inner-city hospital emergency wards. To be
effective, the emergency room workers must be cool and clinical
when faced each day with an overflow of sick or bleeding bodies.
Hospital workers who were shocked every time a stabbing victim
staggered into the room, overly distracted by cries of pain, or
panicked at the sight of blood would be of little value in this station. Cases that in a nonemergency medical setting receive immediate attention are treated in the emergency room as routine cases
that can wait. In all probability, experienced emergency-room staff
guard the operation against both new workers who show signs of
not being "cut out" for the job and veteran colleagues who show
signs of "losing their stomachs" for it. What to the uninitiated
visitor seems like "callous" or "unfeeling" staff behavior may be a
mark of seasoned professionalism.

By the same token, if prison workers were upset or became
angry every time they passed by a convicted murderer or rapist,
they would be unable to perform their duties properly. Just as it
may chill the emergency-room visitor to hear a nurse tell a man
with a severe cut to sit on the side of the room with the "less
serious" cases, the visitor to the prison may be chilled to hear some

heinous criminal called a "good guy" by prison officials. Similarly, what to the uninitiated may seem like a prison riot is to the prison workers a "routine flare-up." An injury that might send the average citizen scurrying off to a hospital emergency room is treated by the bleeding correctional officer as a "scratch or two" requiring medical attention only because regulations require it. New correctional officers who enjoy "riding" inmates are reprimanded by veteran officers for inciting unwanted trouble, while seasoned corrections officials who become cynical about their work lose the respect of their peers. As one Michigan official stated, the keeper approach "just makes sense. You have to take a more humane approach. You can't look on these people like animals, even though some of them may behave like animals."

Prison workers in each system prided themselves on their inmate success stories, instances where being a good keeper was rewarded with an inmate's gratitude or good behavior. Some had saved notes of thanks sent to them over the years by inmates. In *Dialogues*, a news publication for employees of the Michigan Department of Corrections, a few letters of thanks from ex-inmates were published. One letter came to a superintendent of the Muskegon Correctional Facility. The letter read in part: "I must admit I expected the experience of incarceration to be one of a negative, if not destructive, nature. I've found just the opposite to be true . . . a result of the experience and dedication which emanates from your office."[2]

To corrections workers, the keeper approach distinguishes them from other criminal justice authorities, particularly law enforcement officers whom they sometimes characterize as "catchers." The effort of California officers to be viewed more on a par with state troopers is not inconsistent with this observation. Precisely because they do not simply catch and process criminals but are responsible on a daily basis for both the "care and custody" of a community of criminals, CDC officers claim to walk "the toughest beat in the state" and share pride in being "more than just cops." In each state, prison workers were quick to assert that they could outcompete workers from other criminal justice agencies. In Texas, for instance, an administrator responsible for training the system's elite special forces—a group of officers who wear all-black combat uniforms and are used to handle violent inmates, douse major disturbances, and guard dignitaries at events such as the annual prison rodeo—was thrilled to report that workers from other criminal justice agencies "couldn't keep up with our people" at a joint training session. "We sure outdid those catchers," he beamed. A veteran Michigan correctional officer who had had a career as a policeman rejected forcefully the "stereotypical idea" that "prison guards were cops who couldn't make it," and then went on to give examples of where, in his long career as a correctional officer, he was forced to do more of a complex and dangerous nature "than any dozen cops."[3]

While the keeper philosophy thus serves to bolster the self-image of correctional workers, it does so at the cost of fostering among them certain dysfunctional myths about the nature of their task. One is the myth of inmate dominance, the notion that "the inmates can take over whenever they want to." In a remark only slightly less typical of Texas prison officials than those in Michigan and California, a seasoned Michigan administrator asserted: "You can't control everything. I've been stabbed with a pencil. A man can kill you with a bar of soap in a sock. . . . Sure, it would help to get rid of springs in beds, metal scraps, but you just can't do away with everything that might be made into a weapon." To some degree, the belief that, as one Texas officer said, "the inmates will ultimately decide what happens," is correct. But anyone who spends much time observing prison workers inside the institutions or talking with officers in or out of them can see how this belief acts as a sort of self-fulfilling prophecy. To offer just one example, a Michigan official assigned to take visitors on a tour of Jackson prison noted that a metal rake was left in the corner of a heavily trafficked area of the prison. He gave a casual order to an officer that the object be removed and stored safely. Hours later he returned, saw that the rake had not been removed, and simply shrugged his shoulders. Even in the Texas Walls unit and at CMC, a number of seemingly obvious and easily remediable threats to security were treated lightly and justified by resort to the myth of inmate dominance. Of course, if the return of kitchen utensils is monitored, if inmates do not have easy access to tools, if cells are searched thoroughly and frequently, if officers do not lean against the bars, if idle gatherings of inmates are dispersed routinely, and if other basic measures are taken to minimize the instrumentalities and opportunities for prison disorder, then there probably would be less tragic evidence, systematic and anecdotal, to feed the myth.

A second and related myth shared by keepers is the myth of inmate society. Without exception, present and retired prison workers in each system held the view that inmates are bound to enter into some sort of prisoner society complete with its own language, leaders, and laws. While there were differences among prison officials about how to handle inmate society—differences that were manifested in the control, responsibility, and consensual models of correctional management—none doubted for a moment that such inmate groupings were inevitable in contemporary prison settings where inmates work, play, shower, and interact in numerous other ways, official and illicit. As one top-ranking Michigan official argued: "The sociologists are correct. You simply cannot prevent inmate society. You can try to make sense of it, understand, and make it work for the good." As noted in the opening chapter, while there is a germ of truth in this belief about the propensity of confined persons to associate and to identify themselves in opposition to their keepers, it seems rather clear that the extent and destructiveness of inmate society will vary inversely with formal attempts to check, control, and atomize it. Inmate society in its various manifestations—prison gangs, con bosses, informal inmate-officer alliances, and so forth—will become a potent force only where keepers are unwilling or unable to govern the prison themselves.

A third myth shared by keepers is the myth of general or underlying causes. As noted in the section on understanding prisons, for years scholars, journalists, and others unschooled in the particulars of prison administration have been telling the public that prison conditions are determined by forces having little or nothing to do with how prison workers do their jobs—a lack of funds, sentencing laws, overcrowding, dilapidated buildings, and so on. Prison workers themselves have been overly eager to agree with this prison cosmology and far too reluctant about accepting credit (or shouldering blame) for the quality of life inside the nation's penal institutions.

As noted earlier, the Texas, Michigan, and California prison systems have been subject to court orders and serious criticisms levelled by a variety of outside groups. While the three departments responded to these orders and criticisms with varying degrees of cooperation and denial, in each case their responses were conditioned by a sort of wounded pride as keepers. As we shall see in the next chapter, this was especially true of the response by Texas prison officials to the federal court's sweeping ruling in the *Ruiz* case. But in California and Michigan as well, corrections officials have been stung by the misconceptions of their detractors on the bench and elsewhere. For instance, California's William Barkdull, a central office administrator who began his career in the 1950s under Director Richard A. McGee, spoke of how he and his colleagues in the department were puzzled and hurt by the barrage of criticism that began in the mid-1960s. For years, recalled Barkdull, "the only voice for the inmates was the agency itself. Then came the legislature, the ACLU, the Attorney General, the Prisoners' Union, and so on. Soon we looked relatively unprogressive. . . . Glib, young reformers made our agency look bad. . . ."

The keeper philosophy is a set of beliefs and myths held in common by corrections officials which lead them to take a nonpunitive approach to incarcerated offenders, seeking to provide convicted criminals with the most safe, humane, and productive life of confinement possible. There were, however, basic and systematic differences in the way that Texas, Michigan, and California keepers answered certain fundamental questions about their role as keepers.

To paraphrase from the earlier quote of Michigan's Ron Gach, how much should keepers "forget the crime"? Should the inmate be viewed more as an incarcerated citizen or as a confined criminal? Is the rule-abiding prisoner entitled to all, some, or none of the privileges of free, law-abiding citizens? Should privileges be given to him gradually as a reward for good behavior, or all at once upon entering the prison? Do inmates have any right to rebel? Do keepers have a duty to sculpt the moral character of the inmates, or is it enough for them to prevent overt violence and to encourage rule-abiding behavior? Is criminality caused by such things as deviant personality development and poor economic conditions? Or are most criminals rational actors who believe that crime pays? Or is there yet a spiritual dimension to criminality such that some criminals can be understood as wicked souls who delight in preying upon the life and property of others? Texas, Michigan, and California keepers each held a set of ideas on these topics that bound them together and distinguished them from their peers in the other two states. Their differing ideas about the duties of keepers gave rise to their respective models of correctional management.

TEXAS KEEPERS AND THE CONTROL MODEL

Whenever two or more men live together,
rules and regulations are necessary for
governing their lives. Whenever a social
group is without rules, anarchy prevails.

—DIRECTOR W. J. ESTELLE, *Rules and*
Regulations and Grievance Procedures

To understand the philosophical lifeblood of the Texas control model, two treatises are essential reading. One is Warden Joseph Ragen's *Inside the World's Toughest Prison* (1962). This semi-autobiographical book describes the correctional principles and practices of the famous ruler of Stateville Penitentiary in Illinois. The other is Martin Luther's *Secular Authority: To What Extent It Should Be Obeyed*, written in the first half of the sixteenth century. Luther, of course, was no prison warden. He was one of the great figures in the Reformation who left behind a magnificent body of political and theological writings and founded the Protestant faith that bears his name. If you were truly interested in probing the control model's philosophical roots, you might add to your list certain works by Aristotle, John Stuart Mill, and, last but not least, Chester I. Barnard's *The Functions of the Executive* (1938), a masterful, if boring, treatise about organizations and how they are sustained, written by a man who was president of Bell Telephone. Or you could dispense with this eclectic reading list and talk to Dr. George Beto, the model's founder and a man whose mastery of these works influenced how Texas prisons were governed.

As we have seen, the control model involved the strict enforcement of discipline and a daily routine in which the inmates had virtually no say. All inmates would wear regulation white uniforms. All would have short-cropped hair. All would shave and bathe regularly. All who were illiterate would, like it or not, go to school at least one day each week. All would work in the fields for their first six months. All would address the officers as "boss" or "sir," and so on. Prisoners had certain minimal rights, but beyond that everything was to be earned as a privilege that could be taken away by the authorities without any extraordinary hearing process. The Texas authorities made no pretense that this regimen would automatically lead most inmates to rehabilitation. Rather, they believed that it might lead a few inmates to what Warden Bobby D. Morgan of the system's Pack I unit called "habituation," the formation of respectful, lawful behavior through forced adherence to rules mandating such behavior. In chapter three, Major Scott of the Walls unit was quoted about "rehabilitation" as "making people who were never responsible be responsible." This idea was a pillar of the control system and, like virtually all of the system's other operational precepts, it was put in place by Beto. As Beto explained:

> Observe these inmates. Most of them have simply never known discipline, internal or external. The internal kind is moral, a form of personal virtue which can be instilled through a good upbringing. The other is external and is based mainly on the fear of getting caught in some illicit act. . . . In prison, these men, most of them for the first time in their lives, are made to experience external discipline. They must take a bath each day. They must shave. They must wear fresh clothes. They must wait in lines and be respectful to others. We hope that they come to learn the benefits of doing such things . . . [and] turn away from their former lives and ways of behaving.

Under the control model, Texas keepers were to "forget the crime" only insofar as that meant refraining from any imposition of extralegal pains on the inmate. Inmates were to be kept wholly secure from any abuses by other inmates or the staff. But Texas keepers did not forget the kind of character flaws that, they assumed, had brought the man to prison. Each prisoner was to be viewed less as an incarcerated citizen and more as a confined criminal. The tight controls on inmate movement, the clear superior-subordinate relationship between inmates and their "bosses," and the point-incentive system whereby inmates could, through hard work and overall good behavior, earn a trustyship, were institutionalized not only in the interests of security but as a reflection of the inmates' standing vis-à-vis the law-abiding society they had offended. Inmates, it was reasoned, had violated the trust on which any free society must ultimately be based. The regime of the prison, the closely monitored daily round of inmate life, was to be a living reminder to all concerned of the type of society that would be necessary if citizens could not trust one another. Inmates had abused their liberty. The prison was to be run in a way that, while affording inmates an opportunity to better themselves and to get back into society's good graces, never let them forget the moral outrage of the law-abiding community that had banished them from its midst. "I never shake hands with an inmate," Beto noted. "You must keep some social distance between the inmate while an inmate and the free, law-abiding citizen. They neither are nor ought to be viewed as equals." Only on the day of a man's release would Beto offer his hand and only then would the crime be "forgotten."

Virtually none of the Texas keepers looked beyond the individual offender in explaining criminality. They were well aware of the social, psychological, and economic explanations of criminality, but they rejected them in favor of explanations that laid greater stress on the criminal's personal culpability. Beto's successor as director, W. J. Estelle, remarked:

> Some criminals are people who, for a variety of reasons, are radically present-oriented, who don't or won't see the connection between what they do today and what happens to them tomorrow. They don't perceive how their actions affect others. . . . They'll steal or kill without considering the gravity of the act, its morality, or its consequences from the standpoint of self-interest. But not all criminals fit the sociopathic, psychopathic, or other such molds. There are those who turn to crime because they believe that it pays and pays well . . . these criminals are all too aware of the costs and benefits of crime, all too rational for their good and ours. Crime pays and they act accordingly.

This rational actor explanation of criminality was echoed by most other Texas keepers. One central office administrator recalled: "I had an inmate tell me, 'Hell, my mamma was a fool! Working her ass off all day for nothing. . . . Why work ten hours for what you can take in ten seconds?' That is the way most convicts think." To underscore this point, Texas keepers pointed out that many inmates who had acquired job skills and obtained well-paying jobs returned to crime nonetheless: "Do they seize the opportunity and lead a lawful life? Some do, but many don't. The repeaters will tell you directly why they steal or rape or even murder. They'll tell you that crime pays."

Texas prison workers offered a second explanation for criminality that was consistent with this rational actor explanation to the extent that it held the offender to be conscious, willful, and hence fully culpable for his misdeeds, but different in that it ascribed such criminal calculations to wickedness or spiritual depravity. This was clear from the comments of many correctional officers, more than one of whom began by saying "These men aren't in here for singing too loud in the church choir on Sundays!" Beto spoke of inmates who suffered from a "corrupted courage," a form of moral weakness that leads them to enjoy preying upon defenseless persons. At the burial of one Texas inmate, a small group of inmates and prison officials gathered as the prison minister spoke as follows: "In life and in death there's always a boss. In life if you are bad and insubordinate to your boss you're going to have trouble. And in eternity—the Lord is boss!" "Boss," of course, is the Texas term for a prison worker, particularly a correctional officer.

Beto did not believe that inmates had any right to rebel against prison authorities. As Martin Luther wrote, "If wrong is to be suffered, it is better to suffer it from rulers than that the rulers suffer it from their subjects."[4] Any aggressive collective action by inmates, whether in the form of a refusal to work ("work-buck") or a threat to do violence, was to be met with swift official counterforce. As Beto explained: "Inmates must know that you will respond swiftly and appropriately to any such challenge—not tomorow, not the next day, not with the National Guard, but then and there with officers exercising the authority vested in them by the state."

The idea of giving inmates a say in how the prisons run was an anathema to Beto and other Texas keepers. Inmates were to be seen as persons who had a demonstrated inability to be self-governing. The control model was intended to instill in them two habits that were considered prerequisites to the right and ability to be self-governing—the habit of obedience to duly constituted authorities and the habit of laboring for one's life necessities. To give the inmates a choice in these matters, it was maintained, was tantamount to giving people who had abused freedom and shirked responsibilities when free an invitation to do likewise inside prison. In no case were inmates to be permitted to participate in making management decisions. Echoing Beto, former director Estelle lumped inmate self-government schemes with other prison "activities which result in unrealistic expectations. . . . A prison which dabbles in the 'democratic process' or participative management, in my opinion, is borrowing trouble."

Rarely, if ever, did Texas keepers attempt to justify their prison services as a means of reducing the likelihood that inmates will recidivate. Unlike the California and Michigan systems, the Texas system did few studies of the effects of its educational and work programs on recidivism rates. The programs were to be available to inmates for the same reason that clean, safe living conditions were to be provided, namely, as things to which every person in the custody of the state was entitled. To fail to provide these services would be to deprive inmates of an opportunity to lead more productive, civilized lives while behind bars. As Beto explained: "Recidivism rates are not an appropriate measure of prison performance. . . . While education, say, might not keep a man from returning to prison—who really can say?—it has an intrinsic value. . . . The state should provide the inmates with as much education as it can reasonably afford, as much as the inmates can accept."

Through his association with Warden Ragen of Stateville, Beto deepened his belief in the necessity of running a very tight ship administratively, one predicated on the kind of attention to the nitty-gritty details of prison life evidenced in our discussion of the Walls' Warden Pursley. Beto, like Ragen, was as interested in checking staff abuses as he was in checking abuses by inmates. Everyone, inmate and officer alike, was to be monitored by some superior.

As noted in the opening chapter, the idea that compulsion might be conducive to inmate treatment, that inmates ought to be prevented from associating on their own terms and dressing, talking, and working (or not working) pretty much as they please, has begun to gain currency among some academics and commentators. Among Texas keepers, the idea that orderly prisons were the sina qua non of treatment and that inmates ought to be forced, if necessary, to behave in a civilized fashion while in state custody was institutionalized in the control model and applied for most of the two decades ending in 1984. The control style of prison administration was based on a correctional philosophy with roots stretching in time and place well beyond east Texas. The control model was a purposeful attempt to civilize unlawful persons by encouraging and, if necessary, forcing them to live their lives under a strong prison government that demanded lawful behavior from those who lived under and worked for it. The prisons were to be run as benevolent, paternalistic despotisms in the interests of the orderly, humane, and just treatment of convicted criminals.

MICHIGAN KEEPERS AND THE RESPONSIBILITY MODEL

We hope that you will take advantage of
the opportunities open to better yourselves,
increase your knowledge, develop a useful
trade or to develop creative talents."

—INTRODUCTION, *Prisoner Guide Book*

In his 1977 essay, "The Role of the Penal Quarantine in Reducing Violent Crime," Michigan corrections chief Perry M. Johnson began by quoting the following words from John Stuart Mill's *On Liberty* (1859): "The principle is, that the sole end for which mankind are warranted individually or collectively, in interfering with the liberty of any of their members, is self-protection."[5] In the lines immediately following these words, lines not quoted in the director's essay, Mill stressed that a person "cannot rightfully be compelled to do or forbear because it will be better for him to do so, because it will make him happier, because in the opinions of others, to do so would be wise, or even right. These are good reasons for remonstrating with him, or reasoning with him, or persuading him, or entreating him, but not for compelling him. . . ."[6] In the very next paragraph, however, Mill added this crucial if somewhat self-contradictory qualification: "It is perhaps hardly necessary to say that this doctrine is meant to apply only to human beings in the maturity of their faculties. . . . Despotism is a legitimate mode of government in dealing with barbarians, provided the end be their improvement, and the means justified by actually effecting that end."[7]

The essential difference between George Beto, the control model, and Texas keepers, on the one hand, and Perry Johnson, the responsibility model, and Michigan keepers, on the other, is the difference between these two philosophical faces of John Stuart Mill. Johnson knew and quoted the part of Mill that emphasizes that individuals ought to be restrained only so far as is necessary to keep them from doing harm, physical harm, to others. Beto knew and subscribed to the part of Mill that emphasizes the duty to restrain individuals who are not yet fully civilized or in the maturity of their faculties. To Johnson, restraints were to be minimal and to be undertaken for the sole purpose of protecting others. To Beto, restraints were to be tight enough to protect others from the criminal and to compel the criminal, for his own good, to behave in what former TDC director Estelle termed "a socially desirable manner, a morally upstanding way."

Under the responsibility model, it was enough for inmates to refrain from violence and to participate, if they so desired, in the treatment and work opportunities offered to them by the state. Under the control model, it was expected that inmates would be made to follow the rules, refrain from violence or other illicit acts, come to obey and show respect for duly constituted authority, and work and educate themselves when and how prison officials decided. To Michigan keepers, rehabilitation, if it was to happen at all, could only come from a sort of revelation on the part of the inmate, a revelation encouraged perhaps by the sensitive treatment that his green-blazered officers and counselors gave him, and by his participation in programs. To Texas keepers, rehabilitation might or might not be produced in this way, but while in prison, the criminal would be habituated to the norms of a noncriminal, essentially middle-class way of life and would not be permitted to look or act the way he did "on the streets."

Throughout his tenure as Michigan director, Johnson's responsibility model of correctional management was paired with his belief that the sole purpose of imprisonment was incapacitation, that is, to keep the public safe from dangerous criminals. In a 1984 speech before the American Correctional Association (ACA), Johnson stated: "I feel strongly that prisons should be used only to house criminals so dangerous, or persistent, or unmanageable that they must be restrained to protect the public or gain compliance with criminal sanctions. . . . So 29 years of prison work has convinced me that incapacitation is the *only* proper reason for imprisonment."[8]

Johnson was also an outspoken opponent of the death penalty. Department spokespersons were given a kit containing statistical information and position papers. One of the papers by Johnson was entitled "Capital Punishment—A Futile Act." In it, Johnson argued that executions do not "frighten potential murderers" and "may stimulate, rather than deter, potential murderers." The death penalty does not "protect the public any better than Michigan's current penalty for first degree murder, which is life in prison."[9]

Johnson's beliefs that imprisonment was solely for incapacitation and that the death penalty was but a futile crime control strategy were shared by most of the system's upper administrators and by about half of the correctional officers. Texas keepers, on the other hand, believed that prison was for more than incapacitation. Taking their cues first from Beto and then from Estelle, Texas prison workers saw clear retributive and "habilitative" value to imprisonment. Overwhelmingly, they favored the death penalty, not as a crime control or deterrence strategy, but as a form of just deserts. Indeed, many of them would favor capital punishment for heinous crimes even if it could be indisputably shown to increase the homicide rate. Contrary to Johnson, Estelle did not favor life imprisonment without chance of parole as an alternative to the death penalty. On a public television forum about corrections, featuring some of the nation's leading criminal justice practitioners, Estelle spoke of not wanting to keep prisoners "without hope."[10]

For years, Michigan prison officials had argued for prison services as a way of reducing recidivism rates. As had happened in California about a decade earlier, however, in the early 1980s, their own departmental studies began to show rather conclusively that the effects of these programs on recidivism rates were ambiguous, negligible, or nonexistent. Still, the department continued to provide counseling, mental health services, work programs, and educational opportunities.[11] The stress on incapacitation gave way to the keepers' commitment to do more than simply "warehouse" inmates. As one administrator at the Michigan Reformatory (MR) stated: "If we don't act as agents of positive change, we leave them to themselves and to each other to degenerate further. Since 1958 we've run over 180,000 people through these prisons, 12,000 of them through here. I don't believe we are here to warehouse these people." Citing the necessity of learning opportunities, the warden of MR, John Jabe, observed: "God does nothing to a man's mind when that man is imprisoned."

Almost without exception, the Michigan prison authorities were opposed to the idea, widely held among Texas keepers, that prisoners should be viewed and treated more as convicted criminals than as incarcerated citizens. Unlike Beto, Warden Jabe and his colleagues in Michigan saw little reason to relate to prisoners as anything other than confined fellow citizens. As Jabe said: "I'll shake an inmate's hand. It's important to touch. It's important to know what both elements (inmates and officers) are feeling." Nor did Michigan keepers see any reason to strictly monitor or tightly supervise either the inmates or the staff. Opinions about the legacy of Warden Ragen of Illinois were almost uniformly negative, even among those Michigan correctional officers who knew of him and had argued the necessity of greater controls on inmates and a more paramilitary operation. The kind of close security and attention to detail that Ragen symbolized were embraced by Texas keepers. But Ragen's correctional legacy was roundly rejected by Michigan keepers as embodying overly pessimistic assumptions about human nature, fear of the inmates, and a lack of genuine trust and confidence in department personnel. As Warden Jabe noted: "As we progress in corrections, we will need more genuinely professional administrators. We will move about as far as possible from the likes of Warden Joe Ragen and his style of management." Warden Redman of HVMF echoed Jabe: "Joe Ragen is no model for me or any other prison manager. I can't see how a prison could be run along those lines. It's absurd . . . a product of a different age really than the one in which we operate. We try to make the place as natural as possible."

Michigan keepers saw little reason why inmates should not be allowed to participate in making the decisions that affected their lives. Nor did they believe in doing anything to discourage the inmates from lodging complaints or issuing demands about prison conditions. Michigan correctional officers were more prone than their administrative superiors to argue against such measures, but as a group, they were far more supportive of such practices than were their Texas counterparts. As one Reception and Guidance Center official noted: "We 'educate' our inmates. That's a revolutionary thing in this field. We tell them their rights and make them more sophisticated protectors of those rights." Indeed, the very first line of the Michigan *Prisoner Guide Book* "Rules of General Conduct" read: "All prisoners are expected to obey directions and instructions of members of the staff. If a prisoner feels he/she has been dealt with unfairly, or that he/she has received improper instructions, he/she should first comply with the order and then follow the established grievance procedure outlined later in this booklet." Later in the booklet a passage under the heading "Prisoner Representatives" read: "Prisoners are encouraged to make informed and responsible decisions affecting their future, and not become dependent on the institution except as it relates to security, good order and discipline." The equivalent prison manual for Texas inmates continued no such passages. Instead, it contained several lines such as the following: "In the Texas Department of Corrections you must learn to respect authority, therefore, it is imperative that while in the Diagnostic Center you accept this fact. . . . Do not waste food in the dining room. You must eat all that you take on your tray. . . . Keep your feet and shoes off the wall. . . . Fighting, scuffling, etc., will not be tolerated and violators will be punished. . . . You will be required to obey officers at all times."

The stark differences in Michigan versus Texas prison management were reflections of such profound and systematic differences in correctional philosophy. While it is true to say that Michigan officials had less of a sense of mission than Texas officials, this observation must be qualified in light of the fact that each department had a distinct notion of what its mission was. The Texas control model was based on a keeper philosophy that called forth tight security, paramilitary organization, and regulations covering everything down to how an inmate buttoned his uniform. The Michigan responsibility model was based on a keeper philosophy that called forth more relaxed organizational measures including the virtual absence of inmate dress and grooming standards. To Beto and his Texas keepers, governing prisons was a form of soulcraft in which orderly conditions were to provide the foundation for the inmates' enforced habituation to a civilized round of daily life. To Johnson and the majority of his Michigan keepers, governing prisons was a more limited enterprise, taken up mainly for the sake of public protection but wherein inmates would be gently persuaded to think and act in productive, noncriminal ways.

CALIFORNIA KEEPERS AND THE CONSENSUAL MODEL

> *This is a reminder that the basic idea at this facility is to help you return to your community, your family, and your friends as soon as possible. . . . We will assist you if you let us, but it will require your patience and commitment to stay out of trouble. Thank you.*

—C.T.F. SOLEDAD, CONCLUSION, *Inmate Handbook*

Much like many Michigan prison officials but unlike most of those in Texas, California keepers generally viewed criminality as a complex phenomenon with roots deeper than the individual criminal's decision to break the law. As one CDC administrator said: "Hell, they drift into it; they don't choose it. They want a piece of the American dream, a cut of the pie. They reject their lower power and status. They are mesmerized by material things dangled before them on TV, in magazines, all over." At the same time, however, most CDC officials were quick to stress that neither they nor anybody else with experience in corrections can be willing to excuse the criminal for his deeds or to run a prison on the assumption that the incarcerated offender will, if only given the chance, cooperate voluntarily. Sara Bruce, Associate Superintendent of Soledad's North unit, observed: "California does not have a system run by liberals. I'm not one. I doubt that you'll find any real liberals in this business. That's no more true today—a time of growing conservatism—than it was in the sixties—or whenever it was that California prisons were supposed to be so liberal."

The correctional philosophy of California prison officials, like the model of prison management that springs from it, represents a sort of middle ground between the penal ideas embraced by Michigan keepers, on the one side, and Texas keepers, on the other. Many California prison workers knew something about the Texas system and made observations such as the following: "We in California could run prisons the much-heralded Texas way. We choose not to. It's our choice. . . . The Texas system is oppressive and coercive. In the last analysis, all prisons are coercive, but Texas makes a virtue of this necessity." One veteran CDC correctional officer stated: "The inmate is a human being. He's like you and me, entitled to every respect." Research director Bob Dickover observed: "Unlike Texas, we don't attempt to enforce a strict uniformity. We don't wish to debase or to degrade. We don't insist that prisoners wear outfits, prisoner outfits. I wear my jeans at home because they're most comfortable—why shouldn't an inmate do the same? . . . How somebody looks may be vital to his self-image. Why tear that down? Why incite them over such a triviality?" Asked why inmates at most of the prisons had such easy access to weight-lifting equipment, a CDC administrator explained: "It builds their self-image and adds to their self-esteem. They'll send pictures to their girls."

While central office administrators and the staff at Soledad echoed more of the Michigan correctional creed, the staff at CMC echoed more of the beliefs shared by Texas keepers. CMC's Warden Wayne Estelle said of rehabilitation: "I don't carry that in my dictionary." But he was a strong believer in making inmates work:

"We'll show them what it is to do a day's work." More than most California prison officials, Warden Estelle had positive things to say about Stateville's Joe Ragen. Like Ragen, he emphasized a concern with the seemingly trivial details of prison administration. He shared the Texas keepers' rejection of inmate self-government schemes: "To run a prison well requires all the skills that it takes to run any large institution well. The only management style that may work in other settings but will almost certainly fail in prisons is participative management. You can't have it in a prison. You must have quasi-military operations. . . . Unfortunately, to maintain order there must be controls and regulations at almost every turn."

Some of the staff at Soledad believed that it was necessary to structure the inmate's daily routine in a way that might encourage him to behave in a lawful, obedient way. Soledad's Captain Rutherford observed:

> We must teach by example. We must stand for society's ideals
> whether we think those ideals are good or questionable. In
> this society, using foul language indiscriminately, smelling
> bad, wearing dirty clothes, not wanting to work hard. . . .
> These traits will get you nowhere. . . . I guess you could call
> it teaching social conformity, though that may have some
> connotations I don't intend when I speak of teaching by exam-
> ple.

This view, however, was more common among the staff at CMC than it was among the staff at Soledad. At CMC, they took this correctional notion a few steps further by not simply exemplifying or teaching but requiring inmates to behave in socially acceptable ways.

As noted in the previous chapter, prohibitions against cursing, wearing headgear in the dining hall, and reacting aggressively to officers were more strictly enforced at CMC than at Soledad. While CMC, like Soledad, had an inmate council, it was generally agreed that the council at CMC had less of a real voice in prison affairs than its Soledad counterpart. At Soledad inmates who "acted out" at disciplinary hearings or were hostile toward staff members were often given the benefit of the doubt and reasoned with by staff; at CMC such behavior was simply not tolerated. As Warden Estelle observed:

It's not just for the sake of order that we don't permit any nonsense from inmates. It's because the world out there doesn't reward such nonsense. That's a lesson which they need to learn and which maybe we can do a little bit to teach.

CORRECTIONAL LEADERSHIP

Organizations are largely the shadows of their executives. . . . It does not matter whether one is talking about Harvard University, the Chrysler Corporation, or the Texas Department of Corrections. The executive's skills and abilities, his sense of mission and dedication to duty, are decisive in determining how—and how well—an organization runs.

—DR. GEORGE BETO

Within California and among the Texas, Michigan, and California prison systems, what correctional officials thought about the purposes of imprisonment influenced how they ran their prisons. Correctional workers in each state shared what was described as the keeper philosophy but interpreted the duties of keepers differently. Their respective models of correctional administration reflected these philosophical differences.

We now turn to examine a closely related dimension of correctional administration: leadership. It is the leaders of corrections agencies who are most responsible for articulating and institutionalizing a vision of how prisons ought to be governed.

Social scientists are naturally suspicious of explanations that attribute important happenings to the works of a single individual. Alexis de Tocqueville suspected that they would be so suspicious. While the thinkers of earlier times were "inclined to refer all occurrences to the particular will and character of certain individuals," Tocqueville predicted that the scholars of our age would be inclined to "attribute hardly any influence to the individual" and would instead "assign great general causes to all petty incidents."[12]

Contemporary students of organizations, however, have been more than a little sympathetic to what some of their social science colleagues frown upon as "great man" (or "great woman") explanations. The role of individual leadership in shaping and sustaining certain organizations has been almost undeniable—J. Edgar Hoover's FBI, Hyman Rickover's atomic navy, Lee Iaccoca's Chrysler Corporation, Robert Moses's Triborough Bridge and Tunnel Authority, and so on in a list that could run for pages. None of these leaders was solely responsible for how their organizations developed and performed. None of them was capable of bending every internal and external constraint—political, legal, technological, or financial—to his organizational ends. But each of them shaped the life of his organization in significant and consequential ways. As political scientists Jameson W. Doig and Erwin C. Hargrove have observed, such leaders do some or all of the following: identify new missions and programs for the organization; develop and nourish external constituencies to support new goals and programs; create internal constituencies via recruitment systems and key appointments; motivate and provide training for members; identify and remedy points of trouble—mismanagement, corruption, budding outside opposition—and take remedial action.[13] In many cases, of course, it is difficult to sort out and measure the leader's impact on the organization's development and performance. In other cases, however, it is equally difficult to avoid ascribing too much of the organization's success or failure to its leader.

The leaders of prison bureaucracies have rarely received the sort of attention that has attended the leaders of other criminal justice agencies or other public and private organizations generally. Warden Ragen of Stateville penitentiary is perhaps the most notable exception. In the leading scholarly portrait of his administration, Ragen emerges as a consequential leader who was yet only the "master" of his prison's quiescent political and social environment.[14]

Prison executives are subject to a variety of statutory constraints. They preside over a public agency that is, except in the days immediately following some spectacular escape or disturbance, low on the political agenda. They are generally assumed to have little to say regarding the broader issues related to imprisonment. It is not surprising, therefore, that their role has been ignored or downgraded. But as we have already seen through our discussion of correctional philosophy and management in Texas, Michigan, and California, they are more efficacious than is generally supposed; the individual who heads a prison, or a prison system, can shape the organization in ways that help to determine the quality of prison life.

CORRECTIONAL LEADERSHIP IN CALIFORNIA

Anyone even vaguely familiar with the history of the California Department of Corrections will agree that without the leadership of Richard A. McGee, California prisons of the period 1944 to 1967 would have been run much differently and would probably have been far more violent, filthy, and corrupt than they actually were. McGee oversaw the construction of nearly a dozen new prisons, introduced inmate classification concepts, created staff training programs, pioneered inmate work programs and prison industries, and cultivated the relationships with the state's political and business leaders that gave his agency the legal and fiscal tools with which to expand and improve. Retired CDC official Jim Kane was the system's first psychologist-social worker. He assumed that position in 1949 after coming to California from New York. McGee had recruited him to the agency. As Kane recalled: "I came to California from New York because I'd heard that it wasn't corrupt politically. I didn't believe it, so I came to see with my own eyes. You know what? It really wasn't corrupt, not even the prison department! Everything wasn't patronage. Can you imagine that!"

As Kane noted, most prison agencies have been, and continue to be, politicized. New governors enter, and prison directors change, and with every change any long-term plans or commitment to a way of doing things "goes right out the window." Kane, retired CDC official Jim Park, former CDC prison official turned scholar John P. Conrad, and other correctional officials in California and elsewhere have credited McGee with insulating his department from such disruptive political pressures.

Shortly before he died, McGee published a book which instructs prison directors on how to combat political pressures and direct their institutions. In his *Prisons and Politics* (1981), McGee warned prison officials that their organization's environment is "a political jungle in which the rules are vague, friends and enemies are often indistinguishable, and little is predictable."[15] McGee preached to his correctional colleagues what he had tried to practice: "Of all institutions, public or private, probably none has the imperative to be organized as tightly and operated as efficiently as the prison. Not to do so inevitably results in political and legal attacks from the outside, or blowups and insurrections from within. . . . Instead of talking about abolishing prisons, we should be finding ways to make them safe, manageable, and fit for human occupancy."[16]

As noted previously, as important and influential as McGee was in shaping the course of California corrections, he was unable to institutionalize many of his ideas and his successors led the department in a variety of directions, more often reacting to internal and external forces than mastering them. Even the colorful and popular Raymond Procunier, who stayed at the helm of CDC for nearly a decade, was not a pro-active director but rather made ad hoc and often contradictory responses to political pressures, the prison gang problem, the commitment to rehabilitative programs, and other issues that were most salient during his administration. Not until 1983 and the appointment of Daniel J. McCarthy did the California prison system experience the kind of forward-looking leadership it had had under McGee.

As mentioned earlier, McCarthy looked to McGee as something of a model. McCarthy's reputation inside the department was made largely through his successes as warden of CMC. As a warden, McCarthy was one of the few CDC institutional heads who would not comply automatically with central office decisions that offended his correctional judgment. For instance, in 1971 following a bloody incident at San Quentin, Procunier reacted by ordering every prison in the state to lock down. McCarthy defied Procunier's order. The reason he gave for his defiance was simple: the inmates at his prison did not deserve that type of treatment. The staff at CMC, he argued, was in control, and the inmates had, as usual, been complying with the rules. Even with the lockdown, San Quentin and a few other prisons experienced trouble. At CMC, however, the daily routine went as always, and the prison remained calm.

McCarthy accepted the directorship of the system reluctantly. After the resignation of Ruth Rushen, Republican Governor George Deukmejian appointed a former Ohio corrections official to the directorship. The legislature, however, rejected this candidate, citing his record on minority hiring and affirmative action. Everyone then looked to McCarthy as the only person who had a reasonable chance of rescuing the system's drift into increasing violence, decreasing staff morale, and poor public relations. McCarthy had spent thirty-four years in CDC and, as he noted, had "the ulcers and scars to prove it." It took a concerted and dramatic personal appeal by McCarthy's mentor, Richard A. McGee, before the renowned warden of CMC agreed to take the post; shortly thereafter, McGee died.

In chapter three's discussion of the evolution of the California model of correctional administration, we detailed some of the managerial changes being engineered by McCarthy's immediate subordinates. Like his successor as warden of CMC, Wayne Estelle, McCarthy spoke of himself as an "overpromoted prison guard" and recalled how he had begun his career in the department without any real formal training. "Basically, they just gave you a firearm and some keys and said 'Go.'" Like many veteran correctional officials, McCarthy wished to be a part of whatever measures would make correctional management more up-to-date. We shall evaluate such measures in the concluding chapter. For now, however, the point is that McCarthy was able to lead the department's personnel into acceptance of more "professional" management techniques. As one veteran CMC officer said: "Look, we have a bunch of numbskulls in Sacramento who are bringing in people who don't know anything about prisons. These people managed the department of birds and bees or have know-it-all degrees. They're making a mess and putting more pressure on those of us who know what the hell is going on. We have to compensate for their well-intended stupid decisions. . . . I can't figure it. But if Dan McCarthy is in charge, then maybe there's more to this than any of us clowns can see. If he weren't overseeing this stuff we . . . the seniors, the unions, the other supervisory staff . . . we'd buck it and break it tomorrow."

McCarthy has been described by his colleagues as "a tough Mission Street Irishman," a reference to his roots in the Irish neighborhood of San Francisco that also was home to California's two governors Brown. McCarthy is an unassuming man who reportedly has a "long fuse." When he makes his mind up about something, however, he is said to be "as tough as nails" and unyielding.

Part of McCarthy's correctional creed is that a prison which has to lock down or otherwise break its routine is a prison that is improperly managed. Not only did he refuse, as mentioned, to lock down CMC in 1971, but he locked down the entire prison only twice in his dozen years as its warden. Both times the lockdown was caused not by inmate disturbances or uprisings but by correctional officer job actions that affected other institutions as well.

For years CDC had been angling towards the establishment of a new training academy, but this plan was brought to fruition only after McCarthy had assumed the directorship. Appropriately, the training center, located in Galt, California, was named the Richard A. McGee Training Academy. Under McCarthy the state has moved on the most massive prison construction project in penal history and has taken initiatives to alleviate the ever-worsening gang problem. He has forced the agency to respond in a prompt and cooperative way to a barrage of unfavorable court rulings. At the same time, however, he has stood up for the agency against court orders which he deemed "ill-considered, unworkable, and dangerous." Finally, he has instituted measures to deal with the problem of stress among the system's correctional officers, a high percentage of whom retire from the agency on what is referred to as "stress disability."

CORRECTIONAL LEADERSHIP IN MICHIGAN

The role of correctional leadership has been no less pronounced in the Michigan Department of Corrections. As we have already seen, Perry M. Johnson, the department's director from 1972 to 1984, was a chief architect of the responsibility model of correctional administration. As noted, Johnson's policies have not been universally popular either within the department or among the state's political leaders. The point, however, is that Johnson was able to steer his agency in a way that reflected his own correctional beliefs. Largely through Johnson's efforts, the department has enjoyed administrative stability at the top and has normally received a cut of the state's budget that rouses the envy of corrections chiefs in most other states. MDC's Richard McKeon, an assistant to Johnson who had worked in the Michigan state legislature, explained:

> It's not a politicized department. . . . We've fared well mainly because of Perry Johnson. He's smart, articulate, and like-

able. Michigan, you know, is the first state into a recession and the last one out. Yet Perry managed to protect the department and lobbied to get its fair share. He brought the legislators inside to see what was happening.

Not only did Johnson invite legislators and other important outside constituencies to learn about or visit the department and its prisons, over the years he sent his top staff persons to speak to all manner of community groups and prison reform organizations. One public relations kit used by MDC spokespersons was an orange folder stuffed full of departmental statistics, a brief agency history, and position papers. Pasted to the cover of the "Speaker's Resource Kit" was a sticker reading: "If Corrections fails, you lose (again)."

During his tenure as director, Johnson was highly active in the American Correctional Association (ACA) and saw to it that the prisons sought ACA accreditation. A true believer in the ACA's approach to correctional administration, Johnson selected and put in place institutional personnel, particularly wardens, who also favored (or at least would not publicly dispute) the accreditation effort. As a number of MDC central administrators observed, however, there were other reasons for the department's enthusiastic embrace of the ACA. One top administrator explained: "Texas, as you must know, has or had an outright prohibition on accreditation. We, on the other hand, bought into the ACA in a big way. Perry was an ACA governor. He himself helped to establish the guidelines. Also, we have a female warden who was an ACA director of accreditation systems. . . . Having these efforts under way was a good shield against litigation."

As we shall see in the next chapter, many judges, including the one responsible for effecting massive changes in the Texas prison system, have embraced the ACA's manuals and used them in rendering judgments about both the operational quality and the constitutionality of prison management systems. The close alliance between the ACA and the Michigan Department of Corrections did not keep the agency out of court. Indeed, to some extent it backfired, as judges ordered the department to follow complex and detailed ACA-inspired policy directives, which was in many cases (e.g., property rights and property control) virtually impossible. Nevertheless, the existence of such weighty and impressive-looking manuals together with the ongoing accreditation drive was enough to forestall the kind of sweeping court decisions faced by other systems where the actual quality of prison life was at least as good as in Michigan.[17]

Johnson was instrumental in expanding the officers' training program. During his tenure, preservice and inservice training increased both quantitatively and qualitatively. While he advanced a plan intended to recruit and promote more women and minorities within the agency, he opposed vigorously a rule by the State Civil Service agency that lowered correctional officer preservice educational requirements in accordance with affirmative action goals. Following the 1981 riot at Jackson prison, it became clear that some personnel in key positions were barely literate. Johnson used this as leverage to get Civil Service to reinstate its high school preservice standard.

As noted in chapter three, after stepping down as director Johnson assumed the post of deputy director of the department's Bureau of Field Services. Throughout his tenure as director, Johnson was careful to project an image of the department as the agency responsible for virtually all forms of postsentencing supervision, not just prisons. Because of this, the department was less subject to attacks by those who, for whatever reasons, were ill disposed towards prisons and those who run them. Indeed, Johnson himself emphasized that because of their human and financial costs, prisons were to be used as little as possible.[18] In California, where the corrections director is also responsible for parole and related functions, much less has been done to highlight the department's nonprison operations, and most people think of CDC as a prison agency.

Johnson was under no external pressure to step down as MDC director. To be sure, his responsibility model of prison administration had taken a severe drubbing in the 1980s in the form of union opposition, overcrowding, rising violence, a spectacular riot, court intervention, rising costs, and an increasingly conservative state electorate. Not even his sternest critics, however, underestimated Johnson's personal impact on the department and its prisons. Curiously enough, the only one who questioned the extent to which he had led the department was Johnson himself:

A lot of people have asked what it has been like to run, or try to run, a major corrections department for twelve years. . . .

I don't have anything to compare it to. About as close as I can come is to liken it to a story Mark Twain used to tell. . . . This fellow worked in a carpet-weaving mill . . . a whole factory full of gears and spindles. Well, it seems he got his sleeve caught in the machinery and was taken on a tour through the entire works. . . . As Twain said, it was, no doubt, an interesting and educational experience, but not one a person would be inclined to repeat.

The difference between Johnson and the carpet weaver, however, was that the "machine" was largely of Johnson's own making, the product of his own extraordinary talents as a correctional leader.

CORRECTIONAL LEADERSHIP IN TEXAS: "WALKING GEORGE"

Like McGee in California and Johnson in Michigan, the correctional legacy of Dr. George Beto, director of TDC from 1962 to 1972, is vast. Several years ago, Judge Frank Johnson relied on Beto for advice as he set about ordering massive changes in the Alabama prison system. Director of the Federal Bureau of Prisons Norman A. Carlson has looked to Beto as a model administrator, one whom he has tried to emulate in his own lengthy career as a prison executive. Beto has been engaged by leading scholars including Simon Dinitz, Bruce Jackson, James B. Jacobs, and many others. During his tenure as director, CBS News set out to do a documentary on Texas prisons but ended up doing one on Beto,[19] a tall, lean Lutheran minister and college president turned prison chief who was as comfortable with a prison manual as he was with a Bible and could quote the classics one minute and chew out a subordinate the next.

Beto earned the nickname "Walking George" for his habit of showing up at the prisons every day, usually unannounced. A young dentist who years earlier had worked in TDC's summer intern program told of how he learned about Beto's roving. The warden of the prison to which he was assigned told him, "Son, I'm going to give you a real important job. You sit over yonder and listen to the calls that come in over the intercom system. Now, you can ignore all the calls that come in except one, number 1101. Son, when you hear that number 1101 you get yourself up and run as fast as you can and find me." Of course, Beto was number 1101, and the warden, the veteran H. H. "Hal" Husbands, wanted an early warning system to let him know when Walking George was in the vicinity.

In his ten years as TDC director, Beto took only one brief vacation.[20] His devotion to duty also deprived him of other pleasures. One evening, for instance, Beto was invited to the governor's mansion for a gathering of the state's political and business elite. Beto, a man who loved power and being around the powerful, wanted to attend in the worst way. The evening of the party, however, there was a killing at the system's Ramsey unit. Without hesitating, Beto went straight to the prison and forgot about the lavish affair in Austin. In this and other respects, Beto practiced what he preached about the all-encompassing nature of a prison official's responsibility for what happens inside his institution. Beto has stated:

> We are by nature creatures who tend to absolve ourselves of any responsibility for failures while laying claim to all surrounding successes. We are prone to blame our stars, not ourselves. . . . That is the great problem with most prison managers, past and present. The institutions deteriorate, problems mount, and they find excuses where they should be searching for and finding real solutions.

Beto held himself strictly accountable for the quality of life inside the prisons and saw to it that his staff followed suit. One of Beto's policies was that every warden was to handle any disturbance immediately and in perfect accordance with the relevant official procedures. They were not to call the director until the problem had either been resolved or gotten completely out of hand. Early in Beto's tenure, a group of inmates refused to go to work on the prison farm and threatened violence. To meet what he considered to be a "test" by the inmates, and to give his wardens a first-hand demonstration of the kind of prompt, proportionate action he was henceforth to require of them, Beto summoned a half-dozen wardens to the prison. He spent a few minutes reasoning with the inmates about their action, its illegality, and the disciplinary consequences of their refusal to work. When they did not respond, he ordered the wardens to mount horses and equipped each of them with a weapon. He then commanded them to put "number one hoe squad" to work immediately, "defending yourselves as necessary." Before the wardens had ridden more than a few feet the inmates resumed their work. Word of this incident spread like wildfire throughout the system. As one long-term TDC inmate recalled: "Old Beto couldn't be beat, the preacher man with a baseball bat in one hand, a Bible in the other."

Beto had several reasons for that action. One was his belief that in prison settings a swift and overwhelming show of official force, backed up by the resolve to use it if necessary, will almost always preclude the need to use any force and cause the inmate insurgents to "back down before too much of their ego has been invested and too much damage has been done." A second reason was the widespread doubt about his toughness. In the debate preceding his appointment, Beto was opposed by figures such as the police chief of Hamilton, Texas who wrote a letter to the Board of Corrections describing Beto as "a fine and capable man" but continued: ". . . please believe me, convicts don't need a preacher or a professor at the head of a penal institution."[21] A third reason had to do with Beto's belief about the value of such histrionics to the executive's ability to get cooperation from the staff. Staff, he reasoned, are more inclined to follow orders if they respect, admire, or are in awe of the one who issues them, and if they believe that the person in charge would himself be able and willing to carry out the orders under similar circumstances.

To a large extent, the control model grew out of a simple set of assumptions about the nature of human association that Beto had developed before becoming prison director. As Beto explained these assumptions:

> When Robinson Crusoe was alone, he was a law unto himself.
> But when Friday arrived, things had to change. When there
> are two or more people, there must be some way, tacit or
> overt, to regulate social intercourse, to distribute rights,
> privileges, and so on. This is true of all human institu-
> tions. . . . It is especially true in prisons since prisoners are
> generally people who have not been successful at complying
> with such rules or norms of behavior in the past.

Beto saw tight controls as the requisite condition for the success of work, education, and other inmate activities. "Prisons," he said, "must be safe and lawful. . . . Because you can't have other things unless and until you've got control. I've always been a prison reformer, but not the kind that blithely ignores the need for order as a condition for treatment." In a similar vein, Beto justified his policy of designating all prisons as maximum-security facilities on the grounds that any inmate classification system, even the most sophisticated one, is bound to make some errors; aggressive, predatory inmates may end up in lower-security settings while weaker inmates may end up in "heavier company." Moreover, Beto reasoned, the implicit message embraced by those who work in lower-custody prisons is that rules can be bent and supervision can be relaxed. "A relaxed prison administration," he averred, "is one that is looking for trouble." Finally, he argued that "it is always easier to loosen controls than to tighten controls."

But the control model was anchored in something more profound than the simple desire for control. As Beto himself often observed, if control of the inmates were the only goal, then the rest of TDC's correctional program—the educational services, the emphasis on work, and so on—would have been unnecessary at best, irrational at worst. Instead, it was Beto's religious beliefs as a Lutheran theologian and minister that called forth the control system's multiple dimensions. In eulogizing his friend and political ally, State Representative W. S. "Bill" Heatly, Beto unintentionally but eloquently expressed these beliefs. He began with the words of Saint Matthew 25:35–36: ". . . for I was hungry and ye gave me meat; I was thirsty and ye have me drink. . . . I was in prison, and ye visited me." Beto eulogized Heatly as a man who had anguished over the downtrodden and the dispossessed. Heatly, said Beto, "demanded fair and humane treatment for the poor, the stupid, and inept in our prison system. . . ." Heatly had fought for those who had "no alumni association, no lobby, no economic vested interest to plead their cause." Then, in the most touching and revealing part of his eulogy, Beto noted that Heatly had been called a "ruthless practitioner of political coercion": "If that assessment were true, (and it isn't), then let it be said loudly and clearly today that he exercised that coercion in behalf of those whom our Lord characterizes as the hungry, the thirsty, the sick, the stranger, the naked, and the imprisoned."

The same could be said of Beto's leadership as director of TDC. At the base of his political and administrative initiatives was a belief in the moral necessity of seeking and wielding worldly power to protect and guide those who, for whatever reasons, were unable or unwilling to protect and guide themselves. To discipline men who had behaved badly, to educate them, to instill in them a respect for duly constituted authority and a spirit not averse to hard labor, and to do so even against their will was to Beto the natural administrative course. To interest powerful outside interests in the welfare of the inmates, to court governors, key legislators, journalists, and others who might aid his mission was to Beto the only proper political approach.

To this day, both the control model and the man who fathered it are held in reverence by many TDC veterans. Especially among line correctional staff, however, this reverence is tempered by the feeling that, as one officer said, "Dr. Beto was a great man who everybody admired, but he wasn't at all like one of the boys. He made everybody do right. He could freeze a man—convict or boss—with a stare . . . like he was looking into your heart, finding evil, and putting you back to honesty." Another veteran TDC official seemed to grasp the nature of Beto's leadership: "He was as tough as nails, but he had a big ol' bleeding heart. . . . You know Dr. Beto calls himself a liberal? I don't know, but I guess it's true. He's the only damn liberal I ever thought the world of."

Beto's predecessor as director was another dynamic, if more conventional, prison leader, O. B. Ellis. Ellis ran the system from 1947 till his death in late 1961. It was under Ellis that TDC's massive agribusiness complex was started and preliminary efforts were made to develop prison industries. Beto viewed Ellis as a mentor worthy of emulation, but he did not agree with many of Ellis's practices and changed them quickly, often riding roughshod over wardens who liked "the way Mr. Ellis had done things."

Shortly after coming to office, Beto formed a group to study the system's disciplinary practices and, finding that rewards and punishments were administered differently from prison to prison, drafted rules and procedures to remedy the situation and saw to it that they were followed to the letter. Under Ellis, hundreds of inmates had been labelled "incorrigible" and were kept under conditions that prevented them from working, going to school, or doing much of anything beyond sitting in their cells. Beto ordered that they be released and put to work. Those who refused to work were placed in solitary confinement on a bland diet until they "saw the light." He hired doctors and other professionals to identify the system's mentally disabled and made special provisions for these inmates. He curtailed the rather liberal inmate property policy that had existed under Ellis, ordering that inmates be deprived of radios and other nonessentials.

Under Beto's leadership, the system's prison industries were developed and soon TDC became the country's most economically productive correctional agency. Everything from food to inmate clothing was produced, as Beto phrased it, "by the inmates for the inmates." Such dramatic measures were possible only because Beto was forever reaching out to the state's political and business leaders for help and winning their unqualified support. During his first year as director, for instance, Beto lobbied key legislators for a law that would enable the system to sell its industrial goods. Senate Bill 338 was passed. It created an industrial revolving fund and made it incumbent upon other state agencies to purchase products from TDC, provided that the quality was satisfactory and the price was right. Beto also obtained funds for a number of major construction and renovation projects. Five years into his directorship, Beto moved the department into new headquarters built directly across the street from the Walls unit. In the same year, Senate Bill 35 was passed, creating the first fully accredited prison educational system in the country. Throughout his tenure Beto instituted programs for special-needs inmates such as "Operation Kick-It" for drug abusers. Ever sensitive to the need for high staff morale, Beto initiated a host of service awards, many of which he presented personally.

A list of Beto's initiatives as director would run on for several pages. To mention just one more, in 1969 he engineered the passage of House Bill No. 535. This bill created a work-release program which allowed selected inmates with a remaining sentence of six to eighteen months to be employed in a nearby community, returning to prison at the end of each work day. The point is that few of these measures could have been taken without the unflagging political support garnered by Beto. Walter L. Pfluger, a member of the Texas Board of Corrections for over twelve years, recounted:

> Dr. George Beto was a strict disciplinarian and a man of high character and ability. Under his leadership, the Texas prison system became a model for other states. . . . He surrounded himself with highly competent staff, he had the full cooperation of the Board of Corrections and a good rapport with the members of the Legislature.[22]

Dorsey B. Hardeman, who served on the Senate Finance Committee for twenty-two years, related his "very high regard for Dr. Beto." Beto had enlisted Hardeman's support on a number of projects. Hardeman, in turn, had relied on Beto for help in getting parole laws changed.[23] Another former board member, Fred W.

Shield, recalled Beto's successes in mustering outside support while taking "care of the inmates in the finest way possible."[24]

In chapter three, we noted the favorable opinions of Beto held by former Texas governors John B. Connally and Preston Smith. Another former Texas governor, Price Daniel (1957–1963), also expressed a high opinion of Beto's political skills as a prison executive. Daniel's involvement in Texas corrections stretched back to 1947 when he helped then Governor Beauford Jester bring O. B. Ellis to Texas. Daniel recalled:

> Every governor from then on took a sincere interest in the system, but I must say that during my administration every bit of credit goes to Dr. Beto and Pete Coffield and his Board members. Beto and Coffield were responsible for the Legislature's interest in the system, and they also kept the Governor and the media informed and supportive. What I am trying to say is that these and other strong individuals influenced the political environment, and that the resulting favorable environment nurtured the system well.[25]

Even after resigning as corrections director in 1972, Beto continued to wield major influence in the state. Beto had no small hand in picking W. J. Estelle as his successor. He was also influential in bringing Lane McCotter to the helm. Texas governor Mark White relied on Beto for advice on a wide range of criminal justice issues.

Beto's political skills were, so far as one can tell, self-taught. His practices within the organization, however, were influenced heavily by Stateville's Warden Joseph Ragen, whom Beto had known personally and admired deeply. According to Beto, Ragen reinforced his belief that, when it comes to managing prisons, there is no substitute for an attention to the details of what is happening inside the institutions. The "little things," as Beto described them, were manifest in the way that prison authorities related to inmates and paid attention to their concerns. As one example, Beto told of visiting two units on the same day, each of which was serving the same meal of hot dogs, french fries, and assorted relishes. "At one unit," he recalled, "the rolls were served warm, the hot dogs were served individually, and the servers had a calm, friendly disposition. At the other unit, the hot dogs were placed in buns that had just exited the refrigerator, thrown together in a heap on a tray, with few condiments and some rather mean-spirited servers. The inmates at the former prison had a pleasant meal pleasantly served, and it showed in their behavior; the inmates at the other prison had a miserable meal served in a miserable fashion, and they behaved more miserably."

As Beto walked the institutions, any inmate was allowed to approach him with a question or, more importantly, give him an uncensored letter requesting some favor or reporting some impropriety. Beto would follow up on each and every one of these letters. "These encounters," said Beto, "were a source of useful intelligence and a barometer of conditions." During one of his Sunday morning tours, an inmate told Beto that hot biscuits were no longer available at the prison. Apparently, the inmate kitchen workers had complained that making the biscuits required them to rise too early and to work too hard. Beto ordered the warden to order the inmates to make the biscuits or the inmates would find themselves working back in the fields, while the warden might find himself working back in the cellblocks.

Beto was both director and chief chaplain of the Texas prison system. He built temples and other places of worship inside the prisons and ordered his subordinates to permit the inmates regular and easy access to religious services. Beto's dedication to religious services, however, was a distant second to his dedication to prison order. Religious activity among inmates that might in any way lead to violence or conflict was not permitted. Beto wrote and implemented a regulation that read:

> In any society there is the liklihood of occasional, or even frequent, conflict between an individual's religion-inspired inclinations, or obligations, and the need to comply with civil authority. . . . Institutional rules, regulations and policies in regard to the safety of the individual, the safety of the institution, and acceptable conduct of committed offenders shall apply to all services of worship, religious activities and meetings of a religious nature . . . as deemed necessary for administrative control. . . . Growth in the stability and moral strength of inmates may be . . . founded upon the acceptance of basic religious beliefs. . . . This must be accomplished within the context of the requirements of maintaining security, safety and orderly conditions in the institution.

The question of whether prison officials have any affirmative duty to accommodate inmates of all religious affiliations has reached the Supreme Court only once. In the 1972 case of *Cruz* v. *Beto*, the

Supreme Court held that Texas prison authorities acted improperly when they prohibited a Buddhist inmate from worshiping in the prison chapel and proselytizing among the other inmates.[26] Beto maintained that the action was justified on the grounds that the inmate's religious activities had led to conflict among the prisoners. He stressed that other inmates, a majority of whom were Christians, were also strictly prohibited from distributing religious materials or displaying medals or symbols that might create disciplinary or custodial problems.

Beto fought attempts from whatever quarter that might weaken the control system. The thing most likely to weaken it, Beto had maintained, was a failure of executive leadership. When he assumed the director's post in 1962, he announced that he would resign in ten years. In 1972, despite his enormous popularity and cries from state officials, the staff, the press, and a number of prison reform groups to stay on, Beto did what he had promised. Strong executive leadership, he reasoned, could not be sustained for more than a decade. "For one thing," Beto said, "you lose your courage. You come to know your subordinates too well. You learn too much about the legislature and so become too schooled in 'the art of the possible.' The prison director must attempt the impossible. . . . Fresh ideas and energy fade with time."

In the early 1970s prison systems throughout the country were faced with a barrage of seemingly intractable management problems—increasing inmate populations, violence, court intervention, correctional officer unionization, deteriorating physical plants, rising costs, the prisoners' rights movement, prison gangs, tighter budgets. Scholarly treatises and popular writings challenged the morality of imprisonment and raised tough questions about whether prisons rehabilitate, deter, or even punish offenders enough to justify using them so extensively. Beto had done what he could to, as he put it, "manage and master" these developments. "Any prison executive," he argued, "must be pro-active. . . . If you are good at the job, you will be able to anticipate court intervention and take steps to forestall it, you will be able to work through political and budgetary constraints in the interests of safe, lawful prisons." Virtually alone among the nation's leading corrections figures, Beto blamed prison managers for the troubled state of the nation's penal institutions. Most of all, he blamed the "thoroughgoing incompetence" of those who led the nation's prison systems. "Your good prison director," he insisted, "must be a wise prince. . . . He must

Correctional Change: The Case of Texas Prisons

In late 1985, Dr. George Beto, for thirteen years a professor of criminal justice at an east Texas university minutes from most of the prisons he had run, sat motionless as members of his graduate seminar who worked in TDC lectured the class about their experiences. Beto's head drooped as they described in graphic detail how common it now was for Texas prisoners, especially new ones, to be raped or gang raped; how every shakedown of cells turned up hundreds of weapons and other contraband; how certain inmate leaders ran prostitution and drug rings; how prison gangs were putting out contracts on—that is, hiring inmates to kill—staff and other prisoners; how most of the staff was neither willing nor able to prevent violence; how inmate classrooms and work places were, like the cellblocks, sites of inmate idleness punctuated by disorders; how the officers, fearing inmate reprisals for disciplinary action and with little more than personal survival and a paycheck in view, were ignoring most rule violations, major and minor.

Beto's sullen reaction to this information was surprising, since two years earlier, he had predicted that the quality of life inside Texas prisons would take such a dramatic nosedive. In 1983, Beto said: "The Texas prison system is not slipping but has already begun to fall. It is only a matter of years, maybe months, before we hear the crash and see the rubble. I do grieve a bit over the death of the control model. . . . If Joseph Ragen were alive he would no doubt feel the same way about the prisons in Illinois, especially Stateville. He is probably turning in his grave."

In 1984 and 1985, a total of fifty-two inmates were murdered and over 700 were stabbed in Texas prisons. More serious violence occurred in those two years than had occurred in the previous decade. As the disorder mounted, inmate participation in treatment and educational programs became erratic, inmate living quarters ceased to sparkle, and recreational privileges were curtailed. Hailed only a decade earlier as one of the nation's best penal systems, TDC became one of the very worst.

The process of correctional change in Texas was driven mainly by three interrelated factors: a major flaw in the control model created by Beto (the building tender system); a landmark court case which changed both the internal operations in the prisons and the agency's perception in the political community; and changes in personnel and managerial philosophy. The particulars of this instance of correctional change are complex and interesting in their own right. Our reason for analyzing them, however, is to discover something of more general import about the administrative conditions that make for safe and civilized prisons. While there are several tragic elements to this case, it teaches a heartening lesson: there is absolutely nothing inevitable about poor prison conditions and much that can be done to overcome them.

THE ROTTEN CRUTCH: TEXAS BUILDING TENDERS

The Texas control model, as we have seen, was a highly disciplined and formalized system of prison management which placed a premium on the rigorous enforcement of rules and regulations. Inmates were rewarded for good behavior, punished for bad behavior, and normally prevented from associating in ways likely to foster individual or group misconduct. Inmates "did their own time," officers went "by the book," and atop the organizational hierarchy sat a hands-on correctional leader who fostered a sense of mission within the agency, rallied the staff around a common correctional philosophy, and cultivated political and popular support beyond the walls.

The one decidedly sociological element in the control model was the so-called building tender (BT) system. As we have already discussed, Beto had fathered the BT system as a way of formalizing what the sociologist Gresham Sykes had described as the informal alliance between inmates and staff.[1] The BT system was a calculated gamble aimed at turning the leaders of inmate society into the official allies of the administration.

Beto did everything imaginable to tilt the odds in the administration's favor. For one thing, he hand picked his "super-trusties." Through his practice of visiting the prisons frequently and unannounced, encouraging inmates to send him sealed letters, and interviewing selected prisoners prior to their release, Beto learned quickly of abuses of official authority, including those involving BTs. The record shows that he initiated prompt investigations (often conducting them himself) and fired immediately any TDC officials who, in his judgment, had violated their official trust.

Under Beto, any BT who grasped or demanded illicit privileges in return for his help in turning cell doors, providing information, or watching the officers' backs, was normally found out, demoted, and in some cases, sent back into the fields to do stoop labor flanked by "fish" (new inmates). As several veterans of TDC (both inmates and staff) recalled, Beto permitted neither BTs nor staff to "get too big for their britches." As Beto himself explained:

> The control model was, at heart, a system in which power was highly centralized. Power can be used well or ill, but unchecked it tends, as has been observed by better minds, to corrupt. It was therefore imperative that abuses, most especially abuses by staff members, be uncovered quickly and stopped. . . . I assumed a personal role in this both to protect the inmates from illicit coercion and to show all concerned that I condemned corruption and had the means, and the will, to eliminate it.

When Beto resigned from TDC's top post in 1972, most parts of the control model were well institutionalized—the paramilitary procedures; the liberal awarding of good time; the stress on inmate discipline, work, and education. The BT system, however, was never a well-integrated part of the model. Throughout his tenure, Beto and his close aides were aware that, without unremitting efforts to keep it honest, the BT system could easily degenerate into the very situation of inmate dominance and corrupt inmate-staff relations that it was meant to forestall. As one high-ranking TDC veteran recalled:

> The tenders were always like a sort of sore thumb of the control model. . . . I mean here you had the bosses and the "Yes sirs" and the steady discipline, all of it done formal-like and run by the authorities. The line between the authorities and the convicts was clear as could be . . . we didn't even shake hands till they were released. But then there were the tenders, inmates who were "first among equals" so long as they did our bidding and didn't step out of line or grow cocky or get favors. . . . But you know Dr. Beto, he'd never let it get out of control! . . . No inmate who, like they say, "rape a snake through a brick wall" could be a BT, no boss could let him with "Walking George" around.

Beto's high degree of personal involvement in keeping the BT system from degenerating into a con-boss system or some other species of inmate self-rule was a symptom of its essentially prebureaucratic nature. The fact that Beto had to exploit fully his blanketing and charismatic leadership merely to keep the system on an even keel was an early signpost of its weakness. Virtually every other part of his control model could be mastered by any competent and dedicated team of successors, and be made to work under changing conditions; but not so the BT system. In deference to sociological theory, Beto had, in fact, rested his otherwise strong formal system of administrative control against a delicate and dangerous managerial prop. In the BT system, the control model contained the seeds of its own destruction.

Under Beto's hand-picked successor, W. J. Estelle, the number of TDC inmates multiplied by the thousands and the agency's prison stock more than doubled. Though in most respects a brilliant prisons man, Estelle was no Beto. Under Beto, the BT system was like an overly sharp knife wielded by a master chef in a calm kitchen. This knife was handed to Estelle who, by comparison, was a good short-order cook behind a busy counter.

By the late 1970s, administrative authority in TDC had become more decentralized than at any time since prior to the Beto administration. Wardens became more autonomous and the administrative regimen inside TDC began to vary somewhat from prison to prison. For instance, in response to legal challenges, the agency had adopted a more elaborate inmate grievance procedure than anything known in the Beto era. In some TDC prisons, this new procedure was followed to the letter; in others it was ignored; in still others even the rudimentary system of filing and adjudicating inmate complaints that had existed under Beto was forgotten. Estelle, a younger man with a mostly officebound style of executive leadership, was no "Walking Jim." Word of abuses did not always trickle up to the central office in Huntsville, and there was no upward-flowing, independent channel of information which would have enabled Estelle and his aides to check the veracity of reports from the field, or caused them to ask why no such reports were forthcoming.

Predictably, while most other parts of the control model survived and were even strengthened under Estelle, the BT system ran amok. By the mid-1970s at some TDC prisons, the BT system had become nothing more than a con-boss system. As in other such systems, BTs were allowed to carry weapons and were given illicit privileges for "keeping things quiet." In some instances, this meant administering beatings to fellow inmates who had defied an officer or refused to work. At a few institutions, the administration became a virtual hostage to the BTs, relying on them to perform many or most custodial functions. In at least one prison, the weekend staff consisted of only a dozen officers who supervised some forty BTs who opened cell doors, made counts, searched cells, and performed other essential functions.

By the late 1970s, the BT system had given rise to horrible abuses of inmates by their specially annointed peers and had permitted, even encouraged, the victimization of inmates by staff. The corruption of the BTs was infectious. Inmates abused by staff, or by BTs at the behest of staff, were often unable to get a fair hearing (or any hearing at all) within TDC. In a perversion of the ésprit de corps and sense of mission which had characterized the agency, wrongdoers at some prisons were shielded by their coworkers and, in some cases, by their administrative superiors.

It is important, however, to note that, contrary to popular interpretations and the perceptions of many TDC insiders, the BT system was never a major systemic feature of Texas prison management. Estelle was not Beto, but neither was he blind nor totally incapable of identifying problems and disciplining those who created them. Except for those few TDC prisons where the BT system evolved into a full-fledged con-boss system, the centrality of the BTs to TDC operations, even in the last days of the Estelle

administration, has been exaggerated wildly, no less by the
agency's defenders than by its harshest critics. The BT system
was an administrative cancer that spread unevenly throughout the
Texas prison bureaucracy.[2] The BTs were never more than a marginal, if ultimately corrosive, feature of the tight formal system of
rules and regulations that was the heart of the Texas control model
and that had enabled TDC to run cost-effective prisons where an
inmate could "do his own time," live safely, take advantage of
treatment opportunities, work, and (like it or not) habituate himself to norms of civility and law-abidingness.

In their failure to acknowledge this crucial fact, Texas scholars,
national journalists, certain of TDC's "old guard" advocates, and
William Wayne Justice, the Federal District Court Judge who
eventually condemned the agency and ordered an end to the BT
system, became strange but certain bedfellows. Together they
fostered a powerful myth, one which was later used to explain the
explosive upturn in prison violence that followed the abolition of
the BT system; namely, that the demise of the BTs created a
"power vacuum," which was filled inevitably by a new, more vicious, less controllable cadre of inmate leaders who headed budding, California-style prison gangs. This pseudo-sophisticated but
appealing argument, like Beto's original justification for the BT
system itself, was predicated on the constellation of sociological
ideas about prisons discussed in the opening chapter of this book.
It gave rise to the deadly and self-defeating fallacy that, as one
journalist captured it, "the state needed the BTs and both sides
knew it."[3] In truth, from the very beginning, the BTs were nothing but a rotten crutch, a species of inmate self-rule that contributed nothing essential to TDC's control efforts.

Judge Justice had worried publicly about what would happen to
TDC once the BTs were removed from the cellblocks. Indeed, in
1983, he saw to it that two sociologists were hired to analyze the
situation. They concluded that more guards should be hired, and
quickly. Assuming that hiring more officers will necessarily improve the administration of a prison is like assuming that hiring
more violinists will necessarily improve the sound of an orchestra.
The new TDC "violinists" were hurried into the cellblocks, many of
them without even the most basic preservice training. Their in-
service training amounted to a socialization in the false but self-
fulfilling prophecy that, without the BTs, nothing could be done to
gain (or regain) control. There was a rapidly shrinking minority of

veteran TDC officers and higher-ranking officials who knew better, but only a very few of them cared to fight for and demonstrate the efficacy of the rest of the control model. In short, by the dawn of 1984 the agency's sense of mission had been put asunder.

As shall be revealed in greater detail in the ensuing sections of this chapter, the increase in serious prison disorders which occurred in TDC happened because of the administrative instability and mistakes resulting from a change in the agency's legal and political environment. In essence, it was not because it lost the BTs, but because the Texas keepers clung to them so dearly, that TDC began to fall; it was not because its leaders dismantled the BT system, but because they simultaneously abandoned the formal regimen of controls, that the once-proud and well-performing agency became an infamous one.

Fiercely loyal to his predecessor and to the correctional credo and model bequeathed to him, Estelle defended TDC against all comers, including the federal courts. The defense, like the challenge itself, was undiscriminating. In the minds of its critics as well as its defenders, the BTs were equated with the control model rather than being seen as a diseased part of an otherwise healthy system, a cancer ripe for the cutting. TDC staff at every level— wardens, junior officers, prison doctors, department secretaries— rallied around Estelle. Few believed that he would be driven from his position. By 1984, however, Estelle had left the agency. His legion of supporters in TDC were bitter, demoralized, and confused. In the face of the court's order, and under new and less popular leadership, those TDC administrators who had allowed the BTs to assume a central role in daily operations surrendered not only their corrupt inmate allies but their formal means of control as well. In a comment typical of TDC veterans who lived through the turmoil, one ranking agency official confided sadly:

> We threwed the baby out with the dirty bathwater. We had a good program that didn't have nothing to do with the building tenders. Hell, I worked places in this system where we always made it run by the book, like a military operation. That's the way it was under Dr. Beto and mostly under Mr. Estelle. But then, here and there, we stopped going by the rules cause it just seemed easier that way, and nobody caught on at first. The big thing was the tenders, letting them get away with things they shouldn't. . . . Pretty soon you start to

feel like you can't do without them. You become a hostage, they become "boss." Then you forget how things was done right. . . .

COURT INTERVENTION: THE RUIZ CASE

There is a growing body of commentary on court-induced changes in the way that prisons operate. Little of it, however, is based on empirical knowledge about the causes and consequences of court intervention into penal affairs; and most of it ignores sources of correctional change other than judges. Broadly speaking, there are three schools of speculation. One school argues that the courts have emboldened the inmates and weakened the staff. Members of this school blame the courts for rising tides of prison violence.[4] A second school maintains that the courts have merely forced prison administrators to use their ostensibly vast discretionary authority in ways that secure rather than deny prisoners' rights. Members of this school credit the courts with moving corrections "out of its dark ages."[5] Yet a third school holds that the courts have fostered a codification and formalization of prison policies and procedures resulting in "the bureaucratization of the prison."[6] Most members of this school believe that more safe and humane prisons have followed this court-inspired organizational metamorphosis.

We are numerous studies away from knowing which, if any, of these schools is correct.[7] None of them, however, fares well as an explanation for what happened to Texas prisons between 1972 and 1985. In Texas, the court was neither a villain nor a savior. Instead, it was a force for sweeping administrative changes, some of them good, some of them bad, many of them wholly unanticipated.

The litigation began shortly before Estelle's appointment. Inmate David Ruiz, a chronic offender who had been incarcerated repeatedly, sent a handwritten petition to Judge William Wayne Justice of the Eastern District Court. While in prison, Ruiz stabbed several of his fellow inmates and was often placed in solitary confinement. In his petition, Ruiz charged that conditions in "the hole" were inhumane. He claimed that he slit his wrists so that prison officials would remove him from isolation. Ruiz challenged conditions of confinement in TDC under section 1983 of the U.S. Civil Rights Act. In 1974 Judge Justice combined Ruiz's petition with those of seven other TDC inmates. The case, a class action suit, was titled *Ruiz* v. *Estelle*.[8]

In Texas, plaintiffs in cases involving damage claims are entitled to a trial by jury. Judge Justice separated the damage claims at stake in the case from the injunctive issues, thereby making his control over the litigation absolute. In addition, he instituted a procedure whereby issues not raised by the inmate plaintiffs—crowding, recreational facilities, prison land-use, and many others—came under his review. He appointed a few of the country's leading prison litigation attorneys to represent the inmates and brought in the United States Department of Justice as an adversary to the State of Texas.

The trial began on October 2, 1978, in Houston Federal Court. In the four years preceding the trial, Judge Justice imposed a number of orders on TDC. On December 30, 1975, for instance, he ordered that prison authorities be prohibited from censoring or opening inmates' mail. In 1976, he granted a Department of Justice motion to interview TDC inmates but denied a request by the State to have its attorneys present during the questioning.

The *Ruiz* trial lasted 159 days and spread over much of 1978 and 1979. On December 12, 1980, Judge Justice issued a 248-page memorandum opinion ordering sweeping changes in the way that Texas ran its prisons. Among the scores of specific changes he ordered were the following: an end to the use of the BT system; a requirement that the agency more than double its officer force and retrain veteran officers; a revision and liberalization in procedures governing the awarding of good time; a revision in the procedures for handling inmate grievances and an elaboration of the hearing process; a revision in the system's classification procedures that would reduce the number of maximum-security designations; the provision of a single cell for each inmate.

There were essentially seven major issues in the *Ruiz* case, all of them decided in favor of the plaintiffs. First, TDC was accused of using building tenders to impose a reign of terror on the inmate population. Judge Justice found that building tenders who abused their positions were not disciplined. Some BTs known by officials to be guilty of abuses nevertheless retained their jobs. Second, TDC staff were accused of brutality. Judge Justice cited the testimony of inmates who claimed that they were beaten by officers. He rejected TDC's claims that these were isolated incidents and that personnel found guilty of misusing their authority were disciplined or dismissed. Third, Judge Justice held that TDC was overcrowded. He rejected as contrary to common sense TDC's claim that what constituted a crowded prison was subject to honest debate and that the effects of double-celling on the quality of prison life were not readily apparent. He further rejected TDC's contention that the department had virtually no control over the number of inmates in its custody. He pronounced TDC's efforts to deal with the crowding problem "unimaginative." He noted that TDC could reduce its population by making a more liberal use of good time, by restoring good time to inmates who had lost it through disciplinary actions, and by recommending more inmates for parole. Without comment, he dismissed TDC's pleas that such measures would weaken or destroy the inmates' incentives for good behavior.

A fourth key issue in the case was TDC's disciplinary and inmate grievance procedures. Judge Justice challenged them as arbitrary and overly punitive. He ordered the system to elaborate its disciplinary procedures by holding hearings, establishing more elaborate grievance mechanisms, and abolishing such ambiguous infraction categories as "laziness." Fifth, the judge condemned TDC's classification system as unsophisticated and inadequate. He mocked TDC's focus on age and recidivism as the two main factors in making assignments. He ordered prison officials to take account of such factors as the inmate's "propensities toward violence" and demanded that they reduce the number of inmates designated as maximum-security felons. Sixth, Judge Justice found TDC guilty of numerous violations of fire and safety regulations. Finally, he held that the system had acted wrongly in denying inmates easy access to outside persons, especially attorneys and public officials. He ordered TDC to allow the inmates greater visiting and other privileges.

During the nine-year legal battle leading up to Judge Justice's 1980 ruling, TDC's control model had received mixed reviews. Some experts credited Texas correctional officials with running the only safe, clean, fully employed prison system in the nation. Others denounced TDC as a repressive agency that treated its inmates like slaves. The judge agreed with the system's critics, ruling that TDC imposed cruel and unusual punishment on inmates as a result of the totality of conditions in its prisons. The state appealed parts of Justice's order to the United States Court of Appeals for the Fifth Circuit.

In 1982, a decade after the litigation began, a three-judge panel upheld Justice's central finding about the unconstitutionality of conditions inside Texas prisons, but overturned several provisions of the original order. "Taken as a whole," the panel wrote, "the district court's decree administers a massive dose when it is not yet demonstrable that a lesser therapeutic measure would not suffice."[9] In one pointed remark, the panel reversed Justice's order that the prison hospital at the Walls units be upgraded or closed: "The Constitution does not require that inmates be given the kind of medical attention that judges would wish to have for themselves. . . ."[10] The panel reversed Justice's opinion that each inmate is entitled to his own cell. The appeals court overturned Justice's order, premised on the professional manuals American Correctional Association (ACA), that the department divide its prisons into management units of not more than 500 inmates. Also, the panel denied Justice's orders that TDC get his approval for any construction plans and that the reports of his special master—a court-appointed monitor of prison conditions—be treated as findings of fact.

But the appeals panel upheld most of Justice's orders, including the abolition of the building-tender system, the elaboration of inmate classification procedures, the duty of prison officials to assist inmates in obtaining regular and easy access to courts, counsel, and other outside parties, and the right of inmates to associate more freely. The panel chided TDC officials for their failure to run better prisons and warned that the "implementation of the district court's decree can become a ceaseless guerrilla war, with endless hearings, opinions and appeals, and incalculable costs."[11] The panel also warned Judge Justice and his team of monitors to "respect the right of the state to administer its own affairs so long as it does not violate the Constitution."[12]

Neither the judge and his monitors nor the Texas prison officials heeded fully the panel's warnings. The litigation continued for three more years amidst bitter charges and countercharges. The court claimed that TDC was openly defying its rulings. Prison officials, led by Director W. J. Estelle, charged that the special master and monitors were instigating trouble and provoking the inmates to organize and behave violently. Correctional practitioners outside of Texas were polarized into "pro-TDC" and "anti-TDC" camps. Some cheered at the idea that the court was, as one California prison official remarked, "dragging those good old boy wardens kicking and screaming into the twentieth century." Others rallied to the system's side fearing that if Texas prisons were ruined there would remain little to inspire prison workers in less successful systems. As one Michigan correctional worker stated: "We watched what happened in Texas and prayed that they didn't end up like us."

Thirteen years and over a billion dollars after inmate David Ruiz had sent his handritten petition to the court, the litigation drew to a close. In the May/June 1985 edition of the Texas inmate newspaper,[13] the headline read "Final Ruiz Settlement."* The paper gave a complete statement of the agreement. The back page contained an "Inmate Response Form," which inmates were to use if they wished to comment on any aspect of the agreement, raise new issues, or challenge any of the various stipulations about when and how further changes were to take effect.

ADMINISTRATIVE CHANGE AND ITS CONSEQUENCES

The *Ruiz* case changed TDC's legal and political framework and sent the agency into a state of protracted administrative turmoil and confusion. Popular and scholarly accounts have suggested that the agency purposely dragged its feet in responding to the court's decree. In truth, however, the record shows that while Estelle was making a feisty and celebrated public stand against the court and its special master, Vincent Nathan, his subordinates were directed to scratch wildly for ways to come into compliance with the court order without gutting the control model.

The Estelle administration's efforts to achieve this end were complicated and ultimately blown off course by the political storm that brewed in the midst of the *Ruiz* litigation. In 1983, two of the ten most powerful legislators in Texas were Ray Farabee and Ray Keller.[14] With the case still churning, Farabee and Keller pushed prison reform onto the political agenda. Farabee, considered by many to be the Texas Senate's most respected and influential member, sponsored three prison reform bills. Keller, a Texas House member who was reported to have won neither of the two committee assignments he had sought, used his chairmanship of

*The prison agency's compliance with various provisions of the agreement was, however, still under Judge Justice's scrutiny in 1987.

the Law Enforcement Committee to shake up TDC. Keller trained his considerable political energies on the troubled prison system, rewriting what one Texas publication termed "the traditional legislative script: give prison officials all the money they want and tell the folks back home you're for law and order."[15]

Keller sponsored legislation to take away some $200 million from TDC. He and other lawmakers ridiculed the system's performance and criticized its emphasis on maximum-security operations as ineffective and costly. The House passed a broad-gauged prison reform package without controversy. Indeed, six of the seven bills in the package were given unanimous approval.

Over the life of the *Ruiz* proceedings, TDC's political environment became less supportive and eventually turned hostile. Whereas the agency had once been cradled by its Board of Corrections and powerful legislators like Bill Heatly, it was now the object of attacks by its board and became the bête noire of important legislators such as Farabee and Keller. The litigation, however, was but one reason for TDC's increasingly frostly political climate. Al Hightower, a member of the Texas House who has represented the district where most of the prisons are based, observed that the agency's political troubles were also related to the fiscal crunch caused by declining state oil revenues. Hightower remarked: "We've always said to TDC, 'You have the best prisons in the world.' The people and the politicians said to TDC, 'Do what's best and tell us what it costs.' But now there are questions raised about how great the prisons are. The court business has not helped TDC's standing. On top of that, you have a squeeze on money."

In this fiscal context, the Texas Legislature began investigations into TDC's business practices. Lawmakers, newspaper editors, and several members of the Board of Corrections echoed the charge that TDC's budget had hitherto been treated like a sacred cow. It was alleged that the agency had never been subject to serious legislative oversight and that, as a result, its finances, not to mention its internal operations, had become terribly mismanaged. There erupted a series of scandals, most of them minor, concerning everything from unaccounted for tons of prison beef to the "overly generous" emolument program for TDC employees. The national and state press took note of these developments and linked them to the ongoing reports about unconstitutional prison conditions emanating from Judge Justice's chambers and the plaintiffs' lawyers.

The response of Estelle and the agency's staff to this barrage of criticism was stubborn but far from wholly unyielding. Mainly, the response was a mix of wounded pride and contempt, tempered by muddled perceptions and more than a twinge of self-doubt. As one veteran TDC employee recalled:

> The judge and the politicians and the newspapers was all over us like stink on a skunk. No sooner did we fix one thing, broken or not, then we was told we'd better fix another, and another. . . . We didn't think so much was wrong to begin with, so it just got crazier and crazier. . . . I worked here the better part of my adult life, and, honest to you, I never seen nor heard the half of what they was accusing. . . . If I'd a believed TDC was all they said, I'd a been after it too.

From the director's chair, Estelle challenged the agency's critics to measure TDC's performance in terms of safety, cleanliness, and programs. He defied them to prove their assorted allegations and lambasted what he considered to be their naïve assumptions about the way prisons operate. Several persons close to Estelle advised him to take a more accommodating stance toward the court, the special master, critical legislators, journalists, and others. But during his career, first in California and later in Montana and Texas, Estelle had developed a reputation as a gifted corrections man who would never back away from a fight. For him, discretion was never the better part of valor. He chose to battle the agency's detractors and mobilized his troops to demonstrate that TDC's prisons were "the best, or among the best, in the country, bar none." Estelle recalled:

> Certain state officials responsible for representing the department in adversarial proceedings were more willing to file with the plaintiffs than to contest the charges with facts in hand. . . . For some there was political expediency, for others ideological motives that led them to either tear at or abandon what appeared to be a wounded agency. . . . I was determined, as all of us were, to fight for our ideas about how to run prisons. We had self-proclaimed prison reformers telling us how horrible we were at doing our jobs. Of course, what these people knew about prisons you could fit into a tiny thimble with room to spare. They wanted to effect changes and baptize every change a reform. Well, every change in a

prison setting is not a reform and correctional institutions are ill-equipped to handle sudden administrative changes. . . . We were wrong on some things, short as hell in some areas of the operation. We were willing to usher in reasonable changes and remedies. But we had been doing most things very well and would not be part of simple-minded so-called reforms that, as sure as I'm sitting here, were bound to kill inmates, injure staff, and destroy our programs.

Estelle's principled intransigence was mirrored, albeit crudely, by his staff. The thrust of the court's decree and the other charges against TDC were caricatured and exaggerated by many of the uniformed officers. In a typical remark, one veteran officer stated: "The judge says an inmate can spit in your face. I won't have it. That's no good for the inmate! What's it teach him but to misbehave in the way he's always done?" A warden asserted: "We don't need people coming in here—judges, monitors, politicians, professors—telling us what to do. We have our lives invested in these prisons. Our inmates are kept well. They're not getting raped right and left. . . . But I guess that's what the judge and them others want."

Of course, an increase in rapes, assaults, murders, and other forms of prison disorder was intended by none of those who attacked the system. Their attacks, however, set in motion a series of changes in Texas prison management that had precisely that consequence. But before going any further, it is important to stress that the primary responsibility for what happened rests on TDC itself. For while the judicial and political assaults on the agency made it more difficult for Texas keepers to protect and guide the inmates in their custody, there was absolutely nothing in either the *Ruiz* opinion or, more broadly, in the new legal and political constraints that were foisted upon the agency, that made it impossible to govern prisons well.

As we have seen, the BT system was a flawed feature of Beto's control model that came to roost under Estelle. The most puzzling and perverse aspect of TDC's legal defense in *Ruiz* was its assertion that the BT system—documented in agency pamphlets, experienced by thousands of inmates and staff, and known even outside of Texas as one feature of the control model—did not exist. There was, to be sure, a pale plausibility to this denial, for the BT system was so visibly at odds with the rest of the Texas control model that it was possible to conceive of TDC without it. After Estelle's resignation, the agency's lawyers conceded the existence of BTs and agreed to end their use.

In the wake of the political and judicial tumult, some Texas keepers relaxed the unyielding attention to basic security procedures that had been a hallmark of TDC management. In some prisons, officers started letting inmates congregate freely out on the yards and inside the cellblocks. The formal chain of command and standard operating procedures governing cell searches, contraband interception, and the like, were weakened and in some places abandoned. As one TDC veteran observed: "Nobody felt like keeping it up. All you heard was that we beat the inmates, we didn't care for the inmates, that we let them rip up each other. . . . Then the outsiders are giving us orders left and right. So we let go, let everything go."

Estelle's successor, Raymond Procunier, dismantled the BT system where it still existed. At the same time, however, his administration presided over and quickened the dismantling of the rest of the control model. The first effort was a great administrative blessing, the second a horrible administrative curse. Procunier and his top associates underestimated the degree to which TDC's formal administrative regimen had been weakened. Instead of attempting to rescue and resuscitate what remained of Beto's control model—the tight routine of numbering, counting, checking, locking, searching, and so forth—they allowed it to atrophy, speeding its demise, and further alienating the veteran staff.

Procunier set out to run TDC the way he had run other prison systems, including California's. When he took over TDC, he was billed by the national, state, and local press as a "nonpolitical, nonideological" prison executive. Professional organs such as *Corrections Digest* hailed him as a "fire fighter" on his way to clean up the burgeoning judicial, political, and administrative mess in TDC.[16] Upon his arrival in Huntsville, Procunier's rhetoric was characteristically bold. So were his actions. He fired a number of wardens and central office personnel. He hired and consulted ex-California prison officials to assist him in "cleaning house." He toured the prisons, pumping the hands of inmates and staff alike, stopping to trade jokes with some of the system's most dangerous inmates as if he had known them for a lifetime. When a hostage crisis occurred, Procunier rushed to the scene and offered himself to the armed inmate in exchange for the hostages. Through such gestures Procunier won an initial round of support from all concerned—the court, the legislature, the governor, the press, reform groups, and some TDC personnel at all levels.

But it was not long before Procunier began to introduce policies that eroded his support. He demanded that the field personnel respond immediately to a barrage of administrative changes, some of them mandated by the *Ruiz* decree and concomitant political pressures, but many of them widely known to be the product of his desire to impose what many veteran officers derided as "California management" on TDC. He threatened to fire anybody at any level who did not jump into compliance with his official dicta. He warned the staff that good faith efforts were not enough. His administration, in effect, heaped insult upon injury by, among other measures, forcing the staff to take lie-detector tests. Most TDC workers considered the tests to be a slap in the face, questioning their loyalty to the agency, not to mention their personal integrity. In a typical remark, one officer said: "Mr. Procunier thinks we're a bunch of redneck guards who like kicking the s——t out of convicts. That's his big mistake. You bet there are a few bad apples. But most of us love TDC and he's treating us like a pack of godd——n contraband carriers or liars."

Soon the perception among most of the field staff was that Procunier was allied with the agency's detractors. More damaging still, among the officers it became a bit of conventional wisdom that "Procunier is more concerned about the convicts than he is about us." No matter that this perception was untrue, the staff believed it, and nothing was done to make them feel otherwise. Among uniformed staff, the turnover rate began to rise, jumping fivefold at some prisons. Hundreds of TDC officers took the unprecedented and once unimaginable step of forming a union. For the first time since before the Beto era, TDC staff began to identify themselves in opposition to the system's director and the central office.

From the officers' perspective, their jobs had become unnecessarily complicated, dangerous, and thankless. In chapter three we shadowed Major Scott of the Walls unit. In the wake of the changes, Scott declared: "A place where there's no order is not worthy of the name prison. . . . The discipline here isn't what it was, not even months ago. It's getting to the point where I have to say 'please' and 'sir' to a convict in order to get him to behave right." Whereas Scott used to routinely order inmates from the tiers or command them to disperse out on the yard, he now hesitated.

Inmates would file bogus grievances against officers and make charges against them for simply doing their duty. "You'd be holding hearings all day if you tried to enforce the more minor rules now," Scott said. Furthermore, officers were simply uncertain about what rules were in effect and how, if at all, to enforce them. Another TDC veteran, Major Brock of the Ellis unit, observed:

> I've worked in this business for twenty years, and things have never been worse. . . . If an officer sees a fight between inmates he has to stop and ask himself, "What's my authority today? Can I stop it? How can I without being made a patsy for some fake brutality claim?" . . . There were rules to cover every aspect of the operation. . . . But today we have to let the little things go. This is something new here though I've heard that's the way they've been doing it in some places for years. I would be afraid to enter prisons in other states, and I've seen it all. I pray that Texas doesn't go that way, to the point where officers are afraid and the inmates fear each other.

A central office administrator echoed Scott and Brock's observations: "Compliance of staff to our orders or of inmates to staff orders was never really a major problem here. . . . But now, with the court action and the rest, every day has become a goal line defense. . . . Officers must look at the bulletin board each day to see if the essence of the job they had the other day has changed. . . . How would you like to be given a new syllabus every day to teach from? One day you emphasize one theme, the next day another. Pretty soon everyone is confused; people get disgusted, some quit, and things just break down."

Gradually inmates began to taunt the officers about the confused state of official authority. "Every time you turned around," one officer remarked, "some inmate would say, 'Try to make me do that motherf——r and I'll write a writ on your ass.' It didn't make no never mind whether you was telling him to button his shirt proper or to stop hanging around another inmate's cell. You act on him, and another one would say you was the instigator, that you whipped him or something. Then nobody at the top backs you up. So you feel like, 'Hell, I'll let them do whatever and just protect myself.' What else you going to do?" Even proud and dedicated veterans like Major Scott of the Walls unit adapted to the administrative confusion and dwindling officer authority by acting less and less on non-life-threatening inmate rule violations: "You've got to know when you look at your wife and kids in the morning that you will be coming home that night. You try to do things like before, and you may come home, but you will be ornery and exhausted. So I look after mostly the big things now and take it one day at a time."

For the average TDC officer, life inside the prison had indeed become more complex, less predictable, harder, and less rewarding. But there was nothing about the new administrative regime that made it less possible for staff to keep a close watch on the tools in the industrial plant, to frisk inmates regularly, to install metal detectors, to swiftly segregate inmate predators, to identify and bring special charges against prison gang organizers, to limit the flow of inmates in and out of the cellblocks or around the dining halls, to reward inmates for good behavior, or to take the scores of other basic measures that would prevent or reduce individual or group misconduct. But the inspiration for the demoralized ranks to take or reinstitute such measures would have had to come from above. In particular, the director would have had to take the lead in shoring up staff confidence against the unceasing criticism and rewarding staff for the kind of attention to formal rule enforcement that had once been the norm inside Texas prisons.

The Procunier administration, however, took few such measures. As we have already seen, Procunier was not the kind of executive who paid a great deal of attention to the details of a problem. Rarely did he follow through to see whether one of his ad hoc responses to a correctional conundrum had produced the desired outcome. Instead, "the Pro" was celebrated as a leader with some kind of sixth sense for handling certain types of prison problems. Michigan's Ron Gach likened Procunier to a less well-known Michigan prison official, the late Ben Luma: "I looked to Ben Luma . . . the way that some in this business look to Procunier. Luma was more of a Joe Ragen type of guy than Procunier apparently is. But Luma, like Procunier today, was known for his correctional instincts. He could spot a lifer who wouldn't run if placed in a lower-custody joint."

Not surprisingly, therefore, Procunier did little to study systematically the internal and external needs of the agency or to cast his policies and actions accordingly. To the extent that he made more than brash, shoot-from-the-hip responses to TDC's problems, his administration's efforts amounted to a wholly counterproductive attempt to transform TDC into what students of organizations call a means-oriented agency. In simplest terms, a means-oriented agency is one that controls the behavior of its members mainly by specifying the procedures they are to follow. A goals-oriented agency, on the other hand, controls the behavior of its members mainly by evaluating the results of their work. Throughout most of the two decades prior to Procunier's directorship, TDC was both means and ends oriented. Institutional staff were trained and promoted according to both how well they followed TDC's rules and regulations, on the one hand, and how safe, clean, and productive their prison (or area of the prison) was, on the other.

One of the foremost examples of Procunier's effort to make TDC over into a more strictly means-oriented agency was the establishment and implementation of a new inmate classification system modelled along the lines of that which had existed in California. In late 1984, the Texas inmate newspaper ran a feature story under the heading "Curbing the Violence." Procunier's Deputy of Operations and future successor, O. L. (Lane) McCotter, had outlined for the inmates how the new classification system was bound to stem the rising tide of murders and stabbings inside the prisons. The inmates reported:

> . . . McCotter contends that there is concern in the administration over the present trend of violence and steps are being taken to curb it. He points to the new classification system that will be implemented throughout TDC beginning November 1. This is the "key" to a system of "staff control" that brings TDC one step closer to a goal of maintaining a safe prison system.[17]

There was indeed a genuine desire in the administration to curb the then incipient violence. But in stressing new classification procedures as the "key," Procunier, McCotter, and those outside of TDC who cheered the effort ignored one outstanding fact: the same essential procedures had been used in other systems where violence was rampant. Indeed, California's classification methodology as it existed under Procunier in the early 1970s was at least as sophisticated as the model he brought to TDC, yet there were some fifty-nine murders in CDC prisons between 1973 and 1975. Pseudo-scientific efforts to group inmates according to past behavior had done little or nothing to improve the quality of prison life in other systems. But installing a new, more elaborate classification system in Texas was a popular, progressive-sounding idea that could be devised, announced, and implemented with relative ease.

Similarly, it was easier for the Procunier administration to focus on fattening the system's policy manuals than it would have been for it to resume genuine responsibility for the care and custody of its inmates. While expressing little interest in the extent to which officers actually followed the existing procedures governing the control of inmate movement, the oversight of inmate work sites, and so on, Procunier and his aides pushed the department to issue new, more detailed administrative directives and guidebooks. Procunier spoke publicly about his shock that the TDC central policy manual measured only one inch, saying that it ought to be at least four times as thick.[18] In the early days of his administration, a multi-million dollar final report by an independent consulting firm, commissioned under Estelle, circulated among the agency's new cadre of top managers. Entitled "Strengthening TDC's Management Effectiveness," it was an anathema to veteran TDC officials who, like Dr. Beto, voiced the opinion that "any organization that needs or heeds a management study needs new management. If the people in charge don't know what's going on, it hardly helps to tell them."

As per the court's decree, Procunier oversaw the hiring of more officers and established a new training regimen. In addition, his administration instituted new financial planning measures and started to upgrade the department's management information systems. The connection, if any, between these types of measures and what was actually happening in TDC's cellblocks, was never really examined by Procunier or his central office staff. On paper at least, TDC was being transformed into a better, more modern, less "medieval" prison agency. For the moment, the court, key legislators, and others who had criticized the agency were satisfied. There was talk of bringing TDC "up to ACA standards" and seeking accreditation for some of the department's prisons. Board of Corrections member Harry Whittington proclaimed success: "Everybody was doing things 25 different ways in 25 different units. Procunier has put in a set of procedures and standards that cover every kind of incident and remove the possibility of violence, whereas before we did not even have any guidelines."[19]

Paper "guidelines," however, do not seem to have much of a direct bearing on rates of prison disorder. For years numerous correctional agencies around the country had precisely the kind of elaborate documentation, written procedures, and official lists of standards that TDC under Procunier had rushed to establish. In effect, in the two years following Estelle's resignation, the nitty-gritty business of running decent prisons with a demoralized and beleaguered staff was left almost entirely to chance, while the central office fiddled with measures more likely to tickle temporarily the agency's critics than to protect its inmates or to rededicate its workers.

During Procunier's tenure, violence mounted, programs were disrupted, costs escalated, prison gangs emerged, and outside contractors were brought in to do the agricultural and other work once solely the province of TDC inmates. For the last nine months of his brief reign, Procunier came under attack from the governor, other state political leaders, and the press. More officers were on line, new classification procedures were rolling, and new business and accounting techniques were in place. But more inmates were dying, and more staff were quitting. The system was in the latter stages of compliance with the *Ruiz* decree, but the "totality of conditions" inside the prisons, the quality of prison life in Texas, was worse than it had been at any time since the pre-Beto era. Procunier quit TDC and retired from corrections.

Procunier was succeeded by Lane McCotter. McCotter, like Estelle but unlike Procunier, was brought to TDC largely through Beto's influence. Beto had supported McCotter to succeed Estelle, but Governor White and other responsible officials favored Procunier. Procunier had a major reputation in corrections and was all things to all constituencies—a hard-nosed administrator, a compassionate reformer, a seasoned manager, an energetic executive who liked to shake things up. Given the political, legal, and administrative quagmire into which TDC had fallen by 1983, someone of Procunier's stature was a natural choice to succeed Estelle.

When hired as TDC's second-in-command, the 43-year-old McCotter's most recent assignment was as commandant of the disciplinary barracks at Fort Leavenworth, Kansas. McCotter, who had achieved the rank of Army colonel, took over at Leavenworth when the prison was in a shambles. Drug running, inmate violence, and undisciplined activities by the staff were the norm before McCotter arrived. Within six months, however, McCotter had tightened the operation enough to bring these disorders to a virtual halt. Beto, who had visited the prison, was impressed with the military nature of McCotter's operation. Inmates were made to obey orders, work productively, and earn privileges. The staff was "all shine and polish" and McCotter was, as Beto recalled, "on top of the inmates and his subordinates down to the last detail." It was a more genuinely military version of Beto's paramilitary control model, and it left Beto deeply impressed with the young colonel.

McCotter, however, had little experience in dealing with the kinds of political and public-relations pressures that any director of a major prison system must handle. His first year in the system was spent under Procunier. McCotter was a loyal subordinate, who came to respect and admire "the Pro." When Procunier resigned from TDC, McCotter continued with his predecessor's policies. Rather than managing TDC's prisons in the "hands-on" way he had managed Leavenworth, McCotter focused more on the elaboration and codification of procedures. The prison gang problem was not addressed except by occasional lockdowns of entire prisons. Officer morale continued to sink, and the unionization effort strengthened.

AFTERMATH AND OPPORTUNITY

Prodded gently by Beto and a few veteran TDC officials, McCotter and his aides slowly began to shed the emphasis on pseudo-bureaucratic measures. In late 1985, they started to pay greater attention to what was actually happening in the field. Moved by a vision of a return to the control model minus the BTs, McCotter and his aides held more staff meetings, circulated encouraging intradepartmental memos, and launched more critical but sympathetic on-site inspections to insure that officers were behaving in accordance with the officially prescribed routine. TDC began to make extensive use of metal detectors (ordered under Procunier), imposed tighter restrictions on inmate movement, curtailed legally the free flow of inmate mail (used by the gangs to order "hits" on staff and prisoners), and saw to it that inmate grievances were handled formally. An elite team of specially outfitted (black fatigues and combat gear) officers, trained to handle unruly inmates and disturbances with a minimal use of force, was strengthened and became a source of pride. Turnover rates dropped, and officers began competing in earnest for a spot on the elite squad. The prison artifacts in the lobby of TDC headquarters, removed under Procunier, were dusted off and put back on display. Inside the prisons, signs were hung with the message: "Through These Gates Enter The Finest Correctional Officers." In a gesture that was as much symbolic as substantive, several wardens saw to it that the green lines which ran down the sides of the prison hallways, and within which inmates were required to walk, received a fresh coat of paint.

It is far too early to say whether these and related measures presage a better quality of prison life than existed in TDC from 1983 through most of 1985. Thus far, however, the results are mildly encouraging. Between September and December of 1985, having begun what one veteran TDC official welcomed as "a return to a few of the basics," the system experienced no murders and fewer stabbings than in any three-month period since Estelle's last days. By January of 1986, levels of order, amenity, and service inside Texas prisons began to improve. In the first nine months of that year, the prison homicide rate shriveled almost to zero as only two of the nearly forty thousand inmates were killed. Rates of assault and other measures of disorder declined as well, even at the system's worst institutions. The agency's fields, factories, and classrooms started to hum while inmates enjoyed better access to athletic equipment, good food, and most other amenities than they had over the last few years.

There are several morals to this story, several generalizations to be wrung from this case analysis. First, there was nothing preordained about the murderous violence and inhumane conditions that TDC experienced in 1984–1985. Neither is there anything fated, magical, or necessary about the recent improvement in conditions; if Texas prison management slips, so will the quality of life inside TDC's institutions. "Maybe," observed a ranking correctional officer, "nobody is right. Maybe all we ever need to do is run these prisons like we know how, with the grey uniforms working to keep the white uniforms safe and sound and busy. Maybe everybody— judges and politicians and lawyers, old bosses and new—just has to be like good keepers."

Secondly, there was nothing about the court's intervention, least of all Judge Justice's order to abolish the BT system, that made good prison government a "mission impossible." While many parts of the court's intervention were ill informed, ill timed, and ill advised, and while the judge and his helpers acted in ways that seemed almost calculated to breed ill will in the agency, nothing "Willie Wayne" did was directly responsible for the hellish conditions inside TDC's prisons. By the same token, however, nothing he did was directly responsible for the at least temporary respite from violence; nor, more broadly, was there anything in his opinion that guaranteed that TDC's prisons would become better governed after *Ruiz*. In essence, the court's intervention resulted in the imposition of hitherto unknown legal constraints on the agency. If the judge were more judicious, his information better, his appreciation for what TDC had achieved in the past less unkind, and his preoccupation with its sores less total, or if he and his aides had troubled themselves to consider the possible unintended consequences of their sweeping actions, there can be little doubt that things would not have degenerated as they did. The new legal framework imposed on TDC was not, as some of the "old guard" have claimed, a "straightjacket"; rather, it was more nearly a poorly tailored and ill-fitting suit which the agency was rushed into wearing and which eventually, and predictably, burst at the seams.

Much the same can be said for the political assaults on the agency. They made it more difficult, but far from impossible, for Texas keepers to do their jobs well. The agency's detractors had many legitimate complaints and were far from entirely misguided. But their analysis of the situation, their proffered solutions, and their criteria of success left much to be desired. In early 1985, Representative Ray Keller, one of the agency's most important critics, proclaimed that since 1983 the system had undergone "tremendous improvements."[20] But 1984 was second only to 1985 in the number and severity of disorders as well as disruptions to education, work, and other more desirable inmate activities. By 1985, inmates who entered TDC found it very difficult to "do their own time." Nor could they rely on the administration to protect their lives or to provide them with opportunities to work, get an education, and better themselves. Instead, they would have to affiliate themselves with one of the gangs or in some other way find protection. For this situation, the Texas keepers themselves were to blame; but TDC's assorted critics did little more than shout fire, fan the flames, and credit themselves for helping to extinguish a blaze that was in fact raging out of control. Their role in TDC's incipient return to a greater emphasis on managing the institutions in a way that may presage better overall conditions behind bars was marginal at best.

In the aftermath of the scandalous revelations about the BT

system, the court's intervention, and the associated changes in the agency's political environment, personnel, and philosophy, it became clear that what bad prison management had wrought, good prison management could undo. The opportunity, but not the promise, of better prisons was clearly on the horizon.

SUMMARY AND CONCLUSION

In January of 1986, some twenty years after CBS News had done its its aforementioned documentary on Beto and his successes, the same network devoted a segment of its "60 Minutes" program to the horrors of life behind Texas prison bars.[21] Whereas the former program had focused mainly on the agency's leadership and administration, the latter one focused mainly on the inmate gang leaders who had come to control much of what happened inside the system. Both programs made errors of fact and interpretation, but each was essentially correct in what it portrayed.

In the early 1980s, the inmate population of TDC did not change much in racial and ethnic composition. Between 1980 and 1985, the percentage of serious or dangerous offenders in TDC's custody did not change significantly. Nor was there any discernable change in the political culture of the prisoners, at least not of the kind that has so often been posited in explaining the California prison disorders of the late 1960s and early 1970s.

What had changed in Texas was formal prison management. Controls were relaxed. Rules that once checked inmate misconduct were underenforced. Minor infractions were ignored. Prison gangs were permitted to organize. Rewards and punishments were no longer administered in a swift, certain, and significant manner. The care and custody of inmates was left to chance. In short, in 1984 and 1985, TDC stopped governing prisons. It did less than it had done at any time since before Beto to protect and guide those in its custody. The management regime began to crack as BTs became con bosses. Through a series of administrative errors committed in the face of enormous external pressures, TDC went from a mostly benevolent despotism run by prison officials, to a malevolent anarchy of competing prison gangs. At each moment, however, the fate of the system was in the hands of the Texas keepers themselves. By returning to a more formal administrative regime, and by rekindling the sense of mission and ésprit de corps among its officers, TDC may yet improve substantially the quality of life inside its prisons.

This analysis of correctional change in one major prison agency neither vindicates nor condemns any of those who were a part of it all. In 1984, at the 114th Congress of Corrections, Beto was selected to introduce Judge Justice. In his opening remarks, Beto noted that he had heard "snide remarks . . . regarding my appearance on this platform today. . . . How is it possible for someone like George Beto to introduce someone like Judge Justice?"[22] He then expressed to the audience his personal admiration for the judge and his belief that, with respect to prisons and any other institution, the judiciary must take those actions that it deems necessary to uphold the Constitution and the rights of American citizens, including those incarcerated. In his speech, Justice returned Beto's compliments and praised correctional officials for carrying out the incredibly demanding public service with which they are entrusted. He stressed that "the courtroom is a less than ideal setting for the development of correctional policy" and mentioned a "growing awareness of the centrality of the role of corrections administrators in the process of maintaining prisons that are safe, lawful, and humane."[23]

The important task—morally, intellectually, and practically—is to draw the right preliminary lessons about improving prisons from the experiences of Texas, Michigan, and California keepers.

THREE

IMPROVING
PRISONS

*In framing a government which is to
be administered by men over men, the
great difficulty lies in this: you must
first enable the government to control
the governed; and in the next place
oblige it to control itself.*

—JAMES MADISON, *Federalist* No. 51

⑥

The Prison as a Constitutional Government

There is nothing inherent in the nature of prisons or their clientele that makes better prisons impossible. There is nothing about spending more money, hiring more staff, erecting modern buildings, increasing hours of formal training, or reducing inmate populations that makes better prisons inevitable. Low levels of order, amenity, and service in prisons are neither expressions of amorphous social forces (internal or external) nor by-products of public apathy or the insensitivity of corrections officials. Poor prison conditions are produced by observable and, it appears, remediable defects in the way that prisons are organized and managed.

If one is interested in improving the quality of prison life, then the best way to think about the prison is not as a mini-society but as a mini-government. What James Madison argued with respect to the government of society at large applies with equal force to the government of the prison. Prison managers must effect a government strong enough to control a community of persons who are most decidedly not angels. At the same time, however, prison managers must be subject to a vigorous system of internal and external controls on their behavior, including judicial and legislative oversight, media scrutiny, occupational norms and standards, rigorous internal supervision and inspections, ongoing intra-departmental evaluations, and openness to outside researchers.

Where prison government is concerned, the depth of the constitutional challenge—striking and maintaining the proper system of restraints on the behavior of both the inmates and their keepers—is clear from the fact that for most of our history, prisons have bounced between the poles of anarchy and tyranny; between the Hobbesian state of inmate predators and the autocratic, arbitrary regime of iron-fisted wardens. But the history of prisons, including our examination of the different policies and practices tried by corrections officials in Texas, Michigan, and California, gives us cause for hope. It may be possible to discover and implement forms of prison government that are likely to maximize order, amenity, and service while minimizing the human and financial costs of imprisonment.

INTERNAL CONTROLS: PRISON BUREAUCRACY

There is nothing magical about any particular type of organizational structure. Whether business firms, schools, armies, and other institutions achieve their objectives depends ultimately on their ability to attract and hold onto able executives, talented managers, and conscientious workers. Organizations, public or private, will normally succeed or fail according to whether pains have been taken to combine good workers with sufficient resources under the right conditions.

All other things being equal, however, how an organization is structured will have a significant bearing on how, and how well, the organization performs. Recognizing this fact, organizations from Congress to General Motors have, from time to time, made consciously planned changes in the way they are structured. The American faith in organizational solutions to public problems may be unjustified, but it stretches back to the Founding Fathers and, for better or for worse, has been at the heart of our thinking about everything from how to improve our national defense to how to preserve our natural environment.

The field of corrections has not been untouched by our propensity to search for organizational solutions to public problems. Between 1965 and 1975, for instance, forty-two states restructured their adult and juvenile correctional agencies; twenty-nine of them did so twice.[1] Those responsible for these major organizational overhauls were mostly unaware of the related activities of other states. Furthermore, these seventy-one reorganizations appear to have had little impact on how correctional institutions were actually run; the boxes on organization charts changed but the daily routine (or lack of routine) in the cellblocks did not. In 1983, the State of Hawaii surveyed some of these experiences and learned nothing that would justify reorganizing its correctional system.[2]

Based on our explanatory study of correctional institutions in three states, it appears that there is some relationship between administrative structure and prison conditions. The proper unit of analysis, however, is less the corrections agency as a whole and more the prison itself; not who reports to whom at headquarters but who works how in the institutions. Contrary to the argument made in much of the existing literature, the best hypothesis seems to be that higher-custody prisons that are organized along bureaucratic, even paramilitary, lines and operated strictly "by the book" will have less violence than those that are organized and run more loosely. A corollary to this hypothesis is that reliance on inmates to control other inmates—whether via building tenders, inmate council representatives, con bosses, prison gang leaders, or other such inmate-staff arrangements—is a recipe for compromising security and violating laws. Where higher-custody prisons are concerned, those govern best who govern most and most formally.

Bureaucracy is a term that has become loaded with so many meanings and connotations (most of them pejorative) that one hesitates to employ it. By bureaucracy I mean essentially what the father of the concept, Max Weber, meant—namely, an organization with the following characteristics: a hierarchical structure in which authority flows from top to bottom and clear superior-subordinate relationships are the norm; a division of labor in which each worker has specialized prescribed duties and responsibilities; a published set of rules, regulations, procedures, and standards to be followed routinely by most members; personnel employed on a career basis with retention and promotion based on performance; impersonal relations.[3]

As Weber discovered, and as Charles Perrow has observed, bureaucratic organizations tend "to routinize, limit uncertainty, increase predictability, and centralize functions and controls."[4] A paramilitary bureaucracy is one in which most members of the organization are grouped according to rank, wear uniforms that designate their rank, and exhibit other organizational characteristics common to military units such as armies.

Those who have argued that court intervention and related pressures have led to the bureaucratization of the prison have employed a "top-down" conception of bureaucracy that focuses more on the trappings of this administrative form—bulky training manuals, elaborate policy directives, and the like—than on the nature of the workers' tasks and how they are actually performed. In a highly bureaucratic organization those who perform the critical tasks of the agency—in this case the line correctional officers—have little discretion. The successful performance of the organization's task is not highly contingent on the character, personality, integrity, keen wit, or any other special talents of the workers.

The task of most of today's correctional officers, however, is by no means simple or routine. They have been made responsible for inmate care and custody, operate under literally thousands of often contradictory and virtually impossible-to-enforce rules, and exercise vast discretionary powers in deciding how to handle inmates, whom they are simultaneously encouraged and discouraged from relating to on a personal basis. The American Association of Correctional Officers (AACO), a national fraternal organization and lobby, published an "officers' creed" which reflected the complex nature of the officers' work. The creed read in part: "To speak sparingly . . . to act not to argue . . . to be in authority through personal presence . . . to know that I cannot be fair simply by being firm, nor firm simply by being fair." The creed was echoed in the manuals of Michigan, California, and (to a lesser degree) Texas officers. At Soledad, the institutional orders read in part: "No manual can be used as a substitute for sound employee performance, nor can it be expected to answer all questions that occur in daily operations on the job." The prison's post orders read: "The correctional officer's attitude toward the inmates should be one of dignity and of authority combined with a desire to help."

In most prisons, what correctional officers do and how they do it depends largely on their personalities or temperaments. They must exercise judgment on a wide range of matters. Because of this, one officer may ignore an inmate rule violation, while another may treat it as an offense worthy of a major disciplinary report; one may spend most of his shift at his desk, while the next may spend most of his roaming about the cellblock or trading jokes with the inmates; one may emphasize the custodial aspects of the job, while another emphasizes its "human relations" aspects. As even most of the departmental training personnel admit, under existing conditions, there is little that can be done to make officers behave alike or to equip them with the personal skills necessary to succeed: the correctional officer in most prisons is not a bureaucrat or a professional but a sort of craftsman the successful performance of whose task requires certain unique and nontransferrable talents.[5]

In a more highly bureaucratized prison, officers would behave according to a manageable number of simple operational rules. Theirs would be a tight, stable, uniform routine of monitoring inmate movement, frisking inmates, searching cells, and so on. Officer training would take place in an abbreviated "boot camp" where this routine would be memorized and practiced, physical training and self-defense arts would be mastered, and the basic principles of security management, from key control to riot control, would be learned. Preservice educational requirements would be minimal.

In the genuine prison bureaucracy, officers would be more "impersonal" in their relations with inmates, but that is the same as saying that they would be less able to discriminate against inmates whom they disliked. They would be more "restrictive," but that would make even-handed treatment of inmates more imperative and the threats to security less acute. In short, a prison bureaucracy would involve organizational patterns of superordination and subordination that minimize the exercise of arbitrary power or inequality in prisons. Uniformed prison workers at all but the highest levels would be neither professionals nor craftsmen but bureaucrats in the same sense that soldiers are bureaucrats.

The need for formal organization varies inversely with the level of human trust and the likelihood of spontaneous, uninduced cooperation among people. Formal rules and regulations, laws and sanctions, are most necessary where lawful, civilized behavior is least likely and little can be left to informal understandings or norms of conduct. The attempt, therefore, to run prisons informally by winning the mass support of convicted criminals, or by coaxing their leaders, or both would seem bound to jeopardize any possibility for safe, lawful, smooth-running correctional institutions. In fact, prison administrations that have relied on inmates to control other inmates have always paid for this administrative mistake in the currency of higher levels of disorder, illicit activities, and an eventual loss of custodial control. There seems to be an inevitable slide from special arrangements or tacit alliances with the inmates to a situation in which prisoners dictate the character of daily life behind bars.

Strong organizations are usually those in which workers share a belief in the worth and rightness of their tasks.[6] Such organizations are said to have high ésprit de corps. Organizational ésprit de corps means more than just high morale.[7] It refers to the workers' attachment, based on experience, to a particular way of doing things.[8] Such an attachment or sense of mission normally develops where workers are rewarded for their dedication to duty and ability to "get the job done."[9]

Our exploratory study revealed that prisons where employees shared some sense of mission were less disorderly than prisons that were organized more loosely and had a lesser sense of mission. In this connection, it is worth noting that a 1977 thesis by a Texas correctional officer noted how armed forces veterans were attracted to TDC because it allowed them "to function in a similarly structured environment."[10] Prisons in many other systems, however, have borne little or no resemblance to military units.

In much of the literature, any case for more highly structured forms of prison administration is ruled out of bounds by such observations as the following:

> While bureaucratic forms support accountability functions essential to a correctional program in meeting its control obligations, the same forms restrict the highly adaptive and infinitely varied kinds of organizational response which are essential to a dynamic treatment process.[11]

> The prison is often an extreme example of bureaucracy as managers sometimes try to control people as easily and effectively as they would a manufactured commodity. . . . The extreme preoccupation of many wardens and staff with rules, power, and coercion is responsible for . . . poor communication, poor morale . . . and self-protectiveness on the part of the staff. . . . Inmates are forced to develop their own lifestyle in their own world in order to retain any sort of self-integrity.[12]

Just the reverse, however, may be true: bureaucratic prisons may foster higher staff morale, better inmate programs, and a more safe and civilized prison environment. But, unless and until far more empirical research is completed, we will not know what, if any, relationship exists between administrative structure and prison conditions. Even if we knew that prison bureaucracy was best able to produce high levels of order, we would still need to know whether bureaucratizing (or militarizing) the prison beyond a given point would improve (or worsen) the overall quality of prison life, and whether this administrative form is superior for both lower- and higher-custody institutions.[13]

CORRECTIONAL LEADERSHIP AND ADMINISTRATIVE STABILITY

To be well governed, it would appear that prisons need not only bureaucratic bodies but stable, nonbureaucratic heads. If the prison is to be a constitutional government, then corrections executives must lead and prison wardens must manage both behind the walls and beyond them. They must make frequent on-site institutional tours (not "visits") and become hostages neither to second-hand reports nor to what one prison official called "iron bars of paperwork." At the same time, they must make frequent and constructive contacts with their organization's outside "coaches, customers, and critics."[14]

Our study revealed the important degree to which corrections executives can influence the philosophical cast, sense of mission, institutional procedures, and political strength of corrections departments. If the person who directs the prison system does not make a sensible estimate of the problems with which he and his subordinates must wrestle, if he is unable to garner and institutionalize political support for the agency, or if his tenure is too short for him to do anything more than announce his departure, then there would appear to be little hope for the kinds of administrative measures necessary to effect and to sustain a high quality of prison life. Even with a correctional philosophy that can be translated first into policy decrees and then into a bureaucratic routine of administrative action, no prison system will perform well unless it can successfully manage those political and other pressures that make for administrative uncertainty and instability. As California's Richard A. McGee observed, "all of the debating in the world will not solve corrections problems without some analysis of the political contexts in which these [publicly] supported agencies have their being."[15]

Compared to most other prison systems, over the last few decades the Texas, Michigan, and California prison systems performed well. Unlike most other systems, each enjoyed a mostly supportive political environment. In each case, one or more directors of the agency played a vital role in cultivating the necessary outside support and improving the department's public image. They did so not by broad-based appeals designed to raise public concern about corrections. Instead, they accepted that corrections has been, and will continue to be, low on the list of public priorities. They thus sought and garnered the support of key people in government, business, the media, and the academy. As McGee had learned, to garner the authority and resources necessary to manage prisons well, top corrections officials must reach beyond the walls to interested and influential persons. Correctional institutions, he argued, could not be improved "by hiding them from view or moving them to remote areas or making them inaccessible to visitors and uninviting to employees."[16]

At this stage, it is impossible to generalize about the kinds of persons who would make successful prison executives. Nor is it yet possible to generalize about the characteristics most common to successful prison wardens or superintendents. There are, however, a few broad observations that may be worth considering. First, successful prison directors and institutional managers are not here today, gone tomorrow. They are in office long enough to learn the job, make plans, and implement them. Second, they are highly "hands-on" and pro-active. They pay close attention to details and do not wait for problems to arise but attempt to anticipate them. While they trust their subordinates and do their share of paperwork, they keep themselves focused on the prisons and what is actually happening inside of them. At the same time, they recognize the need for outside support. In short, they are strangers neither to the cellblocks nor to the aisles of the state legislature. Third, they act consciously to project an image of themselves that is appealing to a wide range of people both inside and outside of the organization. Fourth, they are dedicated and fiercely loyal to the department and see themselves as keepers engaged in a noble and challenging (if mostly thankless) profession.

Even if there were fifty-one such correctional leaders ready and able to assume control of our prisons, it would mean little unless those jurisdictions where prison directorships are still political plums did something to depoliticize their corrections departments. So long as prison directors change every few years and prison wardens play musical chairs, the kind of correctional leadership and administrative stability necessary to better prisons will not be forthcoming.

THE PATH TO BETTER PRISONS: OBSTACLES AND OPPORTUNITIES

For the sake of argument, let us suppose that such correctional leadership was now in place and ready to institute the type of organizational reforms that we have been discussing. This would by no means guarantee us better prisons. For one thing, even energetic and talented corrections administrators have been known to make mistakes. For another, not even the most pro-active, persuasive, and knowledgeable prison leader presiding over the most orderly, humane, and service-oriented prison bureaucracy could compensate for the kinds of negative pressures on prison operations that may be exerted by officer unions, the courts, the media, the legislature, governors, professional bodies, prison reform groups, academics, and prison workers themselves. If we are to achieve better prisons, then each set of actors must cooperate with the others. Those who influence how prisons are governed must examine their own role, the assumptions under which they operate, and how their actions may foster or retard more safe, lawful prisons. To stimulate this enterprise, let us begin with the opportunities and obstacles to better prisons posed by prison workers themselves.

Correctional Workers

In his famous resolution of the problem of how to reconcile the life of the spirit with the life of the mind, Pascal warned: Two mistakes: to deny reason; to admit only reason. We might begin with a similar maxim regarding the nature of prison management: Two mistakes: to deny its special features; to exaggerate its special features.

Nowhere in the world of public or private management do administrators at all levels face the type of thorny problems confronted on a daily basis by prison workers. They operate in a world where normal, everyday objects must be viewed as potentially lethal weapons. A sergeant in a California prison delighted in showing visitors a "book of horrors," a photographic catalogue of inmate weapons and those who made (or were victimized by) them: sharpened plastic combs stuck into bars of soap and used as knives; bullets concealed in a mattress (discovered by a metal detector); a prisoner's "kiester stash" (a homemade gun which the inmate had concealed in his rectum and used during an escape attempt); a shampoo bottle with a wick used as a flame thrower and the charred bodies of those inmates on whom it was used; inmates with weapons in their hair (blacks in their tight braids, whites in their pony tails); and so on.

Those who work in prisons must doubt inmates' motives and look beneath the surface of superficially positive developments. For instance, a Michigan prison administrator spoke of one of the system's newer religious sects as a budding prison gang: "They're not a religion but a pressure group, a racket with a cover. They extort money, sell job assignments. But as a religion they are given rights which enable them to organize and operate freely."

Following personal interviews, former TDC director W. J. Estelle provided a written discourse on prison management in which he concluded: "Now in seven rambling pages I have told you nearly everything I've absorbed over 32 years . . . although I neglected a few pedestrian items such as clearing the count, contraband control, public speaking, budget preparation, construction management, effective application of anhydrous ammonia, use of portable fuel storage tanks, etc. . . . ." Clearly, corrections is unlike any other occupation. At a minimum, to be at all successful in the field requires a willingness to spend a great deal of time inside prisons. Only there can one learn the real ropes of the trade, including some sense of the unique emotional and other job stresses shared by prison workers.

The belief that lessons learned in managing other types of organizations will translate well when applied to prisons seems doubtful. By the same token, the notion that advanced academic degrees in and of themselves make one qualified to manage prisons, or can be treated as surrogates for penal experience, seems fallacious. Presumably, persons with lots of formal schooling and lots of prison experience would normally be better correctional workers than persons with only one type or neither type of preparation. In this vein, the kind of personnel decisions noted in chapter three's discussion of the evolution of the California prison system seem unwise. The efficacy of such seemingly sophisticated management techniques as management by objectives has been found wanting in other organizations and would appear to have little natural application in a corrections department.[17]

To dramatize the point, in a choice between a world in which all of tomorrow's prisons would be governed by administrators with Harvard MBAs but without any experience working in prisons and a world in which all of tomorrow's prisons would be governed by persons without any such degrees but with years of experience in the cellblocks, we should not hesitate to take our chances with the "overpromoted guards." By the same token, in choosing line correctional staff, persons with the kind of experience that comes from a successful tour of military duty but without even a high school diploma ought to be taken in preference to those who have college degrees but little demonstrated capacity to work hard and follow instructions.

Having conceded so much to the uniqueness of the prison workers' task, we should also point out that prison workers have tended to exaggerate it by overstating both the dangers and the overall difficulty of what they are paid to do. Unlike police, firemen, and other public servants who perform vital and often dangerous tasks, what prison workers do is hidden physically from public view and has only rarely captured the public imagination in a favorable way. The popular stereotypes of prison workers, particularly correctional officers, are most unflattering and wholly unjustified. Stressing the dangers of their work and the "powder keg" theory of governing inmates is a way for prison workers to enhance their self-image, add a bit of color and romance to an otherwise monotonous occupation, and, they believe, garner the appreciation of the rest of us. In addition, by perpetuating the myths about inmates and prison governance discussed in chapter four, prison authorities can deflect responsibility for unsafe, unclean, and unproductive prisons away from themselves and onto everything from villainous judges to impersonal social, political, and economic forces over which nobody, let alone the prison staff itself, has much apparent control.

Corrections is by no means a dismal profession. Prison workers perform what is arguably one of the most essential functions of the sovereign state. They are most likely to succeed in raising their status if they act so as to raise the quality of prison life. They can begin by discarding self-defeating myths about prisons in favor of a shared vision of good prison government.

Courts and Corrections

Courts have become the most important external influence on the behavior of inmates and staff. In 1954 a federal circuit court ruled that "courts are without power to supervise prison administration or to interfere with ordinary prison rules and regulations."[18] Over the last few decades, however, courts have abandoned this "hands-off" doctrine. Judges have intervened on a wide range of prison issues including crowding, medical and health care services, staff practices, food services, sanitation, due process protections for inmates, and, of course, the constitutionality of prison conditions. In 1986, for instance, some thirty corrections agencies were operating under conditions of confinement court orders; many had class action suits in progress and population limits set by the courts; fourteen states had court-appointed special masters, monitors, and compliance coordinators.

The rise of judicial intervention into prison systems has been part of a broader expansion of the courts' role in American government. For better or for worse, state and federal judges have taken a major hand in how prisons are governed. There is no reason to suppose that they will ever go back to the hands-off doctrine. Courts and corrections are permanently linked, and the question is how each can help rather than hurt the other. Let us begin to suggest how a better relationship might be developed by identifying the key issues surrounding court intervention into corrections.

Debates over the role of the judiciary in our governmental system are as old as the nation itself. One such debate has concerned judicial activism, that is, the courts' authority to make or change laws, to decide policies, and to oversee their implementation. A more recent but related debate concerns what is sometimes called "judicial capacity." The issues in the latter debate are less philosophical and more strictly empirical; not whether the courts have the right to intervene but whether they have the ability to do so effectively.

In the case at hand, the essential question is whether the courts have the capacity to render decisions that change prison operations and improve the quality of prison life, or whether they are doomed for lack of knowledge and other resources to issue orders that worsen rather than ameliorate prison conditions. As noted in the previous chapter, at this stage we do not know whether, on balance, judicial intervention has changed prison operations for the better, altered correctional practices in a way designed merely to avoid unfavorable rulings in the future, or led to counterproductive or simply unexpected results.

Based on our exploratory study of correctional institutions, however, there are a few general observations we can make. First, few persons inside or outside of corrections dispute the right of the courts to intervene. Prisoners are not "slaves of the state." Where those immediately responsible for providing prisoners with decent living conditions fail to do so, the courts must, if necessary, force them to do their duty.

Judges, however, are rarely in a good position to know the actual state of affairs inside prisons. It has long been a part of the judicial posture that judges, unlike politicians and other policymakers, refrain from first-hand interviews, observations, and fact-finding missions. But if judges are going to make sweeping changes in the way that prisons are governed, then they ought to be willing to break their tradition of viewing the world from the serenity of their chambers. The ethic of a bench that confined itself to reviewing the legality or constitutionality of laws is hardly appropriate for judges who not only find but make and oversee the implementation of laws. Warden Wayne Estelle of CMC recalled:

The cells here were not built for two. A suit was brought by a civil liberties group. The district court judge who was handling the case showed up here unannounced. The result was that the judge refused to grant a temporary injunction. More important, though, was the fact that the judge stayed here for several hours and learned something about what we do, why, and so forth. More judges should do that.

The point is not that judges who take the trouble to enter prisons will find everything to be swell. Rather, they will learn more about the actual state of prison conditions from such first-hand observations than they will from reading books, essays, and neatly typed depositions. They will be in a far better position to predict and weigh the real costs and benefits of any court-induced changes and to appreciate the constraints under which prison administrators operate.

Far too often, judges have delegated their responsibility to aides who by inexperience or predisposition were unfit to be the "eyes and ears" of the court. In one case, for example, a judge ordered state prison officials to end double-celling at certain units. To comply, the officials would have had to release into the general inmate population inmates whom they knew to pose serious and immediate threats to security. Nevertheless, the judge stood by his order and appointed a young former law clerk with no experience in this area to hold hearings that would decide which inmates were released. Luckily, the state legislature refused to appropriate funds to pay for this irresponsible exercise of judicial authority. In other cases, however, prison officials have been forced to act where court edicts contradicted both correctional judgment and operational reality.

It is imperative that judges recognize the current limits of our policy-oriented knowledge about prisons. Too often they have fallen prey to what are at best pseudo-scientific and presumptuous statements about how best to govern prisons. To illustrate, in his 1984 speech before the American Correctional Association, Justice William Wayne Justice, author of the sweeping *Ruiz* decision discussed in the previous chapter, spoke of an "emerging emphasis upon deference to correctional expertise" and referred to the ACA as "reflecting the current state of professional thinking on the subject of correctional management."[19] Court intervention in corrections, he said, has "to a very large extent, simply filled a vacuum created by inattention by elected officials" to prison problems.[20] Judicial opinions in correctional cases, Justice noted, "have done nothing more than articulate progressive, current correctional thinking. Few, if any, judicial decisions, for example, go beyond the standards you as a profession have recognized and approved for the operation of correctional institutions."[21]

It is no disrespect either to Judge Justice or to the ACA to point out that neither the ACA nor any other group has accumulated anything that even remotely resembles a body of proven knowledge about how to manage prisons well. In the first place, there is no discernable consensus among correctional practitioners that the ACA's voluminous publications and accreditation activities are based on an accurate assessment of how best to operate prisons. Correctional institutions where the quality of prison life is dismal have received and retained accredited status, yet judges have been relying on the "expertise" behind the accreditation standards in rendering their decisions about prisons. Much of the ACA's management training doctrine, for instance, is based on what even the most charitable reviewer must describe as badly borrowed principles from outdated and never tested academic theories.

While the battery of materials available from such credible bodies as the ACA are impressive, and while there are any number of legitimate scholars who by virtue of their research have some sensible notions about prisons, judges are fooling themselves if they believe that there exists anything more than fragmentary knowledge and untried opinions about how to improve prisons. If the ACA and related enterprises spent less time and energy making blueprints and quasi-academic speculations about prisons and more in the way of gathering data on precisely what different prison systems have already tried and how well (or poorly) it has worked, and if they then disseminated this information widely, they would be performing a genuinely valuable service to courts and corrections and possibly stimulate the beginnings of a policy-oriented body of knowledge about how prisons work and how we can act to improve them.

In at least some instances, courts have played a positive role in checking the behavior of prison officials and securing prisoners their rights. They can, no doubt, help to improve the quality of prison life. One area where the courts might lend a hand is in solving the prison gang problem. For years in states such as California and Illinois, and more recently in states such as Texas and Iowa, prison gangs have terrorized fellow inmates, injured and killed staff members, trafficked in drugs, and disrupted the delivery of prison services. Legislatures might grant and the courts might uphold (or even order) a delegation of extraordinary powers to prison officials who are attempting to combat prison gangs. In years past, state prison authorities have sent particularly troublesome inmates to federal prisons. Also, states have swapped prison gang members. Judges might act to assist prison officials in wrestling with the legal, administrative, and even political hurdles that have often impeded such arrangements. They might, in addition, assist police and other law enforcement authorities in dealing with the development of prison "street gangs," criminal organizations that are headquartered in prisons but which have active members, in some cases tens of thousands of them, operating on the outside.[22]

Correctional Officer Unions

In part as a response to the failure to deal effectively with prison gangs and other dangerous features of work inside correctional institutions, over the last decade or so, officers in most prison systems have unionized. There are a few studies which have attempted to assess the impact of officer unionization on prison operations.[23] To my knowledge, however, no studies exist to tell us how, if at all, officer unions have affected the quality of prison life. Even with more empirical data, it would be years before any such assessments could be made.

In 1967, the President's Commission on Law Enforcement and the Administration of Justice highlighted the importance of the line correctional staff to prison operations. As the commission wrote, those who work the cellblocks are "the most influential persons in institutions by virtue of their numbers and their daily intimate contact with offenders. . . . They can, by their attitude and understanding, reinforce or destroy the effectiveness of almost any correctional program."[24] Given the development of officer unions, these words are doubly true today.

Correctional officers do not like to be called prison guards and do not think of their job as a simple exercise in locking and unlocking doors and "hawking," as they say, inmate movements. As other researchers also have found, and contrary to popular perceptions, correctional officers are highly supportive of the idea that some prisoners can be changed for the better. Like other prison workers, they share what was described in the fourth chapter as the keeper philosophy.

There is, however, nothing about a more bureaucratized officer corps that would diminish the positive influence that officers could exercise over inmates. Officers would still be responsible for inmate "care and custody" but would restrict themselves to officially prescribed routines designed to achieve both ends. While officer unions have bargained for higher wages, many of their demands have been for safer working conditions and more intangible signs of appreciation and respect. There is every reason to believe that greater security is possible through tighter operations. The sense of occupational specialness that officers now get through the myths of inmate dominance and inmate society can be replaced by a more healthy feeling, supported by the facts, that they are, as law enforcement officials, on a par with, say, state troopers. To employ the slogan of the California officers union, correctional officers would still have "the toughest beat in the state." The difference, however, is that they would be organized, paid, and esteemed for running this beat in a thoroughly disciplined way.

Prisons, Politicians, and the Press

In their *The Honest Politician's Guide to Crime Control* (1970), Norval Morris and Gordon Hawkins wrote:

> . . . although the prison or penitentiary as we know it will almost certainly have followed the death penalty . . . into desuetude before the end of the century, institutional confinement in some form will remain necessary for some offenders. . . . The open institution plays an increasingly important part in the prison systems of the world . . . only a very few prisoners require cells and walls to keep them in, and cells and walls grossly increase the social isolation of the prison. . . .[25]

For better or for worse, prisons are still with us and will, if anything, be far more numerous in the year 2000 than they were when Morris and Hawkins predicted their demise. The idea of prisons as "open institutions" or "factories with fences" was inspired largely through the examples of Sweden, Japan, and other countries so unlike the United States culturally and in other ways that it is difficult to imagine how their penal practices could be exported to American shores. Japanese inmates, for instance, refer to their correctional officers as *Oyazisan* ("beloved father"); as we have seen, American criminals have less affectionate names for their keepers.[26] Smaller, more loosely run institutions such as HVMF are not bound to achieve a higher quality of prison life than larger, more tightly operated prisons such as CMC. Where officials have experimented with less restrictive higher-custody institutions, inmates and staff have been afflicted by violence, programs have suffered, and the most predatory inmates have come to rule.

Governors, legislators, and other politicians who may influence the future course of corrections should not be tempted into believing that Big House prisons are going to go away or to metamorphose into some more natural and pleasant form. We did not know fifteen years ago and we may not know fifteen years hence how precisely to identify and separate dangerous from nondangerous offenders. Nor have we yet discovered how to characterize or predict the relationship between an offender's preinstitutional behavior and his institutional behavior, on the one hand, and his institutional behavior and postinstitutional behavior, on the other.

Like it or not, prisons are, and will remain, a major part of our criminal justice system. Politicians (honest or not) ought to act in ways that help corrections officials to govern our expanding stock of prisons better. As should by now be quite clear, to accept prisons for what they are—sad places of human confinement—and to attempt to govern them strictly is not to join with "those who still subscribe to the curious notion that by hurting, humiliating, and harassing offenders we can somehow morally improve them."[27] Rather, it is to acknowledge the harsh reality that, at least in this country, confined felons who are left mainly to their own devices tend to rape, kill, and in other ways diminish the quality of prison life. It is the duty of public officials to take the legal and administrative measures necessary to prevent this and to provide safe, clean, productive prisons where the laws are respected by all.

Despite the greater role of courts, prisoners' rights groups, and other concerned bodies, there is preliminary evidence to suggest that governors and state legislators are relatively autonomous when it comes to most policy matters relating to prison administration. Unlike most other areas of American politics, the politics of prisons does not appear to occur in a pluralistic universe of competing and clashing interests. Instead, the few researchers who have explored correctional politics have found the system to be relatively closed and dominated in each case by the governor, a few key legislators, plus a few top corrections officials.[28] Julia Gordon, for instance, found that in Massachusetts, despite the welter of groups organized to influence prison operations, policy reflected the preferences of "Mike and Mike," Governor Michael Dukakis and Corrections Director Michael Fair.[29]

Politicians, therefore, can do much to set the correctional agenda and to effect reforms in how our prisons are managed. We have already noted the tendency of elected officials, particularly governors, to turn corrections departments into "political footballs" and to change prison directors with every disturbance or change of administration. If prisons are to enjoy the kind of administrative stability that is associated with better living conditions, then politicians must learn to exercise self-restraint in this area. The incentives, unfortunately, are skewed against such moderation by politicians. As Richard A. McGee noted, governors cannot win elections by pointing to well-running prisons, but they can lose elections if prisons are in turmoil, are perceived as too soft on convicted criminals, or drain the public purse.[30] Because of the prison's low priority and mixed popularity with the public, legislators normally do not relish the chance to serve on committees that spend much time on corrections. A legislator assigned to such a committee can advertise himself and claim credit for measures which, regardless of their actual effects on the quality of prison life, "shake up" the prisons and lead to "reforms." Hence, the possibility not only of better prisons but of better correctional agencies in general is contingent in part on the willingness and ability of key political actors to look beyond electoral advantages and to exercise some degree of statesmanship.

Short of statesmanship, one thing that politicians can do to improve prisons is to visit them more regularly (though not, one hopes, as inmates). Holding hearings and drafting reports on prison conditions after some major disturbance has occurred is like attempting to learn about airplanes by studying only those that have crashed. Another thing that politicians can do is to avoid the sort of rhetoric about prisons that is likely to bolster myths about them. In particular, they can avoid attributing prison problems to things over which they allegedly have no control—overcrowding, tight budgets, and so forth. Politicians are largely responsible for the legal framework within which prison administrators must operate; they can therefore ameliorate or worsen prison conditions by what they say and do.

While politicians who concern themselves with prisons must respect public opinion, the public's perception of how prisons operate and what, if anything, can or should be done to improve them, is shaped to a considerable degree by the press. By the press I mean the entire spectrum of print and broadcast journalism, everything from local newspapers to nationally televised programs. Corrections officials are highly suspicious of journalists. Some point to particular instances where the press has "burned" them by obtaining access to privileged information about the institution only to use it in a thoroughly one-sided story that paints prison workers as stupid ogres and inmates as their victims. More generally, however, corrections people feel that most books, movies, and news reports underplay the difficulty of their work and portray those who work in prisons as sadistic or subhuman.

The press, however, is not biased against corrections officials so much for ideological reasons as for occupational ones. Stories about dirty, disruptive, dangerous prisons that can "blow at any minute" make good copy. Inmates are more colorful and intriguing subjects for human interest stories than are correctional officers. Exposés on official corruption and terrible conditions behind bars are more interesting than "fluff pieces" about how, everything considered, prison conditions are pretty decent. A careful report about the complex, underlying factors that lead to prison violence is more credible, more in keeping with "expert opinion," and more likely to bring the reporter professional kudos than a report about a "guard" who made a simple security slip.[31]

The "prison beat" is no more prized by journalists than the prison committee is prized by legislators. Many reporters who cover prisons do not bother to inform themselves of basic facts or disregard those facts in the interests of a more sensational story. To take just one example, following a rash of escapes from Michigan correctional facilities, a local television news crew was given permission to interview prison officials and to shoot some film. Michigan had a rash of escapes, virtually all of them from minimum-security settings. All of the escapees were captured. The reporters were not aware that, in Michigan, prisons have long been graded according to a reasoned estimate of the security risks posed by offenders such that more escapes, known as "walk aways," could be expected to occur at less secure—and hence less expensive-to-operate—institutions. They took pictures of the high walls of a maximum-security prison where no escapes had occurred and presented an alarmist view of how prison officials were failing to protect the public. The reporters could have done a public service by conveying accurate and pertinent information that would truly inform the public, benefit the agency, and assuage the community's unjustified fears about escaped felons. Instead, they miscast the department's record and heightened public excitement.

Prisons, Professors, and Public Policy

If our correctional agencies can attract and hold onto able executives, talented managers, and conscientious workers, if they can
operate according to a realistic management philosophy and are
given sufficient (though not necessarily ample) resources, and if
they can develop a sense of mission, an ésprit de corps, and learn
to manage their power over convicted criminals with common sense
and compassion, then our correctional institutions will probably be
safer, cleaner, less idle, more productive, and maybe even cost less
to operate. In short, prisons can be governed well or ill. We need
to learn much more about how to govern them well with the human
and financial resources at hand.

Prison workers, judges, politicians, journalists, and other concerned citizens have looked to scholars for advice about how to
improve the nation's prisons. Not every academic or intellectual,
of course, is a scholar. A scholar is someone who generates and
tests ideas under rules governing the quality of evidence and in
accordance with the canons of logic.[32] Even scholars sometimes
mistake opinions for evidence and accept an idea not because it is
demonstrably true but because it is stimulating intellectually or
promises deliverance from some or all of the ills which afflict our
society.

Based on my exploratory study of correctional institutions in
three states and my analysis of the existing literature on prisons,
it seems clear to me that prison management may be the single
most important determinant of the quality of prison life and that
prisons are best viewed as mini-governments. With the evidence
at hand, I have suggested that good prisons are possible and denied that bad prisons are inevitable. I have attempted to identify
the administrative conditions under which better prisons are possible and have raised serious questions about the importance of
money, training, and numerous other factors that are claimed to
have a major bearing on the quality of prison life. I have doubted
most of what sociologists have argued about prisons and made
recommendations that run counter to most contemporary ideas
about how best to handle incarcerated felons. Furthermore, I have
claimed that prison order is both good in itself and a necessary
precondition for other valued aspects of prison life. In this chapter,
I have even been so presumptuous as to lecture judges, politicians,
corrections associations, journalists, officer unions, and others on

how they may help to improve prisons by strengthening prison government.

The only finding of this study that, to me at least, seems indisputable, is that, other things being equal, dedicated, security-conscious prison management will yield more in the way of prison order, amenity, and service than less dedicated, more lax prison management; in short, prison management matters. The quality of prison management is influenced mainly, though not solely, by the prison's political environment, its correctional leadership, and its correctional philosophy. Some keepers do their jobs more sensibly and with better results than others, but all of them deserve our admiration and respect for performing an illiberal task in a liberal polity.

A paramilitary prison bureaucracy, led by able institutional managers and steered by a talented executive, may be the best administrative response to the problem of establishing and maintaining higher-custody prisons in which inmates and staff lead a calm, peaceful, and productive round of daily life. Prison workers can simultaneously share a sense of mission, identify with each other, care about the inmates, and perform well a vital service to the people of the law-abiding and tax-paying community.

Whether the hypotheses and prescriptions I have sketched are truly valid can be known only through further research and experimentation. There are good a priori arguments, derived from common sense, that the safety and lawfulness of prisons varies directly with the degree to which prison authorities are organized to effect such conditions. The empirical evidence with which to support these arguments, however, remains quite thin; this exploratory study hints at more than it can prove. Still, a far heavier burden of proof now rests on those who say that prisons do not differ, that all prisons are or have been equally terrible, and that we can do little or nothing to improve prisons short of an unlikely combination of expensive measures and risky reforms.[33]

RETHINKING REHABILITATION

From everything that we were able to learn through our review of the prison literature and our exploratory study of prisons in three states, it appears that little of a desirable nature can happen in prisons unless prison authorities maintain order. Commenting on his experiences in prison classrooms, a Michigan inmate said: "It's hard to look at the blackboard when you're worried about getting stabbed." In prisons where individual or group misconduct is common, there is an atmosphere of fear that is not conducive to schooling or any other treatment or work activity. Furthermore, in disorderly prisons the daily schedule of activities is disrupted so often that programs suffer.

As one veteran CDC official noted, "among correctional people, the idea has been that you really can't have both order and treatment. That's what all the so-called experts like to say too. . . . Slowly, [corrections officials] are beginning to see that to have one you must have both." Despite the studies which purport to show that prison work, education, and other programs have little or no effect on postrelease behavior and criminality, it may be worth rethinking rehabilitation. To my knowledge, researchers have not examined carefully the context in which treatment programs have been offered. Normally, the belief has been that tight custodial regimens dash or hobble treatment initiatives. The opposite hypothesis, however, seems stronger: prisons where there is a strong custodial regime can offer more and better programs, and these programs may in turn help to rehabilitate those inmates who participate in them on a regular basis.

There is no good a priori reason, and to my knowledge no body of empirical evidence, to discredit the possibility that prison inmates, even ones who have a long history of serious offenses, may become more law-abiding if they are made to live, work, go to school, and recreate in productive, law-abiding ways. Enforced adherence to the norms of a civilized, noncriminal way of life, coupled with a rich menu of genuine treatment and work opportunities, would seem bound to have some good effect on inmates' institutional and postrelease behavior. Prison inmates, like the rest of us, may be habituated to desirable ways of behaving provided that they are rewarded and punished accordingly. Prisons cannot make saints out of demons or do for the average inmate what families, schools, churches, and other institutions may have failed to do. But they may be able to modify offenders' lifestyles while in custody, and this experience may help keep some who would otherwise return to crime upon release from doing so. Enlightened self-interest and plain moral duty dictate that any chance that prison may afford to make serious offenders more civil and law-abiding ought not to be discarded without further investigation and debate.

BEYOND RECIDIVISM

For the moment, let us suppose that future research validates some of what has been hypothesized: well-led prison agencies effect security-conscious organizational regimes that produce order; orderly prison conditions are a necessary condition for higher levels of amenity and service. But let us also suppose we have discovered that even the most intensive inmate treatment programs offered under the most safe and humane conditions have no demonstrable effect on recidivism rates. (To make this hypothetical example sharper and more thorny, if less realistic, one might also suppose that credible evidence has been found that prisons where levels of order, amenity, and service are high do less well in terms of recidivism rates than prisons where the quality of prison life is more wretched.) Before abandoning our treatment programs and associated efforts, we might pause to place ourselves in the position of keepers and ask whether a high quality of prison life, and the type of prison government which produces it, are not their own justifications.

One argument would be that it is simply good that felons in the custody of the state are well governed. It is difficult to suppose that most citizens would prefer prisons where convicted offenders behave in violent, vulgar, antisocial, criminalistic ways to prisons where they are made to behave more decently, or would prefer less humane to more humane inmate living conditions. A prison government that is lax in enforcing prohibitions against illicit activities, ignores rule violations, tolerates violence, and encourages offenders to walk, talk, dress, and relate to others in prison just as they did on the streets gives tacit if unintentional moral approval to such behavior and invites the offenders' contempt for the "straight society" that permits and pays for such treatment. Misgoverned prisons either send inmates the wrong moral message or no such message at all. As one California inmate, a veteran of several prison stretches, observed:

> When they [authorities] let things fly that way, let you get over on [trick, take advantage of] them and nail [assault, rob, victimize] each other, what's it say? It says nobody gives a good damn. It says you're a bunch of f——ing convicts beneath worrying about. You may not want to change but they don't make it seem like you even ought to want to. And nobody says you have to. Nobody makes you. It's like what

you're doing—acting bad [acting tough or aggressively], doing wrong—isn't wrong. They don't seem to give a s——t if we act right or wrong. So you act how you always act and wonder why they give a s——t what you do out there enough to put you in here, but don't give a s——t when you pull [do] the same s——t in here on your way to back out there. They don't make you straighten up, so you f——ing know they don't really [care] if you do or you don't.

THE MORALITY OF IMPRISONMENT

Even if we knew for sure how to make prisons more safe and sound, many would still oppose imprisonment or view it as a necessary evil. Liberals tend to believe that prisons are by their very nature oppressive and inhumane; conservatives tend to believe that they cost too much and punish too little. The first complains that prisons brutalize; the second complains that they coddle. To some, knowing that prisons can be improved via better management is like knowing that the guillotine can work better provided that it is well oiled; to others, a concern for anything beyond warehousing convicts bespeaks too much compassion for remorseless offenders and too little for their innocent victims. Both groups view the prison as a morally bankrupt institution.

I disagree entirely. It is possible to justify the expenditure of human and financial resources necessary to effect (or inch toward) decent conditions behind bars. Good prisons are prisons where levels of order, amenity, and service are indisputably high. Such institutions are not only possible but desirable. They represent the best moral option for a people that wants to be both just and merciful towards its convicted criminals.

Traditionally, Americans have wanted a criminal justice apparatus that apprehends and visits harm upon the guilty, makes offenders more law-abiding and virtuous, dissuades would-be offenders from criminal pursuits, invites most convicts to return to the bosom of the community they offended, and achieves these ends in a civilized and financially manageable way. Of the various components of the criminal justice system, only corrections has been expected to somehow embody most of these ends. There is, of course, no clear way to maximize each end simultaneously. The penitentiary was an American invention, and it was invented as a way of optimizing on the disparate aims of American criminal justice.

What are prisons for? Normally, four general answers are given: punishment or retribution; deterrence; incapacitation or public protection; and rehabilitation or reformation. As an agency for any one or any subset of these ends, the prison is an absurd institution; as an agency for all four of them, the prison is the only institution. To begin to understand why, let us consult history and logic.

If we could agree that the sole end of our criminal justice system were to protect ourselves against known offenders, then prisons would be superfluous. If, for example, the medical technology were available, single-minded proponents of incapacitation would have no grounds on which to argue against placing convicted (or known but unconvicted) criminals in a comatose state to be awakened at the end of their terms. By the same token, offenders would be far better incapacitated were they debilitated physically, branded for easy identification, banished to some distant island, or placed in irons. If we want only incapacitation, we cannot, without defying logic, worry about the quality of prison life except insofar as it affects inmates' ability to escape.

Similarly, if we could agree that the sole aim of our criminal justice system were retribution, then history and logic would force us to favor other, more ancient forms of punishment wherein crimes are punished in kind—the hand that steals is forfeited, the community nuisance is banished, the rapist is castrated, the murderer is automatically murdered. Despite the intellectual paternity claimed by certain seventeenth- and eighteenth-century thinkers, the principle that the punishment should be proportionate to the crime is many centuries old; indeed, it is stated as a commonplace by a character in Plato's *Laws*.[34] But against the backdrop of world history, the idea of depriving people of their liberty as a punishment for criminal deeds is novel (barely two hundred years old) and rests on the arguably bizzare, metaphysical notion that one can make the punishment fit the crime by calibrating its severity in the metric of time: say five years for a rape, thirty years for a murder—but why not longer (or shorter) for each?

Analogous problems confront anyone who would embrace either deterrence or rehabilitation as the prison's raison d'etre. If selective deterrence were our only end, then we would without hesitation apply far more draconian sanctions against even the most petty offenders—lashes to complement (or replace) the loss of liberty. The same holds for general deterrence, for if "Peter" is more severely punished, then "Paul" will probably be kept more honest. Finally, if rehabilitation were our only end, then it would make sense to abandon the prison or use it merely as a place in which to subject inmates to a wide range of "treatments," from mandatory psychosurgery to vicious routines of behavior modification.

The simple truth is that most Americans will not settle for a criminal justice system that "only" punishes or deters or rehabilitates or incapacitates. Even those who talk as if they believed that prisons were for just one or some subset of these ends will normally contradict themselves if pressed. For instance, ask those who argue that prisons are for public protection plain and simple if they favor the provision of prison services, care whether inmates' living conditions are decent, or desire that those in state custody be protected from rapes, assaults, and other abuses by fellow prisoners or keepers. Most will answer sincerely in the affirmative. Or ask those who argue that prisons are only for deterrence whether they would be willing to have prisoners undergo mild tortures to enhance the deterrent effects of imprisonment. You will get few positive replies.

There are some serious thinkers who both predicted and derided the ways in which democratic, Judeo-Christian peoples would come to treat their criminals. Over one hundred years ago, Friedrich Nietzsche wrote:

> There is a point in the history of society when it becomes so pathologically soft and tender that among other things it sides even with those who harm it, [with] criminals . . . Punishing somehow seems unfair to it . . . "Why still punish? Punishing itself is terrible." With this question, herd morality, the morality of timidity, draws its ultimate consequence.[35]

In American criminal justice, Saint Francis wrestles Nietzsche with no clear victor. Imprisonment is a way of satisfying the community's (and the victim's) desire for retribution. But it remains bounded by Judeo-Christian morality, a morality in which revenge must be restrained by forgiveness and justice tempered by mercy.[36] There is nothing inevitable or necessary about this way of punishment. Other societies, including many existing ones, have opted for systems of punishment far more single-minded and draconian, systems in which those who break the law or offend common standards of decency are dealt with in ways that most Americans would label "harsh," "inhumane," or "sinful." By the same token, some societies, past and present, have punished in ways that most Americans would say are "too lenient" or provide a "mere slap on the wrist."

Ideally, the prison punishes by depriving the offender of something which he has learned to cherish—freedom, if only the freedom to prey upon the life, liberty, and property of others. Any meaningful justification for the human and financial costs of effective imprisonment must stem from a desire to punish criminals in a way that is at once just and merciful. If we were moved simply by the passion for revenge, then we would return to the offender an evil at least as great as that which he inflicted. This we could do via the prison as warehouse or torture chamber. By the same token, if we were led simply by the passion for forgiveness, then we would return to the offender less evil than he inflicted, perhaps none at all. This we could do via the prison as country club or place where each offender did what he pleased. Revenge culminates in a full measure of justice, forgiveness in a bounty of mercy. But prisons bars are forged by revenge and cooled by forgiveness.

The prison is not, as Hawthorne phrased it, the black flower of civilization. Instead, it is evidence of a civilization which seeks to treat all but its most murderous citizens in a spirit of hopefulness and compassion. Imprisonment is a public ideal, and that ideal, like any other, will go unrealized where it is unmet by citizens willing and able to cooperate toward its fulfillment. In the famous words of Dostoevsky, the degree of civilization in a society can be judged by entering its prisons. It is not enough, therefore, to erect prison walls; the morality of imprisonment is unassailable, but the moral standing of any actual prison will depend on its quality of life.

CONCLUSION: THE DUTY TO GOVERN

Some years ago New Jersey State prison officials started a program intended to discourage juveniles from criminal pursuits. The program was called "Scared Straight." Groups of young persons were taken on a tour of Rahway, a maximum-security prison. They were herded into a room where a number of inmates, some of them life-termers, lectured about the horrors of life behind bars—the filth, the violence, the idleness. The inmates used coarse, vivid language. Some youngsters were told that if they ended up in prison they would be raped, no matter how tough they were. Others were warned that they would have to give up their shoes or any other possessions demanded by inmate predators, some of their lecturers among them. While a portion of what the juveniles experienced was staged to maximize its shock value, most of it was real, an adequate reflection of prison life.

There is no evidence that the program, which suffered from a number of design flaws, had its intended effect. Even if it did, however, it would still be a disgraceful and disheartening symbol of how we have lulled ourselves into accepting poor prison conditions as unremediable. What those children experienced was an attempt to scare them with the government's failure to protect and guide—to govern—those in its custody.

It is easy to think of alternatives to imprisonment and to pursue magic cures for the ills of America's correctional complex. It is much harder to get down to the nitty-gritty business of finding and implementing ways to improve conditions for the hundreds of thousands of people who live and work in our prisons. The former is an exciting enterprise that is in vogue; the latter is a tremendous undertaking that seems hopeless. The first stimulates general ideas and frees us to look ahead; the second immerses us in the particulars of prison management and forces us to learn from our mistakes. The former enables us to theorize about how well we will employ new or additional resources; the latter constrains us to discover and apply practical ways of doing better with what is at hand.

The government's responsibility to govern does not end at the prison gates; nor, for that matter, does its ability. Whether government can or should run cost-effective railroads, engineer economic prosperity, or negotiate us to international bliss may all be open questions. But government can and should run safe, humane, productive prisons at a reasonable cost to the taxpayers. No self-respecting government would abdicate or excuse itself from so central a duty. Prisons are a public trust to be administered in the name of civility and justice. Governing prisons is a public management task that we can learn to perform much better.

FOUR

STUDYING PRISONS

*In life as in death there's always a
boss. In life if you are bad and
insubordinate to your boss you're going
to have trouble. And in eternity—the
Lord is boss!*

—PRISON MINISTER, TDC

Boss: Texas term for correctional officer

APPENDIX

PRISON RESEARCH

There is a small but excellent literature on participant observation among prisoners.[1] For one whose primary interest is prison government rather than inmate society, however, studying prisons poses a different set of challenges and opportunities. What follows is a brief, informal discussion of my research experiences in Texas, Michigan, and California prisons. It is hoped that this account will help to smooth the path of future scholars who are willing to venture behind bars in order to understand and improve prisons.[2]

Gaining Access

For good reasons, correctional people are not highly solicitous of outside researchers. Permitting scholars to roam about freely in their archives, to interview personnel at headquarters and in the field, and to observe operations, does not make their lives any easier. Not only do they worry about how the researcher may disrupt the work of the agency or the prison, they worry about "getting burned" by the researcher who violates trusts, distorts information, and writes a highly negative report which, if published or otherwise disseminated, may damage staff morale and create political or other problems.

Many corrections agencies have a tradition of allowing and over-seeing research on inmates. In most agencies, the process for re-viewing and monitoring such research is well established. By comparison, the criteria and mechanisms for approving and ar-ranging research on prison staff are less well developed. Also, keepers are surprised that anyone wants to study them rather than their charges; often, that surprise is mixed with suspicion.

Originally, I had planned to study a fourth prison system, Pennsylvania's, but my requests for access to the department and its prisons were denied. As it turns out, this denial was a blessing in disguise. I hesitate to think what it would have been like to try and get my straining research arms around yet a fourth prison system; besides, studying correctional administration in that state might have obscured the neat management continuum discovered by comparing the control, consensual, and responsibility models.

In Michigan I had asked to study Jackson prison but was granted two other primary sites, HVMF and the Michigan Reformatory. In California I had asked to study San Quentin but was (mercifully) given Soledad. In California, my initial interviews with officials at headquarters convinced me that, for my purposes, CMC might repay study, so I called Warden Wayne Estelle, and he agreed to let me examine his institution as well. My study of Texas prisons began after a year of waiting and negotiating.

Gaining access to prisons, therefore, may require a research strategy that amounts to "rolling with the punches" and making the best of the people, places, and data available to you. It is good scholarly practice to build a research design before making con-tacts or hitting the field, but that design ought to be flexible.

Gaining access to prisons requires that you be flexible in other respects as well. You must, for instance, be ready to sign agree-ments that cause you to think about the possible life-threatening dangers associated with spending time in a prison setting. For instance, TDC's "Terms and Conditions for Doing Extra-Departmental Research" form required an affirmative answer to the following question:

> Do you understand that in the event you are taken hostage there will be no special consideration made regarding your release?

"Soaking and poking" among lawbreakers is different than soaking and poking among lawmakers.[3]

It is advisable to send your initial request for access straight to the director. This applies doubly if approval of your project will involve a major and ongoing commitment by the department. Normally, your request will be forwarded to the responsible departmental research coordinator. The way most corrections agencies work, approval by headquarters serves only as a "letter of introduction" to those in charge of the institutions. Usually, final approval rests with the institutions.

The best way to gain and to keep access to prisons is to be honest and clear with all concerned about what you want to do and how you want to do it. Several friends and colleagues were surprised that TDC let me into its prisons during the final and most tumultuous days of the *Ruiz* controversy. One said: "How did an Italian boy from Harvard get in and around all those old Texas guards?" The answer is that I never attempted to "get in and around" correctional personnel in Texas or any other place. I simply was forthright with them about the scholarly intentions of my study. People who work in corrections are better than average at judging character and smelling a rat. Most of them have enormous pride and confidence in what they do and are willing, even eager, to share their ideas and experiences with qualified disinterested observers. From my Walpole experience I had learned to respect and admire prison workers, individually and collectively, without (or so I believe) being blind to their shortcomings or mistakes.

It is important for researchers to remain sensitive to the concerns of prison workers. For instance, when I sent an early draft summarizing some of my preliminary findings to a CDC official, the letter she sent in response made it clear to me that in emphasizing the gang problem I was treading on sensitive turf. Rather than ignore this reaction, I corresponded with the official and, as a result, sharpened my understanding and patched up a misunderstanding.

In James B. Jacobs's account of his research at Statesville, he noted that his association with Professor Norval Morris of the University of Chicago, a noted legal scholar and criminologist, was helpful in establishing the validity of his claim to "an independent and legitimate research identity."[4] Similarly, my association with Professor James Q. Wilson of Harvard University, a noted political scientist and criminologist, was helpful in getting my research off the ground. Still, like Jacobs, I was never able fully to resolve the problem of being accepted simply as a scholar. A number of inmates and a few staff members persisted in the belief that I was an FBI agent, a narcotics investigator, or someone from headquarters on a special assignment. But the majority of those with whom I came into contact took me for the outside researcher that I was.

It is unfashionable for social scientists to admit it, but the quantity and quality of one's access to research subjects and pertinent materials may be highly conditioned by how much the researcher is liked by those whom he is studying. I established and enjoyed an extremely good rapport with scores of corrections officials in each state. Many of them, from junior officers to ranking administrators, went out of their way to assist me. In my judgment, there is no formula for cultivating such good relations; they happen by a sort of natural accident or not at all. It helps, however, to be flexible and honest.

Finally, before I had even contacted officials in each of the states, I visited the offices of the American Correctional Association. After my first visit to the ACA, I wrote and asked them for a letter endorsing my study. I did so on the assumption that such a letter would help me to gain access to each system. I received a letter from the ACA responding to my request but never received the association's formal endorsement. As it turns out, this too was a blessing in disguise. While the ACA's endorsement might not have hurt my access to Michigan or California prisons, neither would it have done much to facilitate it. The association's endorsement would probably have hurt me somewhat with TDC, where, as I later learned, the ACA has been held in less than high regard. Also, many correctional workers in Michigan and California had serious reservations about the ACA, suggesting that such a link may have hurt me in those systems as well. Based on my experiences, I would recommend against connecting, or attempting to connect, one's prison research to any outside association, foundation, or other agency.

Gathering Data

What may be termed the "management variable" has been neglected by scholars in part because other variables are easier to study. For instance, it is easier to simply transcribe interview data or to manipulate statistics than to actually observe human behavior in complex—let alone dangerous, dirty, and distracting—settings. Furthermore, the researcher who studies an organization by entering it runs certain risks. In particular, he risks drowning in a sea of particulars concerning highly idiosyncratic events, places, and personalities. Such an experience may satisfy neither the intellectual quest for general ideas nor the practical desire for prescriptions broad enough to be entertained and implemented in disparate settings.

But if we are going to learn more about prison government and how to improve it, then prison researchers must take the plunge. In my own case, I attempted to immerse myself in the life of each department and its prisons. I operated on the assumption that everything—what people said and how they said it, notices buried on departmental bulletin boards, official documents and lunchtime scuttlebutt, pictures on walls, newspaper accounts, statistical reports, and so on—was data of potential significance. Whether I was interviewing a seasoned top official or a new correctional counselor, I asked a series of standard questions about prisons but let the discussion drift in the direction of the knowledge and interests of the interviewee. In social science circles, this is known as the "unstructured interview" technique, but I was simply trying to learn things from people who knew far more about them than I did, and to do so without pestering or boring my subjects more than was absolutely necessary. Inside the prisons, I tried to be all eyes and ears, to see as much of each operation as I could, to observe administrative life in the cellblocks, and to stay out of the way.

While I did not get precisely the statistical or other data that I desired, and while I had to make rather strenuous efforts to get and record certain types of information, for me the problem was not a lack but a superabundance of facts, figures, and impressions. Intellectually, this was a salutary burden because it forced me to sift through and make sense of it all. Practically, however, this posed a slight problem since—not being one to learn from experience—on each trip I had to buy an additional suitcase to cart off all the books, notes, and other materials I gathered.

Just transcribing the interview data took weeks. Ordering and digesting the rest of the material took months. When one does a regression analysis or an equivalent analytic exercise, it is possible to be more or less confident that what one did was done right, if only technically. When one engages in the kind of research and analysis at issue here, such confidence is replaced by the uneasy feeling that a better or more telling use of the various data was possible.

Obviously, gathering data on prisons involves gathering data in prisons—shadowing correctional officers, peering from gun towers, sitting in cellblocks. But much pertinent data on prisons may be had by following prison staff beyond the walls—after-work get-togethers at bars, "bull sessions" at an official's home, Rotary Club luncheons, prison rodeos. To take just one small example, when I attended the state-sponsored funeral of an inmate in Huntsville, Texas, I got to explore with the officials in attendance a side of the keeper philosophy that would otherwise have remained closed to me. Specifically, it was through this encounter, including the words spoken over the gravesite by the prison minister, that I began to see more clearly the side of the Texas keeper philosophy that was devoted to something beyond mere control.

Every prison researcher will at some point be forced to negotiate the tension between his desire for scholarly detachment, on the one hand, and his duties as a citizen, on the other. Inside prisons, situations arise that may require the researcher to put down his notepad and, if only momentarily, become a part of the administration he is studying. To give just two examples, in Michigan an inmate cornered me and complained at length about a particular correctional officer. Considering his tone and his demeanor, it occurred to me that the sum of what the inmate had said constituted a potential threat against the officer's well-being. I reported to the officer and to one of his superiors precisely what the inmate had said. Also in Michigan, a fight errupted in a hard-to-reach wing of a prison. The officer on duty, whom I had been observing and talking to, rushed to the scene but, in his haste, swung but did not close an adjacent cell door; I pulled it shut. The point is not that I was right (or wrong) to behave as I did in these instances. Rather, the point is that such situations arise, and researchers must consider, beforehand if possible, how they will handle (or try to avoid) them.

In interviewing top corrections officials, active and retired, it is a mistake to suppose that they will be able to offer little more than anecdotes and "war stories." Not every official, of course, is Dr. George Beto with his mastery of languages and literatures stretching from the classics to corrections. Most, however, are reflective, articulate, and intelligent persons whose ideas about criminal justice and prisons are worth hearing if only because their ideas influence their actions.

In a similar vein, if one wishes to ascertain the beliefs and attitudes of middle-level prison managers and uniformed prison staff, it would be a mistake to rely heavily upon questionnaires or other such survey devices. When I studied Walpole, I administered questionnaires but also talked to and observed the staff in action. In most cases, their written responses were less interesting than their verbal ones while their actions were more revealing than their words. Just to satisfy myself, however, I administered questionnaires to selected officers in Texas and then interviewed and observed these same workers. Once again I was glad that I was not forced to rely on mere answer sheets. Most people, not just prison workers, are not used to filling out forms or writing essays on complex subjects related to what they think and do. In general, they are better able to respond in person after the purposes of the inquiry have been explained to them. While this strategy requires the researcher to expend enormous efforts meeting, talking to, and explaining himself to hundreds of subjects, this cost must be weighed against the reward of more detailed and accurate data. Not surprisingly, people will respond more fully to a personal, on-site request for information than to a form in the mail. In a similar vein, my experience has been that people will tell you more if you take notes rather than use a recorder.

A perennial question among researchers is whether it is better to preface one's fieldwork by making an exhaustive review of the literature on the subject, or to enter the field as more of an intellectual blank slate, reviewing the literature only after spending some time in the field. Presumably, the former strategy enables one to anticipate problems and to immediately place one's data in a broader context; the latter strategy permits one to get a view of things unfiltered by exposure to any assumptions and biases of previous scholars. There is no easy resolution to this dilemma. Based on my own experiences, however, I would argue in favor of going directly into the field. Normally, there will be time aplenty for reviewing the relevant literatures and debates. This reading and reflecting can be done more profitably after some first-hand observations. When I entered Walpole, I had read some, though by no means most or all, of the prison literature. What I saw motivated me to search through this literature with far greater passion and critical interest than I would have mustered in the absence of any field experience. The best advice, therefore, is probably to soak and poke first and to read later.

There are several pitfalls to gathering data in the ways that I have recommended. One, of course, is that the researcher may be tempted to overidentify with the group being studied. A second is that he may simply "burn out" before the research has been completed. One way to avoid the first problem is to attempt to validate one's information and impressions in as many ways as possible, checking interview data against statistical reports, and vice versa. Another way is to expose one's thoughts and findings to friends and colleagues on a regular basis. It is wise to present one's preliminary findings in seminars or other settings where corrective comments and constructive criticisms are likely to be heard. Since the experience of studying prisons taxes the mind and burdens the emotions more than studying, say, legislatures, the researcher should schedule his field activities and related efforts so that interviews and trips in and out of the facilities are coveted, not dreaded.

Generating Interest

Studying prisons is, to me at least, one of the most exciting and important ventures that a student of public affairs can undertake. As noted in the introduction, however, prisons have generated much interest among sociologists but little interest among other scholars. This lack of interest is surprising.

By most definitions, the state (or government) is the institution in society that has a monopoly on the legitimate exercise of coercive power. Imprisonment represents one of the most concrete embodiments of state power. Through imprisonment and associated forms of postsentencing supervision, the government exercises direct control over a large number of citizens (roughly 3 million in 1986). This represents a major instance of state power virtually ignored by students of politics and government. Moreover, political philosophers have been centrally concerned with the moral bases of crime and punishment, a concern that extends from Plato through Hobbes down to more contemporary theorists. If, as many a distinguished thinker has argued, justice is the central political question, then philosophical inquiries into criminal justice—who the state should punish, for what, and how—ought to be near the heart of discourse on public affairs. Yet few contemporary students of politics and government have made such inquiries.

Prisons, of course, are a major part of the American criminal justice system. That "system" is really a loose confederation of local, state, and federal agencies numbering in the thousands and operating under a mind-boggling array of administrative, legal, budgetary, and political constraints. Studying prisons could thus furnish grist for the mill of scholars interested in, among other things, inter- and intragovernmental relations, courts, state politics, public opinion, agenda-setting, theories of bureaucracy, and policy analysis. Also, as David H. Bayley has argued with respect to studying the police, understanding prisons may provide "an important clue to the character of a political regime" while the development of penal institutions may constitute an important chapter in the history of a country's political development.[5] In short, prisons merit more interest than most students of politics and public affairs have shown them.

Future Research

Future prisons research must address two basic sets of issues, one empirical, the other philosophical. The empirical issues concern the governability of prisons and the conditions under which prisons can be improved. At this stage, the need is for comparative evaluations of prison practices that have already been tried. The present study may serve as something of a model for such works, but only in the way that the Ford Model-T served as a model for the Ford Mustang.[6] The philosophical issues concern the legitimacy of imprisonment as a form of punishment. Even if we knew how to improve prisons, this would not in and of itself justify their existence. At present, the bulk of contemporary writing suggests that imprisonment is a cruel and unusual form of punishment. It remains to be seen whether a compelling case can be made that— given the possibility of prisons where levels of order, amenity, and service are indisputably high—imprisonment is a morally desirable form of punishment.

Finally, scholars ought to ponder more seriously the strengths and weaknesses of different ways of thinking about prisons. The sociological approach encourages us to see prison government as derivative of inmate society and calls attention to the broader social and political currents that may shape the life of the prison.

Notes

INTRODUCTION (pp. 1–9)

1. Thomas Hobbes, *Leviathan*, ed. Francis B. Randall (New York: Washington Square Press, 1976), pp. 84–85.

2. Gresham M. Sykes, *The Society of Captives: A Study of a Maximum Security Prison* (Princeton, NJ: Princeton University Press, 1958), p. 58.

3. Ibid., chapters 6 and 7, especially pp. 120–126.

4. Richard F. Fenno, Jr., *Home Style: House Members In Their Districts* (Boston: Little, Brown, 1978), pp. xiv, 249.

5. For a similar study on police departments, see James Q. Wilson, *Varieties of Police Behavior* (Cambridge, MA: Harvard University Press, 1968). Wilson studied eight cities to illustrate alternative police styles. The cities were selected because they were known to embody those styles in a clear way.

6. Joan Petersilia et al., *The Prison Experience of Career Criminals* (Santa Monica, CA: Rand Corporation, 1980).

7. Among those I consulted were Norman A. Carlson, director of the Federal Bureau of Prisons, and Norval Morris, dean of the University of Chicago School of Law.

8. Such prison research hurdles are nothing new. A quarter-century ago Donald R. Cressey observed: "Entering prison is a trying process, even for the research worker. Men who study prisons must, at a minimum, be so interested in them that they are willing to try to secure data under difficult circumstances." (Cressey, ed., *The Prison: Studies in Institutional Organization and Change* [New York: Holt, Rinehart, Winston, 1961], p. vi). Other prison researchers have made similar observations. For instance, see James B. Jacobs, *Stateville: The Penitentiary in Mass Society* (Chicago: University of Chicago Press, 1977), pp. 215–229. My observations on studying prisons are related in the appendix.

9. James Coleman et al., *Equality for Educational Opportunity* (U.S. Department of Health, Education, and Welfare. Washington, DC: U.S. Government Printing Office, 1966).

10. James Coleman et al., *High School Achievement: Public, Catholic, and Private Schools Compared* (New York: Basic Books, 1982); Ernest L. Boyer, *High School: A Report on Secondary Education in America* (New York: Harper and Row, 1983); Diane Ravitch, *The Schools We Deserve: Reflections on the Educational Crisis of Our Times* (New York: Basic Books, 1985).

11. Edward B. Fiske, "New Look at Effective Schools," *New York Times*, April 15, 1984, Section 12.

CHAPTER 1. **The Governability of Prisons** (pp. 11–48)

1. Similar claims have been made for raising staff-to-inmate ratios, staffing to reflect the racial and ethnic mix of the inmate body, increasing the percentage of noncustodial prison personnel, stiffening preservice educational requirements for both custodial and noncustodial workers, enhancing public awareness and concern about prisons, improving inmate classification systems, subjecting prisons to an accreditation process, and so on. Since the National Commission on Law Observance and Enforcement (Wickersham Commission) issued its pioneering report in 1931, over a dozen other blue-ribbon panels have made such recommendations for improving the quality of prison life. These recommendations have been echoed in scores of reports on prison disturbances as well as in various publications by leading professional bodies, among them the following: *Attica; the Official Report of the New York State Special Commission on Attica* (New York: Bantam Books, 1972); "Reform of Our Correctional Systems: A Report by the Select Committee on Crime" (House Report No. 93-329, 93rd Congress, 1st Session, 1973); "Report of the Attorney General on the Feb. 2 & 3, 1980 Riot at the Penitentiary of New Mexico," parts 1 (June 1980) and 2 (September 1980); "Accredita-

tion: Blueprint for Corrections" (Rockville, MD: Commission on Accreditation for Corrections, February 1979).

2. On abolition, see Jessica Mitford, *Kind and Unusual Punishment: The Prison Business* (New York: Vintage Books, 1974), pp. 295–325; Charles E. Reason and Russell L. Kaplan, "Tear Down the Walls? Some Functions of Prisons," *Crime and Delinquency* 21 (1975): 360–372. On community corrections, see The President's Commission on Law Enforcement and Administration of Justice, *Task Force Report: Corrections* (Washington, DC: U.S. Government Printing Office, 1967); George G. Killinger and Paul F. Cromwell, Jr., eds., *Corrections in the Community: Alternatives to Imprisonment.* 2nd ed. (St. Paul, MN: West, 1977). On inmate participation, see J. E. Baker, *The Right to Participate: Inmate Involvement in Prison Administration* (Metuchen, NJ: Scarecrow Press, 1974) and his more recent *Prisoner Participation in Prison Power* (Metuchen, NJ: Scarecrow Press, 1985); Thomas O. Murton, "Prison Management: The Past, the Present, and the Possible Future," in *Prisons: Present and Possible,* ed. Marvin E. Wolfgang (Lexington, MA: Lexington Books, 1979), pp. 5–53. On construction moratoria, see William G. Nagel, "On Behalf of a Moratorium on Prison Construction," *Crime and Delinquency* 23 (1977): 154–172; Michael Sherman and Gordon Hawkins, *Imprisonment in America: Choosing the Future* (Chicago: University of Chicago Press, 1981), chapter 1. On rehabilitation and treatment, see Douglas Lipton et al., *The Effectiveness of Correctional Treatment: A Survey of Treatment Evaluation Studies* (New York: Praeger, 1975); Susan E. Martin et al., eds., *New Directions in the Rehabilitation of Criminal Offenders* (Washington, DC: National Academy Press, 1981). On incapacitation, see James Q. Wilson, *Thinking About Crime* (New York: Basic Books, 1975), chapter 8. On "selective incapacitation," see Peter W. Greenwood, "Contracting the Crime Rate Through Imprisonment," in *Crime and Public Policy,* ed. James Q. Wilson (San Francisco, CA: Institute for Contemporary Studies, 1983), pp. 251–269. The proposal to afford private firms a greater role in building and running prisons is of recent vintage. For a small sampling of the available information and opinions on privatization, see William G. Babcock, ed., "Corrections and Privatization: An Overview," *The Prison Journal,* vol. LXV, No. 2 (Autumn–Winter, 1985).

3. Mitford, *Kind and Unusual Punishment,* p. 325.

4. Ernest van den Haag, *Punishing Criminals: Concerning a Very Old and Painful Question* (New York: Basic Books, 1975), and his "Prisons Cost Too Much Because They Are Too Secure," *Corrections Magazine* 6 (1980): 39–43.

5. See Blake McKelvey, *American Prisons: A History of Good Intentions* (Montclair, NJ: Patterson-Smith, 1977). Neither McKelvey nor any-

one else, however, suggests that the road to better prisons has always been paved by good intentions. As early as 1835, for instance, Alexis de Toqueville observed: "Some twenty years ago several pious individuals undertook to ameliorate the condition of the prisons . . . While new penitentiaries were being erected the old prisons . . . became more unwholesome and corrupt . . . so that in the immediate neighborhood of a prison that bore witness to the mild and enlightened spirit of our times, dungeons existed that reminded one of the barbarism of the Middle Ages." (Tocqueville, *Democracy in America*, vol. 1, ed. Phillips Bradley, trans. Henry Reeve [New York: Vintage, 1945], p. 268.) Most contemporary observers, however, have offered a more monotone assessment of the American prison experience: bleak past, wretched present, doubtful future. They claim, in addition, to see motives more base than humanitarianism behind most major efforts at penal reform. See, for instance, the brilliant works by David J. Rothman, *The Discovery of the Asylum* (Boston: Little, Brown: 1971), and *Conscience and Convenience* (Boston: Little, Brown, 1980). Similar if less convincing interpretations of the French and English penal experience are contained, respectively, in the following: Michel Foucault, *Discipline and Punish*, trans. Alan Sheridan (New York: Pantheon, 1978), and Michael Ignatieff, *A Just Measure of Pain: The Penitentiary in the Industrial Revolution, 1750–1850* (New York: Pantheon, 1978).

6. Norval Morris, *The Future of Imprisonment* (Chicago: University of Chicago Press, 1974), p. 2.

7. Clemens Bartollas and Stuart J. Miller, *Correctional Administration: Theory and Practice* (New York: McGraw-Hill, 1978), p. 347.

8. Wilson, *Crime and Public Policy*, p. 275.

9. Gordon Hawkins, *The Prison: Policy and Practice* (Chicago: University of Chicago Press, 1977), p. 184.

10. Six texts which together provide a solid introduction to prison sociology are the following: Lee H. Bowker, *Prisoner Subcultures* (Lexington, MA: Lexington Books, 1977); Norman Johnson et al., eds., *The Sociology of Punishment and Correction* (New York: John Wiley, 1970); Richard Cloward et al., *Theoretical Studies in Social Organization of the Prison* (New York: Social Science Research Council, March 1960); Donald R. Cressey, ed., *The Prison: Studies in Institutional Organization and Change* (New York: Holt, Rinehart, Winston, 1961); Sir Leon Radzinowicz and Marvin E. Wolfgang, eds., *Crime and Justice*, vol. III, *The Criminal Under Restraint* (New York: Basic Books, 1977), part 3; Larence Hazelrigg, ed., *Prison Within Society: A Reader in Penology* (New York: Doubleday, 1968). Ten important and representative works of prison sociology are the following: Donald Clemmer, *The Prison Community* (New York: Rinehart and Co., 1958; first published 1940);

Gresham M. Sykes, *The Society of Captives* (Princeton, NJ: Princeton University Press 1958); Terrence Morris and Pauline Morris, *Pentonville: A Sociological Study of an English Prison* (London: Routledge and Kegan Paul, 1963); Donald R. Cressey, "Prison Organizations," *Handbook of Organizations*, ed. James G. March (New York: Rand McNally, 1965), pp. 1023–1070; John Irwin, *The Felon* (Englewood Cliffs, NJ: Prentice-Hall, 1970); Leo Carroll, *Hacks, Blacks, and Cons: Race Relations in a Maximum Security Prison* (Lexington, MA: Lexington Books, 1974); Rose Mary Giallombardo, *The Social World of Imprisoned Girls* (New York: John Wiley, 1974); James B. Jacobs, *Stateville: The Penitentiary in Mass Society* (Chicago: University of Chicago, 1977); John Irwin, *Prisons in Turmoil* (Boston: Little, Brown, 1980); James G. Fox, *Organizational and Racial Conflict in Maximum-Security Prisons* (Lexington, MA: Lexington Books, 1982).

11. Stuart Nagel et al., eds., *The Political Science of Criminal Justice* (Springfield, Ill.: Charles C. Thomas, 1983). For a favorable evaluation of this volume, see the review by Otwin Marenin in *The American Political Science Review* 78 (September 1984): 807–808.

12. As Jean Bickmore White has observed, "Political scientists who become interested in corrections policy soon discover that this interest is shared by few of their colleagues." See White, book review, *Political Science Quarterly* 96 (Winter 1981–1982): 687. A few political scientists, however, have studied prisons. Richard H. McCleery published a major book on administrative change in a Hawaii prison. See his *Policy Change in Prison Management* (East Lansing, MI: Michigan State University, 1957). Barbara A. Lavin has studied correctional policy making in New York State during 1959–1973. See her "Political Theory and Correctional Politics," paper presented at the American Political Science Association Meeting, Chicago, Illinois, September 1983. Jameson W. Doig has studied a broad range of correctional issues. See Doig, ed., *Criminal Corrections: Ideals and Realities* (Lexington, MA: Lexington Books, 1983).

Two fine undergraduate political science theses on prisons are Tamera Marie Stanton, "The Impact of Judicial Intervention in Prison Reform," (senior honors thesis, Department of Government, Harvard University, March 1979), and Julia Gordon, "Under Lock and Key: Correctional Policymaking in Massachusetts," (senior honors thesis, Department of Government, Harvard University, March 1985).

13. For a survey and analysis of the American public's views on crime, see Arthur L. Stinchcombe et al., *Crime and Punishment: Changing Attitudes in America* (San Francisco: Jossey-Bass, 1980). For a cross-national comparison, see Joseph E. Scott and Fahad Al-Thakeb, "The Public's Perceptions of Crime: A Comparative Analysis of Scandinavia, Western Europe, the Middle East, and the United States," in *Contemporary Corrections: Social Control and Conflict*, ed. C. Ronald Huff

(London: Sage, 1977), pp. 78–87. For a survey of contemporary American opinion about prisons, see *Gallup Report* 200 (May 1982): 3–25.

14. Together the following works provide a good introduction to the sociology of crime: Edwin H. Sutherland and Donald R. Cressey, *Criminology*, 9th ed., (Philadelphia: J. B. Lippincott Co., 1974); Sir Leon Radinowicz and Marvin E. Wolfgang, eds., *Crime and Society*, vol. I, *The Criminal in Society* (New York: Basic Books, 1977), parts 3 and 4; Susan E. Martin et al., *New Directions*, pp. 45–53, 63–79. Only mildly dated is the statement by Walter C. Reckless, "The Sociologist Looks at Crime," *Annals of the American Academy of Political and Social Science* 217 (September 1941): 76–83.

15. The split between the sociological and the commonsense view of prisons was made explicit by Terrence and Pauline Morris, *Pentonville*, p. 3.

16. For a sample of sociological views on prison violence see the following: Sykes, *Society*, chapters 6 and 7; Carrol, *Hacks, Blacks, and Cons;* Fox, *Organizational and Racial Conflict;* Lee H. Bowker, *Prison Victimization* (New York: Elsevier, 1980), chapter 9. The sociology of prison violence is discussed in greater detail later in this chapter.

17. Clemmer, *Prison Community*, p. xiii.

18. Sykes, *Society*, p. xii.

19. Rothman, *The Discovery of the Asylum*, chapter 4.

20. Sykes, *Society*, p. 5.

21. Ibid., p. 6.

22. George H. Grosser, introduction to Cloward et al., *Theoretical Studies*, p. 1.

23. Gresham M. Sykes and Sheldon Messinger, "The Inmate Social System," in ibid., p. 11.

24. Sykes, *Society*, especially chapter 2. Richard H. McCleery, "Governmental Process and Informal Social Control," in Cressey, ed., *The Prison*, especially pp. 158–160.

25. Bowker, *Prisoner Subcultures*.

26. Clemmer, *Prison Community*, p. 59.

27. Bowker, *Prisoner Subcultures*, p. 65. Bowker is evaluating Irwin's *The Felon*. Debates among prison sociologists concern not the fact but the developmental pattern of the inmate social system. Is inmate society imported into the prison from the streets or does it grow up behind the walls? See John Irwin, "The Big House: the Great American Prison," in Huff, ed., *Contemporary Corrections*, pp. 15–39. Irwin (pp. 37–38) contends that earlier sociologists underestimated the influence of "pre-prisoner orientations" and calls for "a new sociology of the prison." Some sociologists have argued that the "prizonization curve" is "U-shaped,"

meaning that inmates are most "prostaff" (or least a part of any inmate subculture) towards the beginning and end of their terms; others argue just the opposite. See Bowker, *Prisoner Subcultures*, pp. 20–21, 47–48.

28. Erving Goffman, *Asylums: Essays on the Social Situation of Mental Patients and Other Inmates* (New York: Doubleday, 1961), p. xiii.

29. Idem, "Of the Character of Total Institutions: The Inmate World," in Cressey, ed., *The Prison*, p. 16.

30. See David Reisman, "Some Observations on the Limits of Totalitarian Power," in *Individualism Reconsidered* (Glencoe, IL: The Free Press, 1954). I am most grateful to Professor Reisman for bringing this essay to my attention.

31. Sykes, *Society*, p. xv.

32. Donald R. Cressey, foreword to Clemmer, *Prison Community*, p. ix.

33. McCleery, in Cressey, ed., *The Prison*, pp. 153, 164–65.

34. Ibid., p. 153.

35. Ibid., p. 185.

36. For a small sample, see the following: Norman Polansky, "The Prison as an Autocracy," *Journal of Criminal Law and Criminology* 35 (May–June 1942): 16–22; Clarence Schrag, "Leadership Among Inmates," *American Sociological Review* 19 (February 1954): 37–42; Idem, "A Preliminary Typology," *Pacific Sociological Review* 4 (Spring 1961): 11–16; Fox, *Organizational and Racial Conflict*.

37. Sykes, *Society*, p. 123.

38. Ibid.

39. Fox, *Organizational and Racial Conflict*, p. 5. Like Polansky and other sociologists who had written decades earlier (see note 36 above), Fox asserts that in institutions where the administration enforces tight discipline, prisoners are more hostile and the most aggressive, antiauthority prisoners rise to positions of leadership.

40. Clemmer, *Prison Community*, p. 131.

41. Ibid., p. 314.

42. Ibid., p. xiii.

43. Ibid., p. 186.

44. Ibid., p. 190.

45. Ibid., p. 186. Clemmer took these words from Lewis E. Lawes, *Twenty Thousand Years in Sing Sing* (New York: Ray Long and Richard R. Smith, 1932), p. 106.

46. Ibid., p. 190.

47. Irwin, *Prisons*, p. xxiii.

48. Ibid., chapter 5, especially pp. 124–126.

49. Ibid., p. 248.

50. Ibid.

51. Ibid., pp. 241–248.

52. Kathleen Engel and Stanley Rothman, "Prison Violence and the Paradox of Reform," *The Public Interest* 73 (Fall 1983), p. 96.

53. See Irwin, *Prisons*, especially chapters 2 and 3, and John R. Faine and Edward Bohlander, Jr., "The Genesis of Disorder: Oppression, Confinement and Prisoner Politicization," in Huff, ed., *Contemporary Corrections*, pp. 54–77.

54. For brief accounts about these gangs see the following: "Profile/California," *Corrections Magazine* 1 (September 1974): 3–43; "Prison Gangs Formed By Racial Groups Pose Big Problem in West," *Michigan Corrections Association* (Spring 1984), pp. 143–147, 151–153; Robert Lindsey, "They're Behind Bars But Not Out of Business," *New York Times*, June 2, 1985, p. 2E.

55. John P. Conrad and Simon Dinitz, "The Prison Within a Prison: Discipline at the Impasse," (Columbus, Ohio: Academy for Contemporary Problems, March 1978), p. 16. On the same page they add: "The new prison has become a place where guards and convicts have a reason to fear each other. The tacit truce can no longer be relied on."

56. Engel and Rothman, "Prison Violence," p. 97.

57. Sykes wrote that the ability of prison administrators to govern "is defective, not simply in the sense that the ruled are rebellious, but also in the sense that the rulers are reluctant." See Sykes, *Society*, pp. 53, 58.

58. Conrad and Dinitz, "The Prison," describes three models of correctional management, among them the "shared-powers model" born in the wake of the prisoners' movement of the 1960s.

59. Janowitz, in foreword to Jacobs, *Stateville*, p. ix.

60. Sykes, *Society*, p. 134.

61. Bowker. *Prisoner Subcultures*, p. 125.

62. Richard W. Wilsnack, "Explaining Collective Violence in Prisons: Problems and Possibilities," in *Prison Violence*, eds. Albert Cohen et al. (Lexington, MA: Lexington Books, 1976), and an unpublished essay by Wilsnack and Lloyd E. Ohlin, "Preconditions for Major Prison Disturbances," preliminary draft of unpublished research report, Center for Criminal Justice, Harvard University Law School, undated.

63. Ibid.

64. Ibid.

65. Ibid.

66. Wilsnack and Ohlin, Ibid., p. 10.

67. Sykes, *Society*, p. 126.

68. Ibid., p. 111.

69. Ibid., pp. 111–120.

70. Ibid., p. 115.

71. Ibid.

72. Ibid., p. 120.

73. Ibid., p. 121

74. Ibid.

75. Ibid., p. 122.

76. Ibid. (emphasis deleted).

77. Ibid.

78. Ibid., p. 124 (emphasis deleted).

79. Ibid.

80. Ibid., p. 123.

81. Ibid., p. 129.

82. Vernon Fox, *Violence Behind Bars: An Explosive Report on Prison Violence in the United States* (Westport, CT: Greenwood Press, 1956).

83. Ibid., p. 315.

84. John Bartlow Martin, *Break Down the Walls* (New York: Ballantine Books, 1954), and "Why Did It Happen: The Riot at Jackson Prison," *Saturday Evening Post* (June 13, 1956).

85. Robert D. Vinter, "The Michigan Department of Corrections," (October 1961), p. 3.

86. Indeed, in the preface to the 1958 edition of his *The Prison Community*, Clemmer notes that there were "105 prison riots or serious disturbances in American prisons since 1950." That prisons were incredibly violent during the age of the legendary "cohesively-oriented" inmate leader is clear from G. David Garson, "The Politics of Collective Violence in America, 1863–1963" (Ph. D. Dissertation, Department of Government, Harvard University, 1969).

87. *Report of the Attorney General, 1980 Riot at Penitentiary of New Mexico.*

88. Ibid., part 2, p. 11.

89. Ibid., p. 6.

90. Ibid., Citizen's Advisory Report, p. 3.

91. Michael S. Serrill and Peter Katel, "The Anatomy of a Riot: the Facts Behind New Mexico's Bloody Ordeal," *Corrections Magazine* 6 (1980): 6–16, 20–24; Mark Colvin, "The New Mexico Prison Riot," *Social Problems* 29 (1982): 449–463; Wilbert Rideau and Billy Sinclair, "The Lessons of Santa Fe: Two Louisiana Lifers Look at the Bloodiest Prison

Riot in American History," *Dallas Times Herald*, February 2, 1981, pp. 1, 6; Roger Morris, *The Devil's Butcher Shop: The New Mexico Prison Uprising* (New York: Franklin Watts, 1982); W. G. Stone as told to G. Hirliman, *The Hate Factory: The Story of the New Mexico Penitentiary Riot* (Agoura, CA.: Paisano, 1982).

92. Engel and Rothman, "Prison Violence," pp. 93–94. For a report on conditions two years after the riot, see Timothy Leland, "N.M. Prison— 2 Years After a Slaughter," *Boston Globe*, October 20, 1982, pp. 1, 30.

93. *Report of the Attorney General*, part 1, p. 15.

94. Ibid., part 2, p. 10.

95. For descriptions and commentaries on the Graterford incident see the following: *The Report of the Governor's Panel to Investigate the Recent Hostage Incident at Graterford State Correctional Institution* (Pennsylvania, August 1981); David Zucchino, "Probe of Graterford Incident Finds that Answers Raise More Questions," *Philadelphia Inquirer*, February 14, 1982, p. G-3; William Robbins, "Guards 'Shake Down' Graterford Prison for Arms," *New York Times*, November 4, 1981; Tom Fox, "Prisons, Crime: No More Studies Needed," *Philadelphia Inquirer*, November 29, 1981; Chuck Stone, "Guards and Jo-Jo Bowen's Victims," *Philadelphia Daily News*, November 21, 1981, p. 2. Three years after the incident the prison remained troubled. See John Woestendiek, "On Graterford's E-Block the Smell of Violence Thickens," *Philadelphia Inquirer*, May 6, 1984, pp. 1, 20A.

96. Lawrence T. Kurlander, *Report to Mario Cuomo: The Disturbance at Ossining Correctional Facility, January 8–11, 1983* (Albany, New York, 1983), pp. 225–226. Also see the following: "Governor Orders Inquiry By State On Ossining Siege" and "Cuomo Faces Prison Issues," *New York Times*, January 12, 1983, pp. 1, B4, B5; "Report Says Ossining Guard Probably Sparked Uprising," *New York Times*, September 9, 1983, p. B3; "Legal Group Asserts Attica Is In 'Emergency Situation'," *New York Times*, November 22, 1983, p. B3; "State Panel Calls For Changes At Attica, Including Fewer Prisoners," *New York Times*, March 20, 1984, p. B28; Latique A. Jamel, "Fuses in New York Prisons," *New York Times*, June 25, 1984, op-ed page. On the 1971 Attica uprising, see the report of the McKay Commission, *Attica; the Official Report of the New York State Special Commission on Attica* (New York: Bantam Books, 1972). For a recent commentary on prison violence focused largely on New York prisons, see Steve Lerner, "Rule of the Cruel," *The New Republic*, October 15, 1984, pp. 17–21.

97. *July 1982 Update Of The Department of Corrections Response To the Report Of The Governor's Special Committee On Prison Disturbances* (Lansing: Michigan Department of Corrections, July 27, 1982).

98. For brief accounts of recent episodes, see the following: "Prisons

Security Lax Before Breakouts, Tennessee Reports," *New York Times*, April 17, 1984; Erik Ingram, "Quentin Guard's Death—Charge of Neglect," *San Francisco Chronicle*, June 28, 1985; Mary Crystal Cage, "Combs Become Weapons at Folsom Prison, Panel Told," *The Sacramento Bee*, June 20, 1985; David Ashenfelter et al., "Michigan Prisons: From Bad to Worse," *Detroit Free Press*, November 9–13, 1986.

99. James B. Jacobs, "Prison Violence and Formal Organization," in *Prison Violence*, p. 82.

100. Wilsnack, "Explaining Collective Violence In Prisons," in ibid.

101. A good selected bibliography of leading studies of prison violence published between 1972 and 1980 is contained in Marvin E. Wolfgang and Neil Alan Wagner, *The Violent Offender in the Criminal Justice System* (Washington, D.C.: National Institute of Justice, December 1981). But neither these studies nor others produced since enable us to make any confident generalizations about the underlying causes of prison disorder.

102. For an example of the kinds of demands presented to state prison officials, see "The Folsom Prisoners' Manifesto of Demands and Anti-Oppression Platform," in James E. Turpin, ed., *In Prison* (New York: New American Library, 1975), pp. 201–208.

103. American Correctional Association, "Causes, Preventive Measures, and Methods of Controlling Riots and Disturbances in Correctional Institutions" (Washington, D.C.: October 1970).

104. Some scholars, however, have discounted this evidence. For instance, in the early 1970s the California prison system experienced a rash of killings by inmate gangs. Then Director Raymond Procunier responded by tightening administrative controls. Prisons where the violence was worst were locked down for several weeks. Violent inmates were placed in "Management Control Units" while movements of the general population were supervised more closely. These and related measures did not stop the violence but did succeed in stabilizing it. This might be taken as wholly inconclusive but suggestive evidence in support of the hypothesis that tighter security measures and prison violence vary inversely. Howard Binda, however, has stressed the extent to which these management changes failed to squelch certain types of violence. See his "Effects of Increased Security on Prison Violence," *Journal of Criminal Justice* 3 (Spring 1975): 33–45. In his *Prisoner Subcultures*, Bowker (p. 115) cites Binda's study as one which "shows the limitations on any attempt to solve prison problems by merely changing administrative and custody procedures."

105. Particularly interesting in this regard is the Michigan Department of Corrections. The staff training materials on "race/human relations" and "working with people" are as long as those dealing with security and custody. Most of the former are derived directly from sociology and

social psychology texts. Also in this connection, it is interesting to note that the California Department of Corrections has offered inmates in selected institutions courses on radical sociology.

106. Chief among them is Jacobs, "Prison Violence," in Cohen et al., eds., *Prison Violence.*

107. Murton, "Prisons," in Wolfgang, ed., *Prisons: Present and Possible,* p. 24.

108. On recent violence in California's Folsom prison, Murton was quoted as follows (*The Sacramento Bee,* June 20, 1985): "The problem isn't knives on a board. . . . The basic problem isn't steel and concrete. It isn't weapons. It's the way you treat people." Also see his *The Dilemma of Prison Reform* (New York: Holt, Rinehart, and Winston, 1976).

109. Donald R. Cressey, in foreword to Irwin, *Prisons,* p. ix.

110. Ibid., p. viii.

111. Ibid.

112. Irwin, *Prisons,* p. 241.

113. Ibid., p. 246.

114. For a discussion of modern approaches to management addressed to correctional administrators, see the following: Alan R. Coffey, *Correctional Administration: The Management of Probation, Institutions and Parole* (Englewood Cliffs, NJ: Prentice-Hall, 1975); C. H. S. Jayewardene and D. J. N. Jayasuriya, *The Management of Correctional Institutions* (Toronto: Buttersworth, 1982); William G. Archambeaut and Betty J. Archambeaut, *Correctional Supervisory Management: Principles of Organization, Planning, and Law* (Englewood Cliffs, NJ; Prentice-Hall, 1982); David B. Kalinich and Terry Pitcher, *Surviving in Corrections: A Guidebook for Corrections People* (Springfield, IL: Charles C. Thomas, 1984); Clemens Bartollas, *Correctional Treatment: Theory and Practice* (Englewood Cliffs, NJ: Prentice-Hall, 1985).

115. Harry Elmer Barnes and Negley K. Teeters, *New Horizons in Criminology* (New York: Prentice-Hall, 1952), pp. 438–439.

116. Sykes, *Society,* p. 25.

117. Gresham M. Sykes and Sheldon Messinger, "The Inmate Social System," in Cloward et al., *Theoretical Studies,* p. 19.

118. Oscar Grusky, "Organizational Goals and the Behavior of Informal Leaders," *American Journal of Sociology* 67 (1959): 67. A report by Grusky on the same subject and based on the same research was sent to Michigan prison officials under the heading "Inmate Leaders: Cooperative or Hostile?" (March 1958).

119. Ibid.

120. Grusky, "Inmate Leaders," p. 8.

121. Grusky, "Organizational Goals," p. 66. In the published article, Grusky claimed that "data collected at Camp Davis and a comparable prison camp which did not have a program of treatment revealed that the inmates of the former were much more favorably oriented to their camp and to their officers and staff than were the inmates at the control camp—to a statistically significant degree" (p. 66). From both the published essay and the unpublished report submitted to Michigan prison officials, this claim does not seem entirely well justified. In addition, given the small numbers involved in Grusky's study, even the tentative conclusions about "Camp Davis" drawn from the statistical analysis are not terribly convincing.

122. For instance, see David Street et al., *Organization for Treatment: A Comparative Study of Institutions for Delinquents* (New York: Free Press, 1966); Bernard B. Berk, "Organizational Goals and Inmate Organization," *American Journal of Sociology* 71 (1966): 522–534; John M. Wilson and Jon D. Snodgrass, "The Prison Code in a Therapeutic Community," *Journal of Criminal Law, Criminology and Police Science* 60 (1969): 472–478.

123. Stanton Wheeler, "Socialization in Correctional Institutions," in *Crime and Justice*, vol. III, *The Criminal Under Restraint*, eds. Sir Leon Radzinowicz and Marvin E. Wolfgang (New York: Basic Books, 1977), p. 209.

124. Ibid.

125. John McCoy, *Concrete Mama: Prison Profiles From Walla Walla* (Columbia, MO, and London: University of Missouri University Press, 1981), p. 193.

126. Ibid.

127. Charles Stastny and Gabrielle Trynauer, *Who Rules the Joint? The Changing Political Culture of Maximum-Security Prisons in America* (Lexington, MA: Lexington Books, 1982), p. 4.

128. Ibid., p. 214.

129. Baker, *The Right to Participate*, p. 246.

130. Ibid.

131. Ibid.

132. Ibid., p. 251.

133. More accurately, the reformers so credited themselves. See, for example, Warden Clinton T. Duffy, *The San Quentin Story* (Garden City: Doubleday, 1950).

134. Grosser, in Cloward et al., *Theoretical Studies*, p. 4.

135. Ibid.

136. Ibid. Also see the following: Donald R. Cressey, "Contradictory Directives in Complex Organizations: the Case of the Prison," *Administrative Science Quarterly* 4 (1959): 1–19; Cressey, "Prison Organizations," in March, ed., *Handbook;* Sykes, *Society,* especially chapter 2; David Duffee, *Correctional Management: Change and Control in Correctional Organizations* (Englewood Cliffs, NJ: Prentice-Hall, 1980). Richard McCleery (in Cressey, ed., *The Prison,* p. 187) asserts that the "rehabilitative institution must permit a degree of initiative to its inmates that the purely custodial institution denies," leading to an inevitable conflict between "treatment officials" and the security forces.

137. Sykes, *Society,* chapter 2.

138. Charles E. Silberman, *Criminal Violence, Criminal Justice* (New York: Vintage Books, 1978), p. 564. In general, however, Silberman takes a mostly sociological perspective on prisons. For instance, he explains the post-1960s rise of prison violence by reference to a change in inmate social structure: "In effect, inmates have withdrawn the consent on which prison government has always rested. . . ." (p. 546).

139. William E. Amos, in foreward to Sawyer F. Sylvester et al., *Prison Homicide* (New York: Spectrum, 1977), p. xv. Others have made similar observations. Paul Tappan cautioned that the treatment versus custody dichotomy was a false one. Discipline, he argued, was essential to treatment. See his *Crime, Justice, and Correction* (New York: McGraw-Hill, 1961).

140. By the late 1970s many of the nation's inmates were doing just that. For one interesting account, see David C. Anderson, "The Price of Safety: 'I Can't Go Back Out There,' " *Corrections Magazine* 6 (1980): 6–15. This article tells of the rising tide of inmates who requested "protective custody" (PC) so as to be better protected against the predatory behavior of other inmates. In most prisons, inmates in PC have fewer privileges and far less freedom of movement than those in the general population. As is clear from most published accounts as well as from my own research, the inmates who live in fear and make requests for greater protection fit no stereotype but come in all races, sizes, and crimes of conviction.

141. Interview with the author, June 1984.

142. Sutherland and Cressey, *Criminology,* p. 511.

143. Bowker, *Prison Victimization,* p. 165.

144. Lerner, "Rule of the Cruel," p. 21.

145. Bartollas, *Correctional Treatment,* p. 285.

146. Sykes (*Society,* p. 38) chided the officials of the New Jersey State Prison as "indifferent to the task of reform, not in the sense that they reject reform out of hand as a legitimate organizational objective, but in

the sense that rehabilitation tends to be seen as a theoretical, distant, and somewhat irrelevant by-product of successful performance of the tasks of custody and internal order."

147. This idea can be found at several points in the corpus of Aristotle's writings, most especially in *Ethics*, Book 10, chapter 9. For a representative sampling of Mill's ideas, see *Essential Works of John Stuart Mill*, ed. Max Lerner (New York: Bantam Books, 1965). For an overview of how the findings of modern psychology relate to the subject, see the following: Gregory Kimble, Norman Garmezy, and Edward Zigler, *Principles of General Psychology*, 5th ed. (New York: John Wiley, 1980); Gerald C. Davidson and John M. Neale, *Abnormal Psychology: An Experimental Clinical Approach*, 3rd ed. (New York: John Wiley, 1982).

148. Lipton et al., *The Effectiveness of Correctional Treatment;* Martin et al., *New Directions*. Less publicized studies by the Michigan, California, and other state corrections departments have reached similar conclusions about the weak or nonexistent relationship between treatment programs and recidivism rates.

149. Jacobs, *Stateville*, p. 2.

150. Joseph Ragen and Charles Finstone, *Inside the World's Toughest Prison* (Springfield, IL: C. C. Thomas, 1962).

151. Irwin (*Prisons*, p. 27) counts Ragen among such highly touted prison reformers as Thomas Osborne and San Quentin's Clinton Duffy, men who "pushed the prisons toward humanity in their tenure as wardens." In his foreword to Irwin's book, Donald Cressey (pp. vii–viii) pays Ragen the high compliment of saying that, if he "had to do time," he would prefer to do it in Ragen's "Big House" and not in the "contemporary prison." Jacobs (*Stateville*) is as scrupulously neutral toward Ragen as any analyst so close to the subject could be. However, he characterizes Ragen's regime as "totalitarian." This misleading characterization is adopted wholesale by Silberman, *Criminal Violence*, chapter 10. Among prison practitioners, Raymond Procunier, former director of several state prison systems including those of Texas and California, does not think of Ragen (whom he met briefly once) as someone to emulate. On the other hand, George Beto, former Director of the Texas prison system, considers Ragen (whom he met with on more than one occasion) a positive guide for prison managers. Procunier's less than stellar opinion of Ragen was shared by most officials in Michigan and California while Beto's higher opinion of Ragen's legacy was shared by many of those in Texas, including former Director W. J. Estelle.

152. Jacobs, *Stateville*, p. 73.

153. Ibid., p. 78.

154. Ibid.

155. Ibid., p. 204.

156. Ibid.

157. Ibid., p. 209.

158. Kevin Krajick, "At Stateville, the Calm is Tense," *Corrections Magazine* 6 (1980): 6–19; Paul A. Gigot, "Assaults, Drug Traffic and Powerful Gangs Plague a Penitentiary," *Wall Street Journal*, August 20, 1981, pp. 1, 19.

159. Clemmer, *Prison Community*, p. 182.

160. McCormick, as cited in American Correctional Association, "Riots and Disturbances," p. 71.

161. Gustave de Beaumont and Alexis de Tocqueville, *On the Penitentiary System in the United States, and Its Application in France; With an Appendix on Penal Colonies, and also, Statistical Notes*, trans. Francis Lieber (Philadelphia: Carey, Lea and Blanchard, 1833), pp. 49, 106.

162. Ibid., p. 55.

163. Ibid., pp. 58–59.

164. Ibid., p. 87.

165. Ibid.

166. Echoing Aristotle, Edwin Corwin argued that the first task of students of government is "criticism and education regarding the true ends of the state and how best they may be achieved." See Corwin's "The Democratic Dogma and the Future of Political Science," *The American Political Science Review* 23 (1929): 569–592.

167. Richard A. McGee, *Prisons and Politics* (Lexington, MA: Lexington Books, 1981), p. 1.

CHAPTER 2. **The Quality of Prison Life** (pp. 49–95)

1. Chief Justice of the United States Supreme Court, the Hon. Warren E. Burger, foreword, "Our Crowded Prisons," *The Annals of the American Academy of Political and Social Sciences* 478 (March 1985).

2. Quoted in Jack Waugh, "Two Views of One System," *Christian Science Monitor*, December 16, 1971.

3. Marvin E. Wolfgang, "A Prologue to Prisons," in Wolfgang, ed., *Prisons: Present and Possible* (Lexington, MA: Lexington Books, 1979), p. 1. Many others have made similar observations. For instance, Leonard Orland has written: "Literally and metaphorically prisons are houses of darkness; dark in their secretness; dark in their filth and overcrowding; dark in their policies, which are premised, at best, on blind ignorance." (*Prisons: Houses of Darkness* [New York: Free Press, 1975], p. 41.)

Sheldon Krantz has described adult corrections as "a scandalous aspect of America's criminal justice system . . . its facilities are barbaric and its personnel are underpaid, undertrained, and overwhelmed." (*The Law of Corrections and Prisoners' Rights in a Nutshell* [St. Paul, MN: West, 1983], p. 1) David J. Rothman has argued that Jacksonian-era Americans invented the penitentiary not "as places of last resort," but "to join practicality to humanitarianism, reform the criminal, stabilize American society, and demonstrate how to improve the condition of mankind. . . ." (*The Discovery of the Asylum* [Boston: Little, Brown, 1971], p. 79.) But to many interpreters, the prison is the American invention that failed. Also see the following: David J. Rothman, *Conscience and Convenience* (Boston: Little, Brown, 1980); W. David Lewis, *From Newgate to Dannemora: The Rise of the Penitentiary in New York, 1796–1848* (Ithaca, NY: Cornell University Press, 1965); David Fogel, *"We Are the Living Proof . . .": The Justice Model for Corrections* (Cincinnati: W. H. Anderson, 1975).

4. Bruce Jackson, *Law and Disorder: Criminal Justice in America* (Urbana, IL: University of Illinois Press, 1984), p. 240.

It should be noted, however, that the rate at which Michigan's parolees are victims of homicide is over ten times that of prisoners. In other words, for convicted criminals in Michigan, prison is a much less lethal environment than the free community.

5. Joan Petersilia et al., *The Prison Experience of Career Criminals* (Santa Monica, CA: Rand Corporation, 1980), p. 16.

6. Stan Redding, *Houston Chronicle Magazine*, January 22, 1978, as quoted in David B. Gulick, untitled copy of Ph.D. dissertation draft (Criminal Justice Center, Sam Houston State University, February 1984), p. 4.

7. Waugh, "Two Views."

8. Kevin Krajick, "Profile/ Texas," *Corrections Magazine* 4 (1978).

9. John P. Conrad and Simon Dinitz, "The Prison Within a Prison: Discipline at the Impasse," (Columbus, Ohio: Academy for Contemporary Problems, March 1978), p. 29.

10. R. Craig Copeland, "The Evolution of TDC." (Masters thesis, Criminal Justice Center, Sam Houston State University, August 1980).

11. Clemens Bartollas, *Introduction to Corrections* (New York: Harper and Row, 1981), pp. 306–309.

12. Carol Anne Murphy Veneziano, "Stress and the Line Correctional Officer: An Empirical Examination" (Ph D. dissertation, Criminal Justice Center, Sam Houston State University, December 1981), p. 175.

13. Michigan Department of Corrections, *1981 Annual Statistical Report* (Lansing, MI), p. 8.

14. For a small sample, see the following: Michael Vines, "TDC: Cracks in the Myth," *The Texas Observer*, May 31, 1985, pp. 7–11; Michael Vines, "Inmate Reveals Why Violence Stalks Texas Prison System," *San Antonio News*, August 30, 1984; J. T. Sullivan, "Estelle's Era," *The Echo: Texas Prison Newspaper*, August /September 1984; McKinsey and Company, *Strengthening TCD's Management Effectiveness: Final Report* (Dallas, TX, May 14, 1984).

15. Petersilia et al., *Prison Experience*, p. 69.

16. Ibid., p. 68.

17. Petersilia (Ibid., p. 64) notes that the literature points to "a strong inverse association" between age and prison disciplinary problems. This conclusion holds as well for the literature produced since 1980.

18. For instance, see V. C. Cox et al., "Prison Crowding Research: The Relevance for Housing Standards and a General Approach Regarding Crowding Phenomena," *American Psychologist* 39 (1984): 1148–1160.

19. Sheldon Krantz lists "increasing the numbers of correctional officers" among the range of judicial remedies that judges have used. See Krantz, *Corrections and Prisoners' Rights*, p. 283.

20. Joan Mullen and Bradford Smith, *American Prisons and Jails*, vol. III: *Conditions and Costs of Confinement* (Washington, DC: National Institute of Justice, October 1980), chap. 4, p. 108.

21. Texas Department of Corrections, *A Survey of Personnel and Institutional Data from Selected Criminal Justice Agencies as Compared to TDC* (Huntsville, TX, January 1978).

22. In light of this fact it is interesting to note that in a major federal court decision Texas prison officials were, among other things, ordered to reduce the system's inmate-to-staff ratio. See *Ruiz* v. *Estelle*, 503 F.Supp. 1265 (S.D.Tex.1980).

23. Correctional officials are in uniform agreement that architecture matters a great deal, and some believe that it "makes or breaks" the operation.

24. Conrad and Dinitz, "The Prison," p. 27.

25. Ibid.

26. Gresham M. Sykes, *The Society of Captives: A Study of a Maximum Security Prison* (Princeton, NJ: Princeton University Press, 1958), chapter 4.

27. An excellent survey of the subject is made by James B. Jacobs, *New Perspectives On Prisons and Imprisonment* (Ithaca, NY, and London: Cornell University Press, 1983), chapters 3 and 4.

28. Blue Ribbon Commission For The Comprehensive Review Of The Criminal Justice Corrections System, *Preliminary Report to the Governor* (State of Texas, 1982), p. 5.

29. James Q. Wilson, *Thinking About Crime*, rev. ed. (New York: Basic Books, 1983), p. 7.

CHAPTER 3. **Governing Prisons in Three States** (pp. 99–164)

1. For a more detailed description of good time and the point-incentive program see *Texas Administrative Code*, Annotated, Part 2, sections 61.15 and 61.51 (State of Texas and McGraw-Hill, Inc., 1982).

2. J. T. Sullivan, "Estelle's Era," *The Echo: The Texas Prison Newspaper*, August /September 1984, p. 6.

3. *Texas Department of Corrections: 30 Years of Progress* (Huntsville, TX: Texas Department of Corrections, 1974), p. 4.

4. Among observers of the Texas political scene, Heatly's support for TDC and his ties to Beto were well known. See, for instance, Molly Ivins, "The Late Duke of Paducah Touched Every Texan's Life," *Dallas Times Herald*, February 28, 1984.

5. A representative list of these reports and other news stories related to Texas prisons is presented at the end of the notes for this chapter.

6. Hon. Governor John B. Connally of Texas, letter to the author, August 28, 1984. Interestingly, W. J. Estelle himself made a similar observation a decade earlier: "What remains unchanged is the formula necessary to realize our goals. As in the past, we must have the continuing support of the Texas citizenry; the intelligent support of the legislative and executive branches of government; a strong Board of Corrections, populated by leading business and professional persons . . . ." (*Texas Department of Corrections: 30 Years of Progress*, p. 72.)

7. Hon. Governor Preston Smith of Texas, letter to the author, August 28, 1984.

8. It is worth mentioning here that organization analysts, students of public administration and management among them, have only recently "discovered" that there are important connections between an organization's internal life and its political, economic, or other external circumstances. The reader who desires an explicit theoretical framework within which to place my account of each agency (particularly Texas) will find congenial candidates in the following: Gary L. Wamsley and Mayer N. Zald, *The Political Economy of Public Organizations* (Bloomington, IN, and London: Indiana University Press, 1976); Richard H. Hall, *Organizations: Structure and Process* (Englewood Cliff, NJ: Prentice-Hall, 1972), especially Part 4. I make no explicit or consistent use of any particular organization theory or mode of analysis because to do so would bog us down in esoteric conceptual and methodological issues, and because, to my knowledge, there is no such theory, which, if used in this way, would

help rather than hinder clear understanding and exposition. The single theory which comes closest is known as "contingency theory." For an overview of this theory, see the following: Fred Luthans, *Introduction to Management: A Contingency Approach* (New York: McGraw-Hill, 1976); Roy R. Roberg, *Police Management and Organizational Behavior: A Contingency Approach* (St. Paul, MN: West, 1978); Claudia Bird Schoonhoven, "Problems with Contingency Theory: Testing Assumptions Hidden Within the Language of Contingency 'Theory' ," *Administrative Science Quarterly* 26 (1981): 349–372.

9. Patrick Crimmins, reporter for the *Huntsville Morning News*, letter to the author, July 4, 1984.

10. Michigan Department of Corrections, "Purpose and History of the Michigan Department of Corrections," *Employee Handbook* (1979), p. 2.

11. Michigan Department of Corrections, "Introduction," *Pocket Guide For Prisoner Rule Violations* (1981).

12. Michigan Department of Corrections, *Policy Directive: Supervision of Prisoner Groups* (PD-BCF-30.10), December 1, 1981.

13. For an example of the kind of elaborate procedural guidelines on inmate processing necessitated by this classification system, see Michigan Department of Corrections, *Procedure: Intake Processing and Psychological Screening of R&CG* (Reception and Guidance Center) *Commitments* (OP-R&CG-40.07), July 15, 1983.

14. For some idea of what the officers have bargained for and won, see *Security Unit Agreement Between the State of Michigan and the Michigan Corrections Organization SEIU Local 526-M, AFL-CIO* (January 13, 1983 and September 30, 1984). The first page of the employee handbook cited in note 10 above states in large letters: "Any agreement that may be made between Unions . . . [and] the Department Employee that has been determined to be in conflict with the subject matter contained herein will take precedence over the contents of this book."

15. For a summary of the settlement between the Michigan prison system and the U.S. Department of Justice, see Michigan Department of Corrections, *Deadline* (January 19, 1984).

16. For an extensive description of the EPA and the problems and controversy surrounding it, see David Ashenfelter et al., "Revolving Prison Doors," *Detroit Free Press*, September 22–28, 1985. For a fair description of recent troubles inside Michigan prisons, see David Ashenfelter et al., "Michigan Prisons: From Bad to Worse," *Detroit Free Press*, November 9–13, 1986.

17. For a detailed description of the California classification system, see California Department of Corrections, *Review and Analysis of Departmental Classification System* (April 1984).

18. Procunier's remark and a decent overview of the California system as it existed in the year before he left the department can be found in "Profile/California," *Corrections Magazine* 1 (September 1974).

19. At least in Enomoto's case, however, the newcomer label was more the perception than the reality. He began his career as a social worker in 1952 and a few years later became a counselor in San Quentin. He then held administrative posts at several other CDC prisons including Soledad. Also, he was the agency's chief of classification from 1966 to 1970. Interestingly, however, most veteran CDC staffers, especially the correctional officers, were unaware of Enomoto's background or discounted it as marginal.

20. Procunier also served in California's welfare and social services agency.

21. William Darryl Henderson, *Cohesion: The Human Element in Combat* (Washington, DC: National Defense University Press, 1985); Martin von Creveld, *Fighting Power: German and US Army Performance, 1939–1945* (Westport, CT: Greenwood Press, 1982): David Evans, "The U.S. Military Forgets that Wars Are Won By Men," *New York Times*, February 4, 1986, p. A23; Arthur T. Hadley, *The Straw Giant: Triumph and Failure: America's Armed Forces* (New York: Random House, 1986).

22. Folsom, it should be noted, has had a far higher rate of homicides and other serious incidents than Soledad. Some inmates, however, apparently are comforted by the greater gun coverage that obtains at the former prison.

23. R. Craig Copeland, "The Evolution of the TDC," (Masters thesis, Institute of Contemporary Corrections and the Behavioral Sciences, Sam Houston State University, August 1980).

24. Other observers have noted the lack of conflict between security and treatment personnel in Texas. Commenting on how officers and counselors have administered TDC's programs for mentally retarded inmates, Miles Santamour, a member of the President's Committee on Mental Retardation, noted the lack of animosity between treatment and custody personnel in Texas. No other state, he observed, has ever tried to merge its security and treatment staffs the way the Texas program does. Santamour stated: "I've never seen a security staff so excited about treatment." See Mary C. Bounds, "A Way Out From Within: Texas Program Aids Mentally Impaired," *The Dallas Morning News*, October 28, 1984, pp. 1A, 4A.

25. The Soledad officers' negative feelings were due in part to the fact that Soledad staff have suffered a disproportionately high percentage of the assaults on staff by inmates. For instance, with about 10–12 percent of the system's population in 1981 and 1982, CTF-Soledad's North and

Central units suffered 21 percent of the system's assaults in 1981 and 19.6 percent in 1982. See Research Unit, *Study of Inmate Assaults On Staff During the First and Third Quarters of the Years 1981 and 1982*, California Department of Corrections, March 18, 1983.

26. Min S. Yee, *The Melancholy History of Soledad Prison* (New York: Harper's Magazine Press, 1973).

27. John P. Conrad, "A Lost Ideal, A New Hope: The Way Toward Effective Correctional Treatment," *The Journal of Criminal Law and Criminology* 4 (Winter 1981), p. 1714.

28. See, for instance, the following: "SEIU—Running Scared," *The Unionist*, May/June 1984; "SEIU Helps Cover-Up," *The Organizer*, June 6, 1984.

29. Director Robert Brown as quoted by Michael A. Lewis and Howard Warren, "Did Laxity Help Fuel Prison Melee?," *Detroit Free Press*, Saturday, September 7, 1985, p. 3A.

Unnoted Sources

Other sources of information on Texas, Michigan, and California prisons were helpful in writing this chapter. A representative sample of the other newspaper accounts and documents consulted appears below.

Texas Department of Corrections

Newspapers

The Echo: The Texas Prison Newspaper.
June 1975–October 1985.

The Huntsville Item.
January 1965–June 1985.

New York Times.
Wendell Rawls, Jr., "Texas Presses Bid to Kill Prison Suit," December 13, 1981; "Tough Prisons, in a Tough Bind" (editorial), December 18, 1981; Stuart Taylor, Jr., "U.S. Judge Awards $1.71 Million In Legal Fees in Texas Prison Case," and "U.S. Judge in Texas Draws Widespread Hostility With Liberal Rulings," November 20, 1982; Wendell Rawls, Jr., "Texas Officials Ease Resistance to U.S. Court Order on Crowded Prisons," May 21, 1983; "Texas Using a New Formula to Guide its Prison Releases," December 11, 1983; Robert Reinhold, "New Chief Shaking Up Prison System in Texas," June 22, 1984; Wayne King, "Governor Intervenes in Texas Prison Violence," August 12, 1984; Robert Reinhold, "Texas Prison Chief Quits After a Year," June 18, 1985; Robert Reinhold, "Texas Copes With the Cost of Criminals," June 30, 1985.

Bryan Eagle.

"Is Prison Violence Out of Hand?," August 16, 1984; Janet Warren, "Activist Says Counties Contribute to Prison Overcrowding, Violence," August 22, 1984; Dana Palmer, "Union Files Suit Against TDC Rules," August 23, 1984; Sam Logan, "Where I Do I Get Article Ideas? From Experience," August 30, 1984; Sam Logan, "Prison Inmates' Civil Rights Cost Them Their Lives," September 13, 1984; Sharon Herbaugh, "TDC's Top Man Is No Stranger to Prison Problems," November 4, 1984; "White Supremacist Gang Linked to Latest Fatal Prison Stabbing," November 24, 1984.

Waco Tribune Herald.

Rep. Ray Keller, "Pretty Patina Turns to Tarnish When Spotlight Shines on TDC," March 8, 1984; Linda Anthony, "TDC Officials Want Changes for System," November 8, 1984.

San Antonio Light.

"We Have Confidence in Procunier Prison Job" (editorial), September 26, 1984; Don Yaeger, "Solution to Violence Escapes Corrections Department Leaders," September 24, 1984; Stephen Sharpe, "New Prison Board Member Says Views Changed," interview with Ruben Montemayor, October 21, 1984.

Dallas Morning News.

"Report Assails Texas Prison Projects," May 7, 1983; Rep. Ray Keller, "Reform Package Designed to Control Growth of State Prisons," May 8, 1983; Sam Kinch, "TDC Misused Funds, Legislator Says," November 23, 1983; Monica Reeves, "Problems Toppled TDC Chief," December 4, 1983; Richard Fish, "Legislator Urges TDC Investigation," December, 15, 1983; Mary C. Bounds, "1974 Study Pointed to Today's TDC Problems," February 18, 1984; Mary C. Bounds, "6 Texas Prisons to House Most Violent Inmates," August 25, 1984; Anton Riecher, "Texas Prison Official Notes Changes Since His Stabbing," October 15, 1984; John Gonzalez, "White Wants Prison Panelist to Do Job or Quit," October 23, 1984; "Prison Workers Signing Judge's Order," November 11, 1984; Mary C. Bounds, "Prison Board Criticized; Procunier Won't Last, Legislator Predicts," November 16, 1984; Mary C. Bounds, "Procunier Faces Toughest Challenge," November 18, 1984; Mary C. Bounds, "Prison Director Talks About His Turbulent First Six Months," interview with Raymond Procunier, November 18, 1984; "Procunier Has Brought Changes for Texas Wardens," November 2, 1984; "Texas Prison Guard Fired For Passing Marijuana to Inmate" and "Prison Board Chief Expects to Lose His Post" and "TDC Inmate Slain During Argument in Cell," December 5, 1984; Mary C. Bounds, "Party Politics, Activism Shaking Up Prison Board," December 16, 1984; Mary C. Bounds, "Warden Hopes Prison

Strife went Out With the Old Year," January 3, 1985; "Prison Reforms: The Breaking Point," (editorial), January 10, 1985; G. Robert Hillman, "White Calls Summit to Discuss Prisons Progress," January 12, 1985; Terrence Stutz, "Legislature OKs $500,000 Study of State Prisons," January 15, 1985; Mary C. Bounds, "Prison-Suit Pact Signed," May 17, 1985.

Houston Post.

Felton West, "Texas House OKs Court, Prison Reforms," May 3, 1983; Fred Bonavita, "TDC Board Member Says Prison System 'In a State of Crisis,'" May 4, 1983; "Governor Signs Prison Legislation," May 26, 1983; Doug Freelander, "Prison Officers Receive Blame for Abuses," November 6, 1983; Richard Vara, "TBC Chairman Raps Criticism of Prisons," January 10, 1984; "Shadow over TDC" (editorial) January 27, 1984; Fred Bonavita, "Are Inmates Likely to Riot?," February 5, 1984; Fred Bonavita, "Report Notes TDC Progress," September 28, 1984; Eduardo Paz-Martinez, "Prisons Safer Than Reported: TDC Chief Says News Exaggerated," September 28, 1984; Fred King, "Procunier Resigning, Sources Say," June 15, 1985; Fred King, "McCotter Named TDC Director," June 18, 1985.

Dallas Times Herald.

Molly Ivins, "Lege Has Seen the Light, Felt the Heat of Prison Reform," May 24, 1983; Patti Kilday, "Maverick Sparks Controversies on Prison Board," May 29, 1983; "Legislator Wants Prison Managers to Make Full Financial Disclosures," January 13, 1984; Arnold Hamilton, "Ex-Prison Chief Scolds, Challenges Critics," February 3, 1984; Patti Kilday, "W. J. Estelle Jr.: Fallen Hero of TDC," February 6, 1984; Patti Kilday, "Cell Left Unlocked Before Killing; Guard Fired" and "Disgruntled TDC Workers Flock to Union," August 23, 1984; Dale Rice, "Procunier Accepts Job's Challenges, Wins Confidence," November 25, 1984; Molly Ivins, "Texas in Justice,"December 14, 1984; Patti Kilday, "TDC Admits to Shortages, Prison Squalor," January 20, 1985; Patti Kilday, "Prison Lawsuit Leaves $7 Million Legal Tab," May 15, 1985; Peter Larson, "Prison Suit Filled Judge's Life with Controversy, Appeals," May 15, 1985.

Austin American-Statesman.

Candice Hughes, "Prison Board Defies White Budget Plea," November 11, 1983; "Prison Officials Getting the Word," editorial, November 14, 1983; "Prison Brutality Inquiry Reopened," November 30, 1983; Candice Hughes, "Morale Level of Prison Staff Breeds Worry in Huntsville," January 30, 1984; Mike Hailey, "Prison Board Chief Admits Frustration," March 5, 1984; "Unarmed Violence Fails to 'Alarm' Prison Chief," September 16, 1984; "15th Inmate Slain in Prison Stabbing," September

29, 1984; "Governor White's Odd Reform Message" (editorial), October 18, 1984.

Houston Chronicle.

Glenn Smith, "Prison Reform Bills Met with Almost No Opposition," May 2, 1983; John Toth and Frank Klimko, "Inmate Gangs Intimidating, Killing Inside State Prisons," January 29, 1984; Clay Robinson, "High Time to Deal with TDC," January 29, 1984; Raul Reeves, "TDC Director Vows Get-Tough Policy to Re-Establish Order," August 25, 1984; Tim Sheey, "Ex-Con's Book Details Brutality of Prison Life," September 23, 1984; John Toth, "Warden, Assistant Resign at TDC Darrington Unit," October 24, 1984; John Toth, "TDC Goes Outside System to Fill Post," October 26, 1984; Evan Moore, "TDC's Fraternities of Fear," part one of "Hard Times in TDC," November 18, 1984; Evan Moore and Frank Klimko, "From Bones to Bombs," November 19, 1984; John Toth and Evan Moore, "Prison Different as 'Life on Mars'," November 20, 1984; Cindy Horswell, "Inmates, Families Live in Fear Because of TDC Dangers," November 20, 1984; John Toth and Frank Klimko, "Changes Frustrate TDC Guards," November 21, 1984; John Toth and Frank Klimko, "Possible 'Hit List,' Gun Found in Prison," November 22, 1984; Frank Klimko, "Procunier Working to Curb Violence" and "Fiscally, TDC Still Has A Lot To Brag About," November 22, 1984; Don Sneed, "Something Good Inside Texas Prisons," December 10, 1984; John Toth, "Wire Mesh Screens Installed on TDC High-Security Cells," January 23, 1985; Frank Klimko, "TDC Board Chairman Gunn Patches Differences with Governor," January 16, 1985; Clay Robinson, "Officials Endorse Settlement in 13-Year Old Lawsuit," May 17, 1985; Clay Robinson and Frank Klimko, "TDC Staff Warned to Toe Line or Face Firing," May 17, 1985.

Fort Worth Star Telegram.

Karen Hastings, "Prison Chief Puts Pacification Before Reforms," August 5, 1984; Thomas D. Denton, "Violence and Decay of Prisons Won't Be Shouted Away," October 28, 1984.

Huntsville Morning News.

Partick Crimmins, "Audit Shows TDC's Fiscal Complexity," May 28, 1984.

The Houstonian.

(Sam Houston State University).

Loretta Davies, "Beto Recalls TDC," November 8, 1984.

DOCUMENTS AND REPORTS

Apart from newspaper reports, a broad body of departmental materials were consulted. A representative sample of the more interesting and important materials appears below.

Texas Department of Corrections, *Annual Report.* 1963 through 1984.

Texas Department of Corrections, *Annual Statistical Report.* 1970 through 1984.

Texas Department of Corrections, *Newsletter.* 1978 through 1984.

Texas Department of Corrections, *Texas Prison Rodeo: Official Souvenir Program.* 1968 through 1985.

Texas Department of Corrections, *WYNOT* (Quarterly publication of TDC substance-abuse program). 1980 through Holiday Issue 1983.

Texas Department of Corrections, Technical and Research Reports of the Research, Planning, and Development Division (later Management Services Division), 1972 through 1984.

Texas Department of Corrections, Inmate Classification and Testing Forms. 1978 through 1983.

Texas Department of Corrections, *Employees Manual of Rules and Regulations.* September 1978.

Texas Department of Corrections, *Rules and Regulations and Grievance Procedures.* February 27, 1978.

Texas Department of Corrections, *Pre-Service Training Syllabus and Outline.* Undated.

Texas Department of Corrections, *In-Service Training: Summary and Outline.* Undated.

Texas Department of Corrections, *Affirmative Action and EEO Plan.* September 1, 1978.

Texas Department of Corrections, *Tenth Annual Inmates Art Festival, 1983.*

Texas Department of Corrections, *Rules and Regulations: Huntsville Unit.* March 1983.

Texas Department of Corrections, *Memorandum: Alternatives to TDC's Overcrowding.* March 1983.

Texas Department of Corrections, *TDC Unit Operations Manual For Compliance With Ruiz Stipulation Concerning Use Of Support Service Inmates.* May 1982.

Texas Department of Corrections, Executive Division, *Ruiz v. Estelle Critical Date Guidelines and Assigned Responsibilities.* 1983.

Texas Department of Corrections, *Report on Population and Housing.* May 1, 1981.

Texas Department of Corrections, *Chronology of Ruiz Case, June 1972–June 30, 1982*. Undated.

Texas Department of Corrections, *Facilities Study*. January 1983.

California Department of Corrections

NEWSPAPERS

Sacramento Bee.

Claire Cooper, "Prison Overcrowding Inaction Prompts Interim Chief to Quit," March 8, 1983; Judy Tachibana, "Safety Risk Forces Prison Faculty Shift," February 9, 1984; "Panel OKs Corrections Chief Nominee," February 10, 1984; Claire Cooper, "Gang-Mixing Deliberate, Ex-Folsom Warden Says," February 17, 1984; "Prison Workers Reject CSEA Bid Again," March 4, 1984; Claire Cooper, "US Warns Duke on Folsom Prison Violence," April 24, 1984; David Kirp, "Commentary: Prison Politics," May 14, 1984; Laura Mecoy, "Why 'the hole' is Place to Be in State Prison," November 24, 1985; Kent Pollock and Laura Mecoy, "Rifles Hold the Line in California Prisons," November 24, 1985.

San Francisco Examiner.

Bruce J. Adams, "Prisoners Are Back to Work, But Complaints Continue," March 1, 1983; Guy Wright, "Will We Need New Prisons?," March 30, 1983; "Time-bomb in the Prisons" (editorials), April 4, 1984; Tom Hall, "Folsom Denies Staffing Problems," April 24, 1984.

San Francisco Recorder.

Kevin Gallagher, "State Bar to Support Prison Clean-Up Suit," March 29, 1983.

San Francisco Chronicle.

Jack Viets, "San Quentin's Inmate Workers Go On Strike," February 16, 1983; "The Prison Crunch" (editorial), April 13, 1984; David Coulter, "Business Is Booming in 'Prison Industry'," May 19, 1984; "Quentin Lockdown for Blacks, Hispanics," June 19, 1984.

San Diego Daily Californian.

"Prisons Can Be Workplaces" (editorial), January 1, 1984.

San Bernardino Sun.

Art Wong, "Prison Workers Vote to Stay with Small Union," March 3, 1984; "Prisons Show More Strain" (editorial), May 6, 1984.

San Jose Mercury News.

Armando Acuna, "Prison Crisis Strains State," April 3, 1984; "The Price of Prisons," editorial, April 5, 1984.

Van Nuys Daily News.
"Presley Now Urges Shorter Prison Terms," December 25, 1983; "Many Ex-Cons Get Job-Injury Awards," February 20, 1984.

Monterey Peninsula Herald.
"Conservation Camp Proposed at Soledad Facility," February 15, 1984; "The Soledad Shuttle" (editorial), March 21, 1984.

San Luis Obispo Telegram Tribune.
Phil Dirkx, "New Superintendent of CMC Turns Loose Some of His Ideas," February 9, 1984; Alan Mittelstaedt, "More Doubling Up for CMC," March 27, 1984.

Sacramento Union.
Bob Taylor, "Convict Work Plan Outlined," January 31, 1983; Anne Richards, "State Appeals Court's Prisoner-Move Order," March 31, 1984; Scott Reeves, "Prison Violence Likely, Former Director Warns," April 10, 1983.

Folsom Telegram.
Rosemay Younts, "Prison Gangs: Way of Life for Inmates," January 26, 1983; Kristine Angelli, "Correctional Officers Displeased with Judge," June 12, 1985.

San Rafael Independent Journal.
"Prison Frills? Tell the Judge" (editorial), February 21, 1984.

Ontario Daily Report.
"Prison Officials Given Broad Transfer Rights," March 8, 1984.

Los Angeles Times.
John Hurst, "Four Days in Prison: One Man's Story," June 7, 1981; John Hurst, " 'Model' Prison System Degenerating," June 8, 1981; John Hurst, "State Prison System's Future Uncertain," June 9, 1981; "It's Hell" (editorial), June 14, 1981.

Los Angeles Daily Journal.
Alan Ashby, "Profile: Daniel J. McCarthy," December 19, 1983.

Modesto Bee.
Jim McClung, "Nuestra Familia Strikes Terror No More," February 14, 1983.

Record Gazette.
Jim Johnson, "A Trip Behind the Wall," January 24, 1984.

Wall Street Journal.
Stanley Penn, "Prison Gangs Formed By Racial Groups Pose Big Problem in West," May 13, 1983.

MAGAZINES

Peter Collier and David Horowitz, "Requiem for a Radical," *New West* (March 1981), pp. 64–71, 133–147.

Aric Press and Richard Sandza, "A Lockdown at San Quentin," *Newsweek* (July 9, 1984), p. 62.

Fred Nichols, "Sentence: Life Imprisonment," *Sacramento* (August 1984), pp. 22–29, 42–43.

Adriana Gianturco, "Prison Construction: A Program Gone Wrong," *California Journal* (June 1985), pp. 230–233.

Dan Goodgame, "Mayhem in the Cellblocks," *Time* (August 12, 1985), p. 20.

DOCUMENTS AND REPORTS

California Department of Corrections, *An Annotated Chronology of the California Department of Corrections; Draft # 7*. December 2, 1977.

Rules and Regulations of the Director of Corrections. November 1982. Published as State of California, *California Administrative Code*. Title 15. Crime Prevention and Corrections. Division 3. Department of Corrections. Chapter 1.

California Department of Corrections, *California Department of Corrections, 1984*. June 1, 1984.

California Department of Corrections, *California Prisoners*. 1973–1984.

California Department of Corrections, *Institutional Personnel Survey*. April 20, 1984.

California Department of Corrections, *Departmental Recruitment*. Undated.

California Department of Corrections, *California Men's Colony*. October 10, 1984.

California Department of Corrections, *Population Projections Fiscal Years 1983–1984 through 1987–1988*. February 29, 1984.

California Department of Corrections, *Newscam*. 1983–1984.

California Department of Corrections, *Administrative Bulletin*. January 11, 1984–May 14, 1984.

California Department of Corrections, *Review and Analysis of Departmental Inmate Classification System*. April 1984.

California Department of Corrections, *Mission, Goals and Objectives*. April 16, 1984.

California Department of Corrections, *Final Plan to Implement the Findings of the Court; Wilson V. Deukmejian, Phase II Report.* April 16, 1984.

California Department of Corrections, *Correctional Training Facility: July Training.* July 1984.

California Department of Corrections, Research Reports of the Research Division (later Research Unit). October 1967–July 1984.

California State Personnel Board, *Specification.* Correctional Officer, April 25, 1979; Correctional Sergeant, May 7, 1975; Correctional Lieutenant, August 16, 1983; Correctional Counselor I, February 5, 1975.

Correctional Training Facility, *Soledad Star* (Inmate Newspaper). 1983–1984.

BOOKS

Lloyd L. Voight, *History of California State Correctional Administration* (San Francisco, 1949).

Warden Clinton T. Duffy, as told to Dean Jennings, *The San Quentin Story* (Garden City, NY: Doubleday, 1950). Theodore Davidson, *Chicano Prisoners: The Key to San Quentin* (New York: Holt, Rinehart, and Winston, 1977).

Michigan Department of Corrections

NEWSPAPERS

All prison-related articles from several newspapers for the period October 1983–May 1984 were consulted, among the newspapers were the following: *Lansing State Journal; Detroit Free Press; Ionia Centinel-Standard; Ann Arbor News; Ypsilanti Press; Detroit News; Jackson Citizen Patriot; Flint Journal; Grand Rapids Press; Traverse City Record-Eagle.* In addition to those more recent articles already noted, the following were helpful: David Ashenfelter and Michael G. Wagner, "Prison Chief Criticizes Stories as Misleading," *Detroit Free Press,* October 2, 1985; Tom Fitzgerald, "Prison Security Changes Proposed," *Ann Arbor Press,* October 20, 1985; "Second SMP Fight Hurts 8 Guards, Inmate," *The Jackson Citizen Partriot,* June 10, 1985; Corey Williams, "8 Prison Officers Hurt in 2nd Fracas," *Lansing State Journal,* June 10, 1985; Elizabeth Cobbs, "HVMF Warden Redman Leaving," *Ypsilanti Press,* August 30, 1985;

DOCUMENTS AND REPORTS

State of Michigan, *Committee on Corrections Report.* 1972.

Michigan Department of Corrections, *Dimsensions.* Fall 1976.

Michigan Department of Corrections, *Policy Directive Manual*. 1974–June 1984.

Michigan Department of Corrections, *Procedure Manual*. 1974–June 1984.

Michigan Department of Corrections, *Memorandum File*. 1974–June 1984.

Michigan Department of Corrections, *Dialogues*. October, 1975–March/April 1984.

Michigan Department of Corrections, *Annual Statistical Report/Presentation*. 1977–1983.

Michigan Department of Corrections, *July 1982 Update Of the Department of Corrections Response to the Report of the Governor's Special Committee on Prison Disturbances*. July 27, 1982.

Michigan Department of Corrections, *Summary Report By the Decree Coordinator*. 1984.

Michigan Department of Corrections, Bureau of Programs, Research Reports. 1973–June 1984.

Huron Valley Men's Facility, *The Huron Valley Monitor* (Inmate Newspaper). 1983–July 31, 1984.

Michigan Reformatory, *Hill Top News* (Inmate Newspaper). 1983–May 1984.

Michigan Department of Corrections, *Handbook for Family and Friends of Michigan Prisoners*. 1984.

BOOK

David B. Kalinich, *The Inmate Economy* (Lexington, MA: Lexington Books, 1980).

CHAPTER 4. **Correctional Philosophy and Leadership**
(pp. 165–204)

1. Other researchers have found traces of the keeper philosophy among correctional workers. Gresham M. Sykes, for instance, noted that there "is no indication in the day-to-day operation of the prison that the officials have any desire to act as avenging angels." See his *The Society of Captives: A Study of a Maximum Security Prison* (Princeton, NJ: Princeton University Press, 1958), p. 31. Based on his study of Illinois correctional officers, James B. Jacobs argued: "No extreme desire to punish prisoners

is evident. Indeed, the guards' opinion as to the causes of crime and the purposes of imprisonment parallels the liberal sociopolitical position." See Jacobs and Norma Crotty, "The Guard's World," in Jacobs, *New Perspectives on Prisons and Imprisonment* (Ithaca and London: Cornell University Press, 1983), p. 134.

2. Michigan Department of Corrections, "The Thin File," *Dialogues*, 45 (April 1981): 16.

3. The newsletter of the American Association of Correctional Officers (AACO) is published in Michigan under the title *Keeper's Voice*.

4. Martin Luther, cited in Duncan B. Forrester, "Martin Luther and John Calvin," in *History of Political Philosophy*, eds. Leo Strauss and Joseph Cropsey, 2nd ed., (Chicago: University of Chicago Press, 1981), p. 311.

5. John Stuart Mill, as cited in Perry M. Johnson, "The Role of Penal Quarantine in Reducing Violent Crime," Michigan Department of Corrections, June 1977, p. 2. Mill's principle of noninterference, Johnson noted, "seems to us to be the only proper basis and goal of imprisonment."

6. John Stuart Mill, *On Liberty*, ed. David Spitz (New York: W. W. Norton and Company, 1975), p. 11.

7. Ibid.

8. Perry M. Johnson, "A Selective Incapacitation Approach to Corrections," speech delivered at the American Correctional Association (ACA) Congress of Corrections, San Antonio, Texas, August 22, 1984 (emphasis in original).

9. Perry M. Johnson, "Capital Punishment — A Futile Act," Michigan Department of Corrections, *Speakers Resource Kit*, Document "L" and "I," pp. 1 and 3.

10. W. J. Estelle, "The Constitution: A Delicate Balance," PBS documentary, taped June 1983.

11. Not only did it continue to provide these services, but in 1984 it began an elaborate study of how academic and vocational education programs were delivered.

12. Alexis de Tocqueville, *Democracy in America*, vol. 2, trans. Henry Reeve, ed. Phillips Bradley (New York: Vintage Books, 1945), p. 90.

13. Jameson W. Doig and Erwin C. Hargrove, *Leadership and Innovation: A Biographical Perspective on Entrepreneurs in Government* (Baltimore, MD: The Johns Hopkins University Press, 1987), chapter 1.

14. James B. Jacobs, *Stateville: The Penitentiary in Mass Society* (Chicago: University of Chicago Press, 1977). Jacobs argued (p. 51): "Thus, in 1961, when Ragen left Stateville, his system of charismatic dominance was unassailable. . . . Yet on the national scene it was clear that the type of regime exemplified by Ragen and his generation was

passing. . . . Change would, no doubt, have buffeted Stateville even if he had stayed on. . . ." As we shall see in our discussion of correctional leadership in Texas, a most Ragenesque leader with close personal and professional ties to Stateville's famous warden, George Beto, came to the helm of TDC in 1962 and did not permit the types of changes occurring in other prison systems to occur in Texas. It is not implausible that Ragen himself could have done the same in Illinois had he not retired.

15. Richard A. McGee, *Prisons and Politics* (Lexington, MA: Lexington Books, 1981), p. 59.

16. Ibid., p. 114.

17. In this connection, it is worth noting that the executives of private corrections firms have taken a page from the book of Michigan and other systems that have used ACA standards and the accreditation process as a hedge against unfavorable court rulings. In an interview with the author, one private corrections official confided: "Look, the Supreme Court has said that the accreditation process, once completed, puts you beyond minimum constitutional standards. There's lots of paperwork, but it's worth it. . . . They don't come back for three years; meanwhile, you've got one hell of a legal fig leaf, a presumption of innocence against inmate suits, big and small."

18. Johnson's message about prisons being only one part of the corrections system — and the part of last resort — was not just for external consumption. In the opening section of the Michigan Department of Corrections *Employee Handbook* (1979), the last paragraph began with "a final and important point. Corrections should not be identified with prisons alone. . . . There is good evidence that community supervision is more effective in terms of public protection than incarceration unless the offense, or the risk to the public, is so serious that incarceration is unavoidable."

19. CBS Reports, 1966. For a more critical look at TDC under Beto, see Danny Lyon and Billy Cune, *Conversations with the Dead: An Exhibition of Photographs of Prison Life* (New York: Holt, Rinehart, and Winston, 1970).

20. Beto's dedication was inspired in part by the example of Stateville's Warden Ragen. Before becoming TDC director, Beto spent a Sunday evening with Ragen at the warden's home. He learned that it was the first Sunday that Ragen had been in town without spending a part of his morning "walking that big yard." Years later, Beto summarized in 26 points his basic principles of correctional management and penal reform. See Beto, syllabus for Criminal Justice 571, "Special Topics in Correctional Administration," Sam Houston State University, pp. 6, 7.

21. Cited in R. Craig Copeland, "The Evolution of TDC," (Masters

thesis, Institute of Contemporary Corrections and the Behavioral Sciences, Sam Houston State University), p. 220.

22. Walter L. Pfluger, letter to the author, August 9, 1984.

23. Dorsey B. Hardeman, letter to the author, July 20, 1984.

24. Fred W. Shield, letter to the author, October 25, 1984.

25. Hon. Governor Price Daniel of Texas, letter to the author, July 28, 1984.

26. *Cruz* v. *Beto*, 405 U.S. 319 (1972). Justice Rehnquist dissented.

CHAPTER 5. **Correctional Change: The Case of Texas Prisons**
(pp. 205–231)

1. Gresham M. Sykes, *The Society of Captives: A Study of a Maximum Security Prison* (Princeton, NJ: Princeton University Press, 1958).

2. One interesting question, hitherto obscured by the popular focus on the unrepresentative sample of TDC prisons that came to rely almost exclusively on BTs, is why the cancer spread unevenly throughout the system. Why, for instance, did BTs play a bigger role at the agency's Eastham unit than they did at its Walls unit? Texas insiders, including some academics, hypothesize a connection between the character of the inmate population, on the one hand, and the rate and extent to which administrators at certain prisons presided over the conversion of the BT system into a classical con-boss system, on the other. Though plausible, this explanation overlooks the apparent fact that, even among the system's "heaviest" institutions — those which confined large numbers of inmates believed to pose serious threats to security — there were differences in how, and how much, the BTs were used. For example, by most accounts, the BT qua con-boss system infected Eastham more than it did the Ellis I unit. Also, a few of the system's "lighter" institutions came to rely heavily on BTs. A different hypothesis is that the BT corruption went farther and faster at those TDC prisons where staff in key positions (sergeants, majors, wardens) had less knowledge of and attachment to administrative operations as they had existed under Beto. One crude way to measure such "knowledge and attachment" would be to comb through TDC's personnel and performance records. Unfortunately, the records are incomplete and do not contain the sort of objective (who was where when and for how long) and qualitative (who performed how under what conditions) data necessary to test this hypothesis. The sociological literature provides few good clues since little empirical research has been done on intersystem, intrasystem, historical, and other developmental variations in the use of con bosses.

3. Aric Press, "Inside America's Toughest Prison," *Newsweek*, October 6, 1986, p. 50. For a small sample of writings on this subject, see the following: Paul Taylor, "When Inmates Quit Running Texas Prisons, Anarchy Came," *The Washington Post*, September 9, 1984; Dick J. Reavis, "How They Ruined Our Prisons," *The Texas Monthly Magazine*, May 1985; Sheldon Eckland-Olson, "Judicial Decisions and the Social Order of Prison Violence: Evidence from the Post-Ruiz Years in Texas," (Department of Sociology, University of Texas, 1985); James W. Marquart and Ben M. Crouch, "Judicial Reform and Prisoner Control: The Impact of Ruiz V. Estelle On A Texas Penitentiary," Revised version of paper delivered at the annual meeting of the Southern Sociological Society (Charlotte, NC, April 1985).

4. See, for instance, Stanley Rothman and Kathleen Engel, "Prison Violence and the Paradox of Reform," *The Public Interest* 73 (Fall 1983): 91–105. The authors argue that the courts have upset the informal inmate-staff alliances upon which, they allege, prison order has been based. Focusing more on how the courts have influenced formal mechanisms of prison governance, former MDC Director Perry M. Johnson hypothesized a connection between declining levels of order and the necessity to provide increasing measures of due process protection for prisoners in disciplinary proceedings. Reflecting on his own experiences, Johnson suggested that disorder and misconduct in Michigan increased substantially as the system attempted to come into compliance with various court decisions and state statutes which increased prisoners' due-process rights.

5. Clemens Bartollas, *Introduction to Corrections* (New York: Harper and Row, 1981), p. 345.

6. See, for instance, James B. Jacobs, *New Perspectives on Imprisonment* (Ithaca, NY, and London: Cornell University Press, 1983), p. 54; M. Kay Harris and D. P. Spiller, *After Decision: Implementation of Judicial Decrees in Correctional Settings* (Washington, DC: U.S. Department of Justice, 1977).

7. For an essay which argues against the idea that prisons have been "bureaucratized," see John J. DiIulio, Jr., "From Prison Guards to Jailhouse Diplomats: Administrative Change and Its Consequences in American Penal Institutions, 1930–1986," unpublished paper, Criminal Justice Research Program, Princeton University, Fall 1986.

8. See *Ruiz* v. *Estelle*, 503 F. Supp. 1265 (S.D. Tex. 1980). The litigation began in the final days of the Beto administration and was closed some thirteen years later under Procunier. For an interpretive history of the case and the litigation leading up to it, see Sheldon Eckland-Olson and Steve J. Martin, *The Walls Came Tumbling Down: A Study of Litigated Prison Reform*, forthcoming. This study traces the record of penal liti-

gation in Texas from 1849 to 1985. The *Ruiz* case, however, should be understood in light of other major cases which mark the road from the "slave of the State" and "hands-off" doctrines to the present era of prisoners' rights and judicial intervention. Among the more important cases are the following: *Ruffin* v. *Commonwealth* (1871); *People* v. *Russell* (1910); *Banning* v. *Looney* (1954); *Monroe* v. *Pape* (1961); *Cooper* v. *Pate* (1964); *Holt* v. *Sarver* (1970); *Pugh* v. *Locke* (1976). To date, no one has explained adequately the major changes in the judicial approach to prison affairs. A decent attempt at such an explanation is made in Robert C. Bradley, "Judges as Bureaucrats: Formulating, Implementing, and Supervising Structual Reforms in State Correctional Institutions," paper delivered at annual meeting of the Midwest Political Science Association, Chicago, IL, April 19, 1985.

9. See *Ruiz* v. *Estelle*, 688 F. 2nd 266 (5th Cir. 1982).

10. Ibid.

11. Ibid.

12. Ibid.

13. Banning K. Lary, *Special Edition, The Echo: The Texas Prison Newspaper* 3, May/June 1985.

14. "The Ten Best and the Ten Worst Legislators," *Texas Monthly*, July 1983.

15. Ibid., p. 115.

16. "Texas Hires Ray Procunier as Chief 'Firefighter,' " *Corrections Digest*, 15, no. 12, 1984: 5–6. Coincidentally, the same issue of the digest contained a segment on Perry M. Johnson's resignation from his directorship in Michigan.

17. J. T. Sullivan and Jim Craine, "Deputy Director McCotter Outlines New Programs: Curbing the Violence," *The Echo: The Texas Prison Newspaper*, October 1984.

18. See Fred King, "TDC Woes Surprised Prison Chief," *Houston Post*, November 18, 1984.

19. Harry Whittington, as quoted in Mike Hailey, "Decline in Inmate Violence Predicted By Prison Chiefs," *Austin American Statesman*, October 7, 1984, p. A18. Whittington was appointed by Republican Governor Bill Clements. Within a year of his appointment, he cast one of the first dissenting votes that the Board had seen in some two decades.

20. Raymond Keller, as quoted in Mary C. Bounds, "Keller Notes Prison Improvements," *Dallas Morning News*, January 1, 1985.

21. The program aired on Sunday, January 26, 1986.

22. Dr. George Beto, Introduction of the Honorable William Wayne Justice, 114th Congress of the American Correctional Association (ACA), San Antonio, Texas, August 20, 1984.

23. Address of the Honorable William Wayne Justice presented to the 114th Congress of the American Correctional Association (ACA), San Antonio, Texas, August 20, 1984.

CHAPTER 6. **The Prison as a Constitutional Government**
(pp. 235–263)

1. Ralph J. Marcelli, ed., *Reorganization of State Corrections Agencies: A Decade of Experience* (Lexington, Kentucky: Council of State Governors, 1977).

2. Susan Claveria, *A Department of Corrections for Hawaii: A Feasibility Study* (Honolulu, Hawaii: Legislative Reference Bureau, Report No. 1, 1983).

3. Max Weber, "The Essentials of Bureaucratic Organization: An Ideal-Type Construction," in *Reader in Bureaucracy* eds. Robert Merton et al. (New York: Free Press, 1952), pp. 18–27.

4. Charles Perrow, *Organizational Analysis: A Sociological Perspective* (Belmont, CA: Wadsworth, 1970), p. 67.

5. W. K. Muir has written about police officers as "streetcorner politicians" whose stock-in-trade is "passion" and "perspective." See his *Police: Streetcorner Politicians* (Chicago: University of Chicago, 1977). In a similar vein, most correctional officers may be thought of as "jailhouse diplomats" whose stock in trade is prudence. The issue of whether correctional reform is better achieved through tighter bureaucratic controls or greater professionalism is addressed in Jameson W. Doig, ed. *Criminal Corrections: Ideals and Realities* (Lexington, MA: Lexington Books, 1983).

6. For the classic statement along these lines, see Philip Selznick, *Leadership in Administration* (Evanston, IL: Row, Peterson, and Company, 1957), especially chapters 3 and 4. For a crisp restatement of Selznick's insights as they apply to law enforcement bureaucracies, see James Q. Wilson, *The Investigators: Managing FBI and Narcotics Agents* (New York: Basic Books, 1978), chapter 1.

7. Wilson, ibid., pp. 13–15.

8. Ibid.

9. Ibid.

10. James R. Cain, "Similarities Between Penal and Military Organizations" (Huntsville, TX: Institute of Contemporary Corrections and the Behavioral Sciences, Sam Houston State University, 1977), p. iv.

11. Harold B. Bradley, "Designing for Change: Problems of Planned Innovation in Corrections," *Annals of the American Academy of Political and Social Science* 381 (January 1969): 97 (italics omitted).

12. Clemens Bartollas and Stuart J. Miller, *Correctional Administration: Theory and Practice* (New York: McGraw-Hill, 1978), p. 66.

13. In 1986, several state and local correctional agencies began considering the option of "boot camp" institutions. For instance, New York City corrections officials began considering such facilities for juvenile offenders, while the State of Georgia ran a 90-day "shock incarceration" facility in which adult offenders lived like soldiers under a strict daily regimen of discipline, work, and vigorous exercise. Such experiments seem premature and may carry custodial imperatives to an extreme. When and if such practices are tried more extensively, great care should be taken to institutionalize limits on the authority of the staff, to measure the progress of the inmates, and to compare the human and financial costs of these institutions to less paramilitary ones.

14. The phrase is from Richard A. McGee, *Prisons and Politics* (Lexington, MA: Lexington Books, 1981), chapter 5.

15. Ibid., p. 3

16. Ibid., p. 114.

17. For a different view, see Mark L. McConkie, *Management by Objectives: A Corrections Perspective* (Washington, DC: Government Printing Office, 1975).

18. *Banning* v. *Looney*, 213 F. 2d 771, 348 U.S. 859 (1954).

19. Address of the Honorable William Wayne Justice presented to the 144th Congress of the American Correctional Association, San Antonio, Texas, August 20, 1984, pp. 9, 14.

20. Ibid., p. 7.

21. Ibid., p. 10.

22. Federal Bureau of Investigation Director William H. Webster has testified that prison gangs "are quasi-military, violence-prone, highly structured criminal enterprises whose influence now extends well beyond prison walls. They engage in a wide range of criminal activities including narcotics and weapons trafficking, extortion, robbery, and murder." *Organized Crime in America: Hearings Before the Committee on the Judiciary, United States Senate, Part 1* (Washington, DC: U.S. Government Printing Office, 1983), p. 54. Top California prison officials noted estimates that the prison gangs that operate inside their prisons may have a combined total of over 100,000 members on the streets.

23. See, for instance, John M. Wynne, Jr., *Prison Employee Unionism: The Impact on Correctional Administration and Programs* (U.S. Department of Justice, The National Institute of Law Enforcement and Criminal Justice. Washington, DC: U.S. Government Printing Office, 1978), and Barry D. Smith, "The Impact on Unionization on Correctional Officer Wages and Fringe Benefits" (Ph.D. thesis, Institute of Contem-

porary Corrections and the Behavioral Sciences, Sam Houston State University, 1981).

24. President's Commission on Law Enforcement and Administration of Justice, *Task Force Report: Corrections* (Washington, DC: U.S. Government Printing Office, 1967), p. 96.

25. Norval Morris and Gordon Hawkins, *The Honest Politician's Guide to Crime Control* (Chicago: University of Chicago Press, 1970), pp. 124–125.

26. On Swedish prisons, see David F. Ward, "Sweden: The Middle Way to Prison Reform," in *Prisons: Present and Possible*, ed. Marvin E. Wolfgang (Lexington, MA: Lexington Books, 1979), pp. 89–167. Also see Chris Mosey, "The Wages of Sin Are Market-Adjusted," *Sweden Now* 4 (1985): pp. 28–31. On Japanese prisons, see Jim Abrams, "Prisons Offer Own Brands to Japanese," *Houston Chronicle*, October 23, 1984, and Atushi Nagashima, "Corrections in Japan," *Proceedings of the 110th Congress of Corrections* (College Park, MD: American Correctional Association, 1980), pp. 95–102.

27. Morris and Hawkins, *The Honest Politician's Guide*, p. 144.

28. Richard A. Berk and Peter Rossi, *Prison Reform and State Elites* (Cambridge, MA: Ballinger Publishing Co., 1977). Barbara Lavin, "Political Theory and Correctional Politics: Policies and Rhetoric," paper presented at the September 1983 American Political Science Association Meeting, Chicago, Illinois.

29. Julia Gordon, "Under Lock and Key: Correctional Policymaking in Massachusetts" (Senior Honors Thesis, Department of Government, Harvard University, Cambridge, MA, March 1985).

30. McGee, *Prisons and Politics*, chapter 2.

31. Occasionally, however, such stories do appear. For instance, see Laura Mecoy, "Even Officers' Simple Mistakes Can Be Deadly," *Sacramento Bee*, November 24, 1985, p. A20.

32. I am indebted to James Q. Wilson for this observation.

33. At a minimum, it would be helpful if participants in the debate over correctional policies and programs stopped painting their generalizations and counter-generalizations about prisons in black and white. For instance, in 1986 Jackson Toby asserted that by comparison with most other nations, "prison conditions in the U.S. today are almost luxurious" ("Worst Thing About U.S. Prisons is the Prisoners," *Wall Street Journal*, June 10, 1986). Edward I. Koren responded to Toby by asserting that prison conditions in the U.S. today are miserable since all we do is "warehouse" inmates (*Wall Street Journal*, June 30, 1986). Clearly, both are wrong; some prisons are decent, many are horrible, and we need to learn more about how to increase the former while eliminating the latter.

34. Klenias in Book Nine. See *The Laws of Plato*, Thomas Pangle, ed. (New York: Basic Books, 1980), p. 249.

35. Friedrich Nietzsche, *Beyond Good and Evil*, Walter Kaufmann, ed. (New York: Vintage Books, 1966), p. 114.

36. As Walter Lippmann wrote: "The rule of justice, which is primary, is then tempered with mercy, which stems at last from the knowledge that we too are sinners and must therefore give to others what we must ask for ourselves." See Lippmann, "The Captains of Their Souls," in *The Essential Lippmann: A Political Reader for Liberal Democracy*, Clinton Rossiter and James Lare, eds. (Cambridge, MA: Harvard University Press, 1982), p. 144.

APPENDIX. **Prison Research** (pp. 267–276)

1. James B. Jacobs, *Stateville: The Penitentiary in Mass Society* (Chicago: University of Chicago Press, 1977), appendix 1. For a more general discussion of participant observation in criminal justice research, see Frank E. Hogan, *Research Methods in Criminal Justice and Criminology* (New York: Macmillan, 1982), especially pp. 46, 110–111.

2. Since writing this account, I have done research in the Federal Bureau of Prisons and other state and local correctional systems. Nothing I have learned from these experiences leads me to modify the advice given herein.

3. As noted in the introduction, the phrase "soaking and poking" is from Richard Fenno, *Homestyle: House Members in Their Districts* (Boston: Little, Brown, 1978), pp. xiv, 249.

4. Jacobs, *Stateville*, p. 218.

5. David H. Bayley, *The Police and Political Development in India* (Princeton, NJ: Princeton University Press, 1969) and his *Patterns of Policing: An International Comparative Perspective* (New Brunswick, NJ: Rutgers University Press, 1985).

6. One seemingly quick and effective way to build this "Mustang" would be to conduct a detailed survey of many, most, or all of the nation's correctional systems. Stated simply, one would first operationalize more sharply the performance indices (order, amenity, service), perhaps adding others (privacy, visiting). Next, one would create (or borrow from the existing literature on organizations) an operational index of bureaucracy, one that would enable us to array prisons and prison systems (and possibly jails and jail systems) on an administrative scale ranging from the most to the least bureaucratic. Finally, one would gather objective information on levels of crowding, treatment programs, and other variables that might relate to (or be included as additional measures of) perfor-

mance. The resulting batch of data would then be ordered largely via statistical analysis, thereby enabling us to map with some numerical precision the relationship (if any) between administrative structures and prison outcomes.

This approach is not quite so outlandish as it may seem to some social scientists and to most nonacademics. Enough progress has been made in the systematic study of organizations and in the creative use of quantitative methods of analysis to contemplate this sort of an approach. (For instance, see Joseph L. C. Cheng and William McKinley, "Toward an Integration of Organization Research and Practice: A Contingency Study of Bureaucratic Control and Performance in Scientific Settings," *Administrative Science Quarterly*, 28 ([1983]: 85–100.) I would, however, caution prison researchers — and other students of organizations, public and private — to keep soaking and poking before engaging in any high-powered computing.

At least in the case of penal institutions, far more exploratory research needs to be completed before we can say with genuine confidence what variables are important, how they relate one to the other, and how (if at all) they can be measured in ways that lend themselves to more experimental research designs. I believe that the day for such research will come, but we ought not to place the quantitative cart before the qualitative horse. Criminal justice agencies are notoriously bad at keeping accurate records and responding honestly to such inquiries about what they do and how (and how well) they do it. In this respect, police departments have improved enormously over the last twenty years, but corrections departments remain among the worst offenders. The quality of the data would be suspect at best and there would be no way, short of an extended trip into the field, for serious scholars to allay their doubts or to weigh the importance of more hard-to-quantify variables (e.g., leadership). Running the numbers through the computer would not correct, except superficially, the conceptual and methodological errors concomitant to this premature approach.

At this stage, the path to policy-oriented knowledge about prisons — ideas about them that are true empirically, interesting intellectually, useful practically, and instructive morally — runs through the gates and behind the walls. If it proceeds intelligently, future research on prisons may, among other things, succeed in fusing two important traditions in the study of public policy and organizations. First, there are dozens of rich, analytical case studies that attempt to explain how a given public institution, agency, or set of agencies, operates, without, however, attempting to make clear connections between administrative behavior and administrative or policy outcomes. Exemplars of this tradition would include Herbert Kaufman's classic *The Forest Ranger: A Study in Administrative Behavior* (Baltimore, MD: The Johns Hopkins University Press, 1960), and James Q. Wilson's *The Investigators* (New York: Basic Books, 1977). Secondly, there are several scholarly journals that are dedicated in part to evaluating the performance of public sector organizations without, however, being much concerned with the administrative life of those organizations. Students of politics and public affairs with no scholarly interest in prisons or criminal justice but with an abiding interest in public management and a desire, as citizens, for good public policy, thus have a real stake in how future prison research develops. In his *Ethics* Aristotle reminds us that it is the mark of the educated person to look for precision in each class of things just so far as the nature of the subject admits. Research in this area, and others as well, is most likely to flourish if we take this message to heart.

Selected Annotated Bibiliography

William Penn warned that too much reading may extinguish the "natural candle" by which we reason and learn. If only because I was born and raised in the city of Philadelphia, where a statue of Pennsylvania's great founder stands atop City Hall, I am inclined to repeat that warning even though, with bloodshot eyes, I must confess to not heeding it myself.

There are thousands of books, essays, theses, and reports on criminal corrections in America. There are probably hundreds of scholars and others who have read and digested a great many of them. As I have suggested in the present book, however, this literature supplies little dependable information to guide policy makers and others desirous of improving the quality of prison life. In offering this bibliography, therefore, I certainly do not mean to imply that the path to better correctional facilities runs first and foremost through the stacks of the nearest well-stocked criminal-justice library or through the terminals of the nearest computer. We need to develop a bank of reliable empirical data about prisons and other correctional institutions, and to do that, fresh empirical research, much of it out in the field, is necessary. Nor do I wish to imply that the few dozen entries below are in any respect representative of the whole literature, or even that fraction of it that concerns imprisonment and penal administration. And, as should become apparent, I have not included every work noted in the present text nor assembled for a final cheer (or slap) those publications that support (or deny) what I have argued. Instead, I made this brief list only to convey some general idea of what is available in the easy-to-reach secondary literature on prisons; put the reader on slightly more intimate terms with some of the works I cited; introduce him or her to a few important monographs I neither cited nor discussed in any of the chapters; and relate entries to the present study where I thought that might be useful.

American Friends Service Committee, The. *Struggle for Justice: A Report on Crime and Punishment in America.* New York: Hill and Wang, 1971.

An influential tract that helped to focus attention on the problems of America's criminal justice system. From the perspective of mthe present study, this report is a mixed bag, and many of its proposals seem as right (or wrong) for today as they were for 1971. Epilogue contains a discussion of prisoners' rights.

Baker, J. E. *Prisoner Participation in Prison Power.* Metuchen, NJ: Scarecrow Press, 1985.

Documents the historical involvement of inmates in the administration and programming of American prisons. Includes state-by-state descriptions. Presents a far more favorable view of participatory prison management than is given in the present book.

Bartollas, Clemens. *Correctional Treatment: Theory and Practice.* Englewood Cliffs, NJ: Prentice-Hall, 1985.

Up-to-date, fairly well-balanced textbook on correctional treatment. Includes interviews with leading policy makers, practitioners, and scholars.

———. *Introduction to Corrections.* New York: Harper and Row, 1981.

Solid introduction to the place of corrections in the American criminal justice system. Includes interviews with leading policy makers, practitioners, and scholars.

Beaumont, Gustave de, and Tocqueville, Alexis de. *On the Penitentiary System in the United States, and its Application in France; With an Appendix on Penal Colonies, and Also, Statistical Notes.* Translated by Francis Lieber. Philadelphia: Carey, Lea and Blanchard, 1833.

If this book had been studied and its general lessons heeded, most, maybe all, of the last century and a half of America's penological follies might have been avoided. In fact, there is no issue in contemporary corrections, and no perspective on prisons, that is not anticipated in this volume. Written as a report to the French government, the authors concluded: "Let us not declare an evil incurable

which others have found means to eradicate; let us not condemn the system of prisons; let us labour to reform them." If only as a window on the later work of Tocqueville, this book is must reading. For one interesting if not wholly convincing statement on the connection of this study to Tocqueville's subsequent writings, see Roger Boesche, "The Prison: Tocqueville's Model for Despotism," *Western Political Quarterly* 33 (1980): 550–563. It would be a pity to read mere excerpts of the Beaumont-Tocqueville study, or to read it without the complete notes of its first translator, Francis Lieber. Avoid abridged editions like the plague.

Bennett, James V. *I Chose Prison.* New York: Alfred P. Knopf, 1970.

Autobiographical account of prison life and administration by the man who directed the Federal Bureau of Prisons from 1937 to 1964. Passionate argument for less restrictive prisons and indeterminate sentencing. Suggests that the keeper philosophy (see chapter four of the present book) was alive and well in the federal system. Concludes with these optimistic words: "I believe there is a treasure in the heart of every man if we can find it — *if we can help him find it.*"

Berk, Richard A., and Rossi, Peter. *Prison Reform and State Elites.* Cambridge, MA: Ballinger Publishing Co., 1977.

Interesting empirical study hinting that the politics of corrections is less pluralistic than the politics of most other domestic issues.

Bowker, Lee H. *Prisoner Subcultures.* Lexington, MA: Lexington Books, 1977.

Superb summary of the literature on prisoner subcultures in institutions for men, women, and juveniles. Contains a brief, thoughtful introductory statement about the evolution of the author's views on prisons.

———. *Prison Victimization.* New York: Elsevier, 1980.

Excellent summary of the literature on all forms of prison victimization, beginning with a chapter on prison rapes. Contains an appendix on how to find out about prison victimization and a selected bibliography.

Carroll, Leo. *Hacks, Blacks, and Cons: Race Relations in a Maximum Security Prison.* Lexington, MA: Lexington Books, 1974.

An exploratory case study of race relations in a small state prison. Argues that reforms increased staff power and examines how the Attica riot changed the prison's race relations.

Carter, Robert M., et al., eds. *Correctional Institutions.* 3d ed. New York: Harper and Row, 1985.

A textbook containing several fine essays by leading experts. Among the most instructive essays are the following: John Michael Keating, Jr., et al. on grievance mechanisms; Daniel P. LeClair on community corrections; and the same author on furloughs and recidivism rates. A concluding section labelled "Scientific Guidance For Correctional Policies" features four essays offering many analytical perspectives, if little "scientific guidance."

Clemmer, Donald. *The Prison Community*. New York: Rinehart and Co., 1958. First published 1940.

The pioneering work of modern prison sociology based on an analysis of the "Middletown" of American prisons. Careful readers will discover that Clemmer's celebrated treatise, known far and wide for its sociological and penological insights and discoveries, also contains the rudiments of a political philosophy of punishment.

Cloward, Richard, et al. *Theoretical Studies in Social Organization of the Prison*. New York: Social Science Research Council, 1960.

Remarkable volume containing essays by the leading scholars of the day. A measured introduction to the sociological perspective on prisons. In the essay by Cloward there is a recognition that, whatever its real or perceived benefits, "inmate social organization" flourishes at the expense of obedience to formal rules and limits the prospects for inmate reform.

Cohen, Albert, et al., eds. *Prison Violence*. Lexington, MA: Lexington Books, 1976.

One of the few good volumes on the subject. Contains especially fine essays by James B. Jacobs and Richard W. Wilsnack.

Commission on Accreditation for Corrections. *Manual of Standards for Adult Correctional Institutions*. Rockville, MD: American Correctional Association, 1977.

A summary of the standards that correctional institutions must follow if they are to get the good-housekeeping certificate. These standards are based on penological assumptions of questionable validity, and it remains unclear whether the accreditation process leads to better prisons.

Cox, V. C., et al. "Prison Crowding Research: The Relevance for Housing Standards and a General Approach Regarding Crowding Phenomena." *American Psychologist* 39: (1984) 1148–1160.

Readable analysis of what scholars know, or think they know, about the basic causes and consequences of prison crowding.

Cressey, Donald. "Prison Organizations." In *Handbook of Organizations*, edited by James G. March, pp. 1023–1070. New York: Rand McNally, 1965.

Unsurpassed theoretical statement about the organizational character of prisons. Contrasts "punitive-custodial" and "treatment-oriented" prisons. The former type of prison is run so as to "minimize inmate choices," maximize the bureaucratic cast of daily operations, and reward the employee "who carefully observes the conduct of offenders and reports rule violations to his superiors for disciplinary action." The latter type of prison is run so as to increase the inmates' "opportunities for self-expression," relax bureaucratic controls, and reward employees who "think for themselves, use discretion," and help inmates to "get well." The present study adds to Cressey's analysis the observations that the administrative gap between treatment and custody may be harder to bridge in theory than in practice and that the virtues of the traditional model may be greater, and its vices fewer, than most prison reformers have supposed.

――――. *The Prison: Studies in Institutional Organization and Change.* New York: Rinehart, Winston, 1961.

Major volume on the sociology of prisons containing essays that go beyond "charts and official lines of command" to explore the "conditions under which various types of organization arise, persist, and change." As Cressey notes in his preface, the essay by Richard H. McCleery is the only one in the volume by a political scientist. "McCleery," wrote Cressey, "is not interested in prisons. Instead, he is interested in governmental processes . . . [which] are studied in prison because studying them there is more efficient than studying them in a larger social system." McCleery himself added that studying prisons "revitalizes the political theory of Hobbes that has been obscured by a concentration on his discussion of force in government." While finding little to agree with in McCleery's basic understanding of politics, government, society, prisons, and (last but not least) Hobbes, his empirical study of a Hawaii higher-custody prison was an inspiration to me, and it is regrettable that so few political scientists have followed McCleery behind the walls and into the study of the most concrete embodiments of state power.

Davidson, Theodore. *Chicano Prisoners: The Key to San Quentin.* New York: Holt, Rinehart, Winston, 1974.

Fascinating account of the role played by Chicano inmates in the life of California's infamous San Quentin prison. Written as a work of cultural anthropology.

Doig, Jameson W., ed. *Criminal Corrections: Ideals and Realities.* Lexington, MA: Lexington Books, 1983.

A superb volume edited by one of the few political scientists who has studied the subject seriously. All fifteen essays are originals, not previously published. Two especially worthwhile contributions are the editor's "The Uses of Government Power: Corrections as Both Typical and Extreme," and Jack H. Nagel's "Crime and Incarceration across American States." Nagel's essay is interesting not simply as a good scholarly analysis, but as an attempt by a social scientist expert in quantitative analysis to test and refine ideas articulated a decade earlier by his father, the well-known prison reformer William G. Nagel (see entry below). Another especially worthy essay in this volume is Candace McCoy's "Developing Legal Remedies for Unconstitutional Incarceration."

Engel, Kathleen, and Rothman, Stanley. "Prison Violence and the Paradox of Reform." *The Public Interest.* 73 (Fall 1983): 91–105.

A provocative if wholly unconvincing essay that blames liberal reforms and court intervention for prison violence. Provides little empirical evidence and relies uncritically on the sociological assumption that prison order is the product of "complex relationships among inmates." Despite other mistakes, redeems itself by emphasizing that inmates have "a right to safe incarceration."

Fogel, David. "*. . .We Are the Living Proof*": *The Justice Model for Corrections*. Cincinatti: W. H. Anderson, 1979.

First published in 1975, this book is a sensible call to think clearly about what correctional institutions can and cannot accomplish. While neither the philosophical nor the empirical arguments for the "justice model" are terribly sturdy, several of Fogel's proposals (e.g., the end of indeterminate sentencing) seem well supported.

Foucault, Michel. *Discipline and Punish*. Translated by Alan Sheridan. New York: Pantheon, 1978.

A much-acclaimed but (at least in translation, and at least to one not steeped in so-called critical theory) hard to follow interpretation of the history of prisons. As Stephen K. White has observed, Foucault's central thesis in this book appears to be that the founders of the penitentiary system did nothing more than exchange one system of "power/knowledge" for another, less conspicuous one. In White's words, "Modern power does not reveal itself spectacularly in the form of the executioner and bodily dismemberment. Rather, modern power operates in conjunction with human sciences, and proceeds by means of the continual and authoritative categorization, grading, and monitoring of human behavior." (See Stephen K. White, "Foucault's Challenge to Critical Theory," *American Political Science Review* 80 [June 1986]: especially pp. 420–421). Whether Foucault succeeds on his own terms I cannot say, but anyone whose primary interest is prisons, how they have worked and how to improve them, can safely avoid this opus. If it is history and historical perspective you are after, see the brilliant treatises by David J. Rothman listed below.

Fox, James G. *Organizational and Racial Conflict in Maximum-Security Prisons*. Lexington, MA: Lexington Books, 1982.

A highly interesting and nicely executed study of five state maximum-security prisons intended to "assess the relationships between management policies (and organizational structures) and the dynamics of prisoner communities in five very different prisons." Contrary to the argument of the present book, Fox suggests that participative management and what he terms a "collaborative-management approach" may help to reduce "organizational and racial conflict" in higher-custody prisons.

Fox, Vernon. *Violence Behind Bars: An Explosive Report on Prison Violence in the United States*. Westport, CT: Greenwood Press, 1956.

An analysis of the 1952 riot at Michigan's Jackson State Prison by a man who worked there at the time. Lists riots that occurred between the November 27, 1855, uprising at Sing Sing and the October 1, 1955, disturbance at Boston's Deer Island Jail. Concludes that "treatment and custody should compatibly intertwine — but custody can't come first." The present book supports the former half of this assertion but reverses the latter — custody and order must come first.

Freedman, Estelle B. *Their Sister's Keepers: Women's Prison Reform in America, 1830–1930*. Ann Arbor, MI: University of Michigan Press, 1981.

An interesting if somewhat flawed study of the role of women in American penal reform from the 1830s through the Progressive era. Unfairly faults the female reformers for not doing more to help imprisoned women and says less than it might have about the imprisoned women themselves.

Giallombardo, Rose Mary. *The Social World of Imprisoned Girls*. New York: John Wiley, 1974.

One of the few first-rate sociological studies of how women interact behind bars. Identifies differences between male and female patterns of prison life.

Glaser, Daniel. *The Effectiveness of a Prison and Parole System*. Indianapolis: Bobbs-Merrill, 1964.

A truly pathbreaking study based mainly on research conducted in the federal prison system during the last years of James V. Bennett's tenure (see entry above). Based on extensive surveys and field research, this study revolutionized scholarly thinking about the causes of recidivism and helped to set the stage for the studies of rehabilitation and correctional treatment programs that were produced in the decade that followed. Many of Glaser's findings stood conventional wisdom on its head (e.g., the legend that two-thirds of all inmates return to prison was rebutted by his finding that about two-thirds do not return). Unfortunately, however, many of his hypotheses were taken as settled findings, and little, if any, specific follow-up work was done. For instance, in his discussion of "Disciplinary Action and Counseling," Glaser offered two distinct sets of hypotheses, one positing the superiority of going strictly "by the book," the other positing the superiority (and the necessity) of "a policy of flexible rules interpreted to fit each case" that "minimizes alienation of the rule-violating inmate from staff." Glaser's "hunch" was that the second hypothesis was correct, but no subsequent study enables us really to know whether his now twenty-three-year-old hunch was right (as most of the sociological literature on prisons would have one suppose) or wrong (as the present study suggests). Similarly, in his discussion of "Group Responsibility and Integration of Inmates," Glaser claimed that the record of experiments with inmate self-government was mixed. He noted that, in several institutions, the inmate rulers were harsher than the staff and the inmates themselves voted to abolish the self-government schemes after they "had become corrupt." "Professional opinion regarding inmate self-government still is divided in the United States," he noted. Glaser, however, came down tentatively on the side of those who favored some degree of inmate self-government, offering as "a conclusion meriting serious testing" a series of hypotheses, among them that inmates' "identification of themselves as noncriminal persons" is enhanced by having them share "with employees the task of running the prison for the maximum long-run benefit of all." Though it has not wanted for adherents, scholarly and nonscholarly, there has yet to be a serious test of this hypothesis; common sense and existing evidence seem to weigh against it.

Goffman, Erving. *Asylums: Essays on the Social Situation of Mental Patients and Other Inmates*. Garden City, NY: Doubleday, 1961.

Classic sociological statement on prisons, mental hospitals, and military organizations as "total institutions" in which "a large number of like-situated individuals, cut off from the wider society for an appreciable period of time, together lead an enclosed, formally administered round of life." Suggests that these "like-situated individuals" associate informally in ways that limit and even subvert the power of the formal administrative machinery that appears to run their lives so completely.

Harris, M. Kay, and Spiller, Jr., D. P. *After Decision: Implementation of Judicial Decrees in Correctional Settings*. Washington, D.C.: U.S. Government Printing Office, 1977.

One of the few serious empirical analyses of how court intervention into penal affairs runs its course. Based on detailed studies of four cases, the book suggests that the assorted changes in management ushered in by the courts "were generally considered beneficial" and notes that "progressive" correctional administrators and others have used prison litigation as a way of making changes above and beyond those ordered by the courts. From the case examined in the present book (see chapter five), a much more complex and less sanguine portrait of the origins and aftermath of the courts' role emerges; though here, too, it is clear that administrators, politicians, and oversight bodies initiated certain administrative reforms not mandated by the court, while the line correctional staff at some facilities responded in unanticipated ways.

Hawkins, Gordon. *The Prison: Policy and Practice*. Chicago: University of Chicago Press, 1977.

An excellent critical survey of the literature on prisons and prison management. The opening chapter offers a balanced account of "The Prison and Its Critics." Also, the chapter on correctional officers — "The Other Prisoners" — serves as a much-needed corrective to those previous studies that ignore, miscast, or malign prison workers. This chapter helped to launch the many fine studies of correctional staff that have been produced over the last decade, and to "rehabilitate" the officers in scholarly eyes.

Irwin, John. *Prisons in Turmoil*. Boston: Little, Brown, 1980.

A critical account of contemporary corrections by a leading sociologist and former inmate at California's Soledad prison. Argues for greater inmate involvement in prison administration.

———. *The Felon*. Englewood Cliffs, NJ: Prentice-Hall, 1970.

A splendid, if not entirely persuasive, study of criminal identities and the convict world. Argues that the correctional system must change in ways that "recognize the felon's viewpoint" and thereby facilitate rather than hinder his successful return to society.

Jackson, Bruce. *Law and Disorder: Criminal Justice in America.* Urbana, IL: University of Illinois Press, 1984.

A wide-ranging statement about the limited capacity of America's law-enforcement bureaucracies. Informed by the author's eclectic research in corrections and other fields. "Prison," concludes Jackson, "doesn't get a chance to succeed or fail until a person gets there in the first place, and expecting prisons and the antecedent agencies to abolish crime is like expecting hospitals to abolish disease and injury." Though Jackson's argument seems unduly pessimistic, his book makes for interesting and sobering reading.

Jacobs, James B. *New Perspectives On Prisons and Imprisonment.* Ithaca, NY, and London: Cornell University Press, 1983.

Ten fine essays authored or coauthored by the scholar who wrote *Stateville* (see entry below). Among the best are "Race Relations and the Prisoner Subculture" and "The Guard's World."

————. *Stateville: The Penitentiary in Mass Society.* Chicago: University of Chicago Press, 1977.

Simply the best sociological study of a prison published since Sykes (see below and chapter one of the present study). Published in 1977, this detailed portrait of Stateville Penitentiary and its administrative evolution is already a classic.

Kalinich, David B. *The Inmate Economy.* Lexington, MA: Lexington Books, 1980.

Describes in detail the contraband markets in Michigan's Jackson prison. Argues that "some contraband may continue to exist even in the most controlled setting." Concludes that in the future "prisons will become more difficult to manage" while inmates "will continue to develop their own informal norms and sub-rosa methods to make their existence more tolerable."

Kalinich, David B., and Pitcher, Terry. *Surviving in Corrections: A Guidebook for Corrections People.* Springfield, IL: Charles C. Thomas, 1984.

Just what the title promises, though many of the survival principles are mutually contradictory.

Lambert, Richard D., ed. "Our Crowded Prisons." *Annals of the American Academy of Political and Social Sciences* 478 (1985).

A foreword by then Chief Justice of the U.S. Supreme Court Warren E. Burger is followed by a word from Raymond C. Brown of the National Institute of Corrections and thirteen essays that vary in quality. Among the most worthwhile essays are "Prison Overcrowding and the Law" by Claudia Angelos and James B. Jacobs, and "Selective Incapacitation?" By Stephen D. Gottfredson and Don M. Gottfredson.

Lewis, W. David. *From Newgate to Dannemora: The Rise of the Penitentiary in New York 1796–1848*. Ithaca, NY: Cornell University Press, 1965.

Detailed historical account that should be read in conjunction with the works of David J. Rothman (see listings below).

Lipton, Douglas, et al. *The Effectiveness of Correctional Treatment: A Survey of Treatment Evaluation Studies*. New York: Praeger, 1975.

A massive survey that examines most studies on rehabilitation published between 1945 and 1967. The authors conclude that the relationship between rehabilitative efforts and recidivism is ambiguous or nonexistent. This study, and an earlier essay by one of its authors (Robert Martinson, "What Works? —Questions and Answers About Prison Reform," *The Public Interest*, 36 [Spring 1974]: 22–54), caused a major stir among scholars, policymakers, and practitioners and led to the demise of the rehabilitative ideal. While some of the studies examined in the survey took account of the institutional context in which the treatment programs were offered, it remains unclear whether the rehabilitative bubble was burst too soon. As the present study suggests, *we still do not know for sure whether meaningful programs offered in the context of tight custodial regimes that enforce adherence to civil norms and secure law-abiding inmate behavior can help to reduce recidivism, or whether the regime itself, independent of or absent any such programs, may produce rehabilitative effects*. Also, the moral argument for the provision of prison services is independent of their utility (or lack thereof) in lowering crime rates; to my knowledge, that moral argument has yet to suffer any serious challenge.

Martin, Susan E., et al., eds. *New Directions in the Rehabilitation of Criminal Offenders*. Washington, D.C.: National Academy Press, 1981.

Concurs with some of what is argued in the previous entry, including the general idea that it may be possible "to find more effective rehabilitation strategies." The "Report of the Panel" contains five interesting essays; see especially "Theoretical Issues and Approaches to Rehabilitation." It is unclear, however, whether the panel's preoccupation with theories about the causes of crime, a preoccupation that also informs most of the volume's commissioned papers, made its attempt to resurrect the rehabilitation question less successful than it might have been otherwise.

McCleery, Richard H. *Policy Change in Prison Management*. East Lansing, MI: Michigan State University, 1957.

A story of efforts to liberalize operations in a Hawaii maximum-security prison, told by one of the first political scientists to study prisons (see earlier entry under Cressey, *The Prison* and chapter one of the present study). About two decades later McCleery published *Dangerous Men: The Sociology of Parole* (Beverly Hills, CA: Sage Publications, 1978), a fascinating study of how parole agents handle case work less according to a true estimate of the parolees' threat to society and more according to often perverse organizational incentives.

McCoy, John. *Concrete Mama: Prison Profiles from Walla Walla*. Columbia, MO, and London: University of Missouri University Press, 1981.

A graphic account of life at Washington's Walla Walla Penitentiary, scene of an experiment in inmate self-government. The text is interesting, but the pictures speak for themselves.

McDonald, Douglas. *The Price of Punishment: Public Spending for Corrections in New York*. Boulder, CO: Westview Press, 1980.

One of the few competent attempts to estimate the real costs of corrections. Should serve as a model for any future efforts.

McGee, Richard. *Prisons and Politics*. Lexington, MA: Lexington Books, 1981.

Sage advice, not all of it supported in the present study, from the man who ran the California Department of Corrections from 1944 to 1967, having first gained experience in other correctional agencies, federal, state, and local.

McKelvey, Blake. *American Prisons: A History of Good Intentions*. Montclair, NJ: Patterson-Smith, 1977.

Good, mostly straightforward account of America's prison experience by one of the most seasoned students of the subject.

Mitford, Jessica. *Kind and Unusual Punishment: The Prison Business*. New York: Vintage Books, 1974.

A ringing assault on America's prisons in which they appear as the oppressive instruments of an unjust society.

Morris, Norval. *The Future of Imprisonment*. Chicago: University of Chicago Press, 1974.

A thoughtful analysis of the future of America's prisons by a scholar with a firm understanding of their past and present. Should be read in conjunction with Morris and Gordon Hawkins, *The Honest Politician's Guide to Crime* (Chicago: University of Chicago Press, 1970), and Michael Sherman and Gordon Hawkins, *Imprisonment in America: Choosing the Future* (Chicago: University of Chicago Press, 1977).

Nagel, Stuart, et. al., eds. *The Political Science of Criminal Justice*. Springfield, IL: Charles C. Thomas, 1983.

There is, as yet, no "political science of criminal justice," but this book comes as close to offering one as any volume extant. Especially useful are the summary essays that preface each of the sections.

Nagel, William G. "On Behalf of a Moratorium on Prison Construction." *Crime and Delinquency* 23 (1977): 154–172.

Influential essay by a practitioner-prison reformer that shaped the debate. For a later, more scholarly presentation of Nagel's ideas, see the entry under Doig above.

Orland, Leonard. *Prisons: Houses of Darkness*. New York: Free Press, 1975.

A critical look at corrections that offers suggestions about how to establish "the rule of law in prisons" by a law professor who has served as a parole board member in Connecticut. As the author notes, the ancient cuneiform symbol for *prison* is a combination of the symbols for *house* and *darkness*. Though it perhaps paints a bleaker view of corrections circa 1975 than is warranted, this book is a hopeful and for the most part sober statement about the need to bring order to an often "lawless institution."

Petersilia, Joan, et al. *The Prison Experience of Career Criminals*. Santa Monica, CA: Rand Corporation, 1980.

A study that provided some of the baseline data for the present work. Using information from official records and the results of a questionnaire administered to some 1,300 inmates in Texas, Michigan, and California, the researchers found that career criminals do not appear to have greater treatment needs than non–career criminals, participate in programs about as much (or little) as other inmates, and are not the biggest source of disorder. The researchers noted that many of the differences they found might be attributable to differences in management practices, but an examination of those practices was beyond the scope of their study. Such an examination was the heart of the present study.

Rand has published several other studies on prison inmates. As of this writing, one of the most recent is Stephen P. Klein and Michael N. Caggiano, *The Prevalence, Predictability, and Policy Implications of Recidivism* (Santa Monica, CA: Rand Corporation, 1986). This study is worth consulting for several reasons. First, it supplies references to many related works by Rand. Second, it provides an interesting analysis of the postrelease history of inmates in Texas, Michigan, and California. Third, it has important implications for the debate over "selective incapacitation" — "extending the time of those offenders who are likely to be serious threats to public safety and reducing the time served by those who were likely to be less serious threats." Finally, it may have some bearing on one of the arguments made in the present study; namely, that we ought to "rethink rehabilitation" (see chapter six and the Lambert [Gottfredson and Gottfredson essay], Lipton, and Martin entries above). The researchers found that inmates in California were far more likely to be arrested, convicted, and incarcerated after release than inmates in the other two states. Over a thirty-six-month period, the average number of arrests per released inmate was 2.63 in California, 1.22 in Michigan, and 1.17 in Texas. The researchers suggest that such differences in recidivism rates may be related to how long a state waits to incarcerate, the nature of its rehabilitative and postrelease supervision programs, and "other factors within the state's control. In short, *state policies may affect recidivism*" (italics mine).

The researchers called for "further research on this issue to identify policies used by states that have especially high and low recidivism rates (after controlling for the seriousness of their inmates' prior records and other relevant background characteristics)." While seconding this suggestion, I would strongly urge that in addition to the collection of official records, survey results, and other data amenable to quantitative analysis, real pains be taken to relate this information systematically to the results of a serious investigation of *how convicted persons in each jurisdiction actually have been managed by jail, probation, prison, and parole officials, or more generally, how they have been made to behave "in the cellblocks and on the streets" while under correctional supervision.* Only through such a complete empirical analysis will it ever be possible to generalize confidently about the relationships, if any, between managerial and other variables over which states have some immediate control, on the one hand, and inmates' postsentencing behavior, recidivism, and crime rates on the other.

President's Commission on Law Enforcement and Administration of Justice. *Task Force Report on Corrections.* Washington, D.C.: U.S. Government Printing Office, 1967.

One of the few government reports on corrections that is really worth reading. Many, though by no means all, of the recommendations were sensible; several have stood the test of time and seem even more cogent today than they were two decades ago. Among other things, this report helped to focus attention on the problems faced by prison administrators and highlighted the vital role of line correctional staff. Unfortunately, the next significant bout of governmental attention to corrections came four years later in the wake of the Attica tragedy. The government reports (national, state, and local) issued following the Attica catastrophe helped to focus public attention on the nation's penal institutions, but at the cost of letting empty rhetoric (e.g., "Attica is every prison and every prison is Attica") and cheap cynicism about correctional institutions (e.g., "nothing works") replace or derail serious and sustained efforts to improve the quality of prison life.

Radzinowicz, Sir Leon, and Wolfgang, Marvin E., eds. *Crime and Justice, Volume III: The Criminal Under Restraint.* New York: Basic Books, 1977.

Useful as an introductory text. Includes the influential essay by Martinson (see Lipton entry above), an excerpt from the official report on the 1971 Attica riot, and several important essays by leading scholars.

Ragen, Joseph, and Finstone, Charles. *Inside the World's Toughest Prison.* Springfield, IL: Charles C. Thomas, 1962.

A very misleading title but a fairly interesting statement by the man who ran Stateville Penitentiary as long and as tightly as he wanted to. Ragen left Stateville in 1961 but remained active as director of public safety until his retirement in 1965 (see Jacobs entry, *Stateville*). Had he remained active, would his autocratic administrative regime have been swept away by the sociopolitical changes of the late 1960s and 1970s? Counterfactual history can be a dangerous game, but I think the answer is that, for better or for worse, Ragen could have persevered where his hand-picked successor, Frank Pate, obviously could not. A more sophisticated but clearly Ragenesque prison chief, Dr. George Beto, gave birth to the Texas control model in the teeth of the same sociopolitical developments; however, those teeth were probably less sharp in rural East Texas than they were in Illinois and other states. In this vein, another counterfactual question worth asking is whether Beto could have handled the *Ruiz* litigation and related developments (see chapter five) in a way that his successors could not. Here, too, my answer is yes; in fact, I believe that, had Beto stayed at the helm, by 1980 he would have dismantled his corruptive building tender system, avoided protracted court battles, and made TDC into a truly model prison bureaucracy.

Remick, Peter, as told to James B. Shuman. *In Constant Fear.* New York: Reader's Digest Press, 1975.

There are scores of accounts of prison life by prison inmates. In my judgment, Remick's is the most important but least celebrated book by a prison inmate published in the last two decades. It is about conditions inside Walpole prison in Massachusetts circa 1975. I can do no better than to review a few key passages of it:

> . . . I live under constant threat of murder — my murder. The threat even penetrates the maximum security cellblock in which I am locked twenty-four hours a day. . . . I have been tempted to destroy this manuscript. But if the story is not told, the knifings, the killings, the riots, and the terror we have lived through at Walpole will continue. . . . Walpole needs the discipline that was in effect five years ago. It wasn't harsh discipline. . . . And discipline was enforced at all levels. . . . When I entered Walpole I had no intention of writing this book. But after seeing how permissiveness has led to the abandonment of rules, regulations, and discipline necessary to protect the lives and secure the safety of those of us in prison, I felt that someone should tell the full story. . . . I place the blame for what happened at Walpole on the authorities and their policies. . . . When it became apparent that Walpole was under a siege of violence, they could have stopped it. Instead, everyone in authority gave in. They let the worst elements in the prison take whatever they demanded until there was virtually nothing left to give. And so the inmates took control of Walpole, which they still hold as I write this.

Unfortunately for all except the inmate predators, the situation at Walpole did not change much until the 1980s. Remick's book is neither a literary masterpiece nor an inflamed political tract. He blames society and the authorities not for his own criminality but for failing to make it possible for him and other inmates to live safely and to prepare for a more decent and successful life after prison. He blames them for letting the prison's "toughest, most brutal" inmates act as quasi-official contacts between the administration and the inmates and for failing to provide basic amenities and services to the whole inmate population. "I would like," wrote Remick, "to serve my time in peace and go straight when I am released." It is a pity that a book like Remick's attracted relatively little national attention while less honest, less courageous, and more pretentious books by convicts and ex-convicts have gripped so many minds and influenced the public debate about prisons.

Rothman, David J. *Conscience and Convenience: The Asylum and Its Alternatives in Progressive America.* Boston: Little Brown, 1980.

A brilliant analysis of the Progressive era movement in criminal justice and mental health. The reformers espoused an "anti-institutional" creed but justified confinement and coercion in the name of individualized "treatment." A strange union was thereby formed between the progressive reformers and the unprogressive administrators; the initiatives of the former served to increase the power and discretionary authority of the latter. The appearance of reform was created as the rule of silence, striped uniforms, and lock-step marching vanished; however, in reality, raw custodial goals were never more in the ascendant.

———. *The Discovery of the Asylum: Social Order and Disorder in the New Republic*. Boston: Little, Brown, 1971.

Why did Americans in the Jacksonian era build "penitentiaries for the criminal, asylums for the insane, almshouses for the poor, orphan asylums for homeless children, and reformatories for delinquents?" This book, the single most important historical account of its kind published in this century, gives the answer. Winner of the 1971 Albert J. Beveridge Award for the best English-language book published in American History, this opus is must reading for anyone with an interest in American corrections, past, present, or future. Should be read in conjunction with the previous entry as well as Beaumont and Tocqueville (see above).

Stastny, Charles, and Trynauer, Gabrielle. *Who Rules the Joint?: The Changing Political Culture of Maximum-Security Prisons in America*. Lexington, MA: Lexington Books, 1982.

An interesting, scholarly account of the failed experiment in inmate self-government at Washington's Walla Walla Penitentiary. Concludes that "more open environments must be created, attuning the prison to democratic values." Should be read in conjunction with the entries under Baker, McCoy, and Remick (see above).

Sykes, Gresham M. *The Society of Captives: A Study of a Maximum Security Prison*. Princeton, NJ: Princeton University Press, 1958.

Classic sociological monograph based on years of research at Trenton State Prison (see introduction and chapter one). Second in a neat sociological trilogy that begins with Clemmer's *The Prison Community* and ends with Jacobs's *Stateville* (see entries above). Incidentally, as of this writing, a few old-timers who worked in New Jersey prisons in the 1950s are being interviewed to see what, if anything, they remember about the administrative life of the institutions at the time of the riots analyzed by Sykes.

Sylvester, Sawyer F., et al. *Prison Homicide*. New York: Spectrum, 1977.

One of the few in-depth studies of its kind. Analyzes data on 1973 prison homicides in adult male institutions housing 200 or more inmates. Among other results, found that homicides are most likely among maximum-security inmates with records of violent offenses.

Von Hirsch, Andrew. *Doing Justice: The Choice of Punishments*. New York: Hill and Wang, 1976.

A worthwhile argument by a contemporary thinker for punishment as retribution or "just deserts."

Wilson, James Q. *Thinking About Crime.* Rev. ed. New York: Basic Books, 1983.

Fully revised edition of the highly influential 1975 book that pierced the conventional intellectual wisdom about crime and articulated the commonsense view that punishment is necessary to deter offenders and to protect the public. Wilson's central arguments have not changed since 1975, but several qualifications, many fresh ideas, and lots of new information are presented in the 1983 edition. If only for the brilliant essay "Crime and American Culture," the 1983 edition is must reading.

In the introduction to this edition, Wilson notes paranthetically that "no one has ever, to the best of my knowledge, explained why some prisons are humane and others are unspeakable." The present study provides a tentative answer. In both editions, Wilson ends by saying that we have trifled "with the wicked, made sport of the innocent, and encouraged the calculators. Justice suffers, and so do we all." If these words apply to criminals in society, they apply doubly to those behind bars.

Wilson, James Q., ed. *Crime and Public Policy.* San Francisco: Institute for Contemporary Studies, 1983.

A useful volume containing fifteen essays written "in order to show how social science might inform the effort to control crime," including one by Daniel Glaser, "Supervising Offenders Outside of Prison."

Index

Index